S0-DVC-024
USED BOOK
UCD
BOOKSTORE
PRICE $ 17.25

2nd edition

HISTORY OF THE DANCE

in Art and Education

RICHARD KRAUS
SARAH ALBERTI CHAPMAN
Temple University

PRENTICE-HALL, INC.
Englewood Cliffs, New Jersey 07632

Library of Congress Cataloging in Publication Data

KRAUS, RICHARD G. (date)
History of the dance in art and education.

Includes bibliographical references and index.
1. Dancing—History. I. Chapman, Sarah, joint author. II. Title.
GV1601.K7 1980 793.3'09 80-16188
ISBN 0-13-390021-5

Editorial/production supervision
and interior design by Barbara Alexander
Cover design by Carol Zawislak
Manufacturing buyer: Harry P. Baisley

Printed in the United States of America

10 9 8 7 6 5 4 3 2 1

PRENTICE-HALL INTERNATIONAL, INC., *London*
PRENTICE-HALL OF AUSTRALIA PTY. LIMITED, *Sydney*
PRENTICE-HALL OF CANADA, LTD., *Toronto*
PRENTICE-HALL OF INDIA PRIVATE LIMITED, *New Delhi*
PRENTICE-HALL OF JAPAN, INC., *Tokyo*
PRENTICE-HALL OF SOUTHEAST ASIA PTE. LTD., *Singapore*
WHITEHALL BOOKS LIMITED, *Wellington, New Zealand*

To Elizabeth Snowdon
and
to Dorothy Ewing,
teacher and friend

Contents

Preface

This is the second edition of a book which was first published in 1969, and which has been widely used over the past decade as a basic text in university courses in dance history and dance education.

Unlike other dance histories, which have tended to focus rather narrowly on dance as a performing art—often within a limited time frame—this book seeks to provide a rounded picture of dance as a fundamental form of human expression. Varied forms of dance are analyzed from a philosophical and sociological point of view, and are described both in terms of their historical development and present status in society. A strong rationale is presented for the use of dance as a vital educational medium; specific dance curriculum trends on three levels (elementary, secondary, and higher education) are discussed in detail. The contributions of leading choreographers, dancers, producers, and educators throughout history and on the present scene are also presented concisely.

In preparing this text, Dr. Richard Kraus, author of the first edition of *History of the Dance in Art and Education,* was joined by Dr. Sarah Chapman, Associate Professor in the Department of Dance at Temple University. Dr. Chapman's rich background in both modern dance and ballet, and extensive experience in dance education—including a special interest in children's dance, the Laban and effort-shape movements, and national dance organizations—have brought new strengths to the second edition. It differs from the first edition in the following ways:

1. It has been brought fully up-to-date in the treatment of dance as an art form on the contemporary scene, including: a. an analysis of recent developments in American and international ballet and b. a description of the changing scene in modern dance, with detailed discussion both of the more established performers and choreographers, as well as newer avant-garde dance companies.

2. A fuller conceptual analysis of dance as a form of human expression is provided in the opening chapters, and a new chapter on social forms of dance (including ethnic, folk, ballroom, and jazz dance) has been added.

3. The book examines the place of dance in modern society in considerable detail. It includes a discussion of the economic pressures that face all performing artists and companies today, along with strategies for survival and obtaining funding support through government, foundations, and similar sources.

4. The treatment of dance in education includes new information taken from: a. a national survey of dance curricula and teacher certification policies, carried out by Dr. Chapman in 1976 for the National Dance Association and b. a survey carried out in 1979 by both authors, which examined current trends and program emphases in colleges and universities throughout the United States. Special attention is given to the role of national and regional organizations devoted to the promotion of dance as a significant cultural form or element in modern education.

As in the first edition, extensive research was done in such publications as *Dance Magazine, Dance News, Dance Perspectives, The Journal of Physical Education and Recreation,* newspapers with significant dance criticism sections, such as *The New York Times,* and other newsletters and magazines. Hundreds of citations have been drawn from the writings of such dance writers as Jack Anderson, Clive Barnes, Selma Jean Cohen, Doris Hering, Anna Kisselgoff, John Martin, Don McDonagh, Marcia Siegel, and Walter Terry. It is assumed that the reader who wishes to do more extensive research in specialized aspects of dance history and education will explore these sources in fuller detail.

The authors wish to acknowledge the assistance they received from hundreds of dance educators who responded to their college survey, sent photographs, or assisted in other ways. It is not possible to name them all.

Finally, the reader should be warned that, given the rapid rate of change in the modern cultural scene, many of the details regarding dance organizations, companies, and curricula are likely to change in the years immediately ahead. Thus, what is accurate at the time of publication may not be so, in some areas, within a few years. With this limitation, and also with the regret that it was not possible to treat the full range of dance history and all of the individuals who have contributed to it as fully and equally as they would like, the authors hope that *History of the Dance in Art and Education* will continue to find a sympathetic and enthusiastic audience. This audience, consisting of dance teachers, students, performers, or spectators with an interest in this most vital and appealing of the performing arts, grows more numerous and knowledgeable each day. It is hoped that the present text contributes meaningfully to that knowledge.

R. K.
S. C.

1 Dance in America: Concepts and Trends

One of the most striking aspects of the cultural scene in the United States today—and indeed throughout the Western world—has been the rapid growth of dance, both as a performing art and as a form of creative education.

Ballet and modern dance companies have been strengthened and have found new audiences by the millions. Hundreds of new performing groups have been established in communities that had never seen creative dance before. In the United States, federal and state governments have moved vigorously into the support of the arts. Both ballet and modern dance have received substantial subsidies to support choreographic work, employment of professional dancers, and performance on varied levels—including touring on a wide scale. Other forms of dance, such as musical comedy or jazz dance, have become increasingly popular in movies, the theater, and on television. Folk and square dance, clog and tap dance, and disco dancing have all gained strikingly in public interest.

This upsurge of interest in dance as a form of cultural activity, entertainment, and recreation has been influenced by several key societal trends of the 1960s and 1970s. The first of these trends was the growth of leisure itself, as a result of the shortened workweek, increased holidays, vacations, and lengthened periods of retirement. This, coupled with a steady advance in the general affluence of society, has meant that interest has expanded greatly in many forms of creative leisure participation, including hobbies, sports, outdoor recreation, travel, and, especially, the cultural arts.

GROWTH OF INTEREST IN THE ARTS

The rapid expansion of higher education has exposed millions of young people to culture, with a striking result. In 1973, a Gallup Poll funded by the National Endowment for the Arts, showed that over one-third of

American students in colleges were considering careers as participants, teachers, or administrators in the arts. In a survey of 20 large cities with major league football, basketball, hockey, and baseball teams as well as museums, theaters, symphonies, dance, and opera companies, it was found that attendance at arts events was higher than sports events by roughly 301 million admissions to 133 million, during the period from 1973 to 1975.

There has been an enormous growth, since World War II, in the number of symphony orchestras, opera, modern dance and ballet companies, art galleries, theaters, and community art centers throughout the United States. It was reported in the early 1970s that the number of arts institutions and organizations had expanded to the point that there were over 1,000 orchestras, 6,000 museums (with about 800 million annual admissions), and comparable numbers of community opera and choral societies, dance companies, and arts councils.

In 1978, an estimated 14.4 million people attended major orchestra performances, while 15 million saw dance performances, and 9.2 million attended opera events. This was a 100 percent increase over the previous seven-year period. Broadway drew 8.8 million spectators in 1978, and professional non-profit theaters played to 12 million. Community arts councils multiplied from 150 in 1966 to 1,800 in 1978, and hundreds of new performing arts majors were established in colleges, universities, and conservatories or other professional schools. In terms of government support of the arts, state subsidies grew from $4 million in 1966 to close to $170 million in 1978, and the National Endowment for the Arts budget increased from $2.5 million in 1966, its first year, to $123.5 million in 1978.[1]

POPULARITY OF MODERN DANCE AND BALLET

The evidence is unmistakable. The period of the 1970s has been an era of remarkable expansion for all the arts—particularly for modern dance and ballet, as von Obenauer points out:

> Throughout the country dance is big business. In the last ten years the number of professional American dance companies with budgets over $100,000 has risen from fewer than ten to over 50. Just three years ago, 70% of America's dance audience was to be found in New York City. Today, 70% of America's dance audience is spread across the country . . .[2]

She points out that the only three performing arts to show continuous growth in the number of touring performances during a four-year period in the 1970s were modern dance (161 percent increase), theater road shows (19.4 percent increase), and ballet (11.9 percent increase). In the late 1960s, the national audience for dance was 1.5 million; by the late 1970s, it was estimated at 15 million. By 1978, some 350 regional and resident dance

[1]For a breakdown of dance companies receiving grants, see *Dance News,* Sept. 1977, p. 3.

[2]Heidi von Obenauer, *Dance Magazine,* March 1976, p. 98.

companies had joined the American Association of Dance Companies—50 in one year alone!

What do all these statistics mean? Desmond sums them up in a report in *Performing Arts Review:*

> Dance is the fastest-growing art form in America. This rebirth of interest in the oldest of the arts has given rise to a rapidly expanding audience of new dance enthusiasts. The image of the middle-aged balletomane, speaking about dance in the well-rounded tones of the "cultural upper-class," is no longer applicable to the majority of today's dance-goers. Within the last 15 years, due to increased funding, greater media exposure, the build-up of superstars (whoever thought that a modern dancer would make the cover of the New York Times Magazine?), and the slow, begrudged granting of its legitimacy as an art form by academia, dance has reached out to a wider audience than ever before.[3]

EXPANSION OF DANCE EDUCATION

A key aspect of the growth of dance on the American cultural scene has been the expansion of dance education in varied forms. In 1978, *Time Magazine* reported that there were thousands of ballet schools, from small studios with a single proprietor–instructor to complex organizations affiliated with the major professional companies. Typically, the American Ballet Theater school, where parents of an aspiring dancer might pay $700 a year for nine hours of classes a week, had 1,000 students, a 25 percent increase over the previous five years. Schools run by the San Francisco Ballet (587 students), the Minnesota Dance Theater (950) and the Ballet West in Salt Lake City (1,000) had all doubled in enrollment.[4]

Similarly, there has been a striking growth of dance activity within the formal curricula of schools and colleges, as part of general education and as specialized training in the arts. More and more experimental programs in dance have been established on secondary school levels, with some states providing special, publicly supported high schools of performing arts (see Chapter 14). Hundreds of colleges today offer bachelor's and master's degree programs leading to performing and teaching dance specializations. Often, these colleges have outstanding professional dancers and choreographers on their faculty, and support special summer dance workshops and excellent touring dance companies.

In terms of community involvement in dance, recent U.S. census figures disclose that there are over 8,000 dance halls, studios, and schools (including professional dance schools for children) throughout the United States. The social forms of dance continue to be extremely popular. Ballroom dance organizations such as the Fred Astaire or Arthur Murray chains have hundreds of franchised studios in cities large and small. Over 25,000 dance teachers are employed in varied types of settings. Disco dancing has captured the interest of millions of Americans both young and adult, in films such as "Saturday Night Fever," and by 1978 this social dance craze had

[3]Jane Desmond, *Performing Arts Review,* Vol. 7, No. 2, 1977.

[4]"Boom at the Box Office," *Time,* May 1, 1978, p. 88.

created an estimated $4 billion-a-year industry. Ethnic, folk, and square dancing also claim many thousands of enthusiasts, with popular dance clubs, festivals, and workshops throughout the nation.

Overall, there has been a steady growth of involvement in dance for students and spectators alike, and for both amateur and professional performers. The interest is nationwide and continues to grow steadily, supported by dance organizations, councils, and regional associations that promote dance as a cultural art or form of education.

A single, vivid illustration of the national recognition that American dance has gained is that the first National Dance Week was declared in April, 1978, accompanied by government proclamations on all levels. To commemorate this event officially, the U.S. Postal Service simultaneously issued four stamps honoring the contribution of dance to this country. Each stamp paid tribute to a major area of dance—ballet, modern, folk, theatrical or Broadway dance. A number of state governors and big city mayors joined in enthusiastically proclaiming National Dance Week, an event which would have been extremely unlikely a few short years before.

UNDERSTANDING DANCE

To fully comprehend the powerful appeal of dance, and the reasons for its growth as a cultural activity in modern society, it is helpful to understand the nature of dance itself. So varied are the forms of dance, and so different the motivations for carrying them on, that it is difficult to offer a single definition or description that encompasses all forms. There are at least six widely found forms of dance, each with a unique character:

1. *Ballet.* The highly disciplined and codified stage art of ballet is based on a centuries-old tradition of movement skills. It has a repertoire today that is drawn from classical performance side by side with the most contemporary themes and choreographic approaches.
2. *Modern Dance.* Often referred to as "contemporary dance," this highly individualistic and diverse form of artistic expression began as a rejection of what its advocates condemned as the formalism and sterility of traditional ballet. Today, it still places emphasis on the artistic expression of the individual performer or choreographer, although an increasing number of companies are performing works by earlier modern dance pioneers. Its practitioners range from those who accept ballet as an indispensable form of training, or those who actually choreograph for ballet companies, to those avant-garde practitioners who, in performance at least, appear to be concerned with non-dance.
3. *Musical Stage Dance.* This hybrid form, found on the Broadway stage, in movies, or on television, usually combines elements of modern jazz, ballet, tap, and even ethnic dance. It tends to be a bright and highly polished form of glamorous entertainment, visually pleasing to a broad audience.

4. *Ballroom Dance.* The most widely found form of participating dance, ballroom dance ranges from the familiar social dances which were popular in past decades, such as the fox trot, waltz, tango, rumba, or other Latin–American steps to the pulsating and physically exciting rock-and-roll or discotheque dances.
5. *Other Recreational Dance Forms.* Many individuals today enjoy performing the traditional folk dances of European or other foreign countries, either because of their own ethnic heritage or because they are part of an international folk dance movement. Similarly, American square and round dancing are practiced by many thousands of enthusiasts in urban and suburban adult clubs. While these forms of dance—when done originally by the common people—were quite simple, today they are often extremely complicated, with new dances constantly being invented and introduced.
6. *Ethnic Dance.* This refers to the type of dance performed by ethnic groups—usually of a highly traditional nature, and often linked directly to religious practices and social customs. It differs from folk dance in that it tends to be performed by touring companies as a form of spectacular entertainment, while folk dance places primary emphasis on performance for the pleasure of the participant.

Thus, we find a wide variety of distinctly different dance forms, ranging from social pastime to concert or theatrical performance. Dance, in one form or another, appeals to all social classes and widely ranging levels of artistic taste. Some dances are centuries old; others were evolved only yesterday. Dance has become an important part of our cultural, recreational, and educational experience. But, at the heart of all this, what *is* dance? Why does it continue to have such a strong appeal on all these levels, for both spectator and participant? What, essentially, is the meaning and purpose of dance in human society?

One might respond in several ways—in terms of the etymological source of the word; or through historical examinations of how dance was viewed in earlier societies; or through the eyes of the philosopher, the psychologist, the anthropologist, the dance critic, or the dancer. All of these viewpoints will be helpful in framing a definition.

To begin with—an examination of the word itself.

According to Lincoln Kirstein, the English word *dance* is related to the French *danse,* which is believed to have been derived from the ancient high German word *danson,* meaning to "stretch" or "drag." Each of these terms, along with other European variants *(dands, danca, danza, tanz)* is based on the root combination of letters *tan,* found in the original Sanskrit, meaning tension, or stretching.[5] However, in a number of definitions dating from the time in which dance was gaining popularity in the courts of Europe, emphasis was given to its spectacular qualities, its social values, or its use as a form of communication.

For example, in Arbeau's famous *Orchesographie* (1583), the author writes:

[5]Lincoln Kirstein, *Dance: A Short History of Classic Theatrical Dancing* (New York: G. P. Putnam's Sons, 1935), p. 1.

> Dancing . . . is to jump, to hop, to prance, to sway, to tread, to tip-toe, and to move the feet, hands and body in certain rhythms, measures and movements consisting of jumps, bendings of the body, straddlings, limpings, bendings of the knees, risings on tip-toe, throwings-forward of the feet, changes and other movements . . .
>
> Dancing or saltation is an art both pleasing and profitable which confers and preserves health, is adapted for the youthful, agreeable to the aged and very suitable for all. . . . (it) depends on music because, without the virtue of rhythm, dancing would be meaningless and confused, so much so that it is necessary that the gestures of the limbs should keep time with the musical instruments. . . .
>
> Practically all the *savants* hold that dancing is a kind of dumb rhetoric by which the orator, without speaking a single word, can, by virtue of his movements, make the spectators understand that he is gay, worthy to be praised, loved and adored.[6]

Other authorities gave stress to dance's elegance, grace, and beauty. John Weaver wrote in 1721:

> Dance is an elegant, and regular movement, harmoniously composed of beautiful attitudes, and contrasted graceful posture of the body, and parts thereof.[7]

Jean Georges Noverre, in 1760, described dance as follows:

> Dancing, according to the accepted definition of the word, is the art of composing steps with grace, precision, and facility to the time and bars given in the music, just as music itself is simply the art of combining sounds and modulations so that they afford pleasure to the ear.[8]

Another early definition that places stress on order, precision, and graceful movement to the accompaniment of music, was found in Diderot's *Encyclopedia* (ca. 1772):

> [Dancing is] ordered movements of the body, leaps, and measured steps made to the accompaniment of musical instruments or the voice. . . .[9]

Clearly, these definitions were based on the kinds of ballroom or theatrical dance which were common in Europe during the 18th century. Dance was chiefly thought of as the graceful, formal, and highly stylized couple or set dances performed by members of the court, or as the equally stylized ballet of the period, performed as entertainment and narrative in its effect. One famed historian of the dance, Gaston Vuillier, made it very

[6]Thoinot Arbeau, *Orchesographie: A Treatise in the Form of a Dialogue* (New York: Dance Horizons, Inc.), pp. 20, 23.

[7]Cited in Anatole Chujoy, *The Dance Encyclopedia* (New York: A. S. Barnes & Co., Inc., 1948), p. 125.

[8]*Ibid.*

[9]*Ibid.*

clear that only these forms were regarded as dance; indeed, among more primitive cultures, there was no dance:

> Like poetry and music, to which it is closely allied . . . the choreographic art . . . was probably unknown to the earlier ages of humanity. Savage man, wandering in forests, devouring the quivering flesh of his spoils, can have known nothing of those rhythmic postures which reflect sweet and caressing sensations entirely alien to his moods. The nearest approach to such must have been the leaps and bounds, the incoherent gestures, by which he expressed the joys and furies of his brutal life.[10]

But a true definition of dance must recognize that prehistoric man *did* dance; indeed, that this was a highly important part of his life, and was the ancestor of dance as we know it today. Sheldon Cheney, a distinguished historian of the drama, points out the significance of dance as an ancient form of primitive artistic expression:

> Man dances. After the activities that secure to primitive peoples the material necessities, food and shelter, the dance comes first. It is the earliest outlet for emotion and the beginning of the arts. . . .
>
> Not only did drama as such—the art of which *action* is a pivotal material—arise out of primitive dance. . . . Music, too, which can hardly be dissociated from the theatre's beginnings, traces its ancestry to the sounds made to accentuate the primitive dance rhythm, the stamping of feet and clapping of hands, the shaking of rattles, the beating of drums and sticks. Dance, then, is the great mother of the arts.[11]

PHILOSOPHICAL ANALYSIS OF DANCE AS ART FORM

To describe dance in terms of a particular form (whether it be the ornate and graceful 18th-century French ballet, or the pounding rhythmic dance of a primitive ritual), gives only a partial picture. It is necessary to determine the essential nature of dance, rather than its outward form. What are the elements that distinguish this from other forms of human experience and expression? Two philosophers, James K. Feibleman and Thomas Munro, have attempted to analyze dance systematically, as a form of artistic experience.

Feibleman suggests that there are seven traditionally accepted fine arts: sculpture, dance, painting, architecture, poetry, drama, and music. Each of these has a basic concern, and a medium through which it finds expression. Thus, drama is the art which deals with the human social relations of life situations. Painting is the art which deals with the colors and qualities of two-dimensional space. Music is concerned with time, making use of sound vibrations in a temporal relationship. Feibleman defines dance as "that art which deals with the motions of the human body." Uniquely, it

[10]Gaston Vuillier, *A History of Dance* (New York: D. Appleton and Co., 1897), p. ix.

[11]Sheldon Cheney, *Three Thousand Years of Drama, Acting and Stagecraft* (New York: Tudor Publishing Co., 1929), pp. 11–12).

is ephemeral, in that it does not have a lasting product or record of performance.[12]

Accepting this as a concise statement which succeeds in distinguishing dance from other art forms, one must then explore the nature of "art." Thomas Munro points out that this is an extremely complex concept. There are many levels of art, ranging from what might simply be a skill, or product of human manipulation, to the liberal arts, the fine arts, and the performing arts. Munro suggests that different types of art have different characteristics, in terms of how they are perceived, what their subject matter is, and whether or not they are directly functional. He suggests that there are:

> Arts of simultaneous perception, such as architecture, sculpture, or painting, where we see all that is there to see, at once.
>
> Arts of successive perception, which continue in time, changing form, such as music, dance, poetry, and drama.
>
> Arts of space; some art forms are stationary, such as sculpture or painting. Others, like theater, or dance, are movable.
>
> Arts that are imitative or non-imitative. Munro suggests that sculpture and painting are imitative, and that music and architecture are non-imitative. This distinction is not as useful today as in the past; however, if it is applied, dance may be both imitative and non-imitative.
>
> Arts that are serviceable or non-serviceable; architecture and crafts are generally seen as serviceable in that they perform a "useful" function. Dancing, while less so, may perform a service, just as music or art may.

Munro discusses dance at length, pointing out that it is partly a theater art, partly a ballroom art, and partly a religious art. Finally, he states:

> Dance is an art of rhythmic bodily movement, presenting to the observer an ordered sequence of moving visual patterns of line, solid shape, and color. The postures and gestures of which these are made suggest kinesthetic experiences of tension, relaxation, etc., and emotional moods and attitudes associated with them. They may also represent imaginary characters, actions, and stories. Dances are performed by one person or by two or more in mutual coordination; some animals can be trained to do simple dances. The movements are usually synchronized with, and partly aided by, musical or other rhythmic sounds. . . .[13]

Munro's analysis tends to be a description, rather than a definition. What is needed is a clarification of *why* dance is done. Suzanne Langer suggests that ". . . the dancer expresses in gesture what he feels as the emotional content of music. . . ." The implication that the music must be the basis for dance performance, and the goal of the dancer merely to reflect what he feels to be the mood or emotional content of the music, is not satisfactory. Most choreographers would reject this view, pointing out that

[12]James K. Feibleman, *Aesthetics: A Study of the Fine Arts in Theory and Practice* (New York: Duell, Sloan and Pearce, 1949), p. 302.

[13]Thomas Munro, *The Arts and Their Interrelationships* (New York: The Liberal Arts Press, 1951), p. 496.

it is the dance which comes first, in most instances, and that music is then composed to accompany the dance. Again, Langer refers to dance as a "plastic art, a spectacle of shifting patterns of created design. . . ."[14] It is an illusion, a vivid representation, created, organized, formal—the play of power made visible.

This approach to analyzing dance has been extended by a number of philosophers using the phenomenological approach to aesthetics. Phenomenology is a relatively new form of philosophical analysis which seeks to eliminate pre-existing biases and assumptions in an attempt to get a pure and unencumbered vision of what a thing essentially is. It is the search for essences that cannot be revealed by ordinary observation. One analyst, Maxine Sheets-Johnston, points out that to describe dance as a *force* in *time* and *space* (a frequently heard construct) does not convey its meaning as a lived experience, but instead suggests a number of separate objective factors with no unifying center or wholeness. Instead, dance must be conceived, in her terms, as *forcetimespace,* an art form which involves both expression on the part of the performer and evocation of feeling on the part of the audience. She writes:

> The dance, as it is formed and performed by the dancers, is a unity of succession, a cohesive moving form, and so it is to the audience. What appears before us is not an externally related series of spatial-temporal befores, nows, and afters, but a form which is *ekstatic,* in flight, in the process of becoming the dance which it is, yet never fully the dance at any moment. . . . Dance is not only a kinetic phenomenon which appears, which gives itself to consciousness; it is also a living, vital human experience . . . for both dancer and audience . . .[15]

The view that emotional expression is at the heart of dance has been expressed by a number of writers in this field, including John Martin, an extremely influential dance critic and author during the early years of dance's growth on the American scene. Martin suggests that no matter what the nature of dance activity and despite many variations in outward appearances, all dance is essentially the same. His concept of "basic dance" is founded on the view that emotional states tend to express themselves through physical movement. Often the movement is not representational, but it is a clue to the feelings of the person possessed by the emotional state. Dance, as Martin sees it, emerges when the dancer:

> . . . allows each of these impulses to express itself in movements which he deliberately remembers and develops in order to be able to convey to others something of his own intuitive reaction which is too deep for words. Thus, at the root of all these varied manifestations of dancing . . . lies the common impulse to resort to movement to externalize states which we cannot externalize by rational means. This is basic dance. . . .[16]

[14]Suzanne Langer, *Feeling and Form* (New York: Charles Scribner's Sons, 1953), pp. 2–3.

[15]Maxine Sheets-Johnston, in Myron H. Nadel and Constance G. Nadel, *The Dance Experience* (New York: Praeger Books, 1970), p. 46.

[16]John Martin, *John Martin's Book of the Dance* (New York: Tudor Publishing Co., 1963), p. 8.

This concept was supported and amplified by the statements of two outstanding modern dance pioneers, Martha Graham and Doris Humphrey. Graham wrote:

> I am a dancer. My experience has been with dance as an art. Each art has an instrument and a medium. The instrument of dance is the human body; the medium is movement. . . . It has not been my aim to evolve or discover a new method of dance training, but rather to dance significantly. To dance significantly means "through the medium of discipline and by means of a sensitive, strong instrument, to bring into focus unhackneyed movement, a human being. . . ."[17]

Humphrey's view of the underlying purpose of dance was expressed in the following statement:

> My dance is an art concerned with human values. It upholds only those values which make for harmony and opposes all forces inimical to those values. In part, its movement may be used for decoration, entertainment, emotional release, or technical display; but primarily it is composed as an expression of American life as I see it today. . . . I believe that the dancer belongs to his time and place and that he can only express that which passes through or close to his experience.[18]

More recently, in a discussion of dance as education, Fowler expressed the following view:

> Dance is a way to feel what it is to be human and to be alive. In that sense it is celebration. It makes something special out of life. It is revelation; some would say, "illumination." Because it involves the self, it *reveals* self. It communicates what one knows of one's own body feeling. Like all the other arts, dance is a code—in this case a structuring of gestures and motions that captures and conveys subjective inner experience. The elements that make up this code are sound, movement, line, pattern, form, space, shape, rhythm, time, and energy.[19]

The view that all dance has as its fundamental purpose the dancer's expression of personal emotions or feelings about life experience would be meaningful if all dance were intended as communicative expression. Clearly, however, it is not. Much dance is simply ritual, practiced again and again as a matter of tribal or societal custom. Other dance involves social interaction, pastime, or simply a display of physical agility and grace. Even in dance that is intended as an artistic or theatrical presentation, there is great variety. Anderson writes:

> Dance is movement that has been organized so that it is rewarding to behold, and the craft of making and arranging dances is called choreography. Out of all the possible movement combinations that exist, the choreographer selects,

[17]Martha Graham, "A Modern Dancer's Primer for Action," in Frederick Rand Rogers, *Dance: A Basic Educational Technique* (New York: Macmillan Co., 1941), p. 178.

[18]Doris Humphrey, in Rogers, *op. cit.,* p. 188.

[19]Charles B. Fowler and Araminta Little, *Dance as Education* (Washington, D.C.: National Dance Association and Alliance for Arts Education, 1977), p. 2.

edits, heightens, and sharpens those he thinks are suitable for his specific purposes. The gestures in some dances may refer to specific emotional states and their sequence may tell a story. Other dances tell no story, but instead present beautiful images of people in motion, the choreographer believing that pure movement in itself is worthy of attention. Because dance can assume so many guises, the viewer should regard each dance he attends with fresh, unprejudiced eyes. All dance styles are not alike, and some, to the uninitiated, may look decidedly odd.[20]

SOCIAL VIEW OF DANCE

Since dance takes so many forms and may stem from so many motivations, how can one probe for its essential meaning? Perhaps the social scientist can help us discover, not so much the purpose of dance for the individual performer, but rather its meaning for society. Sociologists have pointed out that in many cultures, dance is seen as being far more than graceful movement. Instead, it is a profoundly important social experience —a powerful rite shared by all members of the culture, and essential to its well-being. Margaret Mead commented about her anthropological studies in Samoa that "Dancing is the only activity in which almost all ages and both sexes participate, and it therefore offers a unique opportunity for an analysis of education."[21]

A cultural historian, Curt Sachs, has written that in the lives of primitive peoples and in ancient civilizations few experiences or communal functions approached the dance in importance. It is not viewed as an activity that is external to survival; indeed, he writes, it "provides bread and everything else that is needed to sustain life."

> It is not a sin proscribed by the priest or at best merely accepted by him, but rather a sacred act and priestly office; not a pastime to be tolerated only, but a very serious activity of the entire tribe. On no occasion in the life of primitive peoples could the dance be dispensed with. Birth, circumcision, and the consecration of maidens, marriage and death, planting and harvest, the celebration of chieftains, hunting, war, and feasts, the changes of the moon and sickness —for all of these the dance is needed.[22]

So important to the life of primitive man was dance, that it became a primary means of social identification. According to Havelock Ellis, when a man belonging to one branch of the African Bantu tribe met a Bantu of another branch, he would ask, "What do you dance?" The great power of dance for establishing a sense of tribal unity is vividly described in the following passage by anthropologist Ruth Benedict. She writes of the Zuni tribe in the American Southwest:

> The dance, like their ritual poetry, is a monotonous compulsion of natural forces by reiteration. The tireless pounding of their feet draws together the

[20]Jack Anderson, *Dance* (New York: Newsweek Books, 1974), p. 9.

[21]Margaret Mead, *From the South Seas* (New York: William Morrow & Co., 1939), p. 110.

[22]Curt Sachs, *World History of the Dance* (New York: W. W. Norton & Co., 1937), p. 4.

> mist in the sky and heaps it into the piled rainclouds. It forces out the rain upon the earth. They are bent not at all upon an ecstatic experience, but upon so thorough-going an identification with nature that the forces of nature will swing to their purposes. This intent dictates the form and spirit of Pueblo dances. There is nothing wild about them. It is the cumulative force of the rhythm, the perfection of forty men moving as one, that makes them effective. . . .[23]

Among primitive peoples, then, one of the great purposes of dance was to establish social unity and provide a means of collective strength and purpose. Closely linked to this was the function of religious celebration or worship, in which dance was used as a means of communication. It represented a language for communication with the forces of nature—for becoming one with the gods. A number of examples of dance as religious worship among primitive tribes are illustrated in the chapter that follows.

The Collective Unconscious. One theory of the origins of art, which might be used to place dance within a meaningful social context, has to do with what Walter Abell calls the "collective unconscious."[24] In this sense, art—rather than simply representing beautiful designs or melodic musical structures—grows out of the history, traditions, myths, and primordial images of a people. It stems both from cultural realities, social relationships, historical events, and from the full range of folklore, myths, legends, fairy tales, heroes, and ogres that appeared in a nation's past and that often continue, although apparently submerged, to influence human behavior.

To understand a society's culture, Abell writes, it is necessary to apply a psychohistorical method of uncovering the "collective dream in art." This approach would apply equally well to examining works of classical ballet which are based on ancient myths or folk tales, and to much more cryptic or expressionist works of contemporary dance, whose symbolic imagery may also evoke visions of the past, or of emerging societal forces and relationships. As an extremely simple example, even the traditional folk games, songs, and dances that have been passed down from generation to generation through the centuries as forms of children's play may often be shown to have their origin in religious practice, social custom, or historical events of the past.

Dance then, although it may apparently be based on purely contemporary themes or artistic impulses, is also an expression of deeper, hidden psychological impulses and cultural influences. Sometimes, like other art forms, it may express these in somewhat poetic or spiritual terms. Panayotis Michelis, for example, describes the general function of art experience:

> Art materializes ideas or at least expresses the deeper spiritual anguish of man and his highest ideals in eternal symbols. . . . (it) fascinates man and releases him from immediate practical concerns, transports him into the peaceful environment of a transcendental vision and fills his soul with joy . . .[25]

[23] Ruth Benedict, *Patterns of Culture* (New York: Mentor Books, 1934, 1946), pp. 84–85.

[24] See Walter Abell, *The Collective Dream in Art: A Psychohistorical Theory of Culture* (New York: Schocken Books, 1966), p. 45.

[25] Panayotis Michelis, *Aesthetikos* (Detroit: Wayne State University Press, 1977), p. 46.

However, art may also be used to express more immediate and concrete human concerns; typically, it may take the form of political propaganda or social protests. While some may argue that this is an inappropriate function of art, throughout history the artist has expressed the visions, crises, and needs of each period, as commentator or propagandist.

HUMAN MOVEMENT AND DANCE

A unique aspect of dance is that, of all the arts, it is most dependent on human movement. It is believed that a powerful motivation for dance has been the pervasive need to express oneself physically through rhythmic play, and through exploration of one's bodily powers and physical environment. Observe children playing—either toddlers in the crib or nursery school age children in a sandbox or play lot. They are constantly moving, crawling, lifting, clapping, kicking, running, manipulating their environment. Ted Shawn writes, in *Dance We Must:*

> We know that body movement is life itself—our movement begins in the womb before our birth and the new-born infant's need for movement is imperative and continuous. When we sleep there is constant movement, our hearts beat, our intestines work; in fact as long as there is life there is movement, and to move is hence to satisfy a basic and external need. . . .[26]

But movement alone is not enough. The quality of the movement experience is crucial. And dance has the capacity to promote a special kind of feeling—a sense of heightening of life, an exhilaration, a sense of joy. It has a unique capacity to blend, or combine, the physical and emotional aspects of our being in an integrated expression. The ability to release one's feelings in this way is a deeply therapeutic and healthful function. A distinguished psychoanalyst, Joost Meerloo, suggests that dance is such a widely found form of human expression and emotional release that those who cannot dance are "imprisoned in their own ego," and have lost the "tune of life." He describes them as "deeply repressed" and "forlorn." Through the ages, he writes:

> . . . sorrow, pleasure and ecstasy have been expressed by ritualized, festive dances. The rhythm of life brings the dance, and the dance brings the *saltatio,* jump, and the *ludus,* the playful activity. Every dance transforms man's innate passive rhythm—the mechanical beat in him—into the active rhythm of personal music. Dancing promotes man's vital pulsations, it changes mechanical repetitiveness into passionate and ebullient life. It lets man rediscover his body as a tool of expression.[27]

It is this depth of feeling that distinguishes dance from other very similar forms of movement which are often part of choreographed display and entertainment in our society. For example, Fred Schroeder compares dance to other forms of ritualized and disciplined display, such as team

[26]Ted Shawn, *Dance We Must* (London: Dennis Dobson Ltd., 1946), p. 9.

[27]Joost Meerloo, *The Dance* (New York: Chilton Book Co., 1960), pp. 39–40.

games or even such events as bullfighting or professional wrestling, which in many ways represent choreographed movement.[28] Although such activities, or professional ice skating displays or gymnastic competition, may have a common aesthetic with dance, based on physical ability, strength, bodily control, or precision, Schroeder suggests that dance is a *cultivated art form,* marked by "design, meaning, and creativity," and that these elements separate it from other forms of athletic display or movement.

This is, perhaps, an oversimplification, in the sense that some experimental modern dance companies have developed works that appear to bridge the gap between dance and these other forms of physical display. For example, Stephanie Evanitsky's Multigravitational Aerodance Group performs in the air, thanks to scaffolding, cables, and other equipment. John Curry's Ice Dancing Company performs on ice. Both companies clearly regard themselves as part of the spectrum of creative dance performance.[29] At the same time, other avant-garde companies do almost nothing that the typical spectator would be likely to regard as dance. It is clear that, as new movement forms emerge, we will need to continue to reexamine and reshape our understanding of both art and dance.

OTHER FUNCTIONS OF DANCE

What other purposes does dance serve?

A commonly cited function is its role in courtship between the sexes. There is a theory that dance occurs psychologically among primitive peoples as a result of non-repressive sublimation of the libido. It is thus an expression of sexual drive, a means of displaying one's vigor or beauty, and part of the complicated ritual surrounding the entrance into adulthood and the act of courtship. Dancing provides socially accepted physical contact, and is a direct means of expressing sexual attractiveness; indeed, many social dances performed today are frankly sexual and derived from primitive dance movements that were related to fertility symbolism.

But this too is true only of some dances, and there are many forms in which courtship or sexual attraction plays no part.

It is a mistake, then, to assume that *all* forms of dance have a common core or purpose or meaning. Instead, dance may have many functions, but these vary, according to the society, the class, the age or sex, the religious structure, and similar factors about those who dance. Within varied kinds of societies, past and present, primitive and complex, Judeo-Christian or animist, one might find any or all of the following purposes for dance:

Purposes for dance

1. It is a form of social affirmation, a means of expressing national or tribal loyalty and strength.
2. It is a means of religious worship, as a form of ritual and direct means of communicating with the gods.

[28]Fred E. Schroeder, *Outlaw Aesthetics: Arts and the Public Mind* (Bowling Green, Ohio: Bowling Green University Press, 1977), pp. 44–47.

[29]Anna Kisselgoff, "Other Ways of Moving," *New York Times,* Jan. 14, 1979, p. 14-D, and John Gruen, "Can Ballet be Danced on Skates?" *New York Times,* Nov. 19, 1978, p. 18-D.

3. It is an art form, an outlet for self-expressiveness and personal creativity. Within the mainstream of cultural inheritance, it may be the source of great works which are performed as part of a continuing tradition, or a basis for continuing artistic experimentation.
4. It may also be a form of popular entertainment, appealing to a broader audience than when it represents an art form with a high level of aesthetic worth.
5. Dance serves as a means of expressing physical exuberance, strength, and agility.
6. It offers an important social and recreational outlet, both as a means of restoring oneself physically, and of finding social acceptance within group participation.
7. It provides a medium through which courtship can be carried on.
8. Dance serves as a means of education, in the sense that it is taught to achieve the specific purposes of education within a given society, just as art, music, or theater are taught as cultural forms.
9. Dance serves as an occupation; in increasing numbers, it offers a means of livelihood to performers and teachers.
10. Finally, dance serves as therapy; for many it offers a form of physical and emotional release and rehabilitation; therefore, it is provided, along with other therapies, in many treatment centers.

DEFINING DANCE

Blending all of these elements together, one is able to isolate a number of factors that are useful in developing a definition of dance. These include the following:

1. *Use of the Human Body.* Here we are concerned only with those forms of dance which involve people in performance. While, as Langer points out, one might refer to the "dancing" of gnats in the air as a kind of dance motif or patterned movement, and while animals or birds frequently carry on dancelike and even ritualistic movements, in this context we will not consider these forms as dance.
2. *Extends Through Time.* Dance is not a frozen tableau, or a single gesture or picture of movement; instead, it is a continuing sequence of activity, extending through time, and may comprise a few moments, or may last for several hours or days.
3. *Exists in Space.* Dance is three-dimensional; it exists in the general space of a ballroom floor, on a stage, or in a village square; it exists in the personal space *(kinesphere)* of the person dancing.
4. *Exists in Force (Weight).* Dance is a result of energy expenditure; it is viewed as a greater or lesser degree of muscular energy used to articulate movement.
5. *Exists in Flow.* The amount of energy which is restricted within or gathered toward the physical center of movement, or released away from that center, is reflected as *flow* in dance.

6. *Accompanied by Rhythm.* Most dance is rhythmically patterned; it is performed either to the accompaniment of music, chanting, hand-clapping, or percussive beating. Even those dances which may be performed silently, or to the accompaniment of speech or arbitrarily devised or selected sound effects, usually have a rhythmic structure.
7. *Serves to Communicate.* Most dance has communicative intent, ranging from the literal characterization or story-telling of pantomimic dance or traditional ballet, to the expression of personal emotion or physical exuberance. Even dances which are intended as abstract, non-literal forms, convey a kind of meaning to the onlooker—depending on his ability to perceive or translate the movement in personal terms.
8. *Has Movement Style and Form.* Unlike a child's aimless and playlike exploration of movement, most dance has a characteristic movement style, and has a structure or form. This may range from the use of gestures or step patterns which are typically found in a particular type of ethnic or social dance, to the carefully choreographed sequence of individual and group movements that one finds in concert dance.

Using the word "art" in its broadest sense, that of involving human skill, one arrives at the following definition:

> Dance is an art performed by individuals or groups of human beings, existing in time, space, force, and flow, in which the human body is the instrument and movement is the medium. The movement is stylized, and the entire dance work is characterized by form and structure. Dance is commonly performed to musical or other rhythmic accompaniment, and has as a primary purpose the expression of inner feelings and emotions, although it is often performed for social, ritual, entertainment or other purposes.

One final distinction may be made. It has been suggested that there are two types of dance—the kind which is performed by people, usually as a mass activity, without an audience (or in which the idea of performance is secondary to the idea of doing the dance for oneself), and the kind of dance which is *meant* to be performed for an audience. John Martin phrased it in this way:

> Dance falls naturally into two major categories: that which is done for the emotional release of the individual dancers, without regard to the possible interest of a spectator; and that, on the other hand, which is done for the enjoyment of a spectator either as an exhibition of skill, the telling of a story, the presentation of pleasurable designs, or the communication of emotional experience. . . .[30]

According to this view, most dances were originally of the first type and were meant to be performed as communal activity; the second type is con-

[30]Martin, *op. cit.,* p. 20

sidered to have descended from the first. Ballet and modern dance are essentially concert forms, meant to be performed on a stage and before an audience of spectators. On the other hand, such forms as social, folk, or square dance are primarily participant forms. However, this distinction breaks down in some of the present-day uses of dance. Thus, it is not at all uncommon for children or adults to study modern dance or ballet because of the enjoyment and personal benefits this brings to them, without ever doing a performance, other than possibly a recital at the end of the studio year. In contrast, social, folk, square, and especially ethnic dance—which may all be regarded as primarily participant dance forms—are often done on a highly skilled level, and may provide the basis for performances or exhibitions. Often, national performing groups develop their dances to a high level of artistic quality. They may even combine (as in the case of "folk ballet" companies) traditional peasant and regional dance forms with balletic training and complex choreography which makes their performance very attractive to an audience. Too, in a number of concert works on the ballet or modern dance stage, folk and ethnic themes or movements are used as the basis for choreography. In the past, the court dances of the nobility, which were closely linked with the beginning of ballet, were carried on both as entertainment and for social participation; they, in turn, owed much of their origin to the folk forms of peasants.

Perhaps it would be better to say that, rather than dividing dance rigidly into "spectator" and "participant" forms, dance may range from the simple to the complex, and may under one circumstance or another, have as its primary purpose either performance or participation.

SOCIETAL ACCEPTANCE AND SUPPORT OF DANCE

Finally, it should be stressed that society tends to be curiously ambivalent in its acceptance and support of all the arts, and particularly of dance. For example, there is widespread approval of the arts in general, as an important aspect of national life and a significant ingredient in creative education. Yet, economic support of the arts has been weak, and there is a tendency to regard material accomplishment—in the business or professional world, for example—as being of far greater importance and status than success as a writer, fine artist, or performer.

Dance itself, although it has grown tremendously in the number of performing groups, events, school, and college programs, as indicated earlier in this chapter, continues to be understood and supported by a somewhat smaller percentage of the public than the other arts. Perhaps the reason for this is the elite and "highbrow" stereotype of classical ballet as it was seen in the past, or the image of modern dance as a perplexing, murkily symbolic set of long-haired dancers with flowers in their teeth performing incomprehensible gyrations.

Certainly, there is today much greater comprehension of dance and openness to its varied forms than in the past. Yet, with the exception of several major ballet companies and particularly the exception of a limited number of ballet superstars, who can command huge fees, most dance companies and artists have great difficulty in supporting themselves, and must rely heavily on teaching or other forms of income, or on grants and subsidies, in order to carry on their work.

The economic struggle that must be carried on to support dance as a creative art form, as well as the stereotypes that surround it as a career field, can best be understood in the light of past history. Therefore, before presenting a contemporary analysis of dance as a cultural art form or a significant medium of modern education, this text examines its past history. The chapters that follow are devoted to an exploration of dance in primitive societies, and then to its role in ancient Western cultures.

2

Dance in Primitive Cultures

As the preceding chapter has made clear, dance is found among all the peoples and civilizations of the world. Among primitive, pre-industrial or peasant cultures, where its social and religious functions are most clearly displayed, dance plays an important role throughout life. It is important, in examining such societies, to recognize that they are primitive chiefly in terms of their technical, scientific, or economic development. Their patterns of education, religion, or social custom may be highly complex; their arts also may be extremely sophisticated. Such societies are usually tribal in nature, living in rural surroundings, and depending on hunting or agriculture for their livelihood.

Within primitive cultures, past and present, dance has been a major form of religious ritual and social expression—a utilitarian and omnipresent art. Pearl Primus, the black American dancer who went to Africa to study the dance of her forebears, writes with the trained eye of an anthropologist:

> The role of the professional dancer was of tremendous importance in Africa. He was necessary to all ceremonies, all feasts, all occasions which involved the health and well-being of the tribe. In return for his services the tribe fed and clothed him and provided for him in his every need. He was left free to dance. . . . Is it any wonder then that dance stands with music and art at the very top of the list of cultural contributions of the African to the world? Is it any wonder that the dancer developed to such an extent that he could spin his head on his neck so rapidly that the onlooker saw nothing but blur . . . or that he could leap from the ground with feet outstretched in a wide sitting position and land on his buttocks only to spring into the air again unhurt? Is it any wonder that a group of fifty warriors could dance their spear dances and not one finger be out of place?[1]

[1]Pearl Primus, "Out of Africa," in Walter Sorell, *The Dance Has Many Faces* (New York: World Publishing Co., 1951), pp. 256–257.

Why was dance so important to primitive societies? What are its functions? Essentially, they are much the same as those listed in the previous chapter; dance is used as a means of worship, as a way of expressing and reinforcing tribal unity and strength, as a framework for courtship or mating, as a means of communication, and as a therapeutic or healing experience. It is likely that the use of dance as a means of aesthetic expression, with a few skilled artists performing for large audiences, would rarely be found among primitive peoples; rather than form the audience for such performances, they dance themselves. Nor was dance viewed narrowly as a means of recreation after toil. Primitive mankind tends not to make a clear distinction between work and play and, although certainly there were harvest or other celebratory feasts with dancing, rituals and playlike experiences were usually thoroughly integrated with the productive work of the tribe.

ORIGINS OF PRIMITIVE DANCE

How did dance begin among primitive peoples? Douglas Kennedy suggests that the religious aspect of dance generally had as its purpose communication with the unseen forces which provided food, promoted fertility, regulated the weather, gave good fortune in warfare—and thus controlled tribal welfare and human survival. Man danced originally to supplicate the gods, on all important occasions of life. Kennedy writes:

> As the faith behind such primitive religious impulses weakens, the dances which express it are not immediately abandoned, but they gradually change their character. The form of the ritual remains, but some of the magical content departs. The dancer becomes less and less of a medicine-maker and more and more a performing artist. In fact, the ritual changes imperceptibly into art. It was in some such manner that the folk dances in different parts of Europe grew out of old pagan rites as the pagans themselves were converted to Christianity and gradually lost their primitive beliefs . . . in industrialized . . . England, there are still a few ancient rituals directly descended from the pre-Christian era, and retaining, to a surprising degree, their aura of primitive magic.[2]

Probably one of the first uses of dance was as gesture, in order to communicate. Suzanne Langer writes at length of the development of language and symbolic gesture, showing how man developed certain stylized ways of expressing himself. Gradually, the use of expressive gesture, of facial expressions, of a combination of guttural sound and action to reinforce an idea led to the use of dance as a means of telling a story or giving information. Because of the lack of adequate speech, man was probably compelled to use easily recognizable gesture, sometimes supplementing the movement with the cries of animals or other natural sounds, or with whatever basic words he had developed. The elaborate East Indian *mudras,* or hand language used in dance, and the sign language of the American Indian are both examples of this kind of gesture-communication, elaborately systematized.

[2]Douglas Kennedy, *England's Dances* (London: G. Bell & Sons, Ltd., 1950), pp. 31–32.

One of the important sources of inspiration of primitive dance was the movement of birds and animals. Prehistoric and early primitive man was undoubtedly acutely aware of the living things around him. He hunted them for food and clothing, he fought them for survival, and he knew well their courage, their beauty, and their cunning. Most primitive people have an animist religion, in which they believe in animals possessing souls and being very much like people. Indeed, among many tribes the idea of reincarnation, and of transmigration of souls between humans and animals, is completely accepted. All this was woven in with a sense of mystery about the natural phenomena that surrounded man—the sun, the moon, the stars, night, day, the seasons of the year, life, and death. Most primitive tribes were, and many still are, deep believers in magic; they had no other way to explain the growing of a seed, or the entry of disease into a body, or lightning, thunder —or fate.

Primitive man observed animals closely, felt one with them, attributed great powers to them. He also danced them.

Without question, the dancelike movement of animals was one of the inspirations for the dance of primitive man. For it is true that many insects, birds, animals, and even fish carry out ritualized movement patterns that appear to be very much like our conception of dance.

George Wald, a professor of biology at Harvard, has noted that many human behavior patterns have evolved from those of animals. He suggests that fear and rage, for example, grew out of the need to prepare the body for sudden, strenuous action—either to fight or to flee. He has described, too, how certain movement patterns are used by bees, as part of their total social behavior, and as a means of communication and decision-making. His analysis is based on the work of an Austrian investigator, Karl von Frisch, who found that, by certain dancelike routines, a bee can tell others where it has found a rich store of nectar. Now, another researcher

> . . . has discovered that dances are also used in searching for a site for a new hive. Worker bees fan out in this hunt. When they find a likely place, they return and dance before the swarm. The better the spot, the more prolonged and intense the dance. Other workers, told of the site through the dance pattern, go out to investigate and in turn give their opinion by a dance. . . . In this way the swarm achieves a consensus and flies out to build its new home. . . .[3]

Joost Meerloo describes dancing movements among fish, particularly the astonishing breeding behavior and courtship of the Cichlids, whose slow dancing movements, together with their extremely vivid color, provide what he calls a "slow motion waltz." Meerloo also refers to the unusual mass behavior of ants, in which they march in complicated and elaborate patterns and formations.[4]

[3] *The New York Times,* March 15, 1966, p. 40.

[4] Joost Meerloo, *The Dance* (New York: Chilton Book Co., 1960), pp. 45–46.

Sachs has described the dance of an unusual storklike bird, the stilt bird of Cape York in northeastern Australia, only one of many birds which have been observed to fly or move around the ground in rhythmic and graceful patterns which resemble dance. These birds have been observed assembling by the hundreds in a secluded swamp area. In a quadrillelike formation, they move rhythmically and gracefully in unison:

> In groups of a score or more they advanced and retreated, lifting high their long legs and standing on their toes, now and then bowing gracefully one to another, now and then one pair encircling with prancing daintiness a group whose heads moved downwards and sidewide to the stepping of the pair. . . .[5]

Perhaps most dancelike of all are the play forms, almost approaching dance, which are carried on by chimpanzees. A German investigator, Kohler, observed a number of these large apes over a period of time, and describes them as having a variety of behaviors to which newcomers joining their group were introduced. They used instruments and implements for reaching or climbing; carried on a "sort of rhythmic play or dance," and made a variety of murmurs, wails, and rejoicing sounds. Two of the apes in particular, Tschego and Grande, developed a game of spinning round and round like dervishes, in a spirit of friendly play, which the other apes enjoyed greatly. The resemblance to human dance became striking when one ape stretched out her arm horizontally as she spun around, or revolved slowly on her own axis. The group of chimpanzees sometimes trotted around a post, marking a rough rhythm by accenting the movement of one foot.[6]

Wild apes have even been observed to join hands and move around rhythmically in a circle or weaving line, sometimes bedecking themselves with leaves and boughs. Observing the movements of animals carrying on such dancelike activities, it is natural that primitive man would imitate them. He may have believed that by impersonating them, he would gain their strength or cunning—just as, to the primitive mind, obtaining the nail clippings of a person may give him power over that person. His purpose may have been to imitate the animal as part of storytelling, or for amusement, or to recount adventures. In any case, just as animals are personified within folk myths, and appear again and again in primitive carvings, so many primitive dances are based on specific animal themes.

RELIGIOUS ROLE OF DANCE

However, a superficial imitation of the movement of animals, even when costumed by masks, skins, or horns, was not enough. As Suzanne Langer points out, man differs from animal in terms of ritual, feeling, superstition, and scientific genius. His life is impregnated with ritual—a complicated blend of reason and rite, fact, and dream. Gradually, during the

[5]Curt Sachs, *World History of the Dance* (New York: W. W. Norton & Co., 1937), p. 9.

[6]See Suzanne Langer, *Philosophy in a New Key: A Study in the Symbolism of Reason, Rite, and Art* (New York: The New American Library, 1951) p. 114.

performance of ritual, primitive man's simpler imitative movements or gesture language became transformed into a more elaborate structure of symbolic arts, combining dance, acting, singing, and primitive speech, all wrapped around with complicated conventions and undergirded by an unquestioning belief in the efficacy of ceremony. All nature was embraced by such rites. Langer writes:

> The apparently misguided efforts of savages to induce rain by dancing and drumming are not practical mistakes at all; they are rites in which the rain has a part. White observers of Indian rain dances have often commented on the fact that in an extraordinary number of instances the downpour really "results." Others of a more cynical turn remark that the leaders of the dance know the weather so well that they time their dance to meet its approaching changes and simulate "rain-making." This may well be the case; yet it is not a pure imposture. A "magic" effect is one which completes a rite . . . he dances *with* the rain; he invites the elements to do their part . . . if heaven and earth do not answer him, the rite is simply unconsummated. . . .[7]

The power of religious belief among primitive peoples is tremendous. Often it is responsible for phenomena that otherwise could not possibly be explained on rational grounds. A dervish who dances for 12 or 15 hours at a stretch, whirling steadily without faltering, demonstrates a degree of endurance and self-control that is almost beyond belief. A voodoo dancer in the West Indies who sits on a metal frame above a fire, her skin pressed against the glowing iron, is not burned. Trance dancers in Indonesia repeatedly thrust sharp daggers against their bare chests, so forcefully that the weapons are bent; yet they are not injured. Are these tricks? In some cases they may be, but too many illustrations of such primitive rites have been gathered to question the power of such magical belief. Perhaps the answer lies in hypnosis. Yet, for primitive man, the fact that such rites "worked" made him believe in them unquestioningly as a means of gaining divine protection. He sought the favor of the gods, or of nature, in every aspect of his life—for food, shelter, success in warfare, protection against the forces of nature, and in procreation.

A great concern of his, of course, was the magical act of perpetuating the species—of carrying on the tribe. Thus, many primitive dances are concerned with fertility, and are performed at ceremonies having to do with entrance into adolescence, courtship, marriage, and birth. Just as the primitive artist is usually quite representational, except for those decorations which are intended as abstract design, so the primitive dance on such themes is usually quite frank. Tore Hakansson writes on this point:

> . . . primitive art . . . is representational, conventional, and intended to be understood by the audience for which the artist creates. He decorates houses and equipment and he composes ceremonies concerned with birth, puberty rites, marriage, ancestors, hunting, harvestings, the seasons, and war. The primitive artist is really a craftsman. He is well integrated with the community in which he works. Whereas in our civilization the artist is a specialist and an outsider, a rebel against the conventions of his society, in the primitive com-

[7] *Ibid.*, pp. 138–139.

munity art is a necessity, not merely a form of entertainment ... art ... produces an esthetic effect that is both gratifying and vital, and is a useful social phenomenon, leading to participation of the artist-craftsman with the fellow members of his community in the use of his work—generally in dancing, rituals, and feasts.[8]

Hakansson points out that often art portrays dances and rituals which are part of initiation, clearly phallic in nature. Sex and sexual functions are expressed naturally, with a degree of distortion, or abstractly; often abstract decorations of art objects of primitive people are really stylized sex symbols and are recognized as such by the tribe that uses them.

According to Sachs, human fertility dances may be drawn from two different phases of sexual relations—the mating and wooing, and the act itself. In some cases, he says, moments of sexual intercourse may actually be made part of the dance. Quoting Koch-Grunberg, he describes a fertility dance of the Cobéna Indians of Brazil. The dancers have large artificial replicas of the male organ, which they hold close to their bodies with both hands.

> Stamping with the right foot and singing, they dance—with the upper part of their bodies bent forwards. Suddenly they jump wildly along with violent coitus motions and loud groans. . . . They carry the fertility into every corner of the houses. . . . They jump among the women—they knock the phalli one against another. . . .[9]

Sachs describes primitive dance as being essentially of two types: those which he considers to be out of harmony with the body, and those which are in harmony. In general, the dance which is "out of harmony" is one in which dancers work themselves into extreme nervous excitement. The song is panted out; movements are jerky and uncontrolled. The action is wild, eerie, ecstatic. Dancers may actually go into a trance corresponding to a medical description of clonic convulsion—a state of forceful flexion and relaxation of the muscles which may lead to a throwing about of the body in wild paroxyms. He gives as an example the dance of the secret society of the Wayee tribesmen in Unyamwezi, in Africa:

> . . . suddenly the dancers swing into violent motion. All the parts of their bodies begin to shake, all their muscles play, their shoulder blades roll as if they were no longer a part of their bodies. The drums resound louder and louder. Their bodies are bathed with sweat from head to foot. Now they stand as though changed to statues. Only the weird jerking of the muscles over their whole body continues. Then, when the excitement has risen to its highest point, they suddenly collapse as if struck by lightning and remain for a time on the ground as though unconscious. After a short time the play begins anew.[10]

[8]Tore Hakansson, "Sex in Primitive Art and Dance," in *The Encyclopedia of Sexual Behavior*, eds. Albert Ellis and Albert Abarbanel (New York: Hawthorn Books, Inc., 1961), pp. 154–160.

[9]Sachs, *op. cit.*, p. 157.

[10]*Ibid.*, p. 18.

He also classifies as "out of harmony" the type of dance that is based on a weakened convulsive state. Here, what had originally been a complete surrender to frenzy develops into a conscious art form; the movement is subordinated to the dancer's will, and the convulsion, or loss of control, is limited to a portion of the dancer's body. At no point does the dancer go into a full state of trance, nor does he usually inflict great suffering on himself.

In Sachs's terms, the primitive dance that is "in harmony" with the body is the one that does not "mortify or degrade" the body, but "exalts" it. Through repeated movement, the dancer achieves exhilaration. The dance is powerful, with strong motor reactions, every muscle stretched taut; it brings about a release from gravity with buoyant movements forward and upward. Actions involve leaping, lifting, slapping, stamping, striding, and lunging. Such dances are bold and positive.

PRIMITIVE DANCE MOVEMENT

Specific movements of primitive dance may include whirling, leaping, vibrating, rolling of the pelvis, striding, and stamping. Certain dances, particularly in the Orient, tend to have a much narrower range of movement, and the movement itself may be much more subtle. Such dances frequently are performed on a limited base, with swinging, swaying, and suspension, with gesture language of the hands and arms. In certain dances on Pacific islands, particularly in the Marshall Archipelago, women sit on their heels; in others they sit cross-legged. Frequently, dances in such positions involve clapping in complicated rhythms, or the use of coconut shells or other instruments, to create percussive effects.

Early Spanish explorers described Chamorro dancing in the Marshalls in considerable detail. It often involved social rituals and celebrations, with the sexes playing distinctly separate roles. A Father Gobien wrote:

> . . . they meet often together, to regale on fish, fruit, and a certain liquor, made of rice and grated Cocoas, and then exercise themselves in dancing, running, leaping, and wrestling. They recite the heroic deeds of their ancestors, and repeat the work of their poets, which are full of fable and extravagance. The women have also their festivals . . . When they are met, ten or twelve of them form a circle, standing upright without motion. In this posture they begin to sing the verses of their best poets. . . . (then) their song is accompanied with such lively and just action that there is no hearing them without being charmed with their melody.[11]

Often dancers in the South Pacific islands were elaborately decorated. Another observer, in the Carolines, described how young people gathered around their chief's house in the evening to sing and dance:

[11]Mary Browning, "Micronesian Heritage," in *Dance Perspectives,* No. 43, Autumn, 1970, p. 9.

> The men are placed opposite to the women, and move their heads, arms, and legs, in exact cadence. On these occasions they are dressed in all their finery. On their heads they have crowns of feathers, aromatic flowers hanging from their nostrils, and palm leaves from their ears. Their arms, hands, and feet are also ornamented.[12]

The movement quality of much primitive dance has been well described by Agnes de Mille:

> All primitives . . . who go barefoot and hunt unprotected by armor, have certain characteristics in common. They stamp out rhythms. They run crouched low in imitation of animals or of the precautionary attitudes adopted when stalking prey or an enemy. . . .[13]

She suggests that, because of primitive man's nakedness and vulnerability, he bends to the ground to protect his vitals. Rhythm and complex foot movements are often stressed in primitive dance, rather than elaborate visual patterns or body movements. Dancing as part of primitive ritual is carried out over many hours; both endurance and intensity are stressed, as well as exact adherence to the rules for performance.

THEMES AND EXAMPLES OF PRIMITIVE DANCE

The themes of primitive dance are many. As indicated, many are animal dances, often with masks which give the dancer the godlike or magic power of the animal portrayed. Sometimes skins or horns are worn. Such dances are performed as a prelude to hunting, or sometimes as part of fertility rituals. War dances are found in tribes throughout the world; often these are weapon dances, in which the motions of warfare are used, and in which dancers may sometimes work themselves up to a pitch of hysteria or trance. In many cultures ancient myths are acted out—often with the essential theme of the battle between good and evil, life and death, being reenacted. Other motifs for dance often include dances based on astral themes, portraying the sun, moon, or stars.

Among the American Plains Indians, the dancing ground frequently was laid out so that it had four sacred places, each named in honor of the deities who presided over the four cardinal points of the compass. Among the Cherokees, these points were known as the Sun Land (east), the Frigid Land (north), the Darkening Land (west), and Wahala (south). Each of these had a color assigned to it, and each color had symbolic meaning. White and red spirits were usually invoked for peace and health, red alone for success of an undertaking, blue for defeating a cunning enemy, and black for causing his death.

One of the most famous dances of the Plains Indians was the Sun Dance. Radin describes this, as performed by the Oglala Dakota. Basically, it is interpreted as a dance concerned with supplication to the deities for

[12] *Ibid.*

[13] Agnes de Mille, *The Book of the Dance* (New York: Golden Press, 1963), pp. 32–33.

power and success in warfare, and it represents the cruelest kind of testing of the braves who took part in it. It was usually carried out by a warrior in fulfillment of a vow made at a crucial moment in his life when the help of the gods was needed. After a number of secret rites are carried out, to purify and prepare the initiate, there is a ceremonial search for a center-pole for the dance. When the proper tree is found, it is felled, brought to the camp, and erected. There is a period of fasting, prayer, chanting, and offerings to the gods, for several days and nights.

The Sun Dance itself involved a dramatic climax of self-inflicted torture. Medicine men would take up as much of the skin of the breast under the nipple of each dancer as could be held between the thumb and forefinger. A cut would be made and a skewer inserted through the flesh. The skewer would then be tethered to the center-pole, fastened by long ropes of woven hair or thongs. The warriors then danced, straining back against the thongs and staring up into the blinding white sun, until finally the flesh of their chest had torn loose and the thongs and skewers were pulled through.

> . . . as they dance, they hold eagle pipes in their mouths, this being a term for flutes made from one of the bones in an eaglet's wing. They had to be sounded throughout the time the young man was dancing. The dancing was done in the manner of a buck jump, the body and legs being stiff and all movements being upon the tips of the toes. The dancers kept looking at the sun, and either dropped the hands to the sides in the military position of "attention" with the palms to the front, or else held them upward and outward at an angle of 45 degrees, with the fingers spread apart and inclined toward the sun. . . .[14]

This ordeal frequently continued for many hours, until the warrior had proved his manhood by completing the ritual successfully. To understand such a dance, it is necessary to recognize that it is part of a total religious belief, a symbolic representation, a prayer which in many cases is hundreds of years old. In a sense, it is part of an elaborate drama which embraces all the arts and which is performed with the strictest adherence to authentic detail. Fergusson writes:

> Most of the Indian ceremonials are extremely elaborate, lasting for days and ending on the last day or night with the dance. Outsiders are usually permitted to see only the dance. The secret ceremonies take place in the kiva or medicine lodge and are open only to clan members or to the dancers. Sometimes they are historical or legendary in character, presenting the life of the whole people or of a certain hero. Often elaborate altars are erected and painted with symbolic decorations, sand paintings are made and destroyed at specified hours and, with meticulous care for detail, costumes are prepared for the dance, masks are painted and decorated with feathers, prayer sticks are made. The dancers must be purified by means of fasting and medication, bathing the body, and washing the hair. Everything is done under the direction of the

[14]Paul Radin, *The Story of the American Indian* (New York: Garden City Publishing Co., 1937), p. 313.

cacique or medicine-man, whose duty it is to see that nothing goes wrong, as the slightest slip may ruin the effect of the entire ceremony.[15]

American Indians of the Southwest performed dances that ranged from rituals of the utmost solemnity to others of a purely social and humorous character. As observed in the 1930s, certain dances were done for the cure of disease, notably the "medicine sings" of the Navajo tribe. These were elaborate nine-day ceremonials, which included prayers and the making of sand paintings in secret, sweat baths and medications for the patient, and finally the all-night dance. . . . They were conducted by medicine men, who knew every detail of the ritual, every song, every sand painting, word, and movement of the dance.

An impressive example of the use of dance is found in the religious rituals carried on by the Aztec Indians of Central America, before their conquest by Spanish conquistadors in the early 16th century. The invading soldiers and priests found the Aztec culture rich in complex ceremonies for every occasion of a political, religious, or commercial nature, or to mark such events as births, weddings, and death. Gertrude Kurath points out that they dedicated ceremonies to their gods for rain, fruitfulness of the crops, victory in war, success in the hunt, and the tribal dead, with an annual succession of 18 ceremonies based on the ecological calendar. A later observer concluded that the Aztecs believed dance to be "meritorious," like deeds of charity or penance:

> In these religious festivals and their dances, they not only called on and honored and praised their gods with songs but also with the heart and with the movements of the body. In order to do this properly, they . . . used many patterns, not only in the movements of the head, of the arms, and of the feet but with all their body . . . and this they called *maceualiztli,* penance and good deed.[16]

There were several uniquely different styles of dance, as well as certain dances which were extremely spectacular, or which were carried on in connection with ritual sacrifices of animals or humans, held by the priesthood and the nobility. Among these, Kurath describes the *Volador* (flying pole, in which participants swing out widely, suspended by ropes from a high pole), and the *Comelagotoazte,* or small ferris wheel; these ceremonies were associated with shooting arrows at a crucified victim. In contrast, dances of the early Mayan cultures tended to be "artful, gay, and festive . . . part of all public and private festivities . . ."[17]

So varied are the dances of African tribes that it is difficult to characterize or classify them meaningfully. They embrace all the themes and motivations described earlier; war, the hunt, fertility, courtship, marriage, harvest,

[15]Erna Fergusson, *Indian Ceremonials of New Mexico and Arizona* (Albuquerque: University of New Mexico Press, 1951), p. xviii.

[16]Samuel Merti and Gertrude Kurath, *Dances of Anahuac* (Chicago: Aldine Publishing Co., and Wenner-Gren Foundation, 1964), p. 25.

[17]*Ibid.,* p. 26.

birth, initiation into adolescence or adulthood, and burial. Typically, many African dances are derived from motions performed during work. Rhythm also pervades their labor; by singing and moving in unison, such tasks as rowing, carrying heavy burdens, or felling trees are made easier.

Although many of the functions of primitive dance have declined with the coming of civilization, often they are performed as a matter of custom and national or tribal pride. Today, they may no longer be based on a conscious belief in magic; however, they are still seen as talismans of good fortune, and as expressions of patriotic unity.

Typically, in the dry, grassy plains of Mali, lying below the Sahara desert in West Africa, Bambara tribesmen have retained many of their historic dances which are performed with animal masks. These are done as part of elaborate annual festivals, in which different groups compete against each other for tribal acclaim. What was once done as part of secret ritual is now open to all, and essentially a form of social entertainment. However, it remains an important aspect of tribal life, with much time spent preparing costumes and masks, and choreographing the dance performances.

In a number of the emerging nations of Africa, a strong effort is made to retain traditional folk customs—particularly the dance. In 1966, King Sobhuza II, the Ngwenyama, or Lion of Swaziland, joined thousands of his people in a ceremonial six-day incwala, a central ritual in the life of Swaziland, symbolic of the renewal of the people, land, and king.

> The Ngwenyama, who wears three-piece suits when he addresses Parliament or dedicates factories, was dressed like his warriors. That is, he wore a headdress of fancy plumage, a leopard-skin girdle, and a mantle of ox tails. He danced barefoot on the earth of the royal cattle corral, where the ceremony took place. Many sophisticated young Swazis, European educated, took part. One university graduate said: "I used to shy away from these ceremonies. But there has been a remarkable change of late. We all realize now that this is our national land. It's something we've got to support and be proud of. . . ."[18]

In other countries, even those of Western world, where the pagan dances of earlier centuries have all but disappeared, there is a deliberate effort to retain and revive these forms, as evidences of the historical past. One example is England, where the efforts of Cecil Sharp led to the development of the English Folk Dance and Song Society, which has been instrumental in a widespread revival of English country, Morris, and sword dancing. Many of the original dances done by clubs and teams throughout the country date from pre-Christian days; some are directly suggestive of early pagan rituals. Thus, even in a heavily industrialized nation, elements of primitive dance survive in recognizable form. In other parts of the world, where village life, simple handicrafts, and agricultural pursuits have retained their traditional forms, primitive dances still exist and still hold much of their appeal for the peasantry—although the original magical belief that prompted them has largely slipped away.

An example of how varied forms of pagan folklore have continued to persist in Christian religious and social ritual, even in a 20th century Eu-

[18] *The New York Times,* Jan. 13, 1966, p. L–9.

ropean nation, may be found in Poland. Sula Benet describes the cyclical nature of farm life in mid-century Poland, with the peasant's calendar fitted to the recurrent tasks of planting, tending the crops and reaping, with cach season having its own cluster of holidays and observances. She points out that the holidays are not an interruption of the agricultural task, but rather essential to it. Although they consist primarily of worship and religious ritual, they also provide rest and recreation for peasants and their families. Benet writes:

> (The holidays) are rich too in magical rites and observances carried over from pre-Christian days and mingling comfortably with Roman Catholic ritual and precept. All the important holidays that the peasant observes are linked with agricultural festivals initiated by his remote ancestors.[19]

As an example, the Shrovetide festivals that begin the Easter holidays and end after Holy Week are marked by varied dramatizations and celebrations of winter's death and the return of spring. These include symbolic representations of spring by beautiful young maidens, customs which ridicule young unmarried men, carnival-like parades in which many animal and human masks and costumes appear. Typical of the many unique dances with symbolic meaning that has essentially become a social form of amusement is a Shrove Tuesday dance done by married women, originally intended to make the hemp crop grow tall. Benet writes:

> The women gather in the tavern and when they begin to feel the liquor they dance around a barrel on which stands a *koziolek,* or 'little ram'—a small figure made of wood and pieces of cloth. During the dance they try to leap as high as possible, to make the hemp grow higher. The men spur them on, as each woman tries to outdo the others, and the serious purpose of the dance is buried under waves of merriment.[20]

In other countries which have become more heavily industrialized or in which the folklore roots of culture have largely disappeared, the relation of dance to religion is less clear. However, the examples that have been cited here clearly indicate how dance has been inextricably intertwined with ritual and social custom from the earliest periods of human development. This is made explicit as one reviews the major historical eras of our past, beginning with the pre-Christian civilizations that arose in the Mediterranean region of Europe, the Middle East, and North Africa.

[19]Sula Benet, *Song, Dance and Customs of Peasant Poland* (London: Dennis Dobson Ltd., 1951), p. 36.

[20]*Ibid.,* p. 47.

3

Dance in Pre-Christian Civilizations

It is reasonable to assume that prehistoric man danced; indeed, we have records of what appear to be war dances and shaman dances in cave paintings that date back tens of thousands of years, in what is now France. However, because of the limited number of examples, little is known of these dances. Based on other facts known about the culture of prehistoric peoples at various levels of development—in terms of their utensils, tools, weapons—it is possible to draw parallels with primitive tribes existing in the world today. Thus, conjectures may be made about their customs, their means of cultivation, their dwellings and communities, and similar aspects of their lives. However, these are largely speculation. Our first real knowledge of dance comes with the great Mediterranean and Middle Eastern civilizations that preceded the Christian era.

The early Sumerians had a vigorous musical culture; they developed in the third millenium B.C. lyres, pipes, harps, and drums, some of which they passed on to succeeding Babylonians and Assyrians. In Sumer, a sacred dance was practiced in various forms. In one, a procession of singers is recorded to have moved soberly, perhaps around an altar, to liturgies played on flutes. In another, dancers prostrated themselves before the altar or other sacred objects, as part of religious worship.

In ancient Assyria, many depictions of dancing men and women have been found, suggesting that dance was found both as part of religious practice and as part of the social life of the time. Processions led by men playing harps have been noted, and it is known that the great fire festival of Ashtoreth, the goddess of fertility, which was celebrated every spring, was noted for having wine-crazed dancers slash and mutilate themselves with knives to the orgiastic accompaniment of drums, cymbals, and droning oboes.[1] In Babylon, too, the occurrence of temple dancing has been con-

[1]Alfred Sendrey and Mildred Norton, *David's Harp: The Story of Music in Biblical Times* (New York: The New American Library, 1964), p. 14.

firmed; in the text of the Assurbanipal, it is stated that at a religious festival the performers danced a ring-dance, to musical accompaniment, around the idol of the god who was being worshipped.[2]

DANCE IN ANCIENT EGYPT

However, it was in ancient Egypt, a civilization which lasted for 4,000 years, that dance for the first time reached a full flowering, and was richly recorded, in wall paintings and reliefs, and in the literary record of the hieroglyphs. The Egyptian culture was a complex one, and achieved an advanced understanding of astronomy and geometry, sculpture, architecture, and engineering, as well as initiating the use of paper and weaving processes. It also developed for the first time a varied class structure, with royal families, workers and peasants, slaves, a powerful priesthood, and, in later dynasties, troupes of professional entertainers.

Ted Shawn writes that in Egypt, where the priesthood was all-powerful, dance was the chief medium of religious expression. The secret doctrines and mysteries of the Egyptian mythology, based primarily on the annual rise and fall of the River Nile (resulting in a legend of resurrection and belief in human survival) were portrayed through symbolic dance dramas. In these, the central theme of the Egyptian religion—that of Osiris being slain and dismembered, with the parts of his body hidden throughout the earth, followed by the search of his sister-wife, Isis, to find and bury the body of the god—all this "was re-enacted constantly within the temples in dramatic dance form, and the young people were thus given their religious education . . . "[3]

There was a complex and highly ritualized system of worship in ancient Egypt, concerned chiefly with death and rebirth, and attached to certain holy cities associated with the cult. As part of this system, there began to appear trained dancers who performed regularly as part of religious service. Their main purpose was to propitiate the gods, and to re-enact through dance, music, song, and pageantry, the search for the dead body of Osiris and its resurrection. Chiefly, these were connected to rituals of planting and harvest. Lincoln Kirstein points out that annually such a mystery-play or tragedy was produced at Abydos; in the ritual, the priest, or first dancer, becomes the personification of the entire enacted legend. He is aided by a larger group of dancers, performing en masse.[4]

Other religious dances included a traditional festival performed in honor of the bull Apis, one of the most powerful of Egyptian gods. To carry on this ceremonial, a special bull was selected and raised; in his quarters, the Apeum, the priests or priestesses who attended him would perform secret dances, retelling the adventures of the god of whom the bull Apis was

[2]E. Louis Backman, *Religious Dances* (London: George Allen and Unwin Ltd., 1952), pp. 2–3.

[3]Ted Shawn, *Dance We Must* (London: Dennis Dobson Ltd., 1946), p. 16.

[4]Lincoln Kirstein, *Dance: A Short History of Classic Theatrical Dancing* (New York: G. P. Putnam's Sons, 1935), p. 7.

Egyptian dancing girls and a musician. From a tombstone fresco at Karnak, about 1420 B.C.

the living image. In dance parades inside and outside the temples, they would recount the life story of Osiris. Another traditional dance was the Astronomic, or Dance of Stars, which was performed by priests in their temples, without onlookers. This ritual was based on the movements of the solar system, and was extremely significant to the Egyptians who plotted the seasons of the year, and thus regulated control of the dikes that gave fertility to the land.

Since they were so preoccupied with themes of life and death and indeed sought to conquer death by making the body of the buried nobleman immortal, funeral ceremonies were extremely important to the ancient Egyptians. On the occasion of the burial of important personages, a man skilled as a mimic was dressed in the dead man's garments and, having his face covered with a mask as nearly as possible resembling the face of the deceased, he immediately preceded the hearse. As the procession moved slowly along to the sound of solemn music, he performed a pantomimic dance to show the remarkable deeds achieved during the lifetime of the man being borne to his tomb. The mourning ritual was performed mainly by women, some of them probably hired for the occasion, with weeping, wailing, and stylized dance gestures which imitated scooping up earth and scattering it over the head.

But such themes were not the sole preoccupation of dance among the Egyptians. They enjoyed sports, acrobatics, and various forms of entertainment, and had complex orchestras, including copper cymbals, tambourines, bone clackers, drums, pipes, castanets, whistles, and other stringed and percussive instruments. Bands of female performers were attached to temples, and the royal houses also owned troupes of entertainers who performed on both sacred and social occasions. Slaves were taught both dancing and music, and in the later dynasties there developed a class of professional performers who were independent, in that they were neither owned by the nobility nor attached to temples. Alexander Bland points out that the Pharaoh himself took part in sacred dance rituals; ancient paintings show him first sitting on a throne and then removing his robe to dance four times around a field in a short garment.[5] Non-religious dancing was apparently not considered suitable for the nobility, although they enjoyed entertainment by highly skilled professional dancers. Kirstein cites several illustrative examples of Egyptian dancing at various periods of history:

As far back as the first Dynasty (ca. 3000 B.C.) a wooden relief shows King Semti dancing rhythmically to simply instrumental music.

An official of King Assa (ca. 2400 B.C.) brought from a distant land a Pygmy dancer, who was believed to have come from the spirit-world. Such dancers, who performed in a buffoonlike and grotesque style, were prized; there is an ivory statuette of a dancing Pygmy in the Metropolitan Museum of New York, dated about 1950 B.C.

Wall reliefs at Gizeh (ca. 1580–1150 B.C.) show "girls posturing with tambourines, clacking castanets curved and carved to form conventionalized fingers."[6]

Gradually, the practice developed of having dancing as professional entertainment at private dinner parties. Although the upper classes had once danced, they gradually relinquished this practice to slaves or highly skilled paid performers. In the words of Curt Sachs, none of the "vast number of dance pictures and none of the literary sources reveals a real social dance" for the aristocracy. However, dance as entertainment continued to be popular for all classes; in later dynasties one would find in larger cities like Memphis or Alexandria small groups of roving mimes or acrobats who gave impromptu shows in public squares.

In a physical sense, what was the dance of ancient Egypt like? Because of the stylized treatment of figures in all reliefs and paintings, it is difficult to tell whether the poses and movements that are shown give a realistic picture of the actual dances that were done. However, the movement seems to have ranged from quiet, dignified walking steps, with arms outstretched, to difficult acrobatic positions, such as the famous "bridge" position, or handstands. In some cases, vigorous striding, leaping, or running movements are shown. There are hieroglyph names for dance figures and positions. Some of the movements suggest turns in the air, and one wall relief dated about 1500 B.C. seems to show a figure doing what would in ballet be called an *entrechat.* Other acrobatic actions, such as tumbling, somersaults, and splits, were also common.

In less active dances, movement tended to be sinuous and fluid, with much hand movement, particularly after the period of 1500 B.C., when the

[5]Alexander Bland, *A History of Ballet and Dance in the Western World* (New York: Praeger Book Co., 1976), p. 14.

[6]Kirsten, *op. cit.,* pp. 11–12.

influence of Indian dancing was felt. Dancers often performed as soloists, or in groups of two or three; sometimes they formed larger groups of performers.

One such group work was described in a later period (4th century B.C.) as an entertainment seen in the city of Memphis:

> Then came forward a group of dancers who jumped about in all directions, gathered together again, climbed on top of each other with incredible dexterity, mounting on shoulders and heads, forming pyramids reaching to the ceiling of the hall, then descended suddenly one after the other to perform new jumps and admirable somersaults. Without stopping, they danced on their hands, paired off, one placed his head between his legs and his partner then lifted him in turn and returned to the original position, each of them alternately being lifted and, as he fell, lifted his partner up.[7]

What was the influence of Egypt, then, in terms of the development of dance? Certainly, it consisted of the extent to which dance found a formal place in religious practice, as well as its use as a form of popular or courtly entertainment. The scope and variety of dance movement, as well as the development of a professional class of dancers within the increasingly differentiated Egyptian social structure, were additional important developments. Without question, Egypt was influential in terms of spreading its cultural forms throughout the Mediterranean world. Even beyond the Mediterranean, at Cadiz, it seems that dancing essentially Egyptian in character was established. Havelock Ellis writes:

> The Nile and Cadiz were thus the two great centers of ancient dancing, and Martial mentions them both together, for each supplied its dancers to Rome.[8]

DANCE AMONG THE ANCIENT HEBREWS

While there are no wall reliefs or paintings to tell of dance as performed by the ancient Hebrews, there are abundant references to this practice in the Old Testament. Numerous Biblical allusions show that dance was highly respected, and was particularly used on occasions of celebration and triumph:

"And David danced before the Lord with all his might" (2 Samuel 6:14).

"Then shall the virgin rejoice in the dance" (Jeremiah 31:13).

"Let them praise his name in the dance: let them sing praises unto him with the timbrel and harp" (Psalms 149 1:3).

Throughout the Bible, there are such references. When the prodigal son returned home he was welcomed with "music and dancing," to signify reconciliation and joy. When David slew Goliath, the passage read, "Is not this David the king of the land? Did they not sing to one another of him in dances, saying—Saul hath slain his thousands, but David his ten thou-

[7]Bland, *op. cit.,* p. 14.

[8]Havelock Ellis, *The Dance of Life* (Boston: Houghton Mifflin Co., 1923), p. 54.

sands?" Exodus tells of the dance of celebration by Miriam and the other women, with the timbrel in hand, after the crossing of the Red Sea. After the victory of Judith over Holofernes, we read that they put a garland of olive upon Judith and her maid, and that "she herself went before all the people in the dance, leading all the women." And when Israel was depressed by enemies, war, and captivity, the passage goes, "The joy of our heart has ceased, our dance is turned into mourning."

What were the types of dances performed by the ancient Jews? Several forms are described in the Old Testament. A circular, or ring-dance, is the dance around the Golden Calf portrayed in Exodus 32:6,19. In other passages, we are told how David took the Ark to David's City, in a processional march. Along the way, he stopped from time to time to prepare sacrifices, and to dance with all his strength before the Lord and his Ark.

Other dances are described as hopping dances or whirling dances, usually carried on in celebration. And still other passages refer to use of the dance in divine service, although no formal provision was made in the Mosaic law for music or dance in the service of the Lord.

Probably the early Hebrews were strongly influenced by the religious and secular customs of the Egyptians during their four centuries in Egypt; indeed the Jewish cult had come to life in countries in which the Jews were surrounded by peoples who had regarded the dance as an essential element in religious worship. Alfred Sendrey and Mildred Norton write:

> In both religions, processional dances were used in ritual ceremonies. National festivals alike include popular dancing. The harvest festival was celebrated by both people with fertility dancing, the husbandman of Israel rejoicing, like the Egyptian, with palm and willow branches. . . . Even the Egyptian belief that their gods themselves indulged in dancing had its parallel in a conception of the Hebrews. . . . [9]

As evidence that the ancient Hebrews must have danced on every possible occasion, both in daily life and for special occasions and ceremonies, Sendrey and Norton point out that Biblical Hebrew has no less than twelve verbs to express the act of dancing. The Hebrew word most frequently used is *hul,* or *hil,* meaning "to whirl." Sachs interprets this as "to turn," a word used both for a sword swung in a circle, and for the whirlwind. From this is derived the word for dance, *mahol* (the source of the girl's name Mahelah, or, today, Mahalia). At least two psalms have in their headings the instruction, *al mahalath,* suggesting that they were meant to be performed with some kind of dance. Another interesting term is the word *pasah,* which has two meanings: "to pass over," or "to spare" (thus *Pesah,* the Feast of the Passover), and "to limp," or "to dance in a limping fashion." Some Biblical scholars have thus speculated that the Passover ceremony owes its origin to the peculiar limping dance that may have been performed at spring festivals of the early Hebrews.

In addition to ritual processions or circle dances, or dances of celebration, dances were performed on certain other occasions; some of these have lingered as customs throughout the history of the Jews. Wedding dances

[9]Sendrey and Norton, *op. cit.,* p. 207.

were performed in ancient times; centuries later, during the Middle Ages, it was the custom for the bridal party to dance all the way to the house of the wedding. Dignified rabbis were not above dancing before the bridal couple with myrtle and olive branches. Although mixed dancing was common in the earlier pagan cultures, men and women were customarily separated in religious dances. The rabbis of the Middle Ages only permitted those who were closely related (husband and wife, brother and sister, or father and daughter) to dance together. In Eastern Europe during this later period, the extremely orthodox Hasidic Jews made a practice of having the men only dance certain ritual dances during religious worship.

Although no mention is made in the Old Testament of funeral dances, it is probable that these too were carried on by the ancient Jews. Certainly, they had observed them as performed by Egyptians and in other surrounding lands. Even among the modern Sephardim (Jews of Spanish and Portuguese descent) there are funeral customs of walking around the bier while chanting prayers, which suggest that they are derived from earlier funeral processional dances.

Thus we see that among the ancient Hebrews there was great interest in and respect for the dance. However, certain prohibitions began to appear. Dance is not mentioned formally in the Mosaic code. Men and women were not permitted to take part together in certain dances. And, finally, a distinction was made between those dances which are of a sacred or holy nature and those which resemble pagan ceremonies—such as dancing around the Golden Calf, a form of idolatry. This distinction made by the early Jews, whose faith was the first of the great monotheistic religions, was to be made even more sharply by the Christians, in the centuries that followed.

DANCE IN ANCIENT GREECE

Just as among the early Egyptians and Hebrews, dance was held in great esteem by the ancient Greeks. They speculated on its antiquity and saw it as divinely inspired. It seemed to them that the stars and planets in the sky were doing some sort of cosmic dance; indeed, Urania, the patroness of astronomy, was also a Muse and a patroness of the dance. Lillian Lawler points out that the gods were thought of as fathers of the dance, and almost all of their greater divinities were portrayed in literature or art as dancing. In the *Laws,* Plato suggested that dance arose from the natural desire of all young creatures to move their bodies in order to express emotions—especially joy. But, he went on, the sense of harmony and rhythm which actually makes dances out of natural and instinctive movements is the specific gift of the gods and the Muses.[10]

The Greeks did not really think of dance as a separate entity. Instead, it was closely linked with other kinds of experiences. Thus, the word *orcheisthai,* which was translated in English "to dance," actually suggests rhythmical movements of many sorts—the feet, hands, head, eyes, or entire body.

[10]Lillian B. Lawler, *The Dance in Ancient Greece* (Middletown, Conn.: Wesleyan University Press, 1964), p. 14.

It might even describe marching, the playing of games, juggling, or tumbling, just as in Egypt professional dancers were also acrobats. Another Greek word was *mousiké,* the "art of the Muses;" this embraced music, poetry, and the dance, which, to the ancient Greeks, were all part of the same thing.

The sources of information about Greek dance are many. Among the literary sources are the words of songs written for dance, lines of poetry (including the great Homeric epics), the writings of philosophers, and many other forms of literature, including the work of later Roman historians and essayists. Archaeological sources, such as statues, wall reliefs, carvings, and paintings on walls or pottery, all frequently provide actual pictures of dancing. Because of the conventions they employed and their lack of realism, however, most of these do not give an accurate picture of what Greek dance movements were actually like. And, of course, our knowledge of the music that accompanied dance in this early period is extremely limited.

The earliest references to dance within the region of the Aegean Sea are to the dances performed on the island of Crete from about 3000 to 1400 B.C. Archaeological excavations at Knossos and elsewhere on the island show the Cretans performing a variety of games, sports, dancing, and musical activities during this period. So renowned for their dancing skill and agility were the men of Crete that in Homer's *Iliad,* Aeneas says to one of them, "Even though you are a dancer, I might have stopped you with my spear."[11]

One of the oldest of the dances was that of the Curetes, a wild, leaping men's dance, with much shouting and clashing of weapons. Other warlike dances were performed, as well as simple circle dances, patterned dances of women, dances with animal masks or heads, and fertility dances which involved "front and back somersaults, flying leaps and rapid kicks, standing on their heads, standing and walking on their hands or forearms, or bending far backward like wheels."[12] Lawler suggests that so complicated were these actions that it seems likely that the performers had long and rigorous training, and may have been professional entertainers, although members of royal families were also known to dance. Another famous dance of ancient Crete was the "maze" or "labyrinth" which, in its weaving, spiraling pattern, was thought to have been based on the palace of Minos, at Knossos.

Dance in ancient Crete was clearly a form of entertainment and display, as well as religious ritual or military training. Sappho described the "Cretan woman dancing in rhythm around the altar with her delicate feet, treading the soft smooth flowers of the meadow," and paintings of this period show female dancers with elaborate make-up and hair styles, as well as lavish ornaments and display of the body.

The colorful and spectacular dance of Crete was said to have inspired the dance of the Mycenaean Greeks, who came into being during the Bronze Age, on the mainland of Greece. These vigorous and talented warriors fortified their steep hills into impregnable fortresses, and sallied forth to conquer the Cretan cities, as well as other neighboring powers—such as the Trojans, in Asia Minor. Theirs was the civilization which Homer celebrated

[11]Bland, *op. cit.,* p. 21.

[12]Lawler, *op cit.,* p. 38.

there are two kinds of dance and music—the *noble,* concerned with what is fine and honorable, and the *ignoble,* imitating what is mean or ugly:

> He would have all children, boys and girls alike, instructed from an early age in noble music and dancing, and would spur them on with contests. . . . He would give to officials absolute power to exclude from the schools and from public performances all unworthy rhythms and harmonies, steps and gestures. Music and dancing should be consecrated to the gods . . . inasmuch as the gods themselves dance and create dance. . . . Noble dances should confer on the student not only health and agility and beauty of the body, but also goodness of the soul and a well-balanced mind. . . . [15]

The Greeks learned to dance at an early age, with most of the instruction apparently at the hands of private teachers. They practiced a variety of physical disciplines; they were extremely athletic and their movements were full and vigorous. Vase paintings show free running, skipping, and jumping, always in natural, easy poses, with little artificiality or acrobatics for its own sake. Particularly among the boys, dancing was taught as an aid to military education in Athens and Sparta. In the *palaestra* (wrestling school) and *gymnasium,* they took part in Pyrrhic dances and others designed to prepare them to execute battle motions. The dances fell into several categories:

Podism: quick, shifting movements of the feet, to train the warrior for hand-to-hand combat.

Xiphism: mock battle, in which groups of youths would practice the arts of warfare in dancelike form.

Homos: high leaps and vaults, to prepare them for leaping over high logs and boulders, or for scaling walls and fortresses.

Tetracomos: stately group formations, in which soldiers would advance on the enemy en masse, or protect themselves through interlocked shields.

Not only were these dances learned, as in Sparta, at training schools for boys, but they also were performed regularly at the Panathenaic Festivals, and were carried on regularly as part of the continuing training of soldiers. Shawn writes:

> We have records today of some 18 named Pyrrhic dances—solo, duet, and ensemble—which were mimetic warfare dances, by which the soldier attained the mind-body coordinations, the muscular strength, the discipline, which made him supreme on the field of battle.[16]

So esteemed was dance that it was accepted practice for statesmen, generals, philosophers, and other outstanding Greeks of the Periclean Age to perform solo dances before audiences of many thousands, on important public occasions, or on return from a military campaign or victory. Sophocles, the Athenian poet, while still young, was chosen to play the lyre and

[15] *Ibid.,* p. 124.

[16] Shawn, *op. cit.,* p. 18.

in the epic poems of the *Iliad* and the *Odyssey.* Several passa works describe dance as it was carried on by the Mycenaeans. Ir Odysseus orders Telemachus to assemble all the servants in the the slaying of the suitors; a lively dance is held and the palace re the noise.

A vivid picture of dance is given in the eighteenth book where Homer describes the armor of Achilles. Three dances ar as depicted on the shield. One of these portrays a dancing p young men and maidens danced, holding their hands on one wrists:

> The maidens had soft linen garments, and the youths wore well- tons, faintly glistening with oil. The maidens had fair garlands, and had golden daggers hanging from silver belts. And now they ran ar skillful feet, very lightly, as when a potter, sitting by his wheel, whicl hands, tries it to see if it runs. And then again, they would run in lin one another. And a great throng stood around the colorful danc enjoying the sight; and among them an inspired musician was sin playing on his lyre, and through their midst, leading the measure, blers whirled. . . . [13]

As Greece moved into its classical period, the Greeks worshi number of deities cast in the shape of men and women. Many myt rounded these gods and goddesses, each of whom had special attr powers, and cults. Thus, fertility rites were often offered to Dionysı god of fertility and wine; indeed, the term *tragedy* is believed to have nated with the bacchic rites that were offered in his honor. Some mythological companions of Dionysus were believed to be satyrs, or " men;" when dancers performed these roles at festivals, they wore costumes and footwear. The Greek word for "goat" is *tragos,* and dancing contests carried on during the 6th century B.C. came to be kı as competitions in *tragoedia,* or "goat song." Again, the term *orchestra* c nally meant the circular dancing place of the theater.[14]

Among the other deities who had dances and festivals performe their honor were Apollo and his sister Artemis, at Delphi on the islan Delos in the Aegean; indeed, Apollo was said to have dictated the law choreography. Similarly, Athena, Hecate, Demeter, and Persephone were worshipped by their own special cults, at different holidays during year.

One of the most common uses of dance in ancient Greece was education. The leading Greek philosophers strongly supported this art, an ideal integration of the body and spirit. Aristotle defined education as blend of music and gymnastics, and Socrates urged that it be taught mo widely, saying that those who honor the gods most beautifully in dances ar best in war. Plato wrote "to sing well and to dance well is to be we educated," and devoted a great deal of attention to the importance of th dance in education in his treatise on the *Laws.* He emphasizes the fact tha

[13] *Ibid.,* p. 45.

[14] *Ibid.,* pp. 76–81.

lead the victory dance after the battle of Salamis. Epaminondas of Thebes, one of the most distinguished of Greek generals and statesmen, played musical instruments, sang, and danced, and did so before audiences in his adult years. Aeschylus and Aristophanes danced in various performances of their own plays, and the *Dithyramb,* one of the principal dances of the Dionysian festivals, was often led by celebrated poets and statesmen.

The Greek satirist, Lucian (who lived in a later era in Rome), remarked that the Greeks valued dancing to such an extent that:

> . . . the most noble and greatest personages in every city are the dancers, and so little are they ashamed of it, that they applaud themselves more upon their dexterity in that species of talent, than on their nobility, their posts of honor, and the dignities of their forefathers.[17]

There were specific types of dances in Greek drama:

Emmeleia: this was a grave, serious type of dance, typically used for tragic themes; it embodied a code of symbolic gestures through which the dancer could tell the entire story of a dramatic work without speaking.

Kordax: this was the characteristic dance of comedy, and has been described as obscene and ignoble; it involved suggestive rotations of the body, kicking one's buttocks, slapping one's chest and thighs, and similar movements.

Sikinnis: this was the dance typical of the Greek satyr plays during the 6th century B.C. It was lively, vigorous, and disrespectful, with much horseplay and acrobatic movement; often it involved satirical reenactment of mythological themes.

Not only was dance featured in the Greek theater; it also was an essential element in the entertainment of guests known as *Komos,* or *Komoi.* It was the practice to have afterdinner entertainment of singing, juggling, playing musical instruments, and dancing. At first this was done by the host or guests. Gradually, however, a class of professional dancers developed—and these performers displaced the amateurs. By the 5th and 4th centuries B.C., such performers were widely found, and had developed a high degree of specialized skill. In some cases, slaves were trained as dancers and then performed for pay. Apparently, there were star performers even in those days; one inscription on the island of Delos indicates that a single dancing girl was paid far more than an entire dancing troupe that accompanied her.

Following the conquests of Alexander and his return with Eastern captives, Greek dance began to show Asiatic influences, with gesture language used increasingly. During the Hellenistic and Greco-Roman periods, the *pantomimus,* or pantomimic dancer, became highly popular. A solo dancer, wearing different costumes and masks, would make use of flamboyant gesture and mimicry to tell a story in several scenes, each episode being separated by musical interludes. This form of entertainment was found most widely in Rome, during the peak of power of that Empire.

[17]Ethel L. Urlin, *Dancing, Ancient and Modern* (New York: D. Appleton & Co., 1914), pp. 29–30.

In Greece we see a civilization in which dance began as an essential element in religion, and an important and respected means of military training. Gradually, it became part of the developing Greek theater and then of popular entertainment. Always, it was widely respected by the Greeks; one of their seven Muses, on an equal plane with the Muses of epic poetry and music, was Terpsichore, the Muse of Dancing. But the respect held for dance was based on the total philosophy of the Greeks, during the age of Pericles—their belief in the integrity of mind, spirit, and body and their keen interest in all the arts as essential expressions of man's spirit. It was different in Rome.

DANCE IN ANCIENT ROME

Dancing was much less important to the Romans than to the Greeks from whom they borrowed much of their culture. The educated Romans looked upon Greece as the source of culture and civilization; Roman aristocrats spoke Greek, employed Greek tutors, and copied Greek arts and literature. Early Roman art was vigorous, simple, and well-proportioned. However, as the nation grew wealthy and powerful, it ceased to value such qualities in art; indeed, war and lust for conquest brought thousands of captives and great wealth to Rome. The Romans ceased to create and perform within the arts themselves. Instead, they were entertained by their slaves and captives, of many nationalities. When this happened, dance—along with other forms of popular entertainment—became brutal and sensationalized.

Shawn comments that while the Romans were great organizers, military conquerors, and lawmakers, within the arts they were only borrowers. Ultimately, they debased all they touched. So it was, he says, with the dance:

> Here in Imperial Rome we find the dance first completely theatricalized—then commercialized; and as the religious life of Rome gradually decayed and became orgiastic, so the religious dances became occasions for unbridled licentiousness and sensuality. . . . [19]

How did it all begin?

During the earliest period of recorded history in what was to become Rome, the men of certain corporations, or societies, were grouped together under the name of *Salii,* which some have interpreted as derived from *saltio,* the Latin word for "dance," and *saltantes,* the word for "dancers." The *Salii,* who included sowing priests who purified the fields, warriors who performed weapon dances, and the priests of Mars (god of war), carried on spring processionals which had a somewhat dancelike character. During this period, other choral dances were done, with choruses of older and younger men who marched around in a circle to the rhythmic beating of their shields. Other feasts and holidays throughout the year were celebrated, with dancing that was apparently of a dignified and restrained nature:

[19]Shawn, *op. cit.,* p. 17.

> . . . at the Palilia, or festival of Pales, solemn and magnificent dances were performed in the fields by shepherds, who during the night formed circles around blazing fires of straw and stubble. The Floralia, or festival of Flora, gave rise to the May Day customs still surviving in parts of England . . . [20]

These customs continued for centuries. A Roman writer, Suetonius, comments at a much later date on the processionals of the *Salii,* held as a three-week ritual in March and October. Clad in embroidered tunics and high conical caps, armed and bearing shields, they trooped through the public places of the city, dancing and singing sacred songs.

Other customs included the religious festivals of the *Lupercalia,* the *Saturnalia,* and the *Ludiones.* The *Lupercalia* were held during the Kalends of March, in honor of the god Pan. The priests of this cult, the Luperci, danced naked through the streets of Rome, armed with whips, with which they were said to have struck at the crowds of spectators. The *Saturnalia* was a great feast, held in mid-December, in honor of Saturn. It was a time for revelry, feasting, drunkenness, dancing in the streets, and for class distinctions to be set aside. Kirstein comments that this pagan holiday was adopted by Roman Christians for Christ's Mass, or Christmas, and that it became, in ensuing centuries, the occasion for many dramatic dances.[21]

Dance also played a part in the early Roman theater, although much of this was the work of imported Greek performers, or players from Istria who were brought to Rome in the middle of the 4th century B.C., to placate the gods with entertainment, and to distract a population that had been racked by plague. The dancers and pantomimists from Istria were known as *istriones;* their name was the source of the modern word "histrionic." They wore goatskin shepherd's cloaks; the name for these, *saturae,* is said to be the source of the term "satire" or "satirical." Their performances were farcical enactments which parodied the lives of gods, heroes, or everyday men, often in rustic settings. They were carried on usually without speaking, relying on gesture to tell the story. Kirstein comments that dance, in the form of the *choros,* had little place in the Roman theater. Romans preferred the excitement and color of mass spectacles which were provided in their huge circuses and arenas, to the thoughtful and literary works that were found on the Greek stage.[22]

Since this was the case, the stage became unattractive as a profession; actors and dancers in performing companies tended to be Greek or south Italian slaves, formerly owned by rich noblemen and now rented out to theatrical managers to perform. For a long time, no women appeared on the stage; their parts were taken by young men. Later, women, who among the Greeks were not even permitted to take part in tragedy or comedy, appeared in Rome in pantomime.

For a period of time beginning at about 200 B.C., it became fashionable for Roman patricians to dance. Etruscan and Greek choreographers taught private dancing classes, attended by the sons and daughters of the nobility. Dance became an important social grace. Later, dance was inveighed against, as a softening of the fiber of Roman citizenry; indeed, one emperor,

[20] Urlin, *op. cit.,* p. 35.
[21] Kirstein, *op. cit.,* p. 46.
[22] *Ibid.,* pp. 40–43.

Scipio Africanus, closed the dancing schools by edict, in about 150 B.C. However, it was hardly necessary; the Romans had little real inclination or aptitude for dancing themselves. The only real popularity of dance over a period of time was extended to the pantomimic dance which developed as an independent stage form under Caesar Augustus, about 22 B.C. This became a tremendously popular form of entertainment, for two essential reasons.

First, Romans had little real appreciation for dance as an expression of artistic beauty or emotion. However, they enjoyed the lively spectacle of pantomime dance. Second, by the time of Caesar Augustus, Rome was filled with a huge, heterogeneous population of varied origins. They spoke not only Latin, but Greek, Syrian, Gallic, Teutonic, and many other languages. It was impossible to present spoken dramas that could be understood by all these varied spectators, particularly in the huge theaters with poor acoustics. Therefore, the pantomime became developed to an extremely fine degree and achieved immense popularity.

This dance form was much like an early stage of Greek tragedy, in which one actor, with the aid of varying costumes and masks, portrayed a number of characters in a single tale. Instead of speaking or chanting, the pantomimic dancer performed with dance and gestures alone. The typical costume for the pantomime performer was full and heavy, with elaborate embellishments and masks, for almost all roles. Feet and legs were apparently used chiefly for taking dramatic poses and marking the rhythm, while the trunk of the body was gracefully twisted, and the hands and arms used expressively to convey meaning. Lawler comments that the effect on the public was tremendous:

> . . . spectators sometimes sat in the theaters for whole days, watching the dancers almost as if hypnotized; they thought of the dancers as virtually divine, and Seneca calls the craze for their performance 'a disease'—*morbus.* Women swooned, high officials of the state hung on every move, and Roman emperors summoned the dancers for command performances . . . [23]

Vuillier wrote:

> We can form but a faint idea of the perfection to which the art of pantomime attained among the Romans. It ranged over the whole domain of fable, poetry, and history. Roman actors translated the most subtle sensations by gestures of extraordinary precision and mobility, and their audience understood every turn of this language, which conveyed far more to them than declamation . . . the strength, the infinite gradations of this mute expression, made the dancing of the ancients a great art . . . [24]

Among the many performers were two outstanding artists, Pylades of Sicily, and Bathyllus of Alexandria, both former slaves who were freed by their owners. Both were lionized by the public, became extremely wealthy and arrogant, and had admiring cliques which, in different liveries, used to battle angrily in the streets to support the reputation of their favorites.

[23] Lawler, *op cit.,* p. 140.

[24] Gaston Vuillier, *A History of Dance* (New York: D. Appleton and Co., 1897), p. 39.

Public opinion was divided about pantomime artists; some emperors favored them while others opposed or banned them. Marcus Aurelius put a limit on the wages they might be paid and on their production expenses. The developing Christian Church kept up an unremitting attack on them, and yet at one time, when Rome was suffering from famine and even orators and teachers were banished, three thousand dancers were allowed to remain in the city—so vital was this entertainment considered to be. Yet, more and more, moralists spoke out against the pantomime. Lucian, in the 2nd century A.D., had one of his characters, Crato, ask in a dialogue:

> [How can anyone] sit still and listen to the sounds of a flute, and watch the antics of an effeminate creature got up in soft raiment to sing lascivious songs and mimic the passions of prehistoric strumpets to the accompaniment of twanging string and shrilling pipe and clattering heel?[25]

The controversy continued, but gradually the popularity of the pantomimists declined and many of them were forced to withdraw from the cities, and to perform in smaller towns. Probably their last performances were in the late 4th and early 5th centuries A.D. By this time, more and more criticism had come to be voiced of dance itself, which was attacked by many of Rome's leading citizens and writers. "I let myself be taken to a dancing class," said Scipio in the 2nd century, "and there, by God, I saw over 50 girls and boys, including a youth of less than 12 years old . . . who was performing . . . a dance of which any wretched slave would be ashamed." Increasingly, it came to be seen as corrupt, immoral, and inappropriate for a person of good society. Sallust wrote of a noblewoman, "She played and danced more gracefully than a respectable woman should," and Cicero wrote the following condemnation of an art which had indeed declined from the lofty stature it had held in the Greek civilization:

> Cato calls Lucius Muena a dancer. If this be imputed to him truly, it is the reproach of a violent accuser; but if falsely, it is the abuse of a scurrilous railer . . . For no man, one may almost say, ever dances when sober, unless perhaps he be a madman; nor in solitude, nor in a moderate and sober party; dancing is the last companion of prolonged feasting, of luxurious situation, and of many refinements.[26]

In essence, dance suffered from the sickness that had seized the entire Roman empire. The sturdy, simple patriotism of the Roman citizen had given way to a decadence that demanded "bread and circuses." Tremendous public spectacles were staged, featuring the torture and slaughter of thousands of captives and slaves taken during Roman conquests. The taxes of entire provinces were expended on these cruel entertainments, which the public increasingly demanded. A variety of performers offered their talents —singers, dancers, jugglers, musicians, animal trainers, acrobats—but most of all the Roman citizens demanded violent and sadistic spectacles. There were chariot races; gladitorial contests pitting captives of war, condemned prisoners, and professional fighters together; cleverly staged "sea-fights"

[25]Kirstein, *op. cit.*, p. 50.

[26]*Ibid.*, p. 45.

with slave-manned galleys in flooded ditches; and a variety of other brutal spectacles. These were carried on in huge arenas. The Circus Maximus was said to have held at one time 350,000 spectators.

Two emperors, in particular, were identified with these monstrous games: Caligula, who was extremely fond of singing and dancing, and who frequently performed in the circuses, and Nero, under whom the persecution of Christians was unrelenting. Tacitus wrote that many Christians:

> . . . were dressed in the skins of wild beasts, and exposed to be torn to pieces by dogs in the public games, that they were crucified, or condemned to be burnt; and at nightfall serve in place of lamps to lighten the darkness, Nero's own gardens being used for the spectacle.[27]

Dance itself was often used for gruesome purposes. The historian Plutarch records the fact that often condemned criminals, clothed in rich garments and wearing wreaths, were compelled to dance in the crowded arena until their clothing, which had been treated with some secret chemical, suddenly burst into flames and they died agonizingly.[28]

Because of all it represented, the Roman way of life was bitterly condemned by the early Christians, who suffered under it, yet survived it. And, because dance was so integral a part of the corruption of the Romans in their later days of empire, dance too was condemned by the Church Fathers. But this relationship, after the fall of Rome and through the Dark and Middle Ages, was a strangely contradictory one. Dance became linked to the Christian Church in many ways, and at the same time was violently condemned by it, as centuries passed.

[27] *Ibid.*, p. 57.

[28] Lawler, *op. cit.*, p. 142.

4

Dance in the Middle Ages

The history of dance—as of all the arts—following the fall of Rome, is closely linked with the development of the Catholic Church in Europe. As the preceding chapter has suggested, the early Church Fathers were filled with bitter antagonism toward the Roman way of life, and all its cxcesses. By religious conviction, they rejected this hedonistic philosophy, and instead moved toward a fanatical asceticism.

It must be understood that, after the fall of the Roman Empire, Europe was overrun with warring tribes and shifting forces. The organized power of Rome, which had built roads, extended commerce, and given protection to the arts and the centers of learning, was at an end. Within this vacuum, during the Dark Ages, the Christian Church offered a unity and form of universal citizenship in Europe. The church and the feudal lords who emerged, each controlling his own fiefdom, were the sources of authority in this era. They were closely interlocked, and it was the church that was the sole custodian of learning and education, and the source of morals. Margaret H'Doubler suggests that the characteristic feature of early Christian thought was its otherworldliness, placing a sharp emphasis on the reward to be gained after death, and condemning all carnality and hedonism:

> The paramount consideration of all living was to save the soul. Consequently, the body was looked upon as a hindrance. To exalt the soul the body was ignored, punished, and bruised. Anything that expressed the livelier feelings of instinctive human nature or in any way suggested former pagan ways and ideals of living, was banished into the realm of wickedness. . . .[1]

[1]Margaret H'Doubler, *Dance: A Creative Art Experience* (New York: F. S. Crofts and Co., 1940), p. 13.

RELIGIOUS DISAPPROVAL OF DANCE

Theatrical entertainment in particular was prohibited. As early as 300 A.D., with the coming of the first Christian emperors, a council at Elvira decided that the rite of baptism could not be extended to those connected with the circus or pantomime. In 398, at the Council of Carthage, an edict excommunicated those who attended the theater on holy days. So poor was public regard for stage performers that it was almost assumed that female artists would become prostitutes. Kirstein points out that, after the Lombard invasion of 568, shows and games were rarely mentioned in Rome itself. For two or three hundred years, they are reported to have been carried on in the Eastern Empire, and isolated professional entertainers probably wandered through the countryside, but the great spectacles and organized shows of Imperial Rome were at an end.

However, dance continued to be performed under the most unlikely of auspices—within the Church itself. There is much evidence to suggest that the early Christian Fathers approved of the use of dance in religious ceremonials, provided that its form and intent were holy and not profane. Dancing was a formal part of the Christian service and litany until about the 12th century, when the pressures against it mounted and it became widely banned—although even then it continued to be performed in some areas.

What form did dance take within the Christian Church? The earliest examples are described by the Catholic Father Héliot, in his history of religious orders of monks. A number of Christian sects, the Therapeutae, withdrew into the wilderness in order to avoid persecution, assembling on Sundays and other holy days in groves of oases to dance ring-dances and sing psalms and hymns. Since, after all, worship of this kind had been practiced by all those of earlier faiths, it is not surprising that the first Christians engaged in it. The Therapeutae had a highly developed cult dance, according to Backman:

> Following a night watch *(vigilium)*, the participants grouped themselves into two facing choral groups, one of men and one of women. Each group had a leader. During the alternate singing of songs, the singers sometimes remained stationary, sometimes they moved forward, sometimes backward, sometimes to right and sometimes to left, as circumstances required. Then they united in a single chorus. . . .[2]

Dating from about the year 160, there exists a remarkable hymn, known as the *Acts of John,* quoted in the Catholic Dictionary as being known to Augustine. It offers a version of the Lord's Supper in which Christ, taking leave of his disciples, instituted the custom of Holy Communion. However, instead of the traditional symbolic acts of breaking bread and sipping wine, Jesus is described as having his disciples surround him with hands joined, singing and circling around. The word "dance" is actually used in the *Acts of John.*

[2]E. Louis Backman, *Religious Dances* (London: George Allen and Unwin Ltd., 1952), p. 11.

There are many references to dance as part of worship during the 4th and 5th centuries, along with frequent warnings about forms of dance which were considered dissolute.

Epiphanius, who was made Bishop of Salamis on Cyprus in 367, gave a sermon on Palm Sunday on the entry of Christ into Jerusalem. The festival of celebration is described in these words:

> Rejoice in the highest, Daughter of Zion! Rejoice, be glad and leap boisterously thou all-embracing Church. For behold, once again the King approaches . . . once again perform the choral dances . . . leap wildly, ye Heavens; sing Hymns, ye Angels; ye who dwell in Zion, dance ring dances. . . .[3]

Those who have interpreted this work conclude that it describes not only the spirit of the ceremony, but also literal dances done within the Church. This view is supported by the writings of Basilius, Bishop of Caesarea, who lived between 344 and 407. Basilius wrote frequently of the existence of the dance in the time of early Christianity, including one passage which suggested that pagan rites such as dawn ceremonies which greeted the sunrise were also found in the early Catholic Church:

> Could there be anything more blessed than to imitate on earth the ring-dance of the angels and at dawn to raise our voices in prayer and by hymns and songs glorify the rising Creator?[4]

In many other ways, the Catholic Church based its practices on the rituals of earlier religions. When the heathen tribes of Europe and Asia Minor were converted, the missionaries (most of whom were Roman) built their churches on existing shrines or temple sites. Often they established the Christian holy days at the same times as earlier pagan festivals. Such implements of Catholic ritual as the bell, candles, incense, singing, and dancing had all been found in heathen faiths. Thus, it was natural that dance would be included in the services. However, the leading Church Fathers made a point of opposing those forms of dance which they saw as sinful or dissolute, and which smacked of Roman degeneracy.

Ambrose, Bishop of Milan in the late 4th century, wrote profusely in support of church dance, taking his text from Luke 7:32, "We have piped unto you and ye have not danced." However, he also warned against being "snared" by the appeal of indecent dances and the stage:

> . . . No, the dance should be conducted as did David when he danced before the Ark of the Lord, for everything is right which springs from the fear of God. Let us not be ashamed of a show of reverence which will enrich the cult and deepen the adoration of God. For this reason the dance must in no wise be regarded as a mark of reverence for vanity and luxury, but as something which uplifts every living body instead of allowing the limbs to rest motionless upon the ground or the slow feet to become numb. St. Paul danced in this spirit when he exerted himself for us. . . .[5]

[3] *Ibid.,* p. 24.
[4] *Ibid.,* p. 25.
[5] *Ibid.,* p. 26.

Thus, dance, when it expresses vice and luxury, is condemned. When it is virtuous and performed in honor of God, it is praised. St. Gregory of Nazianzus, an eminent theologian of the 4th century who became Bishop of Constantinople, delivered a stern exhortation to the Emperor Julian, which has frequently been quoted:

> . . . if you wish to dance in devotion . . . then dance, but not the shameless dance of the daughter of Herod, which accompanied the execution of the Baptist, but the Dance of David to the true refreshment of the Ark, which I consider to be the approach to God, the swift encircling steps in the manner of the mysteries. . . .[6]

History tells us that the Abbot Meletius, on the advice of Gregory's writings, permitted dancing in his churches in England, during the early 7th century. Records of the famous Echternach processional carried on in Luxembourg during Whitsun week, in which clergy, choir, and congregation danced to the church and around the altar, indicate that this is a survival of a medieval dancing custom. It is carried on in commemoration of St. Wilibord, who lived around 690. Many other illustrations support the view of Curt Sachs that dance continued to be practiced widely by those Europeans who had been converted to Christianity, but who retained many of their earlier pagan customs:

> Even with Christianity the theme and content scarcely change their outer garb. The charms for fertility still occupy the central position; with undiminished power they dominate at Shrovetide, the first of May, and at weddings, at midsummer, and at funeral ceremonies. . . . Maypole and fire dances, sword dances, mask dances. . . .[7]

As the Dark Ages began to draw to a close, there was continuing confirmation of the use of dance in Christian worship. A hymn which dates from the 10 century, for early morning Mass during the celebration of Easter at the Monastery of Moissac in France, has these lines:

> His [Christ's] life, His speech and miracle,
> His wondrous death prove it.
> The congregation adorns the sanctity,
> Come and behold the host of ring-dances!

DANCE CUSTOMS IN THE MIDDLE AGES

A second form of religious dance was to be found in certain church festivals which were carried on in the latter part of the Dark Ages, and apparently through the Middle Ages. These were particularly popular with the lower clergy—the monks, choirboys, and younger priests and subdeacons—and often they were highly disrespectful of the upper clergy. Just as in primitive religions, these festivals included various forms of acting, sing-

[7]Curt Sachs, *World History of the Dance* (New York: W. W. Norton and Co., 1937), pp. 248–249.

ing, dancing, and the playing of games. John Beleth, who lived in the 12th century and was Rector of the University of Paris, described four kinds of dance in use at church festivals: the Deacons' Festival dance on St. Stephen's Day, the Priests' on St. John's Day, the choirboys' on Innocents' Day, and the subdeacons' on the Feast of the Circumcision. It was the last of these which came to be known as the Festival (or Feast) of Fools. This was a New Year's celebration by the lower clergy which became a dramatic burlesque of the regular church service. From the end of the 12th century on, the Feast of Fools (sometimes called the Feast of Asses) spread through France and most of the other European countries. According to the records of Sens Cathedral, the festival typically included dancing, singing, drinking, and the parodying of religious offices—even those of the Cardinal and Pope.

Other ceremonies which were of a dramatic or dancelike nature were carried on outside of the formal service of the church, but with a greater degree of approval by the authorities. A Children's Festival, or Festival of the Choristers, at which a child bishop was elected, was celebrated usually on Innocent's Day, December 28; this custom is believed to have begun in the 12th century. Elsewhere, ceremonies included various games, acting, singing, and feasting—without, however, the ridicule of the higher clergy or the regular service that made the Feast of Fools so objectionable. At the Cathedral of Auxerres, during the 13th century, a religious mystery play was carried out which made use of a sort of ball game played on a labyrinth design on the floor of the cathedral's nave. This custom is believed to have been based on pre-Christian ceremonies in early Greece.

Particularly in France and Germany, there were many great processions which were carried out to ward off distress or bring relief from pain or epidemics. These were recorded as having taken place regularly in the 9th and 10th centuries, and from the 12th to the 16th centuries. As they marched, the worshippers often carried relics of saints and martyrs, crosses and banners, and images of the Holy Virgin. The movement involved rhythmic steps with the procession stopping at certain stations and performing sacral dances: ceremonial greetings, bows, turns, advancing, and retiring. One description of this ceremony describes it as a

> . . . moving chorus advancing in harmony and with a sort of cadence through the various parts of the church. The processions passing through the choir and aisles, swinging the censer, do so to measured movements prescribed in the ritual . . . representing by their symbolical movements and figures holy and mystical dances.[8]

Another source, from the 9th century, uses the phrase, ". . . the holy relics were borne amidst happy dancing." Because they marched with crosses, banners, and relics, and because of their reverence, those taking part in these processions were not condemned by the church.

Kirstein suggests that, with the beginning of the Middle Ages and extending until about 1400, a variety of dramatic activities was carried on with religious themes, but not as a formal part of religious service. These included "mystery plays" which dealt with events found in both the Old and

[8]Backman, *op. cit.,* p. 85.

New Testaments; these striking displays were put on in church squares or public market places. So-called miracle plays tended to be portrayals of the lives of the saints and martyrs. Somewhat later appeared the "morality plays," which were concerned with depicting the truths of moral behavior; essentially, they were allegorical representations of the struggle between good and evil, virtue and vice.

All of these apparently stemmed from earlier pagan sources, although their themes were Christian. Kennedy suggests that conversion to the new faith did not eliminate many of the older forms of religious drama. Indeed many of the earlier pagan rituals were adopted by the early Church Fathers, in the yearly cycle of miracle and morality plays which helped to convert many ignorant and illiterate peasants to Christianity:

> . . . outside the control of the Church popular custom continued to practice one relic of the old religion in the form of a midwinter drama/dance performance, in which was portrayed by the actor/dancers a contest between life and death. The European folk dances performed during the winter season . . . all include some scraps of this old drama of life and death . . . acted on or near Christmas Day, it is a symbolic death and resurrection. This death and revival drama, performed at the turn of the year, is known in every European country. As one would expect, it is found most complete among the primitive peasantry in Eastern Europe.[9]

THE DANCE OF DEATH

Certain phenomena, however, which were carried on outside the control of the Church, and which involved dance, aroused more serious condemnation by religious authorities. One of these was the Dance of Death, or *Toten Tanz.* This was a custom believed to have originated in France, which then filtered into Germany, Italy, Spain, and England. It was carried on throughout the Middle Ages, and apparently was at its peak during the 14th and 15th centuries, when many references to it appear in songs, poems, and dramas, or are depicted on murals in cemeteries, churches, cloisters, and vaults.

The Dance of Death reveals the great preoccupation of mankind during this period with death. Backman points out that among primitive peoples, the dead often were regarded as dangerous and hostile to the living. Legends of vampires, werewolves, and ghosts were found throughout Europe during the Dark Ages, and many customs had been devised to prevent the dead from "returning." These included binding together the feet of the dead, driving nails into their feet, carrying on a death watch—and, in many instances, singing and performing games and dances during wakes or after the grave had received the corpse.

Particularly in northern European countries, it was customary for such rites to include music and dancing. Backman suggests that the belief was that music exorcised the dead, forced them into compliance at being taken to the grave, and prevented them from walking the earth again; church bells were thought to drive demons away, and to comfort and protect the dead.

[9]Douglas Kennedy, *England's Dances* (London: G. Bell and Sons, Ltd., 1950), p. 36.

In addition, there was a widespread folk belief that the dead themselves liked to dance in churchyards and cemeteries in a sort of *danse macabre.* According to this superstition, they attempted to entice the living into the ranks of their ghostly dancing; however, those who danced with them would then die within the year. In the Dance of Death, then, one finds the suggestion that the living themselves dance toward their own death; death is a wedding dance and one dances in death toward the bridegroom.

Henri Stegmaier points out that, in its earliest form:

> ... the Dance of Death is actually a Dance of the Dead ... in which the dead bodies lure the living from the various ranks of society in their midnight frolic. Later, the dead are conceived of no longer as corpses, but each as the personified figure of death himself.[10]

Death appears in the ritual, and in the many songs, poems, and pictures of the Dance of Death, as a dancer. He compels people of every station and age, however reluctant, to dance with him. Each in turn is taken, according to a graduated social scale—saints and sinners, rich and poor, young and old. A document in the archives of the church at Caudbec, France, described a dramatic dance held in 1393, in which actors represented the various ranks and professions and in which, after each repetition of the dance, one of the dancers withdrew and disappeared. In essence, this was a parable, depicting Death as the universal leveler. It says, "Death avenges all wrong, and all, no matter how powerful in the living world, must at last yield to him."

The point was made more explicit when the characters in the dance were assigned exact roles—from pope to emperor to cardinal to the lowliest monk or subdeacon; from kings, princes, and barons to minstrels, peasants, and laboring men. As recorded in France, each dancer steps forward in turn according to his rank; Death dances grotesquely, questions them, and finally leads them all into the tomb.

The Dance of Death has been interpreted as a form of social and religious satire, and the healthy reaction of the people against the strict asceticism of the Church. It is also seen as an evidence of the awakening spirit of democracy in the dying Middle Ages, in that it protested against the tremendous power and wealth of the ruling classes, as well as the miserable lives led by the common folk. In essence, it was "a desperate statement of the common man's disillusionment with the entire social, political, and religious scheme under which he lived; Death leveled all ranks and stations and proved them ultimately vain. . . ."[11]

The Church was well aware of this symbolic meaning. From the 4th century well into the 18th century, there were many prohibitions against dancing for the dead in graveyards, particularly against dances which were ribald and indecent, or which involved drinking and feasting. The Roman Synod under Leo IV ordered at the beginning of the 9th century that:

[10]Henri Stegmaier, *The Dance of Death in Folk Song* (Chicago: University of Chicago Libraries, 1939), p. 6.

[11]John Martin, *John Martin's Book of the Dance* (New York: Tudor Publishing Co., 1963), p. 22.

In witness of the true and living God, the devilish songs which are heard at night on the graves of the dead are to cease, as well as the noise which accompanies them.

And a later resolution says:

Whoever buries the dead should do so with fear, trembling and decency. No one shall be permitted to sing devil songs and perform games and dances which are inspired by the devil and have been invented by the heathen.[12]

However, these and later prohibitions failed to put an end to the Dance of Death. As late as the 1930s, Backman reports a *Bal de La Mort* carried on in certain regions of Catalonia, as part of the church processions during Holy Week. This took the form of a quadrille, performed by twelve men and three women, wearing black clothes on which white skeletons had been painted:

Their faces were covered with masks representing skulls. One of the dancers carries a scythe, another a pendulum clock, and a third a banner. The musician, with only a drum, is clad in armour, enveloped in a black mantle. They follow the Corpus Christi procession and therefore are a part of the popular church dance. The one who carries the scythe must not take part in the dance, but just swings his scythe toward the bystanders. The others dance and hop. . . .[13]

A number of other, similar phenomena appeared during the Middle Ages, reflecting belief in witchcraft, religious fanaticism, and the lingering influence of heathen superstition. In a sense, they represented the common man's primitive fear of death, in the midst of famine, war, and plagues.

"Witch dances," carried on in the dead of night, paid homage to the devil with wild bacchanals, accompanied by grotesque costumes and masks, sacrifices, and sexual excesses (just as angels were thought to dance heavenly ring-dances in honor of God). The *Witches' Sabbath,* carried on during the night of April 30th, was a traditional time for such rites, which took place in dark and lonely places. Another craze which spread over Europe from the 11th to the 14th centuries was *St. Vitus' Dance,* or, as it was sometimes known, *St. John's Dance,* named after the patron saint who was supposed to protect the afflicted. Here, men, women, and children danced in wild delirium; they performed frenzied leaps and turns, writhing as if suffering from epileptic seizures, screaming out uncontrollably and foaming at the mouth. Similar to this was *tarantism,* a form of seizurelike dance which was thought at first to be the result of the bite of the tarantula spider, and which then became deliberately performed in order to avert the effects of the tarantula's poison. Eventually, as the superstitious belief in this 'remedy' diminished, it was continued as a traditional folk dance appearing in many Italian provinces—the *Tarantella.*

The infliction of self-punishment, performed as an act of atonement, was recorded as early as the year 1000, based on the use of the lash in masochistic self-torture as referred to in Paul's Epistles to the Corinthians,

[12]Paul Nettl, *The Story of Dance Music* (New York: Philosophical Library, 1947), p. 44.

[13]Backman, *op. cit.,* p. 153.

"Thus do I tame my body as I make it unconscious of pain. . . ." From the 13th to the 15th centuries, flagellation songs and dances were widely performed in Europe, beginning in Italy and spreading beyond the Alps—often with approval of the church authorities.

DANSEOMANIA

But the most striking and unusual dance expression of the Middle Ages and early Renaissance was the so-called *danseomania,* or dancing mania, which flourished throughout Europe from the 11th to the 14th centuries. John Martin comments that the people of Europe had been so affected by a succession of natural calamities (wars, plagues, fires) that they sought an outlet for emotional strain in the dancing manias:

> Whole communities of people . . . were stricken with a kind of madness that sent them dancing and gyrating through the streets and from village to village for days at a time until they died in agonized exhaustion. . . .[14]

Kirstein refers to the dancing mania as a form of pathological aberration which was widely documented by writings of the 13th and 14th century, particularly in Germany and the Low Countries. Sometimes it affected children, sometimes large numbers of adults. In 1237, a party of German children danced from Erfurt to Arnstadt, many dying along the way. In 1278, a bridge at Marburg collapsed beneath a company of dancers and all were drowned. In 1347, several hundred men and women danced from Aix-la-Chapelle to Metz, despite the efforts of priests to break the spell that had seized them.

Clearly, these outbursts represented some form of possession, equivalent perhaps to what Sachs had described as "convulsive dance," found among primitive tribesmen. There had been instances cited of men and women who began to sing and dance suddenly in the churchyard, disrupting divine service. In some cases, when they refused to stop, they were cursed by the priest to dance the whole year through, until the ban was withdrawn by a higher church official. A 12th-century writer, Giraldus Cambrensis, described such an outburst:

> You may see men or girls, now in the churchyard, now in the dance, which is led round the churchyard with a song, on a sudden falling on the ground as in a trance, then jumping up as in a frenzy, and representing with their hands and feet, before the people, whatever work they have unlawfully done on feast days. . . .[15]

The participants in this ceremony were said to move their limbs stiffly and jerkily, until they fell senseless to the ground. When they awoke, they were "seized with fury," and leaped about "with wild gesticulations." The height of the dancing manias came about when the Black Plague, or bubonic

[14]Martin, *op. cit.,* p. 22.

[15]Sachs, *op. cit.,* pp. 253–254.

plague, raged over Europe, killing thousands and wiping out entire villages and cities. This occurred in the year 1349, and in the decades following, it became customary for huge crowds to wander through the countryside, particularly in Germany and the Low Countries. They danced as if bewitched, and all the rites of exorcism that were tried failed to drive out the mysterious demons which had possessed them. Petrus de Herenthal, a 14th-century monk, described such dances carried on during the year 1374. There came to Aachen, he says, a curious sect of men and women from various regions of Germany:

> Persons of both sexes were so tormented by the devil that in markets and churches, as well as in their own homes, they danced, held each others' hands and leaped high in the air. While they danced their minds were no longer clear, and they paid no heed to modesty though bystanders looked on . . . they cried out names of demons . . . and that they were dying. . . .[16]

Those possessed, who were sometimes called "choreomaniacs," were frequently accused of being heretics, and of flaunting the devil willfully. However, it seems clear that they did not behave in a spirit of revolt toward the Church; indeed, they apparently accepted the efforts of priests to bless or exorcise them. Nor were they apparently punished, as other heretical sects were. Nonetheless, the fact that they were forced to *dance* uncontrollably as part of the spell that had been cast over them confirmed the essential paganism of dance, in the eyes of many Church Fathers.

The dance epidemics continued well into the 17th century, although they appear to have reached their peak of virulence during the 14th and 15th centuries. At a later stage, they appear almost to have been taken for granted as a fairly mild, recurrent illness from which certain people suffered, or as a practice carried on regularly as part of community tradition. The great dance procession at Echternach, the procession of the hopping saints, is considered to be a descendant of this phenomenon of the Middle Ages.

CONTINUED PROHIBITION OF DANCE

As suggested earlier, secular forms of dance had from the very beginning of Christianity been the subject of opposition by the Church Fathers. Gradually, even the dances that were done in the church came under increasing attack during the Dark and Middle Ages. The Council of Toledo, held in 539, urged that dancing and singing at saints' festivals and processions be rooted out of Spain. The Council of Auxerres, 573–702, forbade the public to dance in choir dances, or nuns to sing in them. Again, the Council of Toledo, in 633, attacked the Festival of Fools, with its singing, dancing, and feasting in churches. At the beginning of the 10th century, Patriarch John III threatened to excommunicate women who visited graves to play music and dance. The Council of Avignon decreed in 1209 that, in night watches for the saints, "there shall not be performed in churches play-acting, hopping dances, indecent gestures, ring-dance, neither shall there be sung love songs or ditties. . . ."

[16]Backman, *op. cit.,* p. 191.

Nonetheless, the prohibitions continued—which must have meant that the dances themselves continued to be carried on.

Odo, Bishop of Paris in the 12th century, is reported to have prohibited dancing in churches and processions, and especially funeral dances in graveyards at night. Much later, in 1667, there was a decree of the Parliament of Paris forbidding religious dances in general and particularly the public dances of January 1 and May 1, the torch dances of the first Sunday in Lent, and those which were held around bonfires on the Vigil of St. John. One reason, apparently, why dancing managed to survive was that the clergy, who sold dancing indulgences, and who therefore derived much income from these fees, resented these prohibitions and refused to enforce them.

In Spain, there were concerted attempts to end religious dance, including a decree by the Bishop of Barcelona to prohibit the so-called *eagle dance,* in 1753, and another royal decree in Madrid in 1777, which attempted to end all dancing on holy days in churches or churchyards, or before images of the saints. Backman concludes that, while these attempts were ultimately successful in ending dancing by the clergy, they were never able to suppress popular church dances in which the communicants participated. To this day, such religious dances are still held in Spain, particularly on saints' days and other important holidays. And, until comparatively recently, similar ritual forms have been presented in the Rhône region of France and in Brittany. Ethel Urlin writes:

> Dancing still forms an important part of the Breton Pardons. After the bells have been tolled, Mass said, and the statues of the Saints decorated and clad in national dress, and after offerings have been made to them of corn, flax, sheepskins and cakes, dancing is inaugurated to the sound of the national *binyou* around a moss-grown dolmen.[17]

DANCE AS POPULAR ENTERTAINMENT

Although the Church had condemned dance as entertainment at an early point, and apparently had succeeded in wiping out organized forms of theatrical presentations, there continued to be wandering entertainers during the Dark and early Middle Ages. These performers, who were apparently combinations of singers, dancers, poets, musicians, actors, and jugglers, wandered through the countryside performing in village squares. Sachs points out that such an entertainer was known in Germany as *spielmann,* which is derived from *spielen,* "to dance." Another name was *joculator,* which later became *jongleur,* or "juggler." Sometimes they were known as *minnesingers,* and sometimes as *troubadors.* Increasingly, during the later Middle Ages, as the restrictions of the Catholic Church were less strongly enforced, these entertainers were welcomed in the castles and chateaus of feudal lords.

In addition to the performances of professional entertainers, the common people amused themselves by doing dances that were essentially social

[17]Ethel L. Urlin, *Dancing, Ancient and Modern* (New York: D. Appleton and Co., 1914), p. 41.

Peasant dances at the May feasts. From a 15th-century prayer book miniature in the Bibliotheque Nationale, Paris.

in character. There were two basic types of medieval dancing performed by peasants—the round dance and the couple dance. The round dance, or *Reigen,* was the more popular form. Sometimes called the *Chorea,* or *Carole,* this was usually performed by a long chain of dancers holding each other by the hand, and moving about in an open or closed circle, or in an extended line. Early German dancing, for example, is reported to have been habitually performed in rows or circles. Couple dances were less common, and did not become widely popular until the 15th century—partly because they were considered somewhat scandalous when first seen.

Sachs makes a distinction between the two dance forms—the couple dance is pantomimic in character, whereas the round dance is not. As an example of the former, Nettl cites a poem written in southern Germany, about the year 1000. It describes a dance passage between a young man and a young lady to the music of a harp player; the action is quite suggestive of the Bavarian folk dance, the *Laendler,* as performed today:

> Now the young man gets up, and then the maiden, and then a chasing and hunting begins, sometimes with loud, then with soft music. They fly hither and thither, as when the falcon hunts the dove in the air. He has reached her, the hunt is finished,—but no,—she escapes again, and the game begins anew.

Truly their art would fascinate the critics, so skillfully do the dancers master the dance, the leaping, the gesture of the hands.[18]

The dances performed by peasants were extremely boisterous and robust, often frank in their sexuality and earthiness. Their names and brief descriptions suggest this character:

Hoppaldei: peasants rushing around like wild boars, moving in couples as though they wanted to fly; arms waving, shoulders heaving and rolling.

Ahselrotten: a shoulder-rolling dance, lively, flirtatious, erotic.

Springeltanz: a wild dance in which the performers hopped and leaped about.

Houbetschotten: a shrugging of shoulders, while sliding along the floor, shaking the head.

Gimpel-Gampel: described both as a boisterous leaping dance, and as a skipping dance.

BEGINNINGS OF COURT DANCE

Peasant dances were copied by the nobility, but in more refined and courtly form. Court dances were part of the chivalric way of life, and stressed coquetry, with much posturing and preening. Because of the heavy, long gowns and trains of the noblewomen, and their elaborate headdresses and jewelry, the ladies of the court were not able to move freely. Indeed, their dance steps at first tended to be little more than gliding, curtseying, and posing. Most of the dances done at first were known as *"basse"* dances, which meant that the action was low; close to the floor.

Nettl describes two courtly dances, as described by poets of the German "minnesinger" period, about the 13th century:

> The women carried their trains . . . in their hands and smiled . . . and with their eyes signalled with love-sick and secret glances . . . the knight walked between two ladies, holding each by the hand and the page walked between two maids. The fiddlers stood close at hand. [The dance] is performed slowly with solemn steps, in long peaked shoes. All the dancers advanced like this in a long row with dragging steps, and two fiddlers play the music.[19]

In addition to their robust spirit, the peasant dances tended to have large movements and wide-stepping figures. In part, this may have been because of their costume, as well as the fact that they danced on grass or on the beaten earth of the town square. In contrast, when the court danced in a ballroom (the first of these is reported to have been built at Frankfurt-am-Main in 1350), the smooth floor of wood or polished marble made it possible for dancers to do graceful gliding or turning steps, while maintain-

[18]Nettl, *op. cit.*, p. 51.

[19]*Ibid.*, p. 56.

ing contact with the floor. As an additional contrast, while peasant dances tended to be performed either in couples or rather free formations of both sexes, the courtly dances were precisely defined in group formations.

For example, there was the *"Treialtrei,"* danced by twelve people with four ladies and two gentlemen facing a similar group. In another dance mentioned by Nettl, one gentleman faced two ladies.

In the middle of the 15th century, when the Ottoman Turks captured Constantinople, many of the scholars in this eastern capital of the Roman Empire fled to the West, bearing with them knowledge of the classical culture of Greece and Rome, which they had preserved. They came to the cities and castles of the nobility in France, Italy, Germany, and other lands in Europe, which were ready in spirit for an infusion of artistic elegance, classical learning, and, in effect, a rebirth of culture. Gradually, the severe asceticism and preoccupation with spiritual concerns which had characterized the early Middle Ages gave way to the more worldly-minded spirit of the Renaissance. The gradual rise of a capitalist class produced patrons of learning and art—within a world which was increasingly secularized. No longer did art have to justify itself through religious content.

Within this context, and with a breaking down of the old restraints, the dance which had once been banned by the Church was now wholly accepted in the courts of the early Renaissance. The minnesingers, jugglers, and jesters now became valuable adjuncts to the courts of Italy and France in particular. A special profession developed—that of the dancing master.

> He accompanied the prince or the count to whose court he was attached on all journeys, and, in fact, he occupied a position of trust and confidence in his patron's household. He was at the same time an arbiter of etiquette, where the instruction given the young men and women of noble family was considered an essential part of their education.[20]

Thus, history had come full circle. After a period in which the arts, learning, music, and dance had been submerged beneath the fanatic asceticism of the Church, there was again an atmosphere in which they could flourish and in which music, drama, and dance, in particular, could reach new heights of artistic development and popularity. This was to be the Renaissance.

[20] *Ibid.,* p. 71.

5

Ballet: Early History and Golden Age

With the coming of the Renaissance, most notably in 15th-century Italy and France, all the arts had a rebirth of interest and artistic experimentation. The old restraints were loosened during the Renaissance, and learning, literature, the stage arts, and indeed all creative expressions of the human spirit were no longer dominated by clerical ideals and purposes. Instead, they were to serve the secular goals of the wealthy and powerful kings and queens who had emerged throughout Europe—along with the luxury-loving members of their courts. The revival of interest in classical scholarship and in the arts of ancient Greece and Rome led to a fresh interest in mythology, ancient history, and the great heroes of past centuries. With the invention of printing, it became possible to widely distribute printed dance music; at one stroke, there was a flood of music published for such instruments as lutes, guitars, organs, and other string and keyboard instruments. The character of music itself changed abruptly. As Louis Horst points out, the pale, austere, rhythmically irregular music of the medieval period— as exemplified by the Gregorian chants—shifted to more brilliant and spirited music with pronounced rhythm and a single strong melodic line.[1]

In the 15th and 16th centuries, a great dance movement swept throughout the courts of Europe, accompanied by a surge of creation of new musical forms. Essentially, this movement had two aspects. One was the creation of a variety of new court dances, performed by the nobility themselves as a form of aristocratic amusement and a means of educating courtiers in social deportment and grace. The second was the development of a number of major entertainments, or spectacles, which ultimately gave rise to the art of ballet in France.

[1]Louis Horst, *Pre-Classic Dance Forms* (New York: Kamin Dance Publishers, 1953), pp. 1–2.

The court entertainments did not suddenly spring into life, as a form of extravagant display. Throughout the Middle Ages, there had been customs and performances which held in them the seed of the Renaissance spectacles. Under religious auspices, there had been festivals, miracle and mystery plays, and a variety of other celebrations, many of which were theatrical in character. Banquets in the homes of great nobles had increasingly placed reliance on entertainments by the resident troubador or dancing master and members of the court themselves; often these were elaborately costumed and provided colorful displays. Even the trade guilds of the later Middle Ages had developed the practice of performing allegorical plays which involved singing, dancing, and acting.

Thus, out of the life of the Middle Ages came both inspiration and a readiness for new forms of artistic performance. These took the form of great banquets in the Italian and French courts, usually at times of weddings or as homage to visiting royalty, or in celebration of the coronation of kings. Each of these banquets featured elaborate spectacles, with singing, dancing, and acting, richly costumed and sometimes with specially designed and built stage sets. Sometimes they were held in the castle itself, in the banquet hall, and sometimes at the entrance to the city gates or at a bridge leading to the city. Their themes were diverse, ranging from the acting out of stories from Greek mythology and fables, stories of the Crusades, tales of Roman history, Christian ceremonials, and episodes from the Old Testament.

As these performances flourished, the art of dance itself received fuller attention. In the 14th and 15th century courts of Italy, dancing masters began to develop a theory of dance instruction that systematized its various movements and styles. For example, Domenico de Piacenza, who was attached to the court of Lionello Sforza in Ferrara, wrote a treatise titled *De Arte Saltandi et Choreos Ducendi* (Art of Performing and Arranging Dances) in 1416. This work described the desired qualities of dancers of the period, and outlined various major types of dance and basic dance movements.[2]

Among the leading dance spectacles of the later Middle Ages and early Renaissance were the following:

Charles V of France presented a major spectacle to the German Emperor Charles IV in 1377. Like many other entertainments, it portrayed a major episode of the Crusades. Two heavily armed wagons drove up to the banquet table. One represented the city of Jerusalem, held by Saracen defenders, and the other a galley holding soldiers of Godfrey of Bouillon. After a long, stylized combat, the crusaders successfully stormed the city. Similar pageants were held in England, when Henry V returned from victory at Agincourt in 1415, and when Henry VI and his French wife Catherine returned in 1432 from their coronation as King and Queen of France and England.

In 1462, King René of Provence put on an entertainment that was both religious and social, on the eve of Corpus Christi. Lacking any single theme or plot, it offered tributes to the royalty of the day, and also portrayed, in a series of separate dramatic episodes, the Roman gods, Mars and Minerva, Pan, Pluto, and Proserpine; fauns, dryads, and tritons; King Herod per-

[2]Alexander Bland, *A History of Ballet and Dance in the Western World* (New York: Praeger Book Co., 1976), p. 14.

secuted by devils; ancient Jews dancing around a Golden Calf; Christ and the Apostles; Death with a scythe, and the Magi following a star.

One of the most popular themes of such entertainments was the *Moresca,* or *Moresche,* which depicted the battles between the Moors, or Saracens, and the Crusaders. This was found both as a form of popular folk ritual and as a subject for court displays. Other aspects of the same theme included the reoccupation of Spain by the Christians, and the attack on Jerusalem by the Crusader Godfrey. To illustrate, at the celebration of the conquest of Granada in 1493, a pantomimic pageant with triumphal arches, a procession of Spanish royalty, Moorish dances, and bullfights was performed. Usually in these performances, the Moors were depicted as black men, and it is believed that there may have been a connection between the *Moresca* and the Morris Dance—a traditional English folk dance in which it was the custom for certain of the dancers to blacken their faces.

Throughout all of these pageants, dance served as a means of pantomiming the action. In many of the entrees, or interludes, other dances which had become popular during the Renaissance were performed. These were the so-called court dances, or "preclassic" dances, which were per-

Equestrian ballet, *Guerra d'Amore,* in honor of Cosimo de Medici, Grand Duke of Tuscany. Engraving by Jacques Callot, published 1615. Reprinted with permission of the Dance Collection of the Library and Museum of the Performing Arts at Lincoln Center in New York City.

formed in couples or small groups, and which now covered a wide range of music, mood, and movement styles.

Dancing had become an everyday adjunct to court life in all of the palaces of the Renaissance. Queen Elizabeth of England was said to have made Sir Christopher Hatton her Lord Chancellor, not because of his particular wisdom in the law, but because "he wore green bows on his shoes and danced the pavane to perfection. . . ." During the Middle Ages dancing had become widely accepted in the courts throughout Europe, and training in it was now viewed as indispensable to the education of a nobleman. Agnes de Mille points out that the invention of firearms meant that whereas before brute strength and endurance had been prize qualities for a courtier who also was a soldier, now intelligence and alertness counted for more. Just as the giant Percherons which had formerly been warhorses (to bear the lords clad in weighty armor) were replaced by lighter and more graceful Arabian thoroughbreds, so during the Renaissance, "clothes became lighter, manners daintier, dueling more expert and dancing more skilled. . . ."

De Mille points out that all courtiers took dancing lessons every day. The steps were simple, but precise, with intricate floor patterns and great emphasis on deportment and manner. The sequences were practised endlessly and when they were performed at court functions, there was no improvisation.[3]

A pupil of Domenico de Piacenza, Guglielmo Ebreo (William the Jew) wrote a text in 1463 which specified the qualities of the skilled dancer: *mesura* (rhythm), *partira del terreno* (a sense of space), *aierel* (grace and lightness), *memoria* (memory), *maniera* (style), *movimento corporeo* (plasticity), and *mistico* (mood). He instructed female dancers to keep their heads up and their eyes down, and outlined principles of etiquette and courtly behavior in the dance; finally, he provided a set of seventeen dance tunes by leading composers in his collection.[4]

COURT DANCES OF THE RENAISSANCE

What were the court dances of the Renaissance that preceded and led to the development of ballet as a performing art?

At the outset, they had been divided into two broad categories—the *Basse Danse,* in which the feet did not leave the floor, and the *Haute Danse,* in which there were higher skips and jumps. However, both of these were broad types, with no precisely designed steps or floor patterns. The term "*branle,*" which later described a separate dance, was in the early period only a step sideways with balancing of the body, or swaying. A number of extremely simple dances were described as having been performed during the 15th century by aristocrats of the French, Italian, Spanish, and German courts. Often, they were known by one name in one country, and another name elsewhere. For example, one of the best known early dances was the *Saltarello,* called *Alta Danza* in Spain, and *Pas de Brebant* in France.

[3]Agnes de Mille, *The Book of the Dance* (New York: Golden Press, 1963), p. 63.

[4]Bland, *op. cit.,* p. 155.

Other dances of the period were the *Piva, Saltarello Tedesco,* and *Calata;* however, none of these apparently had prescribed forms. Neither their descriptions nor the music to which they were danced were recorded for history. It was not until the end of the 16th century that rules were formulated for the proper steps for each dance, and for the appropriate dance music to be played. This meant that, in terms of progress in dance, a whole system of movement and a vocabulary of steps and patterns were developed. In terms of music, the need for contrast in rhythm and musical form meant that each dance soon had its characteristic accompaniment; the composers of the period grouped the selections that were played into a certain order, giving birth to the musical suite—which ultimately became the sonata form.

The most famous dances of the period were the *Pavane,* the *Galliard,* the *Allemande,* the *Courante,* the *Sarabande,* the *Gigue,* and the *Minuet.*

Pavane. This was a dance of ceremonious splendor and great dignity, which is said to have originated in the court of Spain during the Inquisition. Its mood was solemn and religious (the name is derived from the Latin *pavo,* or peacock) and it suggests this stately and pompous fowl. The Pavane was apparently used on some religious occasions; Thoinot Arbeau wrote in 1588, in his *Orchesographie:*

> Our musicians play it when a damsel of good family is taken to Holy Church to be married, or when musicians head a religious procession of the chaplains, masters and brethren of some notable guild. . . . It is used by kings, princes and great lords, to display themselves on some day of solemn festival with their fine mantles and robes of ceremony; and then the queens and princesses and great ladies accompany them with the long trains of their dresses let down and trailing behind them. These Pavanes are also used in masquerades (or ballets) where there is a procession of triumphant chariots of gods and goddesses. . . . [5]

The Pavane was a *Basse Danse,* involving a simple walking step performed by one or more couples, advancing and retreating. It was done in a slow tempo, and one source describes it as a "grave kind of dance borrowed from the Spaniards, wherein the performers make a kind of wheel or tail before each other, like that of a peacock." The Pavane continued to be popular from about 1530 to about 1670; it was used as the opening dance of great festive balls, usually being followed by the spirited Galliard.

Galliard. Arbeau described the Galliard as a blithe and lively dance, of which there were at least 20 different versions. Its source was said to be Italy, where it was also called the *Romanesca.* It included a number of leaping, kicking, and leg-thrusting steps, and was most popular from the last quarter of the 16th century to about the middle of the 17th. Sometimes the Galliard was considered to be immodest; one author referred to it as an "invention of the devil, full of shameful and obscene gestures."

When the Pavane, in 4/4 time, was followed by the lively Galliard in 3/4 time, as a customary sequence at court balls, the first musical suite was born. Many musical compositions were composed with this contrasting structure.

[5] Thoinot Arbeau, *Orchesographie* (1588), quoted in Horst, *op. cit.,* p. 7.

Allemande. This dance eventually replaced the Pavane as the first part of what was to become the four-part classic suite. The Allemande is considered to have been a very ancient German dance, simple and grave in demeanor. One writer, in 1584, described it as "knights in armour, treading a warlike almain."

After it was introduced at the French court, the Allemande gained rather flowing and sentimental characteristics; it was usually danced in 4/4 time, played in a slow and dignified tempo. Its unique aspect was that it required partners to keep their hands joined throughout the entire dance, as they turned and performed various patterns; after it was no longer performed as a separate dance, this action was still perpetuated in folk and country dancing. In square dancing today, to turn one's partner or corner by the hand is called an "allemande."

Courante. Destined to become the second dance of the four-part classic suite, the Courante was said to have originated both in Italy and France. The first phase of the Courante came from Italy, and was brought to France by Catherine de Medici. Played with running passages of eighth notes in quick 3/4 time, it was colorfully described: "It is danced with short passages of coming and going, and has a very pliant movement of the knees, which recalls that of a fish when it plunges lightly through the water and returns suddenly to the surface."[6]

The second form originated in France, and was the more popular version of the Courante. It was apparently a pantomime dance; as described by Arbeau, it was danced by three couples in a row, showing gestures of courtship and flirtation. Movements included running and gliding and, as the dance continued to be performed through the years, it gradually became more solemn and noble in its attitudes. The Courante was a great favorite for about two centuries, from 1550 to 1750.

Sarabande. Eventually to become the third dance of the four-part suite, the Sarabande, like the Pavane, was of Spanish ancestry, and was a solemn dance which was widely used in religious processions and Masses. It appears to have been performed as early as the 12th century, although it was not introduced at the French court until about 1588. The dance was like a grave and proud *Minuet,* involving much advancing and retreating, with couples passing between lines of other dancers almost as a processional. Some thought that it originated first with the Moors in Spain, and it was often performed with castanets. The Sarabande was played in two parts, in 3/4 time, in a slow tempo.

Gigue. The fourth dance of the four-part classic suite was the Gigue —a lively and exciting dance which apparently was found in varying forms in many countries of Europe. The earliest form recorded was in Italy, where the name was derived from the *giga,* a small stringed instrument. Horst points out that the German name for fiddle was *geige,* and traditionally the Gigue, or Jig, has always been performed to spirited fiddle music, played in 3/8, 6/8, 9/8, or 12/8 time. The Gigue was most popular in the 16th and 17th centuries, although it continued to be done in later centuries, as a sort of individual folk dance step, or a music hall turn.

[6]Horst, *op cit.,* p. 35.

Other dances described by Horst as being performed during the pre-classic period of the 16th and 17th centuries were the *Minuet* (which continued to be widely performed as late as the 19th century); the *Gavotte,* originally a lively and flirtatious peasant dance; the *Bourrée,* an earthy and vigorous dance, also of peasant origin; and the *Rigaudon,* a light, gay dance with running, hopping, and turning steps.

As court music became more complex and the courtiers more skilled dancers, the original two-part suite of the Pavane and Galliard was replaced, about 1620, by the four-part suite of the Allemande, Courante, Sarabande, and Gigue. Many great composers of the 17th, 18th, and 19th centuries wrote in one or another of these forms, including Purcell, Bach, Handel, Couperin, and Lully; among later composers who derived inspiration from them were Satie, Ravel, Schoenberg, Debussy, and Prokofieff. Although the court dances of the Renaissance were not ballet as such, they may be said to have provided the vocabulary of movement of much of the early ballet in France and Italy.

THE FIRST BALLETS

Dance historians usually assign the date of the first ballet to 1581, when the so-called *Ballet Comique de la Reine* was produced at the court of Henry III of France, at Fontainebleau. It was a tremendously elaborate and expensive spectacle, produced by the queen mother, Catherine de Medici, who, when she came to France to wed Henry II, had brought with her a company of highly trained musicians and dancers from the city of Florence. The *Ballet Comique* was produced in honor of the queen's daughter-in-law; it was the work of Catherine's valet de chambre, Balthasar de Beaujoyeux, an Italian. It was a mixture of Old Testament tales and Greek and Roman mythology; basically, its theme was the legend of Circe, the Greek enchantress. Original music, poetry, and songs were composed by professionals of the court, and elaborate sets and scenic devices, including fountains and aquatic machines, accompanied the performance. Over 10,000 spectators saw the performance, which lasted from ten in the evening until four in the morning, and which cost between three and five million francs to produce.

Although the quality of performance and the splendor of the entire work far exceeded any court entertainment that had been produced before, it was chiefly because the *Ballet Comique* attempted to confine itself to a single major dramatic theme that it is regarded as the first real ballet to have been presented in Europe. The performance was regarded as a major artistic success; copies of its poetry and music were printed and sent to all the courts of Europe.

From this time, France was viewed as the center of the development of ballet, while Italy served as the home of the developing opera of the Renaissance.

The term "ballet" itself was derived from the Italian *ballare,* meaning "to dance," and from the word *ballo,* referring to dances as performed in a ballroom. *Ballate* were songs used to accompany dancing in Tuscany in the 13th and 14th centuries, and Chujoy points out that during the later years of the Renaissance the Medici princes wrote *canzone a ballo,* or dance songs.

The word *balleti* was the diminutive of *ballo,* and is the direct source of the word *ballet.* At first it meant performances of patterned dances and had no specific theatrical meaning. Balthasar de Beaujoyeux, choreographer of the *Ballet Comique,* defined ballet as "a geometric combination of several persons dancing together."

Similarly, in 1641, Saint-Hubert wrote of ballet as an essentially non-dramatic work requiring "subject, airs, dancing, costumes, machines, and organization." About the same time, Marolles emphasized its spectacular character, asking:

> But what is a Ballet of the type today among us? It seems to me that it is a dance of many masked persons dressed in dazzling clothes, composed of diverse entrées or parts which can be distributed into several acts and which relate agreeably to a whole, with some different airs to represent an invented subject where the pleasing, the unusual and the marvelous are not forgotten.[7]

Gradually, the term "ballet" came to mean a form of theatrical story-telling through dance. The *Encyclopedia* of Diderot, published in France about 1772, says, "Ballet is action explained by a dance . . . specifically theatrical, spectacular, and done to be seen. . . ." Another 18th century conception was, "The stage is, as it were, the canvas, on which the composer (choreographer) renders his ideas; the choice of music, scenery and costumes are his colors; the choreographer is the painter."

In addition to considering ballet in terms of its outward form, one might also view it historically, as the traditional concert dance form of the Western world. Conceived in Italy, it came to life in France in the court of Louis XIV in the latter part of the 17th century. It developed through the contributions of individual dancers, choreographers, and teachers, in the centuries that followed, reaching a peak of creativity and popular appeal during a so-called Golden Age, in the 1830s and 1840s. In this period, a complex system of movement and floor patterns was developed, as well as a teaching system that allowed ballet to be taught with relative exactitude in the courts, opera houses, and academies of Europe, and fundamental concepts of form and style which distinguished it from other dance forms.

Following the *Ballet Comique* in 1581, a number of other outstanding court entertainments were presented, none of comparable scope or artistic excellence. One of these was performed in the Salle de Bourbon, in 1615, to celebrate a royal marriage in France. Gaston Vuillier described it thus:

> Thirty genii [being the chamber and chapel musicians of the King], suspended in the air, heralded the coming of Minerva, the Queen of Spain. This goddess, surrounded by fourteen nymphs, her companions, appeared in a mighty gilded car drawn by two Cupids. A band of Amazons accompanied the car and made a concord of lutes. . . . Forty persons were on the stage at once, thirty high in the sky, and six suspended in mid-air; all of these dancing and singing at the same time.[8]

[7]John Baron, "History of the Ballet de Cour and the Court of Louis XIII," *Dance Perspectives No. 66,* Vol. 16, Summer, 1975, p. 4.

[8]Père Menestrier, quoted in Gaston Vuillier, *A History of Dance* (New York: D. Appleton and Co., 1897), p. 90.

Altogether, over eighty such ballets were performed at the French Court of Henry IV (whose reign was from 1589 to 1610), in addition to numerous balls and masquerades. Such works were known in France as Masques, since all the dancers wore masks—a custom that was not abolished in ballet until as late as 1773.

Louis XIII, who followed Henry IV, was another great patron of the dance. Under his reign, many ballets were performed; the king himself played a leading role in *La Délivrance de Renault* in 1617, and composed dance music for other works. A fairly typical work of this period was the *Mountain Ballet,* an allegorical entertainment in which the scenery consisted of five great mountains—the Windy, the Resounding, the Luminous, the Shadowy, and the Alps. In the midst was a Field of Glory, which the inhabitants of the mountains wished to capture:

> Fame opened the ballet and explained its subject. Disguised as an old woman, she rode an ass and carried a wooden trumpet. Then the mountains opened their sides, and quadrilles of dancers came out, in flesh-colored attire, having bellows in their hands, by the nymph Echo, wearing bells for head-dresses, and on their bodies lesser bells, and carrying drums. Falsehood hobbled forward on a wooden leg, with masks hung over his coat, and a dark lantern in his hand. . . .[9]

Such works usually consisted of a series of dances, ranging in number from about 10 to about 30, by different groups of dancers who dramatized related phases of a common theme. At the end, general dancing was held, in which all the members of the court participated along with those who had performed in the entertainment. With the exception of those few professionals who were attached to the court as dancing masters, musicians, and composers, all were amateurs. John Martin points out that during the reign of Louis XIII, a single performance in an evening often was not enough; the king and his fellow dancers trooped from the royal palace to other mansions of the nobility, repeating the performance. Frequently the evening was brought to a close with a final performance on a platform erected in front of the City Hall, with townspeople as spectators. At the end, the king and courtiers stepped down to the street and danced with the wives and daughters of the townspeople. The king's company was all male, since at this time noblewomen did not customarily dance in the formal court ballet. The roles of girls and women were usually taken by boys and slender youths wearing elaborate wigs and masks.[10]

John Baron comments that the court ballet was significant because it represented the most spectacular and often the most artistically successful entertainment at one of the most powerful courts of Europe for almost a century. Its multimedia elements of mask, costume, music, and dance, taken from the court entertainment tradition in both France and Italy's Renaissance past, influenced French dramatic and musical art for centuries to follow, including opera. He writes:

[9]Villier, *op. cit.,* p. 87.

[10]John Martin, *John Martin's Book of the Dance* (New York: Tudor Publishing Co., 1963), p. 29.

The influence of the ballet de cour on the English masque and on international ballet extends the importance of this art form well beyond French borders.[11]

LOUIS XIV, THE SUN KING

A giant step in the progress of ballet was taken during the reign of Louis XIV, the Sun King, who was probably as enthusiastic and helpful a patron as the dance has ever known. The king himself was an excellent dancer as a young man, and delighted in performing himself. He took daily lessons from his dancing master, Pierre Beauchamps, for over 20 years, and, only when he was too heavy to dance gracefully, in middle age, did he stop performing.

Because of his great interest in ballet, Louis employed a number of outstanding musicians and dancing masters, among them Jean-Baptiste Lully, an Italian-born musician and dancer who ultimately became the director of the Royal Academy of Music and Dance. Another key figure was Beauchamps, a brilliant dancer who formulated many of the beginning principles of ballet and became *maître de ballet* at the Royal Academy.

Beginning in 1651, when he was thirteen, Louis XIV danced in public in the *Masque of Cassandra.* He continued until 1670 as a leading performer, dancing in 26 grand ballets, not to mention the intermezzi of numerous lyrical tragedies and comedy ballets. Throughout his reign, many ballets were danced at the Tuilleries and others at the Louvre, at Versailles, and Fontainebleau. One performance, the *Ballet du Carrousel,* was held on a large open space in front of the Tuilleries in 1662; in this ballet Louis XIV danced at the head of the Roman armies, while his brother led the Persians, the Prince de Condé commanded the Turks, and the Duc de Guise the Americans. In other works, such as the *Grand Ballet du Roi,* performed at the Louvre in 1664, figures of Roman mythology and history were portrayed in a conglomerate sequence of tales. In addition to these separate ballets, a number of ballets were danced in the operas of Lully and other musicians of the period.

Dancing until this time had been an amateur art, and was performed, usually, within the ballroom. Typically, the king and his household sat at the end of the hall on a dais. Along the other sides of the room, spectators sat in long galleries on the edge of the floor. There was no stage, and the dancers were close to the audience. The dance movement was fairly simple, being based in large degree on the pre-classic court dances of the period. The dancers were encumbered by extremely heavy wigs, masks, and costumes; some of these weighed as much as 150 pounds. For amateurs, the noblemen of the court were excellent dancers. Every courtier could dance; de Mille comments that their style was always noble and controlled—the demeanor of a king. Gestures were symmetrical and harmonious, all opening from a central axis, based on the turned-out leg and *port de bras* (fencing position).

The nobleman, in de Mille's words, "danced as he was used to moving in all court procedures:"

[11]Baron, *op. cit.,* p. 4.

Louis XIV in the Ballet Royal de la Nuit, 1653. Reprinted with permission of the Dance Collection of the Library and Museum of the Performing Arts at Lincoln Center in New York City.

> . . .[with] movement characterized by arrogant confidence, affected yet elegant, ornate, swift and commanding, highly disciplined; with erect posture, lightness, strength, brilliance, and catlike use of the foot. . . .[12]

But, in the Sun King's view, this was not enough. Realizing that from a technical standpoint ballet could be developed much more fully, in 1661 Louis XIV asked his ballet master, Beauchamps, to establish rules for ballet, to describe the foot and arm positions and all the known patterns of movement. This Beauchamps did, thus establishing the basis for ballet technique that was to develop through the centuries. In addition, in 1661, the king granted a charter to the Royal Academy of Dance, which was to provide a home for professional instruction in the art of dancing. This art, according to the letters patent founding the Academy:

> . . .has ever been acknowledged to be one of the most suitable and necessary arts for physical development and for affording the primary and most natural preparation for all bodily exercises, and, among others, those concerning the use of weapons, and consequently it is one of the most valuable and useful arts for nobles and others who have the honor to enter our presence not only in time of war in our armies, but even in time of peace in our ballets.[13]

[12]De Mille, *op. cit.,* p. 81.

[13]*Ibid.,* p. 90.

PROFESSIONALIZATION OF BALLET: LULLY AND BEAUCHAMPS

In 1671, Lully obtained the charter of the Royal Academy of Music and combined it with the Academy of Dance, to form a single strong organization. Within two years, the new academy which joined both arts was given the use of the Theater in the Palais Royal, built about thirty years before by Cardinal Richelieu, and occupied until the death of Molière by that famous playwright and his company. This magnificent theater was built in the recently developed manner of the new Italian theater; it had an elevated stage on which the action took place, at one end of the hall, beneath a proscenium arch. All the spectators sat in front, rather than on three sides of the dancer, as in the past.

The use of Richelieu's theater had two important effects on the development of ballet as a professional art at this time.

First, since the dancer had only to be concerned with how he would look from one direction, it became necessary to think of the audience, *in front,* as a focus. When moving from side to side across the stage, the best way to do this while facing the audience was to turn the hip and knee out, so the feet pointed to the side instead of straight forward. Gradually, the turnout became more and more pronounced, and became the basis of the five positions of the foot in classic ballet which Beauchamps recorded about 1700 and which are essential to all ballet technique even today.

A second important effect of the new theater and its stage was that for the first time the performers were markedly separated from their audience. No longer did dance represent a somewhat casual, social activity, in which members of the court might intermingle freely with professionals. Over a period of decades, performance became the domain of the professional dancers who were trained in the Royal Academy and who developed an increasingly high level of skill that separated them, more and more, from the amateur performers in the nobility.

In *The Triumph of Love,* women for the first time performed on the professional stage. Lully succeeded in persuading some of the greatest ladies of the court, including the Dauphiness and a number of princesses, to dance professionally—still wearing masks, of course.

The ballet became increasingly professional. Much of the technique was derived from the court dances performed during the pre-classic period. However, gradually it moved from *danse terre à terre* (close to the earth) to *danse haute,* with leaps, springing steps, and such actions as the *entrechat.* The design of movement became vertical, rather than horizontal. Based on the five fundamental positions of the feet and the twelve positions of the arm which Beauchamps had formulated, a wide variety of steps was developed and named; these became the basis of ballet technique and the *danse d'école* —or education in ballet.

Lully, who directed the new company that performed in the Palais Royal, felt that the Paris audience which now was permitted to attend performances in the new theater would enjoy plays that combined both dancing and singing. Thus, in the early days of the Royal Academy, its company performed in so-called lyric dramas. In these, while the dance may have slowed up the dramatic action, it served to carry the plot along. Gradually, however, in the early and middle 18th century, the so-called Opera Ballet came into being. This included both dancing and orchestral music; it dealt with many kinds of subject matter within a single work, and often the content of one act was not related to that of the following act. In essence, the dramatic action almost disappeared, and the stage work became a vehicle for singers and dancers to display their talents. Gradually, as the plot became less important, dancers tended to perform movement that was increasingly decorative and abstract—rather than story telling in nature.

In a sense, this reflected a change in the times. Vuillier writes:

> The art of the new era inclined to artificiality . . . painters sought inspiration in love and joy, in sylvan delights, in dainty idylls . . . great financiers began to patronise dawning talent, and to encourage the growth of a luxurious elegance. It was a reign of daintiness and of taste . . . perhaps a little mincing and affected. Pictorial art lacked energy and deep feeling—lacked greatness, in a word; but it was pretty, it was seductive.[14]

It was at this time that a pattern developed with respect to the role of the sexes in dance, that has often been repeated since. The leading *organizers* of dance—the teachers, innovators, choreographers, theoreticians—were men such as Lully and Beauchamps. Lully was a musician and a dancer, but far more than this, a clever politician, wise in the ways of the court, who was able to mobilize the efforts of the king in his behalf. Further, he produced many works and composed operas and ballets. Beauchamps, while a brilliant performer who had introduced much technique and was known for his elevations, turns, *pirouettes,* and *tours en l'air,* was also a leading codifier of the dance. His system of dance shorthand, or notation, was the first of its kind and it was his analysis of the fundamentals of ballet movement that laid the groundwork for the development of this art.

EARLY STARS OF THE BALLET

While men monopolized organizational roles, women began to assume the role of stars—glamorous and brilliant dancers who won the acclaim of growing audiences. They no longer came from the nobility itself. Instead, they tended to come from poorer families, and to have learned their craft in the Academy. Now they performed on the stage of the Palais Royal before an audience that was still aristocratic for the most part, although with a sprinkling of wealthy bourgeois. Among these talented performers were Camargo, Sallé, and Prévost.

Marie Anne de Camargo, who lived between 1710 and 1770, is reputed to have been the outstanding French dancer of the 18th century. Her style was gay and light, her movements lusty and vigorous, with strong contrasts. Camargo was considered an extremely expressive dancer; she made ballet a vehicle of interpretation. She had a particular ability for elevation, and was able to rapidly cross and recross her feet in the air (an action known as

[14]Vuillier, *op. cit.,* pp. 138–139.

entrechat), and this gave her the courage to modify the traditional ballet costume. At this point, women wore stiff-hooped skirts that were heavily panniered, and reached the floor, as well as elaborate, heavy headdresses, masks, coats, and heeled shoes. In order to give her legs greater freedom, and to permit her ingenious improvisations to be seen, Camargo adopted a much shorter skirt than was the custom, and an undergarment which was the predecessor of ballet tights. In addition, she wore soft slippers which were the forerunners of ballet slippers.

Another great female star of the 18th century was Marie Sallé. Unlike Camargo, her style was not that of a brilliant virtuoso. Instead, she brought to ballet a dramatic realism and a natural expressiveness in movement. She, too, sought to abandon the traditional ballet costume and introduced flowing draperies modeled after Greek sculpture. In fact, it was her intent to abandon the set uniform of ballet entirely and dress each character in its appropriate national style, or in terms of its place in the plot—a reform that has been suggested again and again by ballet innovators. So popular was Sallé, who lived from 1707 to 1756, that Vuillier wrote of her:

> She was idolised. The huge crowds that pressed about the doors of the theater fought for a sight of her. Enthusiastic spectators, who had paid great sums for seats, had to make their way in with their fists. Upon her benefit appearance in London, at the close of the piece, purses filled with guineas and jewels were showered on the stage at her feet. . . . On this memorable night, Mademoiselle Sallé received more that two hundred thousand francs, an enormous sum for that time.[15]

Another leading performer during this period was Françoise Prévost, who danced during the early 1700s, and who was known for her lightness and precision, as well as for her dramatic ability. In addition, there were a number of leading male dancers, such as Louis Pécours, who starred in many of Lully's and Beauchamps' ballets, choreographed a number of works for the Palais Royal, and taught in the Academy. However, without question, it was the brilliant female stars who attracted the most fervently enthusiastic audiences.

As an increasing number of outstanding dancers developed in Paris, they began to travel from court to court throughout Europe, performing and beginning their own ballet schools and companies. It was at this time that rulers in Italy, Austria, Russia, England, and Scandinavia established royal opera houses and theaters, to which ballet companies became promptly attached. This meant that "the companies were established in permanent residence and guaranteed continuity and protection. All are still functioning as the ornaments of the state and repositories of great national works and technical styles.[16] Among the famous theaters and opera houses which were established at this time were: The King's Theater, in Haymarket, London, 1705; the Royal Danish Ballet, in the National Theater, Copenhagen, 1726; the Royal Opera, in Covent Garden, London, 1732; and numer-

[15] *Ibid.*, p. 142.

[16] De Mille, *op. cit.*, p. 91.

ous others in Naples, 1737; Vienna, 1748; Stuttgart, 1750; Munich, 1752; Moscow, 1776; Milan, 1778; and St. Petersburg, 1783.

In some cases, ballet was founded as a separate company, under royal subsidy and protection; in others, it was a valued component of a major company. In each instance, support was assured that meant that a high level of training and performance could be maintained; ballet had now gained status that was to assure its continuity through the centuries.

In a sense, this represented a threat to the continuing creative development of ballet. Just as in any art form which becomes attached to the establishment, its ways became fixed and stereotyped. The choreographers of the early and middle 1700s made no attempt to reform the existing Opera Ballet practices. Every opera had *Passepieds* in its prologue, followed by *Musettes* in the first act, by *Tambourins* in the second, and by *Chaconnes* and *Passepieds* in the acts following (these refer to dances popular during the period). No one dared to violate this formula, according to Vuillier:

> . . . in every opera, each leading character had to dance his special dance, and the best dancer always concluded. It was by this law, and not by the action of the poem, that the dancing was governed. And what intensified the mischief was that poets, musicians, costumiers, decorators, never consulted one another. Each had his prescriptive routine; each pursued his own old path, indifferent as to whether he arrived at the same goal as his neighbor. To reform all this was a Herculean task. No single individual could diverge from the beaten track until all abandoned it. . . .[17]

Few tried. Such famous performers or choreographers of the middle and late 18th century as Gaetano Vestris, distinguished member of a great ballet family; Jean Dauberval, a French dancer and choreographer who composed the famed *La Fille Mal Gardée;* Madeleine Guimard, a leading female dancer toward the end of the century who was extremely popular with royalty and conducted a leading salon; Charles Didelot, a dancer and choreographer in Sweden and at the Paris Opéra; and Salvatore Vigano, a leading Italian dancer and choreographer—all of these were generally content with their lot. It remained for one person, Jean Georges Noverre, to propose a set of sweeping reforms in ballet that ultimately changed this theatrical art in a number of radical ways.

THE REFORMS OF NOVERRE

Noverre, who lived from 1727 to 1810, made his debut as a dancer at the age of 16 in the Opéra Comique and was appointed ballet master four years later. Ultimately, he became a leading choreographer, critic, writer, and reformer of ballet. He was the first to fully envision its artistic possibilities, and to eliminate the conventionalized movements, gestures, and stage traditions. Noverre's book, *Letters on Dancing and Ballet,* published in 1760, stressed that dancing should not only be physical virtuosity, but also a

[17]Vuillier, *op. cit.,* p. 153.

means for dramatic expression and communication. Ballet had become a collection of miscellaneous short dances which tended to be thrown together to casually written music. These were presented at random in operas, with no relation to the action or plot, chiefly because they permitted the stars to show off their special abilities before the large audiences which only a performance of opera could obtain.

Noverre's philosophy (one which he presented so vigorously that ultimately he was compelled to leave Paris and to seek posts elsewhere, in England, Vienna, and Stuttgart) comprised the following ideas:

Balletic movement should not only be technically brilliant, but should move the audience emotionally, through its dramatic expressiveness.

The plots of ballets should be unified in design, with logical and understandable stories that contribute to a central theme, and with all solos or other dance sequences that did not relate to the plot being eliminated.

The scenery, the music, and the plot should all be unified; a reform of costumes was necessary so that they would be appropriate to the theme of the dance and music should be specially written so as to be suitable for the dance as well.

Pantomime, which had become increasingly conventionalized and meaningless, needed to be made simpler and more understandable.

These and many other suggestions were summed up in his writings on the *ballet d'action*—that is, ballet in which the dance actually promotes the dramatic representation, instead of interrupting it for meaningless displays of virtuosity. In his own work, Noverre collaborated with musicians closely. He sought appropriate subject matter first, worked out a libretto or poem, developed dance movements to express the content of the poem, and then explained the plot to the composer and asked that music be composed to fit this work specifically—rather than just setting a dance to existing music.

Noverre wrote:

> A well-composed ballet is a living picture of the passions, manners, habits, ceremonies, and customs of all nations of the globe . . . if it be devoid of expression, of striking pictures, or strong situations, it becomes a cold and dreary spectacle. . . .[18]

Gradually, Noverre's ideas gained influence. When he urged dancers to ". . .break hideous masks, to bury ridiculous perukes, to suppress clumsy panniers, to do away with still more inconvenient hip pads . . ." he lent courage to leading performers who had long wished that costumes might be reformed. Thus, in 1772, when *Castor and Pollux,* an opera by Rameau, was being performed, Gaetano Vestris was scheduled to perform as Apollo, wearing a traditional enormous black wig, a mask, and a big gilded copper sun on his chest. Unable to appear, Vestris's role was taken by Maximilien Gardel who was determined to let the audience know that *he* was playing the role of the Sun God, rather than Vestris. He refused to wear the wig, the mask, and the copper sun. The public approved the change and from this time on, the use of the mask was abandoned by leading dancers.

[18]Jean Georges Noverre, *Letters on Dancing and Ballet,* Translated by Cyril Beaumont (published originally in 1760, republished by Dance Horizons, Inc., New York, 1966), p. 16.

Other disciples of Noverre, including Dauberval and Didelot, applied many of his reforms with respect to the development of ballet plots and the use of meaningful gesture—rather than the stereotyped hand language then in vogue. Noverre never completely succeeded in his wish to make ballet a completely independent theater art, rather than a decorative adjunct to opera. Nonetheless, he represented a force for the revitalization of ballet that was not to be duplicated until Michel Fokine left Russia for Paris, over a century later.

The next major influence to touch and modify ballet was the French Revolution.

The immediate effect of this violent overthrow of the French monarchy was to challenge the place of ballet in public life, as a form of entertainment that was essentially an aristocratic art, and identified with the pastimes of the very royalty that had fled the country in terror, or had been executed on the guillotine. However, dancers, as always, were adaptable. Before long, the Paris Opéra figured in the forefront of a number of fetes of the Republic; there were patriotic spectacles in which the performers were supported by large choirs singing patriotic hymns and cantatas. In one such fete, the Marseillaise was danced as a great public spectacle. In another, during the second year of the Revolution, a festival titled "Festival of the Supreme Being" dealt with revolutionary themes; it was designed by David, conducted by Robespierre, and presented by decree of the National Convention.

While the Revolution caused a temporary cessation to some forms of dance, it did not quench the French passion for this activity as a social art. According to Vuillier, scarcely was the ruthless execution of great numbers of Parisians (known as the Terror) at an end, than 23 theaters and 1800 dancing schools were open every evening in Paris. Mercier, a writer of the period, describes the scene:

> . . .dancing is universal; they dance at the Carmelites, between the massacres; they dance at the Jesuits' Seminary; at the Convent of Carmelites du Marais; at the seminary of Saint-Sulpice; at the Filles de Sainte-Marie; they dance in three ruined churches of my section, and upon the stones of all the tombs which have not been destroyed. They dance in every tavern on the Boulevards, in the Champs Elysées, and along the quays. They dance at Ruggieri's, Lucquet's, Mauduit's, Wenzel's, and Montausier's. There are balls for all classes. Dancing, perhaps, is a means of forgetfulness. . . .[19]

And Parisians had much to forget. Strangely, one festivity was instituted—a so-called *Victim Ball*—to which were admitted only relatives of those who had died on the scaffold as part of the persecution during the Revolution. Mercier asks:

> Will posterity believe that people, whose relatives had died on the scaffold, inaugurated, not days of solemn general grief when assembled in mourning garb, that they might bear witness to their sorrow at the cruel losses so recently incurred, but days of dancing, drinking, and feasting? For admission to one

[19]Henry Fourment, *Paris During the Revolution,* quoted in Vuillier, *op. cit.,* p. 197.

of these banquets and dances, it is necessary to show a certificate of the loss of a father, a mother, a husband, a wife, a brother or a sister under the knife of the guillotine.[20]

When the Revolution came to an end, ballet, which had been suspended except for the sort of patriotic spectacles mentioned earlier, resumed. Now, however, under the Republic, its themes were quite different. There were now ballets dealing with the *sans-culottes* of the Revolution. Other works commemorated the American Revolution, and some ballets were choreographed which criticized religion and the Catholic Church—reflecting the viewpoint of the new government. All this represented not only an accommodation to the existing powers, but also the first breaths of a new idea—political and social democracy. It was linked with a concern with contemporaneous thought, and with the first stirrings of another sort of revolution—the Romantic Revolution. With poetry, music, painting, and literature, the ballet was to be a vital part of this new artistic movement.

ROMANTICISM IN BALLET

In the decades immediately following the French Revolution, ballet continued to change radically, in terms of its aesthetic content and format, technical style, and vocabulary. Instrumental in this development were three leading figures: Salvatore Vigano, Carlo Blasis, and Théophile Gautier.

Vigano, who lived from 1769 to 1821, had been a disciple of Noverre, and of the famed ballet master, Dauberval. He attempted to carry out Noverre's theories of unity of form and dramatic expression, and contributed much to the development of pantomime to replace the conventionalized gestures that were widely used in ballet to develop the plot. He attempted to develop what he called the *choreodrame;* this made use of groups of dancers who were treated in a plastic, almost sculptural way. He composed many of the leading ballets of his era, as ballet master at La Scala, and at other leading opera houses in Vienna, Venice, and other European cities.

Blasis (1787–1878) was, without question, one of the towering figures of ballet history. He was an Italian dancer, choreographer, and teacher, who had been strongly influenced by both Noverre and Vigano. He had danced and composed in both France and England, and returned to La Scala in Milan as the outstanding ballet master of his time. He developed a comprehensive system for practicing and teaching the art of ballet; indeed his method of education is still widely influential today. He developed major theories involving the laws of equilibrium and balance, and geometric schemes governing the body's movement in ballet exercises. In 1830, he published his famous *Code of Terpsichore,* which contained a fundamental system of ballet instruction, a model that every ballet school has since used. In the Imperial Academy of Dancing and Pantomime in Milan, of which Blasis became director in 1837, the following practices were instituted: pupils were not admitted before the age of eight, or after the age of 12 (14 in the case of boys). They had to be medically sound, and of "good stock."

[20]Vuillier, *op. cit.,* p. 196.

Their training was fully mapped out: three hours of practice a day and one hour of mime. They were attached to the school for eight years and after that their careers as performers were assured by an ascending scale of salaries.[21] Blasis was a gifted student of sculpture and anatomy and so clear a writer that in his book he was able to make thoroughly understandable the mechanical basis of ballet technique. In addition to the bar work and other exercises that he developed, Blasis required his students to study character dancing, pantomime, and *adagio.*

Without question, Blasis was the key figure in the development of the *danse d'école* during the early 19th century. It remained for Théophile Gautier to provide the inspiration that helped to plunge ballet into the thick of the Romantic movement in Europe.

Gautier was a poet, journalist, and dramatic critic of the Romantic era in France, with a great passion for the ballet. He took an active part in the development of this art during its so-called Golden Age. As an extremely influential critic, Gautier helped to shape public taste and enthusiasm and influenced the entire course of ballet in the Romantic age.

Exactly what was Romanticism? Essentially, it was a revolutionary movement in art, which overthrew the rigid forms that had been established by the academic schools which had dominated artistic activity in the 18th century. In its origins, Romanticism was a literary movement; every art form became affected by literary sources, particularly by the poems and plays of Victor Hugo. The Romantic poets, artists, and composers were concerned with the occult and the supernatural; they depicted man's pursuit of the unattainable, exemplified in the hopeless love of a mortal for an unworldly being.

During the 20 years that followed the end of the Napoleonic era in 1815, Romanticism conquered all the arts in France, and spread throughout Europe. Earlier conventions were disregarded and new works were produced with meaning and emotional content that appealed to a fresh new audience. In a sense, Romanticism represented an attempt to escape the realities of life as it was. People had suffered badly during the wars of the previous decade; and the developing Industrial Revolution, with its mines and factories, was now bringing new suffering and wretchedness to millions of underprivileged throughout Europe. Thus, the Romantic movement, which offered color, fantasy, fairy tales, and folk legends—romantic love and beautiful dreams—offered a protest against the sordid quality of real life.

In ballet, this contrast between the bitter reality of life and the yearning for fantastic possibilities meant that a new kind of subject matter was to be used. Supernatural creatures fell in love with mortal men; dead maidens rose from the grave to haunt unfaithful lovers; there were moral victories of aerial and spiritual creatures over earthy and sensual beings.[22] Perhaps most typical of all ballets of this era was *La Sylphide,* choreographed by Philippe Taglioni for his daughter, Marie, one of the great ballerinas of this era. *Sylphide* depicted a woodland creature of supernatural origin, who fell in love with a Scotsman; the ballet is the tale of their tragic romance. For this work, a new costume was devised for the ballerina—full but filmy white

[21]Arnold Haskell, *Ballet* (Middlesex, England: Penguin Books, 1951), p. 26.

[22]Martin, *op. cit.,* p. 34.

skirts that reached halfway down to the ankles. Ballets of this type, which filled the stage with white-clad dancers, were called *ballets blancs,* or white ballets, because of the shimmering effect they created.

As part of the yearning for the unattainable, dance itself became increasingly elevated. More and more, the ballerina defied gravity by soaring through the air and dancing *sur les pointes* (on the tips of her toes). In some ballets, female dancers actually "flew" above the stage by being suspended from wires, so that they could glide along overhead. Such devices were useful not only because of the ethereal roles they played, but as a symbol of the spiritual and exalted role which the Romantic ballet gave to women. Indeed, the ballerina was raised to a new height of glamor and popular favor, while the male dancer's role was reduced to being little more than a support for her brilliant solos. Kirstein writes that during the 1840s, male dancers were in a poor position, as compared to the period when Vestris, Dauberval, and Gardel were dancing. Even as partners, their roles were diminished and, with few exceptions, all solos were given to the ballerina, and the male dancer became little more than a support or a background for her.[23]

BALLET BECOMES A FEMALE ART

The predominant tone of the ballet was female, and the critics themselves ridiculed men who performed as dancers. One writer, Jules Janin, summed up the view of his fellows:

> You know perhaps that we are hardly a supporter of what are called the grand danseurs. The grand danseur appears to us so sad and so heavy! . . . He responds to nothing, he represents nothing, he is nothing. Speak to us of a pretty dancing girl who displays the grace of her features and the elegance of her figure. . . . Thank God, I understand that perfectly. . . . But a man, a frightful man, as ugly as you and I, a wretched fellow who leaps about without knowing why, a creature specially made to carry a musket and a sword and to wear a uniform. That this fellow should dance as a woman does—impossible![24]

Even more cruel in his attacks was Gautier, who despised the male dancer almost as much as he worshipped the ballerina. According to Gautier, a ballet without men is the height of good taste, "for nothing is more abominable than a man who displays his red neck, his great muscular arms, his legs with calves like church beadles', his whole heavily masculine frame, shaken with leaps and pirouettes. . . ." The criticism was often inconsistent. On the one hand, Gautier criticized men for their masculine clumsiness; however, when they were too graceful, he attacked them also: "The dancers at the Opéra are of a nature to encourage the opinion which will only allow

[23]Lincoln Kirstein, *Dance: A Short History of Classic Theatrical Dancing* (New York: G. P. Putnam's Sons, 1935), p. 253.

[24]Jules Janin, quoted in Ivor Guest, *The Romantic Ballet in Paris* (Middletown, Connecticut: Wesleyan University Press, 1966), p. 2.

women in ballet [for they affect] that false grace, those ambiguous and revolting mincing manners which have sickened the public of male dancing. . . ."[25]

And finally:

> For us a male dancer is something monstrous and indecent which we cannot conceive. . . . Strength is the only grace permissible to men.[26]

By the middle of the 1840s so strong was the feeling against male dancers that they were eliminated from the corps de ballet whenever a justification could be found. The device of the *danseuse en travesti* (female dancers in male costumes) was then discovered, and women began to play the roles of hussars, sailors, and other customarily male parts. Although many talented male dancers continued to appear in Paris, the standard of their performance gradually lowered, and fewer and fewer young boys entered the Paris Opéra's School of Dance; it was a career that had little appeal for them.

BALLERINAS OF THE GOLDEN AGE

The great stars of the period were five ballerinas, who flourished during the Golden Age of ballet, the 1830s and 1840s, when ballet was at its creative heights in terms of artistic inspiration and an expanding body of technique and brilliant choreography.

Marie Taglioni (1804–1884) was considered by many the greatest dancer of the century. She danced in Vienna, Italy, Germany, and France, and later in her life became a star of the St. Petersburg Imperial Theater. Her outstanding work was *La Sylphide,* which was a sensation throughout Europe and was considered to be the first great Romantic ballet. Taglioni was the first ballerina to develop the art of *pointe* dancing; she was extremely light, almost floating, and had great elevation. She represented the mystical side of Romanticism; her technique was superb—fragile and exquisite.

Taglioni's greatest rival was Fanny Elssler, who lived between 1810 and 1884. She was a Viennese dancer who symbolized the earthy side of Romanticism and was viewed as a "pagan" dancer; the stage image she conveyed was far more passionate than spiritual. Her movement was closer to the earth than Taglioni's, but had great style and precision. She perfected "character" dances of other lands—such as Hungary, Poland, and Spain. When she toured America in 1840 she was a tremendous sensation.

Fanny Cerrito (1821–1899) was a famous Italian ballerina and choreographer of the Romantic period, who danced in Naples, Vienna, London, and Paris. She was a spirited and beautiful dancer, with great technical skill, whose popularity was close to that of Taglioni and Elssler. Lucile Grahn (1821–1907) was a famous Danish ballerina who studied first in Copenha-

[25]Théophile Gautier, quoted in Deidre Priddin, *The Art of the Dance in French Literature* (London: A. & C. Black, Ltd., 1952), p. 41.

[26]*Ibid.*, p. 41.

Pas de Quatre, danced in 1845 in London by Marie Taglioni, Carlotta Grisi, Fanny Cerrito, and Lucille Grahn. Color lithograph by John Brandard, in Cia Fornaroli Collection.

gen and then performed in Paris at the Opéra in *La Sylphide,* competing with Taglioni. She was considered the greatest classic technician of her time, and was noted for a quality of dreamy grace and abandon. Her teacher and choreographer was the renowned August Bournonville; his versions of *Giselle* and *La Sylphide* were among her great roles. Carlotta Grisi (1821–1899) was an eminent Italian ballerina of the Romantic period, who created the role of *Giselle* and was a protégé of Théophile Gautier. In addition to many starring roles in Paris, Grisi was a favorite in St. Petersburg and London, where she performed in Perrot's *Pas de Quatre,* with Taglioni, Grahn, and Cerrito.

Gradually the creative inspiration that had enabled ballet to reach its height in the 1830s and 1840s declined. Innovations were perpetuated as custom, and the great variety of new technical achievements that had been developed served chiefly as a means of displaying acrobatic brilliance. There were no great male dancers; and with the decline of the great ballerinas of the period, interest in ballet itself declined in Italy, France and England.

The typical ballet of the middle and later 19th century was a romance of ancient days or a fairy tale. It usually lasted for the entire evening, with three or four acts and intermissions that often lasted as long as forty-five minutes each, to permit the audience to stroll in the foyer. The plot was told through sign language of the hands, which often was not intelligible to the audience; dance numbers interrupted the ballet from time to time, with little relation to the drama itself. The sequence of performance was usually the same, with the high point of the evening being a grand *pas de deux* by the ballerina and her partner. Uninspired music was turned out in a cut-and-dried fashion by staff composers and artists; the whole point of the performance was to demonstrate the technical skill and beauty of the ballerina.[27]

Small wonder that public tastes declined, and that audiences became apathetic. Haskell comments that "two hundred years after the founding of the Academy, ballet in the country of its birth was artistically bankrupt . . .

Ballroom dancing in mid-19th-century Paris. Lithograph of the Bal Mabille by A. Provost, about 1850. Reprinted with permission of the Dance Collection of the Library and Museum of the Performing Arts at Lincoln Center in New York City.

[27]Martin, *op. cit.*, pp. 38–39.

merely a prelude to flirtation. . . ."[28] In England, where there was no royal ballet or other state institution to support the art, matters grew even worse. Ballet became a popular routine on music hall programs, with poor music, decor, and choreography. In Paris, it hung on as part of operatic performance, although, according to Shawn:

> . . .the "Golden Age" of the ballet was a period when the dancers were the supreme stars of the stage, and a bored public walked out into the foyer while the singing of the opera was proceeding. . . . At the beginning of this present century, the ballet was at a very low ebb indeed. Sterile, artificial, distinguished neither by greatness of execution nor of idea, written down to by the opera composers, it was now during the ballet that the audience preferred to walk about in the foyer, rather than watch the mechanical, lifeless performances. . . .[29]

BALLET IN CZARIST RUSSIA

Only in one country did ballet retain its popularity and prestige; this was in Czarist Russia. Here it remained firmly entrenched as a cherished ornament of the aristocratic regime, with a widespread audience that remained unquestioningly loyal to it.

Ballet in Russia had a long and respected tradition. As early as the time of Louis XIV in France, traveling "Muscovites" had visited his court to observe the court ballets. At the time of Peter the Great (1672–1725) it became government policy to westernize Russia, which had been sealed off from the rest of Europe for centuries. Peter the Great resolved to break down social customs which had kept his nation behind the times. Therefore, he decreed that the boyars (wealthy landowners) must shave their beards and give up their "dignified and cumbersome robes," and that women might join men in social dances and assemblies which had heretofore been unknown. As in France and Italy, an interest in ballet as a stage art soon followed this introduction of social dance in the court. Almost from the beginning, however, it became a professional art, with the importation of distinguished foreign teachers and choreographers, and the training of skilled, paid performers. Arnold Haskell writes:

> The Empress Anne (1693–1740) founded the Academy, which survives today under a different regime, importing a Frenchman, Lande, to direct it, and thinking it of sufficient importance to include dancing in the curriculum of the cadets. . . . The most intense development took place with Catherine the Great (1762–1796) who imported a Frenchman, Le Picq, and the great Italian, Angiolini, to her court . . . enthusiasm and knowledge [of ballet] spread. . . .[30]

In Russia, where there were vast estates, courtiers had to provide their own amusements and cultural activities. Thus, when Catherine the Great

[28]Haskell, *op. cit.,* p. 30.

[29]Ted Shawn, *Dance We Must* (London: Dennis Dobson, Ltd., 1946), pp. 21–22.

[30]Haskell, *op. cit.,* p. 32.

favored ballet, the nobility followed suit, forming ballet troupes of their own, and spreading a great interest in ballet throughout the land. Gradually, these separate companies became merged in the two great ballet organizations in St. Petersburg and Moscow, with the dancers who joined these companies being given their freedom long before the serfs at large. Haskell comments that ballet became the most cherished possession of the Russian Czars, with huge sums being expended to support its performance, and to import foreign dancers, choreographers, and teachers.

Charles Louis Didelot (1767–1837), an outstanding French dancer, choreographer, and teacher, was one of the greatest of these. Though born in Stockholm, he had an extensive career at the Paris Opéra and in London, where he choreographed a number of major works. He was brought to St. Petersburg by Czar Paul as ballet master of the Imperial Theater, and continued at this post into the regime of Alexander I. From 1801 to 1811, and then again after 1816, he remained in St. Petersburg, where he choreographed over fifty ballets. Didelot was an excellent teacher, and during his reign the ballet school in St. Petersburg developed many outstanding dancers.

Other foreign performers who influenced the Russian ballet during the 19th century included Marie Taglioni, Jules Perrot, Christian Johannsen, Charles Saint-Léon, Enrico Cecchetti, and Marius Petipa.

Following the debut of Fanny Elssler at the Paris Opéra, Taglioni left France, to accept a profitable three-year contract at the St. Petersburg Imperial Theater, from 1837 to 1839. While there, she performed in many of the great ballets then being done in Western Europe, and so introduced them to Russian audiences.

Jules Perrot (1810–1892), a leading French dancer and choreographer who had had an outstanding career dancing with the great Romantic ballerinas at the Paris Opéra, went to St. Petersburg in 1848. He was a leading dancer and choreographer there until 1859, producing nearly twenty ballets in that time—many of these based on realistic themes, with strong dramatic plots.

Christian Johannsen (1817–1903), a Swedish dancer and teacher who had studied under Bournonville in Copenhagen, went to Russia to perform in the St. Petersburg ballet in 1841. He became the leading male dancer there, remaining a *premier danseur* until 1869, when he devoted himself exclusively to teaching at the ballet school. In the decades that followed, he taught all of the great Russian dancers who developed in this period.

Charles Saint-Léon, who lived from about 1815 to 1870, was another leading French choreographer, dancer, and musician, who became ballet master of the Imperial Ballet in St. Petersburg in 1859. While there, he produced a number of original works, including the first ballet on Russian themes.

Enrico Cecchetti, an Italian dancer and ballet master, who lived from 1850 to 1928, starred at La Scala in Milan, in London, and was with the first major Italian ballet company to tour the United States. He came to Russia in 1887, where he made his debut at the Maryinsky Theater in St. Petersburg and shortly became the second ballet master at the Imperial Theater and instructor at the Imperial school. He taught many of the great stars of the Russian ballet and became the private instructor of Anna Pavlova. As official instructor for the Diaghileff company he taught such outstanding performers of the 20th century as Leonid Massine, Adolph Bolm, Ninette de Valois, Alexandra Danilova, Anton Dolin, Serge Lifar, and others.

Through the contributions of all these foreigners, the lavishly supported and prestigious Russian ballet gradually gained world eminence. It blended the distinctive styles of the French and Russian dancers into a system of balanced training and performance, and incorporated their strengths into what was to become a vigorous and extended technique of solid substance. In a history of the Russian ballet, one of its leading dancers, Nicholas Legat, wrote:

> The secret of the development of Russian dancing lay in the fact that we learned from everybody and adapted what we learnt to ourselves. We copied, borrowed from, and emulated every source that gave us inspiration, and then, working on our acquired knowledge and lending it the stamp of the Russian national genius, we moulded it into the eclectic art of the Russian ballet. . . .[31]

Without question, the most influential of all the foreign artists who came to Russia was Marius Petipa.

Petipa (1822–1910) was best known as a choreographer of the Imperial Ballet in St. Petersburg, and has often been referred to as the "father of the classic ballet." He studied in France and made his debut at the Paris Opéra opposite Fanny Elssler in 1841. He was regarded as an excellent dancer, with particular strength in the art of partnering. However, it is chiefly for his choreography and direction of the St. Petersburg ballet that he is known. Joining the Imperial Ballet in 1847, he remained active for over 50 years, during which time he became the dominant force in Russian ballet. He choreographed over 60 full-length ballets (which usually had four or five acts and lasted for the entire evening) and many shorter ballets and divertissements. Among his best known works were *Don Quixote, La Bayadère, The Sleeping Beauty,* and *Bluebeard.* He also restaged many great ballets which had originally been performed elsewhere, including *Giselle, Coppelia,* parts of *Swan Lake,* and *La Sylphide.*

In addition to his gift for choreography, Petipa was noted for his detailed research and planning for each ballet he produced. He worked intensively with the composers and set designers who were attached to the Imperial Theater, but placed choreography high above all the other arts which contributed to the ballet. Thus, even in working with a composer of Tchaikovsky's stature, Petipa rigidly dictated the kind of music he wanted —the style, mood, length, beat, tempo, and dynamics. He developed a format for his full-length ballets which he applied consistently through the years: these patterns always involved three repeats of the same technical action and a fourth variant of it to complete the sequence. In the second half of the 19th century, his dominance was unquestioned in Russia, and indeed throughout Europe, for many of the leading dancers throughout the Continent came to study and dance with him.

[31] Nicholas Legat, quoted in Anatole Chujoy, *The Dance Encyclopedia* (New York: A. S. Barnes and Co., 1949), p. 411.

During this period, a class of spectators emerged who came to be known as "balletomanes." These were the enthusiastic and knowledgeable audiences that packed the Bolshoi and Maryinsky Imperial Theaters in St. Petersburg and other ballet houses in Moscow and throughout Russia. Ballet was cherished by the powerful and wealthy, as well as by intellectuals, students, young officers, and all classes that could afford to attend. With the exception of those seats reserved for the royal family and high public officials, all other seats in the orchestra and boxes and loges, as well as some in the balcony, were sold by subscription. These were highly valued and would often remain in the same family for generations; occasionally one would be sold at a very high price. Thus, the dominant audience for the ballet constituted "an exclusive circle" that knew the mechanics and tradition of ballet thoroughly, and was essentially a highly conservative audience that refused to accept change. There was a second kind of audience—the balletomanes who sat in the upper tiers of balconies and galleries who were mostly students, young officers, civil service officials, and clerks. They were dedicated to the ballet (to obtain tickets they usually had to stand in line through most of the preceding night, often in the frigid cold of the Russian winter) and were less conservative in their views.

Through the 1880s and 1890s, ballet in Russia became increasingly stodgy and stereotyped—following the same format that had been in effect for the previous three decades. Pantomimic sign language, that often was incomprehensible to the dancers as well as to the audience, was still used. The *corps de ballet* was usually used for purely decorative interludes that had no relation to the theme of the ballet itself. Costumes, music, and decor were all composed in a cut-and-dried way that contributed to the sterility of the performance and had little vitality or originality.

Finally, reform was not welcomed or even possible under Petipa. Thus it was that when two great Russians of the early 20th century, Diaghileff and Fokine, broke through the hidebound traditions of the past, it was not in St. Petersburg or Moscow, but in Paris.

6 Dance in America: Colonial Period and Nineteenth Century

Meanwhile, what was the development of dance on the North American continent? Certainly what happened in the American colonies prior to the American Revolution could not be considered out of the context of what one historian has called the "Atlantic Civilization." Those who settled in New England, in the Mid-Atlantic colonies, and in the coastal region of the South were all Europeans—and they brought with them many of the attitudes and customs of their homelands. There was a steady flow of traffic back and forth, of colonists, journalists, performers, and publications. Clearly, a stone cast at the French court, or in London, spread ripples abroad.

Yet, there were certain distinct features in the New World that made life here very different—and particularly so for those concerned with the dance as art or recreation. One factor was the distance and danger of the ocean journey; this tended to reduce communication, and prevented vogues in the arts from being seized upon as rapidly in the American colonies as they were throughout Europe. Another factor was the difficulty of living on the North American continent—the fact that the first need of all was to survive. One had to plant crops, to cut down forests and clear fields, to build shelters, to protect oneself against the winter, against hunger, disease, and the sometimes hostile Indians who surrounded the colonies. In such a situation, it was difficult to justify amusements and public entertainment. This was a democratic society; there was no royalty that would view dance, theater, or other arts as a means of amusing itself or enhancing its own prestige, and that would therefore subsidize and protect performing companies.

Then there was the matter of religious attitude.

During the 17th century, there was a widespread condemnation of idleness and casual amusement. Foster Dulles points out that in Puritan New England, where the stern rule of Calvinism prohibited any sort of play, the tradition was that life should be wholly devoted to work. There was no place for an "idle drone" in such a society.[1]

The Puritans had come to the New World in order to set up a society based on a Calvinistic interpretation of the Bible. They believed that they were a chosen people; the early government of Massachusetts, for example, was a theocracy, run by Puritan ministers, who thought that the Bible was the disclosed word of God, and that its meaning and intention on every subject had been made plain and explicit to them. Not all colonists in New England were Puritans, of course, but they were the dominant group and those who resisted them were often punished or banished. Typically, Massachusetts and Connecticut banned dice, cards, quoits, bowls, ninepins, "or any other unlawful game in house, yard, garden or backside. . . . " The theater was completely prohibited in a number of colonies; Connecticut adjudged as common rogues and served fifteen lashes on the bare back of anyone foolish enough to "set up and practice common plays, interludes, or other crafty science."

In particular, the early Puritans forbade mixed dancing (between men and women), dancing in taverns, Maypole dancing (which they saw as an expression of paganism), or dancing accompanied by feasting and drinking.

A group of Puritan ministers in Boston issued a tract against dancing in 1684, titled *An Arrow Against Profane and Promiscuous Dancing, drawn out of the quiver of the Scriptures.* Yet, even as they condemned "mixt or promiscuous dancing," they indicated that dance could be a means of teaching "due poyse and Composure of Body," and that if a parent wished to have his children learn it, he should send them "to a grave person who will teach them decency of behaviour, and each sex by themselves."[2]

The truth is that, despite the reputation of the Puritans for being opposed to any form of dance, they had themselves come out of an English tradition which valued poetry and literature, and in which music and dance formed part of the education of every cultivated person. While in England, Joy van Cleef points out, many of the Puritans, like other members of their social class, had studied dance as a basic skill of the society and a widely accepted pastime. However, it was generally regarded as a private matter, to be enjoyed in the home and family circle, rather than in public spectacles and performances.

The same distinctions that had been made by the Church Fathers during the Dark and Middle Ages in Europe were again made in 18th-century America. The Reverend John Cotton, who was to come to New England in 1633 and become the leading minister of Boston and New England, said while still in England in 1625:

[1]Foster Rhea Dulles, *A History of Recreation* (New York: Appleton-Century-Crofts, 1965), p. 5.

[2]Joseph E. Marks, *America Learns to Dance* (New York: Exposition Press, 1957), pp. 20–21.

> Dancing (yea though mixt) I would not simply condem. For I see two sorts of mixt dancings in use with God's people in the Old Testament, the one religious, Exod. XV, 20, 21, the other civil, tending to the praise of conquerers, as the former of God, I Sam. XVII, 6, 7. Only lascivious dancing, and amorous gestures and wanton dalliances, especially after feasts, I would bear witness against, as a great *flabella libidinis.*[3]

Others were less liberal than Cotton, and the court records during the 17th century, particularly in New England, frequently mention severe punishment for mixed dancing, dancing in taverns, and similar offenses. Yet, in spite of condemnation and punishment, settlers in communities large and small throughout the colonies of the North continued to dance. Beginning in the 1670s, dancing masters began to appear in the New England towns, and people of quality began to give balls. Polite society, particularly members of the less strict Anglican faith, accepted dance wholeheartedly as a form of social custom. Indeed, many ministers sanctioned dancing schools provided that they were conducted by "grave persons" and did not teach " mixt" dancing. The dances that were most frequently taught were drawn from the newly published English work, John Playford's *Dancing-Master*. While these country dances had both men and women dancing together, they were in sets, or formations, and did not involve "couple dancing" as such. Since they taught good manners, and were desired by the more influential people in the community, they were accepted by ministers.

Van Cleef describes these dances, explaining why they were approved by the Puritans while other forms were frowned upon:

> . . . though popular at court, the country dances were not dances of self-presentation like those ordinarily performed by one couple at a time while the rest of the company watched, dancers taking the floor in the order of their rank and position. They were not "show-off" dances. Nor were they extravagant or spectacular like the galliard, nor bold and indecorous like the volta, which required the man to lift . . . his partner into the air while executing rapid turns . . . The country dance was a democratic affair in which a number of people danced together. Its interest lay in the figures, or patterns—sometimes extremely intricate (requiring) a team effort on the part of the whole group, or set, in order to succeed.[4]

DANCE IN THE SOUTH

Further to the South, members of the ruling class in Virginia had much closer ties with England, and were of a higher social class in general, than the Puritans who had settled New England. They had both wealth and leisure because of the nature of the land they settled and the large plantations which were worked by indentured servants and slaves. Thus, they were more inclined toward aristocratic forms of amusement, and able to indulge

[3]John Cotton, quoted in Marks, *op. cit.,* p. 15.

[4]Joy Van Cleef, "Rural Felicity: Social Dance in 18th Century Connecticut," *Dance Perspectives No. 65,* Vol. 17, Spring 1976, pp. 7–8.

their inclinations. While the laws of the colony, applied by Governor Argall in 1618, "strictly banned any Sabbath-day dancing, fiddling, card-playing, hunting or fishing," these laws gradually fell into abeyance. In any case, dancing was permitted on other occasions and even justified, as an important aspect of education.

> Dance served an even more important role than that of social amusement. It was believed to be one of the accomplishments proper for a gentleman, and not having a knowledge of dance showed a lack of the proper education. Writers on aristocratic education expected a gentleman to dance well, but not to become so proficient that he rival the dancing master.[5]

For gentlemen, both dancing and fencing were seen as "ornaments to grace and accomplishment," and for young ladies, it was thought that "to lead a dance gracefully" was a commendable quality. Thus, by the end of the 1600s, Virginia was well supplied with dancing masters, as part of the life of its plantation owners which was closely modeled after that of country squires in the mother country.

During the 18th century, an increasing number of teachers of dancing were found in colonies of both North and South. Marks cites many examples of such masters advertising to the public: In 1712, George Brownell offered the young ladies of Boston, "Writing, cyphering, dancing, treble violin, flute, spinet, etc." Samuel Perpoint advertised in the Pennsylvania Mercury in 1728 and later in 1729 that he gave instruction in dancing and small sword. In Williamsburg, Virginia, Mrs. Neil stated that she was opening a boarding school of young ladies on the English plan, and that "The best Masters will attend to teaching Dancing and writing."

> Dancing masters, like preachers, doctors, lawyers, peddlers and many other trades and professions during the eighteenth and early nineteenth centuries, traveled from town to town, often advertising ahead that they planned to open a dancing school "if there be sufficient inducement."[6]

There continued to be a certain amount of resistance to dancing; one opponent of a school for dancing, fencing, and the violin in Providence, Rhode Island, wrote in 1763 that he would as soon have set up "a public stew or Brothel." But in general, social dancing had become widely accepted both as a form of recreation and as a means of education.

Dance was seen as contributing to the ends of education. A book on education in Philadelphia in 1792 makes clear that ornamental accomplishments were not an end in themselves:

> . . . though the well-bred woman should learn to dance, sing, recite, and draw; the end of a good education is not that they may become singers, dancers, players, or painters; its real object is, to make them good daughters, good wives, good mistresses, good members of society and good christians.[7]

[5]Marks, *op. cit.,* pp. 25–26.

[6]*Ibid.,* p. 40.

[7]*Ibid.,* p. 47.

Toward the end of the century, an increasing number of balls and assemblies were held, particularly in the larger cities. It is probable that the colonists performed both the country dances, jigs, and cotillions which became popular during this period, and also such dances as the Minuet, Courante, Galliard, Rigadoon, and Gavotte, all appeared in Rameau's text, *The Dancing Master,* which was found in libraries throughout the colonies. Certainly when, in 1762, 69 couples attended a lavish ball given by Sir Jeffrey Amherst, which was described as the "most elegant ever seen in America," the dances done were similar to those found in the English court.

Both George Washington and Thomas Jefferson were known as zealous and enthusiastic dancers, who frequently attended concerts and the theater. Washington Irving, in his *Life of George Washington,* told how the "young ladies of Maryland rode to the assembly at Annapolis in scarlet riding-habits thrown over their satin ball dresses, kerchiefs drawn about the great masses of their puffed and pomaded hair, and after dancing through the night rode home again in the shadowy dawn." The young John Quincy Adams, in Newburyport, describes going to a dancing hall with his friends during the 1780s, and dancing continually from seven at night to three or four in the morning.

Clearly, dance as recreation had taken hold in the colonies, by the time of the American Revolution. But meanwhile, what of dance as theater? Here there was less to report.

BEGINNING THEATRICAL DANCE

From the beginning, stage performers—whether they were actors, singers, dancers, or acrobats—were viewed with suspicion in the colonies, especially in the North. Gradually, however, as the early bans against theater were relaxed and a leisure class began to develop, professional performances began to be offered. At first, these were given by amateur or semiprofessional groups, or dancing masters themselves, who seized on the opportunity to earn additional income, as well as to enhance their reputation by dancing before an audience. In time, the first truly professional troupes appeared on American stages; they came from Europe.

The first of these was an English company, headed by Lewis Hallam, which toured the colonies during the mid-1700s, to perform Harlequinades, spectacles, and incidental dances. Shortly thereafter, in 1767, the John Street Theater opened in New York and became the center of week-long performances of drama, pantomime, opera, and "ballet-spectacles" by various visiting companies. These were imported intermittently from Europe and probably visited other cities, performing wherever they could find a hall and a sponsor. There was a cessation of theatrical activity during the American Revolution, due first to a prohibition of theater by the first Continental Congress in 1774, and then to an antitheater law passed by Congress in 1787. However, this law was repealed, and now an increasing number of foreign troupes visited the new United States.

Baltimore was the scene of the first major revival of American theater after the Revolution, with a new theater being built in 1781 that was to boast shortly of having the first resident stock company of professional actors in

America. Numerous dance attractions appeared on its stage. In 1787, the "Baltimorean Boy," the first black theatrical artist to appear in that city, did a number of "slack-rope tricks" called "Strength of the Knee—Mermaid—Skinning the Eel—and Sleeping on the Cord." Also known as the "Incomparable African," he also exhibited "curious Attitudes in jumping and Tumbling on the Floor . . . (balanced) himself with his Hand upon a Chair . . . (played) four different instruments . . . (and concluded) with walking on the Ladder, and acting the Clown."[8]

In 1792, Alexandre Placide, his wife, and a well-trained company presented operettas and ballets. Patriotric spectacles had briefly come into vogue during the Revolution, and Placide's company presented a number of these during the 1790s. Performances were diverse, including such unusual elements as "specialty dancers, acrobats, tightrope walkers," and similar features.

Perhaps the best example of this was John Durang, who gained in reputation during the 1790s and in fact established himself as the head of a famous dancing and theatrical dynasty—the first in the new land. While Durang was known chiefly as a dancer, he was also an "actor, singer, tightrope performer, acrobat, designer and scene painter, puppeteer, circus clown, and author." When he performed individually, he often did specialty numbers like an *Alamande,* or the *Hornpipe* for which he was most noted. Also, he performed in a group number known as *The Touchstone,* or *Harlequin Traveler,* which was an Italian-English pantomime, with such stock characters as *Harlequin, Scaramouche, Columbine, Pierrot,* and others.

The first ballet to be regarded as a serious work in the United States was a performance of *La Forêt Noire,* in the New Chestnut Theater in Philadelphia, in 1794. This featured a well-known French dancer, Madame Gardie; Durang danced in the leading male role as her partner, and also performed in a variety of specialty numbers and character dances, including his famous *Hornpipe*.

By the turn of the century, an increasing number of European companies had visited the United States, and American audiences had become more knowledgeable and demanding, in terms of the dance art. However, there was no real center of theatrical art in the country, such as existed in European opera houses, where ballet had become firmly established. Nor was there any academy for the teaching of dance. The few Americans who established a reputation in this field usually received their training in a fragmentary way, from the European stars who came here to perform.

DANCE IN THE NINETEENTH CENTURY

In the early decades of the 19th century, the leading centers of drama and dance were New York and Philadelphia; by 1830 there were three theaters in the latter city. In Richmond, Virginia, in 1819, a new theater, the Richmond, was built. It was an impressive structure with a dome that was 120 feet in circumference, that was "said to exceed in beauty the elegant

[8]Chrystelle T. Bond, "A Chronicle of Dance in Baltimore," *Dance Perspectives No. 66,* Vol. 17, Summer 1976, p. 5.

dome of the National Theater in New York." Similarly, in other major cities, theaters were constructed and filled, with dramatic, musical, and dance performances.

The French performers began to dominate ballet in America. One of the first of the foreign visitors who captivated American audiences was the ballerina Francisque Hutin, who showed them the first *pointe* footwork, in multiple pirouettes, that had been seen here. Other French artists, including Charles and Ronzi Vestris, and the Ravels, a family of acrobats and ballet dancers, toured the country during the 1820s. Gradually, terminology like *pas de deux* and *corps de ballet* began to enter the language; Americans were becoming somewhat knowledgeable in this new art.

The greatest European visitor of the century was Fanny Elssler, who arrived in 1840 and toured the country for two years. Somehow adapting herself to inadequate theaters and stages, untutored audiences, and makeshift *corps de ballet* (her partner was James Sylvain, an Irish dancer, whom she had brought with her from Europe), Elssler was the inspiration of almost hysterical acclaim. She was a prodigious success wherever she went:

> Champagne was drunk out of her slippers and red carpets were laid at her feet. Congress adjourned because so many of its members were absent, paying homage to the adorable Fanny. President Van Buren received her at the White House and the government treated her like a visiting dignitary. When she went out driving in her carriage infatuated young gentlemen took the horses from the shafts and harnessed themselves in their places. In the theater, Elssler had only to appear to receive an ovation. . . .[9]

In the time she was here, Elssler had a marked effect upon American tastes. She performed a number of the works which had been popular on European stages; her personal style, earthy, close to the floor, highly expressive and dramatic, received great acclaim.

Others who visited included the Paul Taglionis (he was the brother of Marie Taglioni); Jean Antoine Petipa and his son, the eighteen-year-old Marius, who was to become the dominant figure in Russian ballet; and even Enrico Cecchetti, who, traveling with his family, made his debut in 1857 at the Philadelphia Academy of Music, at the age of seven. While the tours of these outstanding European visitors did not succeed in creating an American dance tradition, they helped develop high quality in a number of leading American ballet performers.

Mary Ann Lee was known as the first American to achieve nationwide fame as a performer of the classic ballet. Born in Philadelphia about 1823, she made her debut as a dancer at the Chestnut Street Theater in 1837 as Fatima in *The Maid of Cashmere,* the English version of a French opera. Later, her appearances ranged from Shakespeare to burlesque, from *La Sylphide* and *Giselle* to the *Sailor's Hornpipe.* Both Mary Ann Lee and Augusta Maywood, one of her early rivals, had received training in Philadelphia from the French performer, P. H. Hazard. They danced together and competed for public favor until Maywood left for Europe in 1838, where she was to spend the rest of her career. After performing in such works as *La Bayadère* and

[9]Olga Maynard, *The American Ballet* (Philadelphia: Macrae Smith Co., 1959), p. 18.

La Sylphide (most of the ballets performed at this time were copies of European successes), Lee herself went to Europe in 1844. She studied for a year in the ballet school of the Paris Opéra, whre she took daily lessons from Jean Coralli, an outstanding teacher and the choreographer of *Giselle.* When Mary Ann Lee returned to the United States, she was not only much improved as a performer, but she brought with her a number of other European works, to introduce for the first time in America. Lee toured the leading cities of the United States with George Washington Smith, finally retiring because of poor health in 1847. She was generally regarded as an excellent performer, although not the equal of such foreign visitors as Elssler or Taglioni.

Julia Turnbull was regarded as Mary Ann Lee's strongest rival during the major period of her career. The two dancers starred in an original ballet, *The Sisters,* in 1839. Turnbull was soloist with the Fanny Elssler company during her tour of the United States, and performed principal roles in such works as *Nathalie, La Bayadère, Esmerelda,* and *Giselle,* until her retirement from the stage in 1857.

Augusta Maywood, born in 1825, was regarded as America's first great prima ballerina. She was an expatriate who spent the major part of her career in Europe, where she was ranked as being close in ability to the greatest dancers of the Golden Age. After a brilliant early career in New York and Philadelphia, she went to Europe. In 1839 she made her debut at the Paris Opéra. Regarded as an infant prodigy, she received the acclaim of Théophile Gautier. She toured widely, performing in Paris, Vienna, Lisbon, and ultimately, La Scala, in Milan. Forming her own touring company, she remained in Europe throughout her performing career, and particularly in Italy, where she was regarded as the leading ballerina of the era.[10]

After Durang, who retired from the stage in 1819, the next widely known American male dancer was George Washington Smith. Smith's career encompassed almost two-thirds of the 19th century, since he first danced in public in 1838 and was still a teacher of dancing at the time of his death in 1899. Smith danced in everything from classical ballet works and opera to the circus. He partnered almost every one of the great ballerinas who visited this country, including Elssler, and staged and performed in many of the great romantic ballets, including *Giselle, La Fille du Danube,* and *La Jolie Fille de Gand.* He learned much of his classical ballet technique from Sylvain, Elssler's ballet master, and from Jules Perrot, in New York and Boston. Throughout his career, Smith received equal billing with the American and foreign ballerinas—the greatest of the time—with whom he performed.

In the latter part of the 19th century, no dancers emerged on the American scene to equal these four. Indeed, ballet itself underwent a decline in the late 1850s. While other foreign performers toured the United States, including the company of Dominico Ronzani, who was later to become the leading choreographer at La Scala, ballet never took root here or flourished. America lacked major theaters and houses of opera, state-supported schools, and government patronage. Public taste was willing to support

[10]Marian Hannah Winter, "Augusta Maywood," in *Chronicles of the American Dance,* Paul Magriel, ed. (New York: Henry Holt and Company, 1948), p. 119.

occasional foreign stars and touring groups, but did not value native American performers. Indeed, the major dance phenomenon of the latter part of the 19th century was *The Black Crook,* an elaborate and immensely popular musical play of questionable artistic merit.[11]

THE BLACK CROOK

The Black Crook was performed for the first time at Niblo's Garden in New York in September, 1866. It was based on a melodrama with a trivial plot, which nonetheless provided the basis for a spectacular and original production, using props and decor from another performance whose theater had burned down. The plot included a remarkable hodgepodge of sorcery, demonism, and wickedness, with such characters as an alchemist, the Devil, fairies, demons, and baronial servants. The great feature of the musical was a "Great Parisienne Ballet Troupe," featuring Marie Bonfanti, star of the Paris Opéra and Covent Garden Theater in London; the cast included many other leading dancers, with a company of 80 dancers in all. Part of the attraction of *The Black Crook* was its impressive and spectacular stage sets and effects. Another appealing aspect was the ballet success of "the 'witching Pas de Demons,' in which the demons, who wear no clothes to speak of, so gracefully and prettily disported as to draw forth thunders of applause." The show ran continuously for sixteen months to overflow houses, making almost a million dollars. It continued to be performed with added embellishments for forty years in various forms throughout the country. Throughout its various runs, the ballet remained a highlight of this landmark of the American stage and, while classical ballet was at a low ebb, this continued to keep the dance at a high level of interest in American theaters.

Overall, while occasional ballet performances continued to be offered, the classical dance had little prestige as America approached the turn of the century. In *The Black Crook,* the abbreviated costumes of the dancers had shocked many audiences, and the element of sex in their performance had been widely advertised by the management. Although other popular extravaganzas continued to be performed, with lavish productions and dancing girls on display, the quality of the dancing was of low caliber. Maynard comments that dancers were poorly paid and socially ostracized:

> The American dancing girls of the period had the worst of reputations, especially as the management believed in advertising them as Parisians, and had them masquerade under Gallic names, with the supposed Gallic reputation for amorousness. They were required not only to dance but often to sing, act, and support comedians, trained animal acts, or starred singers, in variety shows. . . . How the performers endured the fatigue of their profession is a wonder. Many of them worked in factories by day and danced in the *corps de ballet* at night. Most of them were waitresses on the side. . . .[12]

[11]George Freedley, "The Black Crooks and the White Fawn," in Magriel, *op. cit.,* pp. 65–79.

[12]Maynard, *op. cit.,* p. 24.

With all this, interest in dance continued to grow, however. One evidence of this was the growth in the number of dancing teachers. In mid-century, there were eight dancing masters in New York City. In 1896, the New York directory listed 63 such teachers, who often combined instruction in the social dances of the time, and in ballet.

During the 19th century, other dance forms, in addition to theatrical dance, had enriched the cultural scene. Three of these are worthy of mention here: the continuing popularity of social dancing, the gradual development of a black dance art that was to make major contributions to entertainment in America, and that strange phenomenon of religious dance carried out by the Shakers in New England.

POPULARITY OF SOCIAL DANCING

At the beginning of the 19th century, social dancing had become widely popular and accepted throughout the young United States. In both North and South, religious objections to it had largely diminished, although, as new provocations appeared, resistance from the pulpit continued to be voiced from time to time. Dancing teachers were flourishing in cities and towns, and balls and assemblies were commonplace. A contemporary historian wrote that dancing had become "the principal and favorite amusement in New England; and of this the young people of both sexes are extremely fond."[13]

In the cities, where dancing masters conducted regular classes, and where education in dance had become a mark of aristocratic upbringing, instruction was formal and disciplined.

But on the frontier and in rural areas, where life was rougher, there were few dancing masters and no formal cotillions or rules of etiquette. Girls and women were scarce and often the action was rough and ready. Dulles quotes a description of the time:

> "None of your straddling, mincing, sadying," wrote Davy Crockett, "but a regular sifter, cut-the-buckle, chicken flutter set-to. It is a good wholesome exercise; and when one of our boys puts his arm around his partner, it's a good hug, and no harm in it."[14]

Dancing was carried on at country fairs, logrollings, and quilting parties, and at special holiday celebrations. After dinner and sports or games, the climax of every gathering was a dance. The men and women of the frontier loved to dance, doing Virginia Reels, country jigs, and shakedowns. It was a favorite form of entertainment everywhere, commented on with surprise by traveler after traveler amazed to find such rollicking gaiety in frontier settlements.

Gradually, new forms of dancing emerged, arousing new condemnation from the moralist leaders. In the 1830s the waltz and polka became

[13]Dulles, *op. cit.*, p. 37.

[14]*Ibid.*, pp. 76–77.

popular on the European scene, and soon were enthusiastically adopted on the dance floors of the New World. These whirling, giddy dances were shocking because they involved dancing in a facing, closed couple position. Ministers preached vehemently against "the abomination of permitting a man who was neither your lover nor your husband to encircle you with his arms, and slightly press the contour of your waist." Nonetheless the exciting new importations won their way into society:

> The *New York Herald* raved about "the indecency of the polka as danced at Saratoga and Newport. . . . It even outstrips the most disgraceful exhibitions of the lowest haunts of Paris and London." But the floor would be crowded on a Saturday night. . . .[15]

It should be recognized that opposition to dance at this time stemmed from a general religious disapproval of many forms of play. One leading preacher of the period, Henry Ward Beecher, attacked racing, the theater, the circus, and "promiscuous balls . . . night-revelling, Bacchanalian feasts, and other similar indulgences." To such attractions, he explained, "resort all the idle, the dissipated, the rogues, the licentious, the epicures, the gluttons, the artful jades, the immodest prudes, the joyous, the worthless, the refuse."[16] However, even Beecher did not object to dancing itself in the form of private dancing parties, or dancing at home.

Gradually, some voices spoke up in favor of dance. One woman editor of a widely read magazine, the famous *Saturday Visitor,* pointed out that no page of scripture either directly or indirectly condemned dance. She went on to describe it as a "good, right, proper" exercise, "well calculated to promote the harmonious development of mind and body," and opposed to the money-loving, hard-crusted spirit of the time. Another leading public figure, Dr. Sylvester Graham, wrote in a progressive journal, the *Regenerator:*

> Dancing, when properly regulated, is one of the most salutary kinds of social enjoyment, ever practiced in civic life; and every enlightened philanthropist must regret to see it give way to any other kind of amusement. The religious prejudice against dance is altogether illfounded; for it is entirely certain that this kind of social enjoyment, when properly regulated, is more favorable to good health, sound morality, and true religion, than perhaps any known in society.[17]

The upper social class had formal assemblies and cotillions; to match these, public balls, with admissions ranging from twenty-five cents to a dollar, came into being. In New York City, there was Mr. Parker's Ball at Tammany Hall, the Third Ward American Republic Ball at the Minerva Assembly Rooms, and the Native American Ball at the Park Theater. And, Dulles points out, there were counterparts of these in every town and city throughout the country; social dancing was the rage.

[15]*Ibid.,* pp. 151–152.

[16]Henry Ward Beecher, cited in Arthur C. Cole, "The Puritan and Fair Terpsichore," *Mississippi Valley Historical Review,* June, 1942, reprinted by Dance Horizons, Inc., New York, p. 10.

[17]*Ibid.,* p. 11.

For the lower classes, there were less respectable dance halls, cheap variety shows, concert saloons, and beer gardens—"branches of Satan's den" as those of Puritan conviction named them. In cattle towns and mining camps in the West, there were "hurdy-gurdy houses," where drinking, gambling, prostitution, and dancing might all be found together.

In the latter part of the 19th century, there were huge society balls for those of wealth and prestige in New York, Chicago, San Francisco, and the major society resorts. Dancing was a universal social pastime for those of the middle and upper classes; trade, professional, and fraternal organizations all gave annual balls. It was accepted that businessmen and their wives would attend dancing classes through the year, which would usually terminate in a *German,* or *Assembly.* Dulles cites a typical program of one such event: *The Lancers, Waltz, Polka, Military March, Quadrille, York, Portland Fancy, Caledonia,* and the *Virginia Reel.* Most of these were set or line dances, with the exception of the waltz or polka. On a grander scale, Ward McAllister wrote in 1890 of a great society ball; the ostentation had begun to approach that of the royal courts of the Baroque era in Europe:

> For one ball the host built a special addition to his home providing a magnificent Louis XIV ballroom which would accommodate twelve hundred. . . . At a reception given at the Metropolitan Opera House, twelve hundred guests danced the Sir Roger de Coverly on a floor built over stage and auditorium, and were then served supper at small tables by three hundred liveried servants. It was a world of jewels and satins, of terrapin and canvasbacks, of Chateau Lafite and imported champagne. . . .[18]

To teach the dances, and to act as arbiters of social taste, there were many successful dancing masters. The best known and most successful of these was Allen Dodworth who, since childhood, had been a member of his family's fashionable band and orchestra. Dodworth was an accepted member of society himself, as founder and first treasurer of the New York Philharmonic Society, and one of its first violinists. He had entrée into the leading ballrooms and private parties of the best society, and operated a fashionable dance academy that catered to the most exclusive and socially ambitious families in New York.

"The dancing school," as Dodworth saw it, "is not a place of amusement. . . ." Instead, it was a place where dance was taught in a rigorous and precise way; Dodworth was the author of a widely respected text on social dancing published in 1885. The precise foot positions, the carriage of the body, and the whole ritual of social behavior were taught inflexibly by Dodworth, who

> . . .battled with the world on the issue of dancing as a medium of education and cultured behavior, including health, morals, and manners. He demanded good teaching and not merely coaching in the transitory fads of the ballroom, and he strongly advocated the setting up of a standard practice.[19]

[18]Ward McAllister, *Society as I Have Found It,* quoted in Dulles, *op. cit.,* p. 232.

[19]Rosetta O'Neill, "The Dodworth Family and Ballroom Dancing in New York," in Magriel, *op, cit.,* p. 81.

Christy's Minstrels in *Skedaddle,* the celebrated "walk-round." Lithograph by H. C. Maguire. Reprinted with permission of the Dance Collection of the Library and Museum of the Performing Arts at Lincoln Center in New York City.

By 1900, there were many other influential and successful teachers, and the private dancing academy was well established as one of the channels through which social-climbing families might pry their way into accepted society.

EMERGENCE OF BLACK DANCE

Another and quite different aspect of dance during the 19th century was the emergence of black dance and music on the North American continent. When African slaves were brought to America, they brought with them their folklore and religious traditions. Although they were converted to Christianity, many of the dances continued to be performed, now for reasons of custom and social entertainment, and also as a tenaciously lingering memory of magical belief. One name for such belief and practice was *Voodoo,* or *Vodun.* Almost as Italian peasants in the early Middle Ages danced the Tarantella to avert the effects of the bite of the tarantula spider, so the slaves in early 19th-century New Orleans were permitted to dance, as a kind of palliative to their subservient condition.

> The Sunday dances of the slaves in Congo Square, legalized by the Municipal Council of New Orleans, were an attempt of the "city authorities to combat Voodooism." They were supposed to act as a kind of safety valve to keep the slaves contented. The dances also became a remunerative tourist attraction at which Voodoo music happened to be played. . . .[20]

Public performances of these black dances were held in a large empty lot known as Congo Square, off and on from 1817 to 1885. Herbert Asbury describes the early days of such performances:

> At a signal from a police official, the slaves were summoned to the center of the square by the prolonged rattling of two huge beef bones upon the head of a cask, out of which had been fashioned a sort of drum or tambourine called the bamboula. . . . The favorite dances of the slaves were the Calinda, a variation of which was also used in the Voodoo ceremonies, and the Dance of the Bamboula, both of which were primarily based on the primitive dances of the African jungle. . . . The entire square was an almost solid mass of black bodies stamping and swaying to the rhythmic beat of the bones on the cask, the frenzied chanting of the women, and the clanging of pieces of metal which dangled from the ankles of the men.[21]

In a somewhat similar custom, slaves on the British-owned Caribbean island of Jamaica were permitted to take part freely in Christmas festivities in the homes of their masters during the 18th and early 19th centuries. Robert Dirks describes a scene of the period in which an English lady lustily played the piano while her slaves

> skipped and pranced around her parlor. . . . Indeed, things often became boisterous, with slaves joining in satirical songs aimed at their hosts or boldly offering free advice concerning plantation affairs. . . . In the evening, the slaves left to dance in their own quarters.[22]

In a related Jamaica holiday custom, believed to have derived from traditional African custom, masked characters known as John Canoes were impersonated by male black slaves. Wearing terrifying masks with boars' tusks protruding from the mouth and ox horns sprouting from the head, and swinging wooden swords, John Canoes roamed entire neighborhoods, stopping at every home to dance. Other slaves took the part of Koo-Koo, or Actor-boy, a Christmas character unique to Jamaica, or engaged in other singing and dancing festivities. There are many accounts of black slaves acting as musicians and dancers on southern plantations during the 18th and 19th centuries. In many areas, an adapted form of the white man's dance was the only kind of dance permitted to him. Marian Winter points out that black music-making and dancing survived at all is remarkable, when one considers the Slave Laws of 1740, which remained among the basic regula-

[20]Marshall W. Stearns, *The Story of Jazz* (New York: Oxford University Press, 1956), pp. 44–45.

[21]Herbert Asbury, *The French Quarter* (New York: Alfred A. Knopf, 1936), p. 243.

[22]Robert Dirks, "Slaves' Holiday," *Natural History,* December 1975, p. 86.

tions for black slaves for a century and a quarter. These laws were instituted after a slave insurrection in South Carolina in 1739:

> A group of slaves attempted an escape to Florida . . . and were captured in a bloody charge. They had marched "with colors flying and drums beating." The laws of 1740 stringently prohibited any Negro from "beating drums, blowing horns or the like" which might on occasion be used to arouse slaves to insurrectionary activity. . . .[23]

When drums were forbidden, black slaves devised substitutes; they used bone clappers like castanets, and other artifacts to provide rhythm: jawbones, blacksmiths' iron rasps—and handclapping and foot beating. The latter, with increasingly intricate heel and toe beats, was based on traditional African step dances.

One of these, the *juba* dance, resembled an elaborately varied jig; it was found wherever blacks settled in the New World. The names *Juba* and *Jube* were slave names traditionally associated with dancers and musicians. Ultimately, "Juba" was to become the sobriquet of the most famous of all black stage dancers.

Black dance routines had long been known (either as originals, or as white men in blackface) on the American stage. Winter comments that by 1810, the singing and dancing "Negro Boy" was established with the traditional clown as a dance-hall or circus character. This role was played by impersonators who performed English or Irish jig or clog steps, to the accompaniment of popular songs which had allusions to blacks in their lyrics. Only rarely did a genuine black appear. Indeed, the original "Jim Crow," known as a famous black performer in the early 19th century, was a white entertainer, "Daddy" Rice, who made an effort to use fairly authentic source materials in his act.

The first actual black to achieve distinction as a performer on the stage was Juba, who was born, probably free, under the name of William Henry Lane, in about 1825. Juba began performing professionally at about the age of 15, having learned much from an older black jig and reel dancer, "Uncle" Jim Lowe, who had not himself appeared in the regular theaters of the day. By 1845, Winter writes, it was widely accepted by professional entertainers that Juba was "beyond question the very greatest of all dancers. He was possessed not only of wonderful and unique execution, but also of unsurpassed grace and endurance."[24]

Winter describes his routine as imitating all the well-known dancers of the day and their special steps, and then going through his original specialties, including a comic "walkaround," in which he impersonated a number of different styles and characters. By 1845, Juba's position was so secure that he was able to tour with four white minstrel players and receive top billing as "Master Juba! The Greatest Dancer in the World." In 1848, he went to London, where he drew immense audiences and such praise as ". . .the dancing of Juba exceeded anything ever witnessed in Europe. . . . The style

[23]Marian Hannah Winter, "Juba and American Minstrelsy," in Magriel, *op. cit.*, pp. 39–40.

[24]*Ibid.*, p. 39.

as well as the execution is unlike anything ever witnessed in this country. . . ."[25] Londoners of every class flocked to Vauxhall Gardens to witness his performance, and the critics were lavish in their praise of his tremendously agile and ingenious dancing.

At least partly due to Juba's influence, the traditional role of the "Gay Negro Boy" was adopted in British, French, and German circuses, and blackface clowns appeared in circuses and fairs. Because his material was essentially faithful to black dance steps and rhythms, as seen on Southern plantations, many white minstrel-show performers imitated him and other black dancers—thus keeping a measure of authenticity in minstrel-show dancing. By contrast, minstrel-show music had little relation to its original source.

Although the American black continued to be the source of inspiration of music hall performances, blacks themselves found it increasingly difficult to find employment on the stage. Winter comments that increasingly, the black was forced into playing a caricature of a superstitious, vain, ignorant, and childlike creature (often wearing a "fright wig," which could be made to suddenly stand on end at moments of "shock"). When he was allowed to appear at all as a musical or dancing performer, he was usually forced to play the role of the happy lazy plantation black, indulging in childish pranks. Sometimes, he was cast as a foreign performer; Zouave dancers and drill teams, or "Koo-i-baba, the Hindoo baritone," were examples of such exotic types that permitted the talented black performer to find a place on the stage.

The final irony, as America moved toward the close of the 19th century, was that blacks were no longer permitted to share the stage with white performers. Racial segregation became increasingly widespread, and it might happen that a black performing group would appear on a stage during the afternoon, and a white group, in blackface, at night. Sometimes light-complexioned blacks found it necessary to use burnt cork to make themselves as dark as white performers who did their act in blackface. Despite Juba's contribution, and the unquestioned ability of many great black dancers, singers, and musicians, there was little opportunity for such performers until several decades had passed.

SHAKER DANCE

A final aspect of dance in 19th-century America relates to a unique phenomenon that joined dancing and religion.

This was the appearance in New England and as far west as Ohio and Kentucky, of an unusual Protestant sect called the Shaking Quakers, or Shakers. Descended from a group called the United Society of Believers in Christ's Second Appearance, which appeared in Manchester and Bolton, England, as early as 1747, the Shakers actually traced their spiritual lineage far back to "an ancient heretical tradition for dancing as part of the adoration of God," as seen in early Christian sects. E. D. Andrews comments that:

[25] *Ibid.,* p. 50.

The worship of many spiritual sects was similar: the early Quakers and Baptists, the French Prophets, the Merry Dancers of England, the Kentucky Revivalists, the Girlingites or Shakers of the New Forest, the Shaker Indians of Puget Sound. . . .[26]

The small band of English colonists who came to be known as Shaking Quakers first made their appearance in this country in the region of Albany, New York, at about the time of the Revolutionary War. They had an extremely strict code; founding a religious order that was separate from the world, they rejected a "corrupt society," and forswore marriage and all "carnal" practices.

The Shakers expanded their order rapidly, developing 11 communities by 1792, with meetinghouses that had spacious halls which would permit expanded ceremonies, and with seats along the walls for outsiders. Gradually, their dancing, which had been based on individualized expression, changed to a more organized and structured form, including first the "square-order shuffle," which was patterned on the vision of angels dancing around the Throne of God. Recognizing that a lively worship ceremony was impressive to onlookers and would help in conversion, the Eastern leaders

Shaker dancing near Lebanon, N.Y. Lithograph, about 1825. Reprinted with permission of the Dance Collection of the Library and Museum of the Performing Arts at Lincoln Center in New York City.

[26]E. D. Andrews, "The Dance in Shaker Ritual," in Magriel, *op. cit.*, p. 4.

of the Shakers began to encourage the composition and performance of lively songs and dances. These included various formations, in circles, lines, and weaving patterns. Pantomime became increasingly used; "gestures, such as bowing, stamping, whirling, acting out "signs" . . . were incorporated into the structure of worship, assuming, to a lesser or greater degree, symbolic meaning. . . ."[27]

Sometimes the ceremony involved acting out "chasing the Devil," in which "true believers" would surround a "backslider," pointing their fingers at him and shouting "Woe, Woe, damn his devil," and attempting in other ways to save him for the Lord.

During the 1820s, the Shakers choreographed specific dances, with names such as the *"Continuous Ring Dance"* or the *"Union Dance."* Damro describes these as follows: The *"Continuous Ring Dance"* consisted of the brethren forming four lines, or ranks, facing in opposite directions, as the sisters did the same. Then all marched forward singing, while turning from one line to the other. The *"Union Dance"* was devised to promote union of the followers and to make the worshipers conscious of the everlasting fellowship they shared. . . . brethren and sisters lined up in two rows facing each other. While the brethren went down (their) line greeting each individual by grasping hands and singing, the sisters were giving the same greeting in their lines.[28]

During the 1840s, there was a great revival of religious belief, and the Shakers developed increasingly complex and elaborate dance forms as part of worship. Andrews points out that a variety of formation dances were used during the "Great Revival"—lines, crosses, squares, stars, and other patterns. But now the dances took on new symbolic meaning:

> The devotees felt that they were indeed marching heavenward, that the circle was the perfect emblem of their union. The "wheel-within-a-wheel," three or more concentric circles turning in alternate directions around a central chorus, became a figure of the all-inclusiveness of their gospel; the outer ring the ultimate circle of truth, the Shaker dispensation; the singers, the harmony and perfection of God that were at the heart of life. In another exercise, "The Narrow Path," a single file of dancers, with heads bowed, placed one feet before the other as they trod the narrow way to salvation. . . .[29]

Gradually, the Shaker communities that had flourished throughout the Northeast and Midwest declined; the songs and dances that were performed as an attempt to reach an ideal communion with God were abandoned early in the present century. In retrospect, the Shakers represented one extreme of religious practice—the use of dance in worship that was typical of pre-Christian or early Christian worship. Much more typical of the 19th century in America, however, was religious opposition toward dance. This varied, according to the particular denomination and the region of the country. Along the eastern seaboard, dance became widely accepted, and aroused

[27] *Ibid.*, p. 8.

[28] Dianne Damro, "Dance of the Shakers," *Journal of Physical Education and Recreation,* May, 1977, p. 47.

[29] Andrews, *op. cit.*, p. 10.

little opposition on the part of the clergy. However, in other parts of the country, fundamentalist Baptist and Methodists viewed dance as one of the great evils that threatened morality and chastity. Typically, one of the tracts distributed during the great religious revivals of the mid-19th century was titled "The Social Evils of Dancing, Card Playing, and Theater-Going."

Such attitudes were not universal. Sometimes it was dance itself that was seen as evil. Sometimes what was objected to was the custom of taking part in dance in crowded dance halls or public balls, with extravagant dress, drinking, foul air, and overheated exercise before going out into the cool night air. Opinion was divided among ministers themselves. In 1894, *The New York Times* carried out a survey of the attitudes of churchmen:

> Among the clergymen the division is as marked and as profound as it is among the laity. There are clergymen of the liberal school who not merely attend balls given by their parishioners but who applaud the waltz and the polka, and deny the responsibility of harm being inherent in either of them.
>
> On the other hand, many clergymen, both of New York and Brooklyn, make no effort to conceal their opposition to all forms and varieties of public dancing, and especially the dances [waltz and polka] so vehemently denounced at the Brooklyn revival.[30]

Among the more liberal clergymen, it was considered acceptable to sponsor dancing in the church gymnasium, and one minister in Jersey City considered opening a dancing school for young people. It was his view that if they were going to dance, it should be in desirable surroundings; he approved of dance as wholesome exercise and a means of promoting graceful movement and carriage of the body.

To summarize the state of dance at the end of the 19th century in America, it was a time when social dancing had become extremely popular on all class levels, and when the dance in education had begun to gain broad acceptance—as a later chapter will describe. In terms of theatrical dance, however, and particularly ballet, the situation was at a low ebb. There was no continuous development or sustained tradition for ballet in America, in contrast to Europe, where the ballet:

> . . .was a venerated art and a formal institution, affiliated with permanent opera companies, amply supported by official or private means and assured of a supply of well-trained dancers from their schools. In America the ballet was entirely left to private initiative, to enterprising impresarios or theatre owners or to the choreographers and dancers themselves. There was little opportunity for aspiring artists to study classic dancing and even less to see good performances.[31]

In America, there was comparatively little ballet as such, and what there was was poor. De Mille writes that the performers were pitied and scorned, and it was at this time that dance gained an unsavory name in the United States. No longer could it command respect as an artistic or theatri-

[30] *The New York Times,* February 18, 1894, p. 12.

[31] George Amberg, *Ballet in America* (New York: Duell, Sloan and Pearce, 1949), p. 9.

cal enterprise.[32] On the music-hall stage, varied forms of dance were shown, ranging from acrobatics to toe-dancing, to variations of the "Little Egypt belly-dancer" theme, or the skirt-dancing and scarf-twirling effects of performers like Loie Fuller. In Europe, while ballet remained an established state institution, thc art had declined markedly both in inspiration and its appeal for audiences.

To this sad state at the turn of the century, two pioneers addressed themselves. One was a European—Michel Fokine, and the other an American—Isadora Duncan. Between them, they changed the face of dance for the century that followed. At the same time, dance began to emerge as a recognized form of education on the American scene.

[32]Agnes de Mille, *Book of the Dance* (New York: Golden Press, 1963), p. 128.

7 Early Development of Dance Education

Some critics have viewed the provision of dance education in American schools and colleges as a comparatively recent phenomenon, stemming from the influence of the "progressive education" movement of the first decades of the 20th century. Clearly, this is not the case. Dance has had a long and honored place in the curriculum, both in primitive societies throughout the world and during the long evolvement of Western civilization.

Margaret Mead has written informatively about the teaching of dance in Samoan village life. It takes place there as a highly individual activity, set in a social framework. Children learn to dance at small informal parties or entertainments, often in honor of visitors or wedding celebrations. Both visitors and hosts take turns in providing music and dancing. The chief's wife or one of the young men calls out the names of children, who come out on the floor to perform in small groups. As a group of musicians perform, everyone present joins in by singing, clapping, or beating on the floor with their knuckles. There is a minimum of preliminary instruction in dancing, and the form of the dance itself is highly varied.

> No figures are prescribed except the half dozen formal little claps which open the dance and the use of one of a few set endings. There are twenty-five or thirty figures, two or three set transitional positions, and at least three definite styles. . . .[1]

Each child apparently uses the dancing of older children as a model for his own performance, although there is no set pattern, and individuals develop their own styles of movement. As the dancing goes on, the audience calls out praise, comments, and suggestions. Younger children are good-

[1]Margaret Mead, *From the South Seas* (New York: William Morrow and Co., 1939), p. 112.

naturedly advised to move in certain ways, or to adjust their costumes, while the more expert older children receive a steady murmur of appreciative remarks: "Thank you, thank you for your dancing!" "Beautiful! Charming! Bravo!"

Within most primitive cultures, dancc is thus learned—as a natural part of growing up, and through participation by children and youth in everyday social occasions or in special festivities or rituals. In some situations, they must learn and practice a special dance in preparation for a ceremony in which they will take part. In some others, where dance has become highly developed as an art form, groups of talented children receive instruction from expert adult dancer-teachers, but this is a less common arrangement.

As indicated earlier, the purposes of dance education were well understood by the ancient Greeks. Socrates expressed high esteem for dance, recommending that it be taught more widely:

> . . . for health, for complete and harmonious physical development, for beauty, for the ability to give pleasure to others, for "reducing," for the acquisition of a good appetite, for the enjoyment of sound sleep. He confesses that he himself dances alone "at dawn," . . . and he openly expresses the wish that he may acquire greater skill in the graceful art.[2]

Aristotle also gave attention to the place of dance in education. Although he did not favor requiring it as a formal educational activity before the age of fourteen, he saw it as affording intellectual and aesthetic gratification of the highest type. In his view, it was useful in purging the young student's soul of "unseemly emotions," and it helped to prepare the future citizen for worthy enjoyment of leisure.

Dance came to the fore as an important aspect of the education of the European nobility during the later Middle Ages and the Renaissance. Michel de Montaigne, the great French 16th-century essayist, wrote in his treatise *The Education of Children,* that education should include training for character and for life; that it should strengthen the body and also cultivate the mind:

> Our very exercises and recreations, running, wrestling, dancing, hunting, riding and fencing will be a part of his study. I would have his manners, behavior, and bearing cultivated at the same time with his mind. It is not the mind, it is not the body we are training; it is the man and we must not divide him into two parts. . . .[3]

The arts of music and dance, along with the skills of warfare and hunting, were an integral part of the education of courtiers in all of the castles of Europe. A leading Italian schoolmaster was Vittorino da Feltre (1378–1446), who was responsible for the education of the sons of Marquis Gian Francesco Gonzaga at Mantua, in 1423. Da Feltre was a humanist, who

[2]Lillian B. Lawler, *The Dance in Ancient Greece* (Middletown, Connecticut: Wesleyan University Press, 1964), p. 125.

[3]Michel de Montaigne, *The Education of Children,* quoted in Emmett A. Rice, John L. Hutchinson, and Mabel Lee, *A Brief History of Physical Education* (New York: Ronald Press Co., 1958), p. 73.

made Latin, Greek, and classical archeology the main body of instruction; youths from most of the princely houses of Italy, as well as the sons of nobility from other lands, came to him for instruction. Typically, he included in his curriculum the characteristic features of knightly education. There were special teachers of dancing, riding, fencing, and swimming, as well as excursions for hunting and fishing, and other sports.

Many historians suggest that the modern physical education movement began with the appearance of a text, *De Arte Gymnastica,* dated 1569, and written by Hieronymus Mercurialis, a famous physician who lived in Rome. In this book, which was read throughout Europe and was widely cited by other authors and school authorities, Mercurialis sought to revive the gymnastic education of the ancient Greeks; among the activities he recommended was dancing. Another influential writer on education, who lived in the following century, John Locke, published a text, *Some Thoughts on Education,* in 1693. In this, he deals extensively with training not only the intellect, but also the constitution and health of the child. In addition to other forms of activity, he writes specifically of dance:

> . . . besides what is to be had from study and books, there are other accomplishments necessary for a gentleman, to be got by exercise, and to which time is to be allowed, and for which masters must be had. Dancing being that which gives graceful motions all the life, and above all things, manliness and a becoming confidence to young children, I think it cannot be learned too early. . . .[4]

Johann Guts Muths, another leading pioneer in the development of German education, published, in 1793, the text *Gymnastics for Youth,* in which he advocated dancing as a means of physical exercise, by writing, "Dancing is an exercise strongly deserving recommendation, as it tends to unite gracefulness and regularity of motion with strength and agility." He promoted dancing vigorously in his gymnasium at Schnopfenthal, and was perhaps the first author to use the term "gymnastic dance":

> A good gymnastic dance for the open air, approaching the heroic ballet for young men or boys, calculated to exercise their strength and ability, excite innocent mirth and youthful heroism and cherish their love of country through the accompaniment of song, is an extremely desirable object. . . .[5]

Other educators who were active in the beginning Turnverein movement introduced the so-called "folk roundel," which consisted of simple marching, hopping, skipping, and running movements and patterns. These were always accompanied by singing and sometimes by music, and were apparently the forerunners of what later came to be considered gymnastic dance in American physical education. Similarly, the director of the Royal Central Gymnastic Institute in Germany, during the mid-19th century, in-

[4]John Locke, *Some Thoughts on Education,* quoted in Fred Leonard, *A Guide to the History of Physical Education* (Philadelphia: Lea and Febiger, 1923), p. 60.

[5]Johann Guts Muths, *Gymnastics for Youth,* quoted in S. C. Staley and D. M. Lowery, *Gymnastic Dancing* (New York: Association Press, 1920), p. 6.

troduced what he called "transition exercises," which seemed to be a blend of gymnastics and dancing, carried on in dance formations and executed according to command.

At the same time, there were many private teachers of dancing throughout Europe, who taught it as an art in schools of ballet, or as a social grace, in the homes of wealthy or royal families of the time.

DANCE EDUCATION IN AMERICA

Meanwhile, what of America? It has already been pointed out that, as religious attitudes condemning dance grew less severe in the American colonies during the pre-Revolutionary period, a great wave of interest in dancing developed. There was a steady growth of dancing schools; many private schools included instruction in fencing and dancing, or music and dancing, for both boys and girls. The purpose of such education was seen as the very opposite of frivolity; indeed, an example of dancing not being learned entirely for pleasure is suggested by an incident at the Philadelphia Assembly in 1781:

> "Come, miss, have a care what you are doing," shouted the Master of Ceremonies to a damsel who was permitting a bit of gossip to interrupt her turn in a contradance. "Do you think you are here for your own pleasure?"[6]

The development of dance in education during the 19th century in the United States was of course closely linked to the expansion of elementary and secondary programs, and to the establishment of private academies, seminaries, and colleges for women. Treatises on education by European authorities became increasingly available in the United States. In particular, the works of Froebel, the German founder of kindergartens and champion of education for girls and women, began to affect educational philosophy here. Increasingly, there developed the conviction that the schools were responsible for physical as well as academic growth of children, and that activities other than the purely academic should be included in the curriculum.

During the first years of the new century, an increasing number of state colleges or church-supported colleges were founded, as well as the first women's colleges (which were founded originally as seminaries) at Mount Holyoke and elsewhere in New England. In all of these settings, dance began to be taught. Some women educators, including Emma Willard and Mary Lyon, attempted to provide some form of physical education for their students. Emma Willard taught during the winter of 1807–1808 at Middlebury College in Vermont. It was an extremely bitter and snowy winter and, according to Marks, she later wrote:

> When it was so cold that we could live no longer, I called all my girls on to the floor, and arranged them two and two in a long row for a country dance;

[6]Joseph Marks, *America Learns to Dance* (New York: Exposition Press, 1957), p. 51.

> and while those who could sing would strike up some stirring tune, I, with one of the girls for a partner would lead down the dance, and soon have them all in rapid motion. After which we went to our school exercises again.[7]

While dancing was, as a rule, found more frequently in programs for girls and women than for male students, one of the first recorded examples of dance as part of the required program for men was in the military academy at West Point. It was included in the course of instruction which was submitted to President Washington in 1783. Its rationale, of course, was that each officer had to be able to conduct himself as a gentleman, and that instruction in dancing would help him do this, and would provide poise and social competence. However, it was not actually taught until 1817 when Pierre Thomas, the Academy's first fencing master, was permitted to organize a voluntary dancing class for cadets who requested it. In 1823, dancing was made a required subject in the summer encampment, with daily lessons for the third and fourth class which were taught by Papanti, a famous Boston dancing master of the period.

During the first quarter of the 19th century, dancing began to be found in schools for young children. It was seen chiefly as a means of acquiring poise, manners, and social confidence. By mid-century, the justification for dance rested chiefly on its healthful benefits. An educational writer of the time, the Reverend John L. Blake, wrote in *The Farmer's Every-Day Book* that dance should be provided in every country school, under the direction of the schoolmaster:

> In the middle of the day, or prior to the commencement of the afternoon studies, let half an hour be spent in this fascinating exercise, as a reward of good conduct as scholars, and the prediction is made with confidence, that neither girls or boys will ever be tardy. Besides, it will refine the manners and the temper of the minds beyond calculation. Instead of diminishing progress in study, it will increase it. The design is by no means to fit them for the ballroom. It is simply to give them a healthful exercise; for boys, instead of playing ball—and the girls, instead of romping.[8]

Dance tended to be found more widely in private academies than in public schools, where it might be challenged on the grounds of utility or morality. Typically, in Cleveland in 1840, a citizen petitioned the city council to introduce music into the public schools. The council denied the request, claiming that it was illegal to teach music in the schools. At the meeting, one of the members of the council said that if music were introduced, dancing might also be taught; however, of the two, he preferred dancing.

In some cases, when dance was taught, it was in fact disguised as a form of musical gymnastics or as calisthenics. Thus, when Mary Lyon published a book of exercises at Mount Holyoke College in about 1853, teachers were warned that the exercises, done to music, should not be performed in a

[7]Alma Lutz and Emma Willard, *Daughter of Democracy* (Boston: Houghton Mifflin Co., 1929), p. 37.

[8]John L. Blake, *The Farmer's Every-Day Book* (Auburn, New Hampshire: Derby, Miller Co., 1850), p. 165.

dancelike fashion—or they would arouse opposition. However, in Lyon's teaching, and also in the calisthenics taught by Catherine Beecher during the 1840s and 1850s in a girls' school in Cincinnati and at Mount Holyoke, the activity resembled dance greatly. The term "calisthenics" was adapted from the Greek *kalos,* meaning beautiful, and *sthenos,* meaning strength. The exercises involved simple movements to be accompanied by music, to produce grace of motion and good carriage.

Between the period of the Civil War and the close of the 19th century, dance became a more fully accepted part of physical education, and thus of general education. Dio Lewis, a popular temperance and health lecturer, developed a system of graceful exercises using light dumbells, accompanied by music or drum beats for rhythm. In his book, *The New Gymnastics,* published in 1862, he praised dance as a moderately strenuous exercise, which developed flexibility, dexterity, and grace. In a school he conducted at Lexington, Massachusetts, girls took part in gymnastics twice a day for half an hour, and also performed dance as such, about three times a week. He described his gymnastics method as follows:

> . . . persons of both sexes unite in all the exercises with great social enjoyment, thus adding indefinitely to the attractions of the place. . . . In the New Gymnasium, everything is set to music. Marches, free movement, dumbells, wands, rings, mutual-help exercises. No apathy can resist the delightful stimulus. The one hundred persons on the floor join in the evolutions inspired by one common impulse. Under the old system each person works by himself, deprived of the sympathy and energy evoked by music and the associated movement.[9]

Lewis did not regard his system of "new Gymnastics" as dancing, commenting that the exercises "are arranged to music and . . . possess a charm superior to that of dancing and other social amusements." However, they clearly resembled a modified form of dance, involving marching, leaping and skipping actions, with partners traveling around the floor together.

There was an increasing readiness to accept dancing in education during the latter decades of the 19th century. This was in part due to the fact that it was a popularly accepted social pastime among all classes in society. Indeed, when it was introduced at such a leading women's college as Vassar, and opposition was expressed, the trustees and officers of the college supported it strongly. Matthew Vassar, the founder of the college, said to the trustees in 1869:

> Years ago I made up my judgment on these great questions in the religious point of view, and came to the decision favorable to amusements. I have never practiced public dancing in my life, and yet in view of its being a healthful and graceful exercise, I heartily approve of it, and now recommend it being taught in the college to all pupils whose parents or guardians recommend it.[10]

Similarly, years later, the president of Harvard University, Charles W. Eliot, wrote in a letter to Charles Francis Adams, "I have often said that if

[9]Dio Lewis, quoted in Leonard, *op. cit.,* p. 261.

[10]Matthew Vassar, quoted in Marks, *op. cit.,* p. 97.

I were compelled to have one required subject in Harvard College, I would make it dancing if I could. West Point has been very wise in this respect. . . ."[11]

AESTHETIC AND GYMNASTIC DANCE

A major influence in helping to bring dance as art into schools and colleges was the work of the French dramatic teacher, François Delsarte. His American followers developed a Delsartian system of exercise which attempted to relate outer movements to inner states of feeling. This method, widely used in the 1890s, was introduced at Chautauqua, the famous adult education camp in upstate New York which began a nationwide movement during the later years of the 19th century and the early 20th century. The Delsartian system stressed freedom and harmony of movement, and had a vague rationale about making the body "a temple for the indwelling soul." Some called it "aesthetic gymnastics." Often it accompanied singing or the recitation of poems. In addition, it included a great many dance movements and maneuvers.

The Delsartian system in turn led to the introduction of a method which was termed "aesthetic calisthenics." This approach was formulated by Melvin Ballou Gilbert, a Portland dance teacher, who developed it as a substitute for regular gymnastic work for women. The method was introduced to physical educators in 1894 by Dr. Dudley A. Sargent, a pioneer in this field, and professor of physical training at Harvard, who organized what later became the Sargent School of Physical Education. Gilbert's method was based on:

> . . . the long-established five positions of the feet and the five positions of the arms, together with the positions of the whole body known as attitudes, arabesques, poses, elevations, groupings, etc. From these precepts are established, whereby the steps, attitudes and motions are systematic and in strict harmony with time and music.[12]

The Gilbert method gradually became known as *aesthetic dance.* During the early years of the 20th century, its practitioners were influenced by the work of Isadora Duncan and sought to make it a highly expressive and artistic form. While aesthetic dance made considerable use of ballet movements as well as such ballroom dance steps as the polka, schottische, waltz, and mazurka—all fitted into series of exercises or routines that might then be performed—it was modified in its level of difficulty so that it might be taught to large classes without difficulty.

Sargent had hoped that the Gilbert method might be used with both men and women. However, as it became increasingly artistic and expressive,

[11]Charles W. Eliot, quoted in Henry James, *Charles W. Eliot, President of Harvard University, 1869–1909* (Boston: Houghton Mifflin Co., 1930), Vol. II, p. 163.

[12]Melvin Ballou Gilbert, "Classic Dancing," *American Physical Education Review,* June, 1905, p. 153.

men and boys resisted it. Thus, "it became necessary to modify the dancing so as to give opportunity for a heavier kind of work. . . ."[13]

This "heavier" and more masculine kind of work became known as *gymnastic dancing.* It rejected the balletic orientation of aesthetic dance; Staley and Lowery wrote of it as "any balance exercise that is free, serial, rhythmical," with coordinated simple movements, strenuous enough to be good exercise, and of a genuinely masculine makeup. The fundamental foot and arm positions, and the terminology of steps found in the aesthetic dance were discarded, along with the turnout, the difficult "technical steps," and the expressive emphasis.

Gymnastic dance made use of the terminology of gymnastics. It could be taught by the "physical director and not by a dancing master." The subject matter of gymnastic dance was drawn from various fields of physical activity: "folk dancing, aesthetic dancing, gymnasium exercises, athletic exercises, play and work."[14] Men, in performing it, wore gym costumes: shorts, athletic shirts, high stockings, and basketball sneakers. The dances were done in solos, couples, sets, and mass groupings. Often, they resembled the old drills of Dio Lewis, in that they involved maze running, skipping steps, galloping, as well as such folk dances as the Virginia Reel, the Hornpipe, the Highland Fling, the Czardas, and dances of other nationalities—usually performed as solo or group routines. Thus, in the early years of the 20th century, two forms of dance became established in college and secondary school physical education—gymnastic dance for boys and men, and aesthetic dance for girls and women. This separation of activity was typical of American physical education, which was one of the few curricular subjects in which boys and girls were divided into separate classes as a matter of custom.

FOLK AND NATIONAL DANCE

A third form of dance that rapidly became popular in the early part of the 20th century was folk or national dance (the term "national" usually referred to those folk dances that were characteristic of a nation, and which were found within its borders, such as the *Irish Jig,* the *Italian Tarantella,* or the *Scottish Highland Fling*). As indicated, these dances had been the source of many of the gymnastic dance routines. Actually, they had been practiced in physical education since 1887 when Dr. William G. Anderson, a pioneer physical educator who was director of the Brooklyn Normal School of Gymnastics, introduced Irish jigs, reels and clogs, the buck and wing, and soft-shoe steps.

At the same time that much of the folk dance material became incorporated into gymnastic dance, it also developed as a separate stream of activity in physical education, and in the early recreational or playground movement throughout the country. Two collectors of traditional folk dances, Elizabeth Burchenal and C. Ward Crampton, did much original research in European countries. They published extensive collections of traditional folk dances

[13]Dudley A. Sargent, quoted in Marks, *op. cit.,* p. 102.

[14]Staley and Lowery, *op. cit.,* pp. 82–83.

which were still being performed in such countries as Germany, Denmark, Sweden, Finland, and the British Isles—as well as traditional American country dances.

These became widely adopted in physical education syllabi and in community recreation programs throughout the country. They were seen as having important recreational values, and also as yielding intercultural benefits in a society whose citizens had come from many nations.

By the beginning years of the 20th century, dance had become widely adopted in schools and colleges throughout the United States. With the exception of a few finishing schools or girls' academies or colleges where it might be taught essentially as a social grace, it was viewed primarily as a form of physical education. Before long, physical educators developed an impressive litany of its benefits. Dr. Luther Halsey Gulick, an early physical educator who, like many of his counterparts, was initially a medical doctor, wrote rather mystically of the background of folk and national dances:

> The movements of folk and national dances . . . are . . . an epitome of many of the neuro-muscular coordinations which have been necessary to the life of the race. They have grown up very slowly through centuries until they have come to fit and express the very soul of the people, embodying its memories, expressing its psycho-physical traits and aspirations. Upon the basic neuro-muscular coordinations have been embroidered, for esthetic purposes, certain finer movements. The movements themselves, however . . . follow long-inherited tendencies toward neuro-muscular coordinations which arose under the selective influence of survival.[15]

The physiological outcomes of dance were further described in great detail:

> . . . dancing . . . exercise removes excess accumulations of fat, replacing the same with healthy muscle tissue, thereby transforming a body that was soft, inactive, and soggy into one that is tonic and elastic. As a means of organic stimulation, dancing can be made vigorous enough to satisfy the most hardy nature. . . . The mental attitude of the dancer makes this possible. The dancer prosecutes the most vigorous steps with no thought for the work he is doing. He is aware only of his pleasure.[16]

Dance was now widely established as part of the teacher training program for both men and women in many departments of physical education throughout the country. It took many and varied forms, as illustrated by this description of end-of-summer performances at Chautauqua in the 1890s:

> The exhibitions by students of the School of Physical Education were the highlight of each Chautauqua season for years. Oldtimers still marvel at the amazing review Anderson's protégés presented each summer at the Amphitheater and on the ball diamond. They drew from six to seven thousand people with standing-room-only the rule. . . . In 1892, "1,000 pupils participated in the exercises closing the course, at which a vast audience was amazed as well

[15]Luther Halsey Gulick, quoted in Staley and Lowery, *op. cit.,* pp. 22–23.

[16]*Ibid.,* p. 24.

as delighted at the feats of strength and agility shown." Old pictures show gymnasts, small dance groups, and large mixed classes of several hundred—including foreign pupils—doing wand drills and dances. Tumblers, Bolin's Swedish class, high bar work, Indian club drills, and the flambeaus (hoops of fire) set the pace with band music to fill any gaps. Minuets by tiny girls, Delsarte Health exercises, and dances—Swedish folk, English Morris, and clog—done to piano accompaniment, excited audiences.[17]

ROOTS OF MODERN DANCE IN EDUCATION

Three educators were to provide the spark that led eventually to the adoption of modern dance in American schools and colleges. They were Gertrude Colby, Bird Larson, and Margaret H'Doubler.

In 1913, Colby joined the staff of the Speyer School, the demonstration school of Teachers College, Columbia University, in New York City. A graduate of the Sargent School of Gymnastics, she was asked to develop a physical education program that would be natural and free, and which would permit self-expression. Gradually, she began to experiment with creative dance based on natural movement and on children's interests, a form that could be integrated with other curricular experiences in the school. Her approach made use of music as an emotional stimulus; it was not based on any carefully designed system of movement, and yet it had great appeal, compared to the stilted aesthetic dance, or the limited gymnastic dance that was in vogue at the time. Colby later joined the staff of Teachers College, where she taught a number of students who became leading American dance educators, including Martha Hill, Mary O'Donnell, Martha Deane, and Ruth Murray.

Colby gave the name of *natural dance* to her new method. In a sense, it was the forerunner of what was to become modern dance in schools and colleges. Before this was to happen, her method was to be influenced by the leading professional dancers of the 1920s and 1930s, and also by other educators who were to provide it with a scientific rationale.

Closely associated with Gertrude Colby was Bird Larson, who was in charge of dance at Barnard College, on the Columbia University campus. While Larson recognized the value in Colby's natural dance, she also felt that there was a need for dance technique that would be based on the laws of anatomy, kinesiology, and physics. Having had an extensive background in corrective physical education, Larson experimented with a system of movement which would have its origin in the torso of the body, and which would in effect represent not a preconceived system of technique and dance patterns but a science of movement.[18] A further extension of Colby's work was the use of rhythm and music, and, for a time, Larson's approach was called "natural rhythmic expression."

[17]Harold L. Ray, "Chautauqua, Early Showcase for Physical Education," *Journal of Health, Physical Education and Recreation,* November 1962, p. 39.

[18]Mildred C. Spiesman, "Dance Education Pioneers: Colby, Larson, H'Doubler," *Journal of Health, Physical Education and Recreation,* January 1960, pp. 25–27.

In 1916, Margaret H'Doubler, who had taught physical education at the University of Wisconsin, came to Teachers College to study for her Master's degree. As a part-time teacher at Columbia University between 1916 and 1918, H'Doubler carefully observed the experimental work of Colby and Larson. When she returned to the University of Wisconsin in 1918, she developed a dance program which was based on a scientific understanding of the nature of physical movement as well as a sound philosophy of creative expression.

H'Doubler succeeded in establishing a major in dance at the University of Wisconsin in 1926, thus achieving formal recognition for the dance in university education and bringing into existence a major center in the Midwest for the creation of a large dance audience. In addition, many teachers were brought into meaningful contact with dance education. H'Doubler wrote extensively, and her texts became influential in the professional preparation of dance educators and physical educators. She also founded *Orchesis,* the University of Wisconsin dance club which served as a model for many college and university performing groups.

During the 1930s, three streams of dance activity were evident: folk and social dance; tap, clog, and character dance; and, most important, the new modern dance.

Proponents of folk and national dance such as Louis Chalif, Mary Wood Hinman, and Elizabeth Burchenal had succeeded in widely promoting this activity in schools and colleges throughout the United States. Burchenal, who was organizer and chairman of the folk dance committee of the Playground and Recreational Association of America, brought a wealth of material to the movement from original sources, and through her authoritative lectures and publications, trained many teachers over a period of several decades. Louis Chalif, through his special courses for teachers and a variety of publications, also spurred this activity forward. Mary Wood Hinman was active in the development of all kinds of dancing: gymnastic, Morris, Maypole, folk, national, and clog dance. She was instrumental in the establishment of Folk Festival Councils in a number of American cities, and fought to gain acceptance for social dancing as a valid activity to be taught in schools.

Clog and tap dancing attained considerable success in schools and colleges during the 1920s and early 1930s. These dance forms were descended from traditional steps found in the jig of the Elizabethan period, the shuffling and foot-tapping steps of Latin countries and the British Isles, and black plantation dances. In its earlier development, the term "clog dance" was used, based on the original use of shoes with wooden soles, which created rather crude and heavy rhythmic patterns. Tap dancing, which made use of leather soles with aluminum heel and toe taps, and of modern, popular music, with faster and syncopated tempo and rhythms, gradually replaced clog on the musical stage and, ultimately, in dance education. Duggan comments that

> Clog is to tap dancing, therefore, what natural is to modern dance—an immediate predecessor to designate this type of rhythmic work in educational institutions. The term *clog* persisted in education long after it had been replaced

by *tap* in professional circles. This was due in part to the school's hesitancy to sponsor an activity associated with the theater. The name persists now partly due to habit and partly due to the fact that much published material was brought out during the period when *clog,* not *tap* dance, was the correct term for school teachers. . . .[19]

CREATIVE DANCE IN THE SCHOOLS

At the beginning of the 1930s, much of the creative dance which was taught in the schools stemmed from the natural dance which had been taught by Colby. It tended to emphasize free and unstructured movement, on self-discovery, and on spontaneous response to music. On the elementary level, many teachers were presenting "creative rhythmic movement" with a minimum of direction or actual instruction; rather, the teacher created the inspiration for the child to move. Teachers were encouraged to undertake the activity with younger children—whether or not they had dance skills themselves. In fact, one influential author thought it could be a positive handicap:

> . . . dancing, like children's art, is not dependent on background. In fact, as in their art, it can be a good thing if the teacher is unencumbered with old ideas on the subject. What the teacher needs is faith and understanding. Faith that there is the capacity within the child to do surprisingly beautiful things when encouraged and freed by the teacher—understanding that children's dancing is not a thing of steps, of artificial movements to be learned by rote. The moment we concern a child with steps, we tie him up, inhibit his free movement, make him fearful, put false emphasis. The walk is ruined if we ask the child which foot he puts forward first. He just naturally walks following a desire within him. So also will the child dance. . . .[20]

Even for students on the high school or college level, many teachers at the beginning of the 1930s encouraged an extremely free approach, based on Colby's natural dance theories. Betty Lynd Thompson wrote of "creative" dancing at this time:

> This form is taught in most large colleges and universities and in many high schools. It is developed along the lines of education and aims at developing personalities rather than dancers. . . . All of the movements are based on natural movements of the body, movements which we normally can do, but which are studied and practiced until they can be done with ease, perfect balance and coordination. . . .[21]

[19]Anne Schley Duggan, "The Evolution of Tap Dancing," *Educational Dance,* February 1940, p. 2.

[20]Natalie Robinson Cole, *The Arts in the Classroom* (New York: The John Day Co., 1940), p. 69.

[21]Betty Lynd Thompson, *Fundamentals of Rhythm and Dance* (New York: A. S. Barnes and Co., 1933), p. xviii.

When the dancer has developed a degree of skill in the control of her body, when she becomes able to "sense the rhythm and the emotion of music," then, according to Thompson, she is ready to create dances herself. Essentially, the emphasis throughout this period was placed on personal creativity, and aesthetic expressiveness—without the conviction that the body had to be trained as a tool, or instrument, before it could perform effectively. The influence, however, of the concert dancers of the 1930s was to create a much greater interest in technical mastery, in expanding the range of dance movement, and in developing a recognition of dance as an art form—rather than a means of catharsis, or naïve self-expression.

How did modern dance come into being? It had its roots in the movement essence of Isadora Duncan, the performance of Ruth St. Denis and Ted Shawn, and the choreographic contributions of Martha Graham, Doris Humphrey, and Charles Weidman in America, and Mary Wigman in Germany. During the middle and late 1920s, two movements existed side by side. On the one hand, educators—primarily physical educators—were teaching creative dance under a variety of names, in the schools and colleges of the nation. On the other hand, professional dancers were presenting their first recitals and concert tours throughout the land.

It soon became apparent that they needed each other. The dance educators in schools and colleges needed the professionals to provide a body of technique, and to explore the artistic potentialities of the new medium; in addition, many of them began to study dance in the studios or special workshops directed by concert dancers. In turn, the professionals needed the school and college people both to *attend* their classes, and to provide an audience for them, particularly on national tours with concert groups, when, it was soon discovered, the college or university town provided a welcome climate for programs that were experimental or controversial.

A more detailed analysis of this process, as well as of the development of modern dance itself, may be found in the chapters that follow.

8

Modern Dance: The Early Decades

As suggested in the preceding chapter, the uniquely American dance form that was to appear in this country during the 20th century, and that was to have a profound effect on dance education, was modern dance.

Beginning with Isadora Duncan, who broke away from the classical ballet and urged a new use of dance as a powerful medium of personal expression, the foundation was laid. Ruth St. Denis and Ted Shawn followed by providing a generation of Americans with their first awareness of dance as an exciting theater art. But it was the small group of dancers and choreographers who burst upon the scene in the late 1920s and early 1930s who may truly be said to have been the first modern dancers. These were the great early figures—Martha Graham, Doris Humphrey and Charles Weidman, Helen Tamiris, and the German dance pioneer, Mary Wigman.

How is modern dance to be defined? At the outset, many viewed it chiefly as a form of dance which rebelled against the formalism, decadence, stereotyped choreography, and productions of classical ballet. They welcomed a form of dance which responded to modern concerns and was an American—rather than imported—art form.

In rejecting the vocabulary of ballet movements and the artificiality of its traditional forms and themes, modern dance was viewed as a true expression of contemporary life—alive, vital, and constantly changing. It was based on natural, expressive, basic movement, through which the dancer was able to express a broad range of feeling—rather than only the decorative, romantic, or pseudotragic emotions of the classical ballet. John Martin wrote that the prime purpose of modern dance was not spectacle, but to communicate emotional experiences, intuitive perceptions, and elusive truths.

Selma Jean Cohen suggested that, although the first modern dancers did not set out to shock their audiences, they had to be extreme to make their point:

They simply had to discard all the trappings of the familiar traditions to make their audience see with fresh eyes. By eliminating the decorative, the superficial, the glib polish, they aimed to dig down to the essence of significant movement; movement that had long been disguised by distortion and ornament; movement that—when laid bare—would be recognized as the symbol of long-hidden realities.[1]

Since there was no universally accepted system of movement, each of the leading choreographers of this early period sought to explore and develop his or her own vocabulary of dance. Martha Graham based her fundamental idea of contraction and release of energy on the basic breathing rhythm of the body, and the effect of inhaling and exhaling breath. Doris Humphrey saw all human movement as existing in a transitional state between equilibrium and disequilibrium, calling the process "fall and recovery." In each case, a language of dance was developed to suit individual creative needs.

The specific skills of ballet, as well as the emphasis on performing extremely difficult feats with an air of perfect aplomb and gracious ease, were rejected. Instead, the movement of modern dance tended to reveal the performer, rather than to mask him. A wide variety of nondiscursive gestures was developed; movement that was harsh, forceful, percussive—often primitive in quality—was developed. Instead of involving highly controlled leaps, turns, and other springing movements in the air, or dancing on the *pointes,* or holding the arms and feet in rigidly preordained poses, the body and limbs became flexible; they were held in any pose, they were wracked, torn, twisted, to suit the purposes of the dance.

Similarly, in terms of the use of the dancing group, the traditional ballet hierarchy of leading dancers—the ballerina and the premier danseur—secondary dancers, and the corps, all performing in a ritualized sequence, in which they played separate and largely unrelated roles, was discarded. Instead, modern dancers almost lost identity in their roles; the group itself was fluid and treated as a sculptural whole. Don McDonagh comments that even though there were "stars," or leading dancers, in modern dance's basically egalitarian structure, it was common practice to:

> treat each of the members of a particular company as being equal and liable to be given individual variations to dance in the course of a piece. The company was considered an ensemble basically, in contrast to the traditional ballet company, which was as hierarchically arranged as an army or a king's court.[2]

In every way, through its stark and simple costumes, its simple and sculptural decor, its music composed by leading contemporary composers in most cases, modern dance was an expression of the contemporary scene. Typically, during one period in the 1930s, the titles of works performed on the modern dance stage included: *Strike, Heretic, Traditions, Stock Exchange, Lynch Town, Work and Play,* and *American Provincials.* But, like modern art,

[1]Selma Jean Cohen, *The Modern Dance: Seven Statements of Belief* (Middletown, Connecticut: Wesleyan University Press, 1965), p. 7.

[2]Don McDonagh, *Complete Guide To Modern Dance* (New York: Popular Library, 1977), p. 18.

such preoccupations were cyclic; at other points, and in the hands of other choreographers, the themes of modern dance works might encompass Greek mythology; ancient or modern poetry, or other literary works; American folklore and legendry; major social issues; interpersonal relationships approached psychoanalytically; historical events; or, simply, abstract and lyrical works that had no theme or story line.

Since modern dance was and is eclectic, drawn from so many sources and subject to so many influences, it is difficult to define it further, either in its formative years or today—other than to describe the dancers and their works, and their influence on the American concert-going public. One final element, however, might be stressed, which characterizes modern dance, and that is—*freedom.* Always, its primary value has been placed on permitting the individual choreographer to develop and express his own art, without regard to pre-existing forms and traditions. This does not suggest, as some have concluded, that modern dance has no discipline. Merce Cunningham has written:

> Since he works with the body—the strongest and, at the same instant, the most fragile of instruments—the necessity to organize and understand its way of moving is of great urgency for the dancer. Technique is the disciplining of one's energies through physical action in order to free that energy at any desired instant in its highest possible physical and spiritual form. For the disciplined energy of a dancer is the life-energy magnified and focused for whatever brief fraction of time it lasts. . . . The most essential thing in dance discipline is devotion, the steadfast and willing devotion to the labor that makes the classwork not a gymnastic hour and a half, or at the lowest level, a daily drudgery, but a devotion that allows the classroom discipline to be moments of dancing too. . . .[3]

Thus, although at the outset, modern dance might have been confused with the natural dance, or "interpretive dance" that flourished in the 1920s, it soon became a disciplined and demanding dance form. Much later, the rejection of ballet that characterized the first years of modern dance gave way to an acceptance of the view that ballet represents a valuable means of training and developing the body for dance.

But what happened at the beginning? Isadora Duncan is usually referred to as the liberating spirit who gave expression to modern dance. Actually, there were a number of other rebels and pioneers who preceded her, and who helped to shape the form of dance that was to emerge. Among these were François Delsarte, Émile Jaques-Dalcroze, and Loie Fuller.

DELSARTE, DALCROZE, AND FULLER

François Delsarte, a French teacher of music and acting, who lived from 1811 to 1871, had a remarkable influence not only on the actors of his time whom he taught, but also on Ruth St. Denis, Ted Shawn, and a generation of 20th-century German and Central European dancers. Delsarte

[3]Merce Cunningham, "The Function of a Technique for Dance," in *The Dance Has Many Faces,* Walter Sorell, ed. (New York: World Publishing Co., 1951), pp. 250–251.

sought to develop a logical system of expressive movement and gesture; in so doing he spent his life observing people in a variety of circumstances, and particularly under stress:

> He even visited morgues and mines, after an explosion, to watch . . . how the bereaved betrayed their grief. From behind bushes in parks he studied children at play and . . . analyzed the differences in movement behavior between the attendants who loved children and those who did not . . . with cold scientific detachment he peered at humanity unconsciously registering its emotions and made copious notes. . . .[4]

Some of the great actors of his day were disciples of Delsarte. He developed a complex system of gesture, based on three zones of the body and of human expression. These were: *mental,* or *intellectual* (head and neck); *emotional* and *spiritual* (torso and arms); and *physical* (lower trunk and legs). In turn, each of these zones had three subdivisions, which were further divided in terms of function. The Delsartian method had nine fundamental laws of gesture on which were based exercises to develop freedom and relaxation of every part of the body, and to serve as a discipline for learning gesture and pantomime.

Delsarte also developed a system of dividing movement into three major orders, or types. These were "oppositions," "parallelisms," and "successions," terms which were widely used in modern dance vocabulary many decades later, as they had been transmitted to German modern dancers by Rudolf von Laban, who studied with a pupil of Delsarte. In addition, Ruth St. Denis and Ted Shawn made use of the Delsarte system by having one of his disciples teach in their school.

It was Shawn's view that Delsarte's teaching was the first to reveal what modern dancers call "tension and relaxation" or "contraction and release;" thus, it was he who laid the foundation for the German modern dance which, in turn, strongly influenced the American modern dance.[5]

Émile Jaques-Dalcroze, a Swiss music teacher and composer who was born in 1865 and continued to have a major influence on the teaching of music and dance from the late 19th century well into the 20th century, was a professor of harmony at Geneva. Concerned over the lack of expressiveness on the part of many music students, he determined to make use of physical movements to accentuate rhythmic awareness and musical creativity. He created a system of bodily exercises and approaches to the teaching of music and movement which strongly influenced many dancers and choreographers.

In 1910, a college for instruction in the Dalcroze method was built in Hellerau, Germany, where Serge Diaghileff observed his students in action. One of Dalcroze's pupils, Miriam Rambach, who later became known in England as Marie Rambert, was assigned to teach the members of Diaghileff's ballet company; in particular, Vaslav Nijinsky was much influenced by the Dalcroze approach, and revealed its effect in his own dancing and choreography. Hanya Holm, Kurt Jooss, Ruth St. Denis, and Mary Wigman were

[4]Margaret Lloyd, *The Borzoi Book of Modern Dance* (New York: Alfred A. Knopf, 1949), p. 29.

[5]Ted Shawn, *Dance We Must* (London: Dennis Dobson, Ltd., 1946), pp. 48–49.

among many other influential dancers who learned through his personal teaching or through his disciples and writing. Many of the 3,000 pupils he graduated scattered throughout the world and taught the Dalcroze method in America, England, France, Sweden, and other lands—usually under the name "eurhythmics." Stated simply, his technique provided a basis for strengthening the dancer's or musician's sense of rhythmic and harmonic structure, through a progressive system of "music visualization" and other exercises.

Of the many other dancers who performed in the years preceding Isadora Duncan, who were not within the mainstream of the ballet idiom, one of the most unusual was an American performer, Loie Fuller, who lived from 1862 to 1928.

There were a number of popular dancers (known as "skirt dancers") in this period, who performed in American and English music halls, where variety performances were presented. Skirt dancing consisted of graceful, somewhat balletic steps, without dancing on *pointe* or executing lifts; the performers rustled extremely full shirts. Loie Fuller's contribution at the outset was to swath herself in yards of luminous veils; gradually she extended this to dance with 100 yards or more of diaphanous fabric which she manipulated with sticks under the play of colored lights. By the time she was well embarked on her career, electric lights had been invented, and she experimented widely with the use of moving lanterns of colored glass.

Although Fuller was said to be a mediocre dancer, who had had less than half a dozen dancing lessons in her life, the effect she created was spectacular. One description from a writer of the time tells how one could see,

> . . . at the back of the darkened stage, the indistinct form of a woman clad in a confused mass of drapery. Suddenly, a stream of light issued apparently from the woman herself, while around her the folds of gauze rose and fell in phosphorescent waves, which seemed to have assumed, one knows not how, a subtle materiality, taking the form of a golden drinking cup, a magnificent lily, or a huge glistening moth. . . .[6]

Isadora Duncan herself met Fuller in Berlin, and was much impressed by the magic that had been wrought with the help of colored lights, fabrics, glass mirrors underfoot, luminescent cloth, and skilled electricians:

> Before our very eyes she turned to many colored, shining orchids, to a wavering, flowing sea flower, and at length to a spiral-like lily, all magic of Merlin, the sorcery of light, color, flowing form. What an extraordinary genius![7]

Perhaps the lesson that Loie Fuller taught was that a single person dancing on the stage could create an image capable of gripping and moving a huge audience—and this without reliance on the traditional classic dance technique that heretofore was the weapon of star ballerinas who captured

[6]Clare de Morinni, "Loie Fuller, The Fairy of Light," in *Chronicles of the American Dance*, Paul Magriel, ed. (New York: Henry Holt and Co., 1948), p. 209.

[7]Isadora Duncan, quoted in Lincoln Kirstein, *Dance: A Short History of Classic Theatrical Dancing* (New York: G. P. Putnam's Sons, 1935), p. 268.

the public's adoration. Isadora Duncan was to demonstrate the same effect —but she accomplished it without the aid of the brilliant stage effects that Fuller used. Her only instruments were her body and the magnetism of her expressive personality.

ISADORA DUNCAN

Isadora Duncan was born in San Francisco, California. Her family was an artistic one; her mother taught music, and the young girl studied ballet as a child, but soon broke away from the classic dance form, which did not suit her spirit. Years later, she was to write about what she felt was the artificial idiom of ballet:

> The whole tendency of this training seems to be to separate the gymnastic movements of the body completely from the mind. The mind, on the contrary, can only suffer in aloofness from this rigorous muscular discipline. This is just the opposite from all the theories on which I founded my school, by which the body becomes transparent and is a medium for the mind and spirit.[8]

At an early age, Isadora began to give dancing lessons. At the age of eighteen, she left for Chicago; then she gave concerts in New York at the Carnegie Hall Studios. In 1899, she danced in London and Paris, and began to develop an interest in Greek vases and statuary. Her fame began to spread; she danced in Budapest, Berlin, Italy, Greece, and then Russia, where she met Diaghileff and Stanislavsky and visited the Imperial Ballet School. Her first appearance in Russia, in 1905, stimulated a controversy between the traditional balletomanes and critics and those who proposed reform of the ballet. She is believed to have influenced Fokine strongly; indeed, throughout her career, many dramatists, directors, painters, and composers were said to have been moved and strongly affected in their own experimentation by Isadora.

There was nothing theatrical about her performance, in the sense of characterization, telling a story, or exhibiting brilliant dance technique. Instead, it was an art of personal expression, in which Isadora threw away the conventional corsets, ballet slippers, and tutus of the period, and danced barefooted and barelegged in a filmy, short Greek tunic. She performed moderate lifts and leaps; ran, and skipped. Her arms were often extended in an upsoaring gesture, never held in a fixed or formalized way; her neck and face were mobile and expressive. Overall, her movement was simple, but heroic:

> She reclined rather than fell; she kneeled to rise again; her movements were mainly upspringing. Although she vitalized the dance, gave it new weight and force, it did not have the dynamic range or accent of today's. It was more a harmonious plasticity, swinging, swaying, flowing rhythms, with no marked dissonances, no little vibratory movements. . . .[9]

[8] *Ibid.,* p. 271.

[9] Lloyd, *op. cit.,* p. 4.

Isadora Duncan in *La Marseillaise.* Photograph by Arnold Genthe, 1916. Reprinted with permission of the Dance Collection of the Library and Museum of the Performing Arts at Lincoln Center in New York City.

The quality of Isadora's dance is well described in her own writing. She had a personal vision of America dancing, in which she saw

> . . . great strides, leaps and bounds, lifted forehead and farflung arms, dancing the language of our pioneers, the fortitude of our heroes, the justice, kindness, purity of our women and through it all the inspired love and tenderness of our mothers, that will be America dancing. . . .[10]

She danced to the accompaniment of great musical works of the time, and of earlier periods—including many selections which had never been considered works that were suitable for dance. For over 25 years, she danced to music by Chopin—Mazurkas, Preludes, and Nocturnes, Ballades, Valses, and Polonaises. She used the operas of Gluck: *Orpheus et Euridice* and *Iphigenia in Aulis.* In 1904, she danced the Bachannal in Wagner's *Tannhauser* at Bayreuth; later, she was to perform to such powerful pieces as Wagner's

[10]Isadora Duncan, quoted in Walter Terry, *The Dance in America* (New York: Harper and Row, 1956), p. 40.

Forest Murmurs, Funeral March, and *Ride of the Valkyrie.* She danced to three movements of Beethoven's *Seventh Symphony,* and in a later period to major works by Berlioz, Bach, Mozart, Scriabin, Rachmaninoff, Schubert, and Tchaikovsky.

She never did exactly the same work twice, and often improvised on the stage, as in her famous performances of *March Slav,* and the *Marseillaise,* at the time of World War I. Indeed, she had no system of dance as such, and no steps that she taught her own classes. Basically, she disapproved of schools, and would not teach her pupils to imitate her own dancing. Instead, she wanted to help them develop movements that reflected their individual styles and preferences.

Isadora continued to dance throughout North and South America and in Europe during the 1920s, until she was killed in a tragic automobile accident in Nice in 1927. Her life was marked by a number of tragedies and unhappy romances; indeed, she rejected the common morality of the time and led an unorthodox life.

What was Isadora's contribution to dance?

Certainly it was not in terms of technique or of a conscious system of dance. For several decades after her death, those who had performed in her group or studied with her, called themselves Duncan dancers. However, Kirstein refers to these "pitiful, aspiring devotees" of her art as giving recitals "which were only shadows of her violent impulse." More recently, in the 1970s, a number of dancers, including Annabelle Gamson, have reconstructed Duncan's art and given performances which have been enthusiastically acclaimed by critics and public alike. However, support of such revivals tends to stem both from interest in their historical meaning and appreciation of Duncan's genius—rather than from Isadora's continuing influence on contemporary dance forms. Certainly, the interpretive dancing that flooded the country in the United States was due partly to her influence; however, it was also linked to the so-called aesthetic dance which was widely found in the 1800s, for which she was not responsible.

Probably Isadora's foremost achievement was to cast dance in a new light. It was now seen primarily as a means of personal expression, as a powerful and emotional stage art, and as something which might be freed from the rigid classical technique and stereotyped performance found in traditional ballet. While she had no direct successors, she set the stage for the next great dance artists who were to emerge—Ruth St. Denis and Ted Shawn.

DENISHAWN

Born in New Jersey in 1877, Ruth St. Denis had little early dance training. It is said that she took only three lessons from Madame Bonfanti, the Italian ballerina who had been a star of *The Black Crook,* decades before. However, she was greatly interested in the theater and, after touring as an actress, skirt dancer, and toe dancer, began in 1904 to take an interest in Egyptian dance art. She created what was first an Egyptian, and then a Hindu dance production—the ballet *Radha*—in 1906. Like her other works in this

Ruth St. Denis (center) in *Egypta.* Photograph by Sarony, New York, 1910. Denishawn Collection. Reprinted with permission of the Dance Collection of the Library and Museum of the Performing Arts at Lincoln Center in New York City.

vein, it was authentically costumed, set to music that was composed with an Oriental flavor, but played with Western instruments. *Radha* was instantly popular, and St. Denis toured with it on the vaudeville circuit in the United States, the British Isles, and Europe. Gradually she composed other numbers, all on exotic themes: *The Nautch Dance; The Yogi;* and *O-Mika,* based on the Japanese Noh drama form. Audiences appreciated the colorful theatricality of her work, which she attributed in part to Loie Fuller, saying:

> She brought appurtenances—lights and veils—to dance and where would I be, pray, without my lights? where would Isadora have been without her simple lighting effects? where would the theatre dancers of today find themselves without Loie's magnificent contributions?[11]

She was greatly influenced too by the great spiritual quality and emotional force of Isadora Duncan, whom she had seen dance in London in about 1900. Later she was to refer to Duncan as having a divine inheritance from ancient Greece, and as being "the embodiment of cosmic rhythm."

In 1914, Ruth St. Denis married Ted Shawn, who became her partner, and thus Denishawn was founded. Shawn had been born in Kansas City, Missouri, in 1891, and grew up in Denver where he entered college to study for the ministry. He was struck by diphtheria, was slightly paralyzed, and took up the study of dance as remedial exercise. Entering the field professionally, he studied ballet, opened a dancing school in Los Angeles, and

[11]Walter Terry, "The Legacy of Isadora Duncan and Ruth St. Denis," in *Dance Perspectives No. 5,* 1959, p. 30.

made an early motion picture of dance. While touring the country he met Ruth St. Denis, and their marriage followed shortly.

These two great individualists remained together as a team until 1932. In that time, they organized 13 major tours of the country, helping to bring about a recognition of the American dance as an independent art form and, in effect, creating a new audience for dance among middle class theatergoers who heretofore had seen only the pioneering Diaghileff tours. In addition to their tours, St. Denis and Shawn founded schools, first in Los Angeles and then in New York; there were a number of other branches and teachers of the Denishawn method in smaller cities throughout the country.

After they separated, Shawn formed his famous men's group which toured the United States in the mid- to late 1930s. In addition, he founded and was director for many years of the Jacob's Pillow School of Dance in Lee, Massachusetts (Norman Walker held this position after Shawn's death). Ruth St. Denis, who had by this time become known as the First Lady of American Dance, continued to run Denishawn House in New York City for a number of years. Later, in semi-retirement, she continued to experiment with, and to perform, works based on a linkage of dance and other related arts with religious service; typically, at lecture-demonstrations, she would perform Psalms using the Indian *mudras,* or gesture language.

What were the major contributions of Ruth St. Denis and Ted Shawn?

First, St. Denis's dance was filled with theatrical appeal; she made great use of color, lighting, scenery, and exotic (and often abbreviated) costuming. She had a great preoccupation with religious themes and mysticism and, although her dance movement in ethnic-based works was not truly authentic, nonetheless it gave a more accurate picture of authentic dance styles of exotic lands than ballet had ever done. St. Denis's movement skills were not highly developed; her technique tended to be largely a matter of "plastiques and poses, of manipulation of scarves and draperies, in decorative costumes, all very pictorial, and all done with an air."[12]

St. Denis had a very personal gift for movement and a facility for improvisation. She also developed a choreographic technique of "music visualization," under which each dancer followed a specific instrument in an orchestral score—more as Dalcroze had done years before. Her talents then, were based chiefly on an instinctive theatrical sense, a quality of religious mysticism, and a great sense of mission, in terms of bringing dance to the American people that would be worthy of them.

Ted Shawn, in contrast, was less mystic and more analytical. He had a considerable respect for technical training in dance and included various elements in the system that was presented in the Denishawn school—a barefoot adaptation of classical ballet instruction, ethnic and folk dance steps and styles, Dalcroze training, and even beginning German modern dance. In 1930, the first course in Wigman dance technique was sponsored in America by Denishawn. All of this was combined in an eclectic but vigorous and impressive style, most visible in Shawn's company and then at Jacob's Pillow.

In addition to his concept of dance training, Shawn made the following important contributions:

[12]Lloyd, *op. cit.,* p. 25.

Ted Shawn and his male dancers in *Kinetic Molpai.* Photograph by Shapiro, Pittsfield, Mass., 1936. Reprinted with permission of the Dance Collection of the Library and Museum of the Performing Arts at Lincoln Center in New York City.

He focused on the need to develop male dancers and fought to obtain recognition for dancing as a worthy art for men, throughout the United States on the concert stage and in colleges and universities.

He began the practice of commissioning music especially for his original dance works; composers such as Charles Wakefield Cadman, Deems Taylor, and Vaughan Williams were among the contemporary musicians with whom he worked. In addition, Shawn was among the first to make use of such composers as Debussy, Scriabin, and Satie.

He made widespread use of themes related to Americana—the early pioneers, the Indians, the American black, and the Spanish Conquistador. *Xochitl,* Shawn's production on an Aztec theme, showed movement that was stylized in the manner of figures seen on ancient Mexican reliefs; both he and St. Denis did intensive research in preparation for their dances. Other compositions of Shawn's were less literal; two of his works, *Labor Symphony* and *Kinetic Molpai,* were vigorous, abstract representations of primitive forces and masculine vigor.

Shawn was a great crusader for dance. He wrote a number of widely read books, including *Fundamentals of a Dance Education* and *Dance We Must,* and taught at a number of colleges, including Springfield College and Peabody—thus helping to gain recognition for creative dance as an educative medium.

Before Denishawn, America had largely been a wilderness of dance art and dance appreciation, consisting of hoofers, skirt dancers, acrobatic dancers,and vaudevillians. The only seriously regarded dance was European, and the greatest of the American dancers, like Augusta Maywood or Isadora

Ruth St. Denis and Ted Shawn in *Siamese Ballet.* Photograph by Lou Goodale Bigelow, 1918–19. Denishawn Collection.

Duncan, spent the major part of their careers in Europe. Denishawn exerted a tremendous influence on the youth of America; it has been commented that it converted as many to this form of dance as Pavlova did to ballet.

A final major contribution of Denishawn was that it provided a training ground for the great modern dancers who were to follow. In Martin's view, modern dance was not so much an outgrowth of Denishawn as a rebellion against it. Martha Graham, Doris Humphrey, and Charles Weidman were all leading Denishawn dancers and were deeply influenced by the training and theatrical experience they received in the company. However, when their original ideas for choreography, and their drive to create independently, were stifled within the Denishawn framework, they declared their independence. Thus, in the 1920s, modern dance as such came into being.

MARTHA GRAHAM

Generally accepted as the greatest single figure in American modern dance, and the symbol of it in the popular mind, Martha Graham has been described by the ballet choreographer Agnes de Mille, her close personal friend, as probably the greatest American choreographer, and an international cultural influence in fields extending beyond her own. Particularly, she has been one of the few persons to create new forms of movement.

> Her invention is prodigious. Like Picasso's, her art has changed deeply in style and technique many times during her career. For every new work, there was

Martha Graham in *Letter to the World.*
Photograph by Barbara Morgan.

> not only a new design in steps, but a new concept in technique and dynamics, a restudying of the basis of movement. . . .[13]

A tenth-generation American of New England stock, Martha Graham was brought up in California, having been born in Pennsylvania in about 1898. As a teen-ager, she saw Ruth St. Denis dance and was impressed by her; in 1916, she entered the Denishawn School as a student and studied intensively with Shawn. Three years later, she joined the company, taking the leading female role in *Xochitl.* For several years, she performed with Denishawn, both in the United States and abroad. Then, in 1923, she separated from their company, dancing in the Greenwich Village Follies, and then teaching dance at the Eastman School of Music, in Rochester.

In 1926, when she offered her first dance concert in New York City, she embarked on a career of choreography and performance that has been unmatched. During the period between 1926 and 1949, she composed over 100 dances, many of them full-scale theater pieces. She explored an extensive range of themes in her dances, frequently becoming preoccupied with one concept until she exhausted its creative potential. Some of the themes dealt with in her earlier years included the following: American Indian and

[13]Agnes de Mille, *The Book of the Dance* (New York: Golden Press, 1963), p. 157.

primitive ritual, American pioneers, tragicomedy, Greek mythology, and both narrative and abstract works dealing with psychological insights and conflicts.

None of her dances can truthfully be assigned to just one thematic category; they are all extremely complex in terms of symbolic meaning, psychological implications, and literary illusion. As a creator of dance, Graham has been unfailingly experimental, uncompromising, often disturbing, and, to the uninitiated audience, frequently the source of bewilderment and angry resistance.

Yet, with it all, critics and fellow choreographers deny that she is deliberately seeking to puzzle or to horrify the audience. Terry suggests that she is concerned with the universality of human emotions and behavior, and with the revelation of human character. He writes:

> Her dance purpose is to give physical substance to things felt, to lamentation, to celebration, to hate, to passion, to the experience of "frontier," to bigotry, to . . . underlying passions, dreams, fears and tragedies. . . . Far from being a cultist or an obscurist, she endeavors to remove the clock of obscurity from the purposes and aspects of human behavior and to reveal in solid dance architecture the architecture of the inner man.[14]

Graham has always avoided having one vocabulary or system of dance movement. She has certain movement principles and sequential techniques for the development of the body to the full range of its potential. These principles and techniques are in complete opposition to the serene and smooth control characteristic of classic ballet, in which all the strain, effort or uncertainty of the body is hidden. Instead, in Graham's technique, the "engineering, the effort" are revealed. "She threw aside all the traditional steps and techniques of ballet, the straight long leg, the pointed toe, the quiet, even hips, the flexed foot, the relaxed hand; she stressed continuous unfolding movement from a central core . . . but added spasm and resistance . . . she made the floor a part of gesture; invented many beautiful falls and recoveries from the ground; she discovered a whole technique of balancing on bent knees, with her thighs as a hinge and the spine cantilevered and suspended . . . she invented turns with a changing and swinging axis. . . ."[15]

Graham has commissioned many of the leading modern composers, including, in an early period, many pieces by Louis Horst, Lehman Engel, and Wallingford Riegger, and, in a somewhat later period, Samuel Barber, Gian Carlo Menotti, Norman Dello Joio, William Schuman, Robert Starer, and Carlos Surinach. She has also danced to classical works by Cesar Franck, Gluck, Mendelssohn, Debussy, Bach, and Handel, among many others. In addition to using orchestral music, she has danced just to the spoken word, and to a variety of forms of accompaniment in between. Many of the musical works composed for Graham's dances have been recognized as outstanding contemporary compositions in their own right, such as Copland's "Appalachian Spring."

Similarly, she has set a whole fashion with respect to stage design and costuming through her own brilliantly imaginative costume designs and

[14]Walter Terry, "Martha Graham," in Anatole Chujoy, *The Dance Encyclopedia* (New York: A. S. Barnes and Co., 1949), p. 216.

[15]De Mille, *op. cit.,* pp. 157–158.

those of Edythe Gilfond, as well as by having leading modern artists and sculptors, such as Rouben Ter-Arutunian, Isamu Noguchi, Jean Rosenthal, Oliver Smith, and Arch Lauterer, design her sets for her. Graham has introduced a number of staging techniques that are now widely used: symbolic props and sets; the use of mobile scenery; the use of sculpturally designed props as a fully integrated part of the movement design of the dance work.

Most of the leading modern dancers of the 1930s and 1940s were members of the Graham company—Erick Hawkins, Merce Cunningham, Jane Dudley, Sophie Maslow, May O'Donnell, Jean Erdman, Dorothy Bird, Mark Ryder, and many others. In more recent years, the leading roles were taken by Bertram Ross, Helen McGehee, Ethel Winter, Matt Turney, Linda Hodes, Yuriko, Mary Hinkson, Robert Cohan, David Wood—all of them superb dancers of outstanding physical presence—many of them gifted teachers or choreographers as well. One of Martha Graham's great contributions to the American modern dance was that she was the first to regularly use blacks and Orientals in her company, in contrast to earlier companies which had established a rigid color line.

Through the 1950s and 1960s, Graham continued to compose and present a number of major works of the American dance theatre—*Judith* (1950), *The Triumph of Saint Joan* (1951), both inspired solo performances; *Seraphic Dialogue* (a 1955 larger version of *The Triumph of Saint Joan*); *Embattled Garden* (1958); *Phaedra* (1962), and too many other critical triumphs to enumerate. Through this period, she continued to operate her school in New York City, to offer special short-term courses for teachers, to present master courses at Connecticut College, and to tour both the United States and Europe to overwhelming acclaim.

In her earlier years a controversial figure, Martha Graham became so widely known and accepted that, if anything, she was regarded by many as traditional—part of the "establishment." Nonetheless, it would be difficult to conceive of a more vital influence than she continued to be. Emily Coleman sums up her impact:

> How is one to say how many dancers, choreographers, actors and directors, have reflected in their own work the impact of Miss Graham's incandescent intensity on the stage? The precise degree of coloration may be impossible to gauge, but it is assuredly present. "Martha Graham is not only a great dancer," says Katharine Cornell. "She is also a great actress. She is one of the two or three great American creative artists in all fields.[16]

DORIS HUMPHREY

During the 1930s and 1940s, the other American modern dancer whose work was regarded as comparable to that of Martha Graham was Doris Humphrey. Born about 1895 and, like Graham, of New England ancestry, Doris Humphrey attended the Parker School in Chicago. There

[16]Emily Coleman, "Martha Graham Still Leaps Forward," *New York Times Magazine*, April 9, 1961, p. 44.

she received early training from Mary Wood Hinman in ballroom, clog, folk, and aesthetic dance. Later, she studied ballet, and began to perform semi-professionally, as well as to teach dance at summer workshops and in classes that she organized herself in Oak Park. In 1917, she went to Los Angeles to study with Ruth St. Denis and Denishawn. Shortly after, she joined the Denishawn company, and danced in many of its leading roles in tours throughout the United States and a number of Oriental countries. In 1928, she and Charles Weidman left Denishawn and founded a school and small performing company in New York.

From that time until 1945, when she retired as a dancer because of arthritis of the hip, Humphrey was active as a dancer, choreographer, and teacher who was extremely influential in the development of dance in education in the United States. Commenting that her dance style was based on the "pseudo-Greek" approach of Denishawn, using light, fleet foot movements, and accompanied by a wide variety of music and expressive sounds, de Mille describes her impact as being more from composition and teaching than from technical development. She is considered to have been one of the greatest teachers of choreography as a fine art; she had the gift of releasing, rather than cramping, creativity.[17]

Her major works, some of which have been revived in recent years, included: *Air for the G String* (1928); *Drama of Motion* (1930); *Dance of the*

Humphrey-Weidman group in *The Shakers.* Photograph by Barbara Morgan, about 1941.

[17]De Mille, *op. cit.,* p. 162.

Chosen (later named *The Shakers*) (1931); *New Dance Trilogy—New Dance, Theater Piece, With My Red Fires* (1935–36); *Passacaglia in C Minor* (1938); *Song of the West* (1940); *El Salon Mexico* (1943); and *Inquest* (1944). Retiring as a dancer in 1945, she continued to choreograph a number of major works for José Limón and his company, including *The Story of Mankind* and *Lament for Ignacio Sánchez Mejías* (1946); *Night Spell* (1951); and *Ritmo Jondo* (1953). During this period, while serving as artistic director of the José Limón Company, she also served on the faculty of the Connecticut College School of Dance and the Dance Department of the Juilliard School of Music in New York. A number of other major compositions were commissioned especially for the American Dance Festival in New London and the Juilliard Dance Theater. In 1958 she died, leaving a final unfinished dance work, *Brandenburg Concerto No. 4,* to be completed by Ruth Currier, and a book on choreography, *The Art of Making Dances,* published posthumously in 1959.

While Doris Humphrey's work was often highly moving, she tended to be less concerned with dramatic representation than with an abstract evocation of mood. She studied movement intensely for years, and developed a personal theory of dance movement as representing an arc between the pull of gravity and equilibrium—between fall and recovery.

She was gifted as a choreographer both in small groupings and in working with large-scale companies; her work ranged from a satirical comment on humanity and its foibles in *Theater Piece* or *Race of Life,* to a serene and abstract design in *Passacaglia.* Both through her own work and as choreographer and artistic director for José Limón, Doris Humphrey made a major contribution to the American dance theater.

CHARLES WEIDMAN

Closely allied to Doris Humphrey during much of her career was Charles Weidman. Born in Lincoln, Nebraska, in 1901, he joined the Denishawn school and company in 1920; Doris Humphrey was his first teacher and soon they became co-performers. His gift for pantomine was evident, and he became recognized as the leading male dance comic and satirist of his day. Weidman's most famous works were: *The Happy Hypocrite, Candide, Atavisms, Flickers, And Daddy Was a Fireman,* and *House Divided,* in which he depicted Abraham Lincoln during the Civil War.

Weidman staged the dances for a number of major Broadway musical shows, as well as separate dance revues. He taught at Bennington and a number of other colleges, was influential in training many dance educators, and numbered among his pupils such well-known performers as José Limón, Sybil Shearer, Jack Cole, and Peter Hamilton. His greatest gift was for narrative pantomime. Extremely inventive, he created movement that was fragmentary, mercurial, comic—making use of abrupt changes of tempo, rhythm, and dynamics. Lloyd writes:

> He jested in stroke and curlicue, lampooning right and left with his pencil-slim body, making jokes with his fingers and witty observations with his bare toes. . . . He could always be counted on to do the unexpected thing. The

movement was choppy on the surface, but underneath flowed the current of human feeling; sometimes the surface, too, was smooth with serious intent.[18]

In such a work as *Lynchtown,* his group choreography had dramatic strength and a charged atmosphere that created a powerful effect; however, most of his work tended to be light, humorous, and entertaining, rather than deeply moving. Following his 20 years spent as a collaborator with Doris Humphrey, Weidman continued to perform with his own small company and to teach at a number of universities. In the mid-1960s, he established, with Mikhail Santaro, in New York City, the Expression of Two Arts Theater, which gave periodic performances demonstrating the linkage of the graphic and dance arts.

RUDOLF VON LABAN

Another major influence on the developing modern dance came about through the work of two Europeans, Rudolf von Laban and Mary Wigman.

Laban was a Hungarian-born scholar who had studied painting in Munich and dancing in Paris, but whose major contribution was as a theoretician of dance and human movement. Beginning in the first years of the present century, he worked on experiments exploring the nature of human movement, and on a systematic analysis of so-called plastic rhythm. As early as 1910, in Munich, his first movement-choirs performed dancing for recreation. He was successful in developing huge civic festivals; throughout his life, he was concerned with the nature of work movements and the effective utilization of effort in labor. After directing his own dance company, which performed a number of experimental works, Laban became Ballet Master of the State Theater in Berlin during the 1920s. However, his most notable work was not in choreography, but in terms of his analysis of the physical laws governing dance movement, and the approach to dance training that he developed with his pupil and collaborator, Kurt Jooss.

According to his theory of *eukinetics,* all movement may be divided into two major categories: "outgoing" and "incoming." Laban developed a number of theories relating to *centrifugal* movement (movement originating in the center of the body and radiating or spreading out to the periphery) and *peripheral* movement (beginning with the extremities and moving to the center of the body). He carefully analyzed movement as to intensity, speed, and direction, making use of the object known as the *icosahedron,* the twenty-faced geometrical form which is a midpoint between a cube and a sphere. The essential concept of the icosahedron was that man's movements are both spherical and related to the three dimensions of space which are represented by the cube. Thus, movement takes place in three dimensions, and also on diagonals and inclines, limited only by the anatomical possibilities of the body; Laban used the imaginary points in space dictated by the icosahedron to develop a complicated movement scale that provided a systematic basis for dance training.

[18]Lloyd, *op. cit.,* p. 89.

Laban also was known for his development of the movement-choir, a form of mass gymnastics somewhat similar to Dalcroze's music visualization, but with a greater degree of aesthetic purpose and emotional content than was found in Dalcroze's system. Following the Nazi takeover of Germany, Laban went to England, where he began an Art of Movement Guild. There, he had a major impact on the theory and practice of elementary education and physical education. Bruce writes:

> . . . his philosophy has impregnated the teaching of physical education, particularly as far as women are concerned. Laban's work has been taken most directly into the teaching of modern educational dance or free dance and dance drama as we see it in many schools and training colleges. Indirectly, his theories have become the basis of schemes of physical education, and have replaced to a great extent, in women's work especially, the anatomical and physiological approach which existed previously.[19]

Laban's major contribution to dance performance was his system of dance notation, called originally *kinetographie,* and now known as *Labanotation.* Of the many types of notation that have been proposed, this is today the best known and most widely used throughout the world.

Kurt Jooss, a German choreographer and dancer, who studied in Paris and Vienna and under Laban at the National Theater in Mannheim in 1921, later became his assistant and principal dancer. Jooss was supervisor of the dance group in the Essen Opera House and other German companies, and later, founded his own Jooss Ballet. However, having worked closely with Laban, Jooss had a concept of ballet that was far from the traditional classic style; in such experimental works as his famous *The Green Table,* the quality of the movement and choreography was very much like that of the beginning modern dance of the period.

MARY WIGMAN

The most influential of Laban's pupils and co-workers, however, was the German dancer, choreographer, and teacher, Mary Wigman.

Mary Wigman is widely regarded as having been one of the great germinal forces underlying the development of modern dance in the 1920s. Although all her teaching was done in Europe, she exerted tremendous influence through her three tours of the United States in the early 1930s and through the many American dancers who came to study with her in Dresden —as well as through the work of her disciples. In terms of a basic philosophy of dance, use of movement and space, teaching ideology, and the content of her dances, she was unique.

Wigman, who was born in 1886, and who continued to teach in Germany when she was well into her seventies, studied with Dalcroze at Hellerau and absorbed much of his teaching, although she rejected his primary emphasis on musical elements. She next studied under Laban, and was his teaching assistant in Zurich, Switzerland, during World War I. While she

[19]V. Bruce, *Dance and Dance Drama in Education* (London: Pergamon Press, 1965), p. 4.

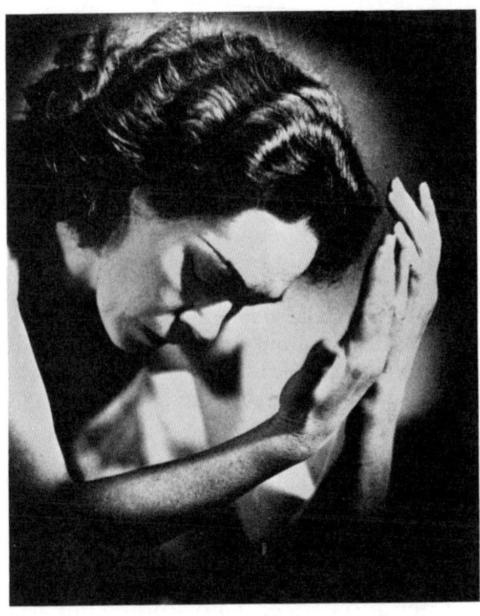

Mary Wigman in *Dance of Silence* from the dance cycle *Autumnal Dances.* Photograph by S. Enkelman, Berlin-Charlottenburg, 1937. Reprinted with permission of the Dance Collection of the Library and Museum of the Performing Arts at Lincoln Center in New York City.

absorbed much of his intellectual viewpoint toward movement, her own approach was a less systematic and more emotional one. Like Laban, she rejected the vocabulary of movement as well as the total artistic viewpoint of classic ballet; her approach to dance, in her first performances in 1919, was almost acrobatic. In part, this was an outcome of the environment in which she worked. Germany had never had as strong a ballet movement as other European countries, and was receptive to new forms of art that were revolutionary in their approach in the tortured years of inflation and political and spiritual turmoil following World War I. In such a setting, Wigman's radical new approach to dance found a welcome audience.

By 1926, she had formed a major school in Dresden, as well as lesser schools elsewhere, and had developed a performing group which became widely known. Her choreography tended toward full-length works, or "dance cycles," that were concerned with fundamental human emotions, superstitions, or relationships. When she performed in the United States in 1931 and 1932, she showed fragments of these larger works, performed by herself alone, without scenery and often without music. They had such titles as *Summer Dance, Witch Dance, Storm Song, Dream Image, Dance of Sorrow, Dance for the Earth, Lament, Death Call,* and *Dance into Death.* These were drawn from larger cycles, including *Visions, Sacrifice,* and *The Way.* In 1933, she appeared in the United States with her twelve-member company (all women) and American audiences had a fuller look at her art.

Her other works included a major antiwar statement in *Totenmal,* performed in Munich in 1930, and such later suites or cycles as *Woman Dances, Autumnal Dances, Bright Queen,* and *Dark Queen.* During World War II, Wigman's career was suspended; however after 1945 she resumed her teaching and choreography on a reduced scale in Leipzig. There, she produced Gluck's *Orpheus* as a dance-drama in 1947. In the years that followed, she taught in Leipzig and in West Berlin, and choreographed for the Municipal Opera in Berlin and the National Theater in Mannheim.

What was the essence of Wigman's dance?

First, in terms of the content of her works, she was deeply concerned with primitive and symbolic themes, treated in a mystical and often grotesque manner; she is said to have had a preoccupation with death and to have used it constantly as a symbol in her dances. Her general orientation was to deal not with intensely individual problems, but rather with the universal elements of life. Lloyd writes:

> . . . it was something primordial, something that dug deep into forgotten roots, an almost atavistic approach to man in relation to his universe, a return to the primitive through layers of civilization. It was something that stirred distant reverberations of things long past, something inexplicable, truly unutterable in words. . . .[20]

In movement, the use of music, and staging, Wigman's approach was unique for her time. Her actions were described as "predominantly low-keyed." She tended to kneel, crouch, crawl, and creep; her head was often downcast, and the arms were rarely lifted high. She avoided all balletic movements and never danced on her toes, although she did use the turned-out knee and foot for the sake of balance.

In a film of several of her shorter solo dances which was assembled by Professor Allegra Fuller Snyder of the Dance Department of the University of California at Los Angeles and shown in the mid-1970s, a somewhat different mood is displayed. Such works as *Seraphic Song, Pastoral, Festive Rhythm,* and *Dance of Summer,* show Wigman's less familiar, joyous, and lyrical side.[21]

In general, the visual effect of Wigman's dance was stark, harsh, and gloomy. Many saw it as ugly and disturbing. Critics referred to her costuming as distressing, but original, and certainly successful in conveying the mood she sought. Costumes were simple, somewhat Asian or primitive in appearance, and usually made from dark, rough fabrics. She used platforms as part of her staging; her lighting was simple, and stage effects in general, other than what could be created by the dancers, had little importance for her. Far more crucial was her sense of space as a vital element in staging and performance. Space, to Wigman, was not simply a vacuum to be filled, or an area in which the dancer moved. Instead, it was a force that was tangible —almost like water, through which the dancer must swim. She constantly saw it as an element which offered resistance to the dancer; in a sense, it represented the universe in which the dancer struggled.

Wigman's approach to music differed radically from that of Isadora Duncan's, in that Duncan had used music as a primary source of inspiration, whereas Wigman often danced without music, or with a simple melodic line of a woodwind instrument, or with primitive percussion accompaniment.

[20]Lloyd, *op. cit.,* p. 15.

[21]See John Mueller, "Films: A Glimpse of Mary Wigman," *Dance Magazine,* March, 1976, p. 96.

Mary Wigman Dance Group in *Der Weg,* about 1932. Hanya Holm Collection. Reprinted with permission of the Dance Collection of the Library and Museum of the Performing Arts at Lincoln Center in New York City.

She made much use of such Oriental instruments as Hindu drums and Balinese gongs, sometimes held in the dancer's hand. Dance and accompaniment were not composed separately, but developed together in an organic fashion.

Many critics and audiences did not readily accept Wigman's viewpoint. Kirstein comments that although her influence on contemporary dancers was powerful, she had little to offer those who were primarily interested in theatrical dancing, or who wished to demonstrate dramatic ideas "larger than their own frustration." Describing her instructional system as basic and semi-acrobatic, he sharply criticizes her custom of releasing students in the studio to freely improvise movements such as joy, terror, or grief, to percussive accompaniment. Unlike the traditional method of ballet instruction, he sees it as neither "brilliant, precise nor capable of repetition." Finally, Kirstein suggests that Wigman's dance was based on the era's "loose thinking" on progressive education and adolescent self-expression.[22]

Nonetheless, Wigman's impact was a major one. She broadened the scope of dance concern and represented a major influence on beginning modern dancers in America, who were operating in an educational and intellectual climate which *did* stress a growing concern with self-expression and a psychologically oriented creativity. In her work with such European

[22]Kirstein, *op. cit.,* pp. 306–307.

dancers as Kurt Jooss and Harald Kreutzberg, a brilliant mime, she strongly influenced a number of performers who were essentially balletic. And finally, through her major disciple, Hanya Holm, she exercised a strong effect on the American dance scene that was to continue to the present day.

HANYA HOLM

Hanya Holm came to this country in 1931 to open a branch of the Wigman School. Originally, she had studied at the Dalcroze Institute, and had been a leading dancer with Wigman's original dance company during the 1920s. Later, she headed the faculty of the Wigman School in Dresden, and acted as assistant director and a leading dancer in Wigman's major work, *Totenmal.*

Holm remained in the United States, fusing Wigman's original theories with her own creative impulses, to develop a new dance art that was uniquely American in outlook. Her major compositions included *Trend, Dance Sonata, What Dreams May Come, Tragic Exodus,* and *The Golden Fleece,*

Hanya Holm Dance Group in *Dance of Work and Play.* Performed at Bennington College. Photograph by Barbara Morgan, 1938.

which was filmed in 1941. As a choreographer she was extremely gifted; her works had a remarkable plastic quality and were marked by originality of staging and much technical excitement. Music was extremely important in her work, and she has had such modern composers as Norman Lloyd, John Cage, and Roy Harris write for her.

While never an outstanding dancer herself, Holm was an unusually gifted teacher, who exposed her students to a logical and detailed development of technique, and to working in various planes, directions, dimensions, and extensions that reflected Laban's original thinking. She stressed the centrality of the body that makes possible unified and integrated movement. At Bennington, Juilliard, at her own school in New York City (in 1936, the original name of Wigman School was changed to the Hanya Holm School of Dance), and especially at Colorado College, where she was in charge of a summer dance workshop for many years, Hanya Holm had a strong influence on American dance educators. She was also one of the comparatively few modern dancers who have been successful on the Broadway stage; two of her best known shows were *Kiss Me, Kate,* and *My Fair Lady.*

There were a number of other major choreographers and dancers during this period, on the American concert stage. Of these, two stand out as being close to Graham, Humphrey, and Wigman in their creative stature: José Limón and Helen Tamiris.

JOSÉ LIMÓN

José Limón, born in Mexico and brought up in California, was without question a towering figure in American modern dance. John Martin has called him "the greatest American male dancer in his field," and Walter Terry has referred to him as "without peer in his generation of men dancers."

From an early interest in painting and music, Limón turned to dance in 1928. He performed and choreographed during the 1930s, mostly for small groups. He joined the Humphrey-Weidman Company, becoming the leading male dancer, save Weidman himself. After World War II, he formed his own company, with Doris Humphrey, who had just retired from active dancing, as his artistic director. The company was well received, presenting a number of major works to critical acclaim, and traveling on several tours of Europe and South America sponsored by the State Department. Limón's work includes the retelling of an ancient legend of the conquest of Mexico by Spain, *Malinche,* with music by Norman Lloyd; *The Moor's Pavane,* the story of Othello, set to music by Purcell; and *Missa Brevis,* to music by Kodály. His own dancing was somber, powerful, and majestic; even when past the age of highest capability, he always commanded respect.

Limón's company originally included Dorothy Bird and Beatrice Seckler; later dancers were Lucas Hoving, Betty Jones, Ruth Currier, and Pauline Koner, all of them outstanding choreographers and heading their own companies as well. In addition to performing, José Limón was a gifted teacher at the Connecticut Summer School of the Dance, at his own studio in New York, and at the Juilliard School of the Dance.

José Limón as the Moor in *The Moor's Pavane.* Photograph by Walter Strate. Reprinted with permission of the Dance Collection of the Library and Museum of the Performing Arts at Lincoln Center in New York City.

HELEN TAMIRIS

Helen Tamiris was another leading modern dance figure during the 1930s and 1940s. Born of Russian parents on New York's East Side, she studied at the Henry Street Settlement House under Irene Lewisohn; in addition to interpretive dance, she had ballet training at the Metropolitan Opera Ballet school. She learned Italian ballet from Rosina Galli and Russian ballet from Michel Fokine. She danced for a period of time in Broadway revues and night clubs, and with the Metropolitan Opera as well, including performances abroad in Berlin and Paris. Then, in 1927, she began a career as a concert dancer. Her aim was to be a dancer of her age and country, and she felt that ballet, ethnic dance, or even Duncan dance could not help her do this. Modern dance could and this indeed, to her, was one of its purposes

—deal meaningfully with modern problems—and motivate audiences to a stage of concern and readiness for action.

Thus, most of her choreography dealt with vital social themes; the works had titles such as *Revolutionary March; Dance of the City; How Long Brethren; Songs of Protest;* and *Adelante,* based on the Spanish Civil War. They were dances of camaraderie, protest, and affirmation, closely linked to the strong left-wing movement of the time. Black spirituals and Caribbean ceremonials were also an important part of her customary concert program. Tamiris was an effective organizer; she brought together a Dance Repertory Company in 1930 which included Martha Graham, Doris Humphrey, Charles Weidman, and, in the following year, Agnes de Mille. While its program was successful and well received, the Repertory Company did not continue. Instead, Tamiris danced independently and later, in the early 1960s, formed the Tamiris-Nagrin Dance Company with her husband, Daniel Nagrin, who had been a featured dancer with her in concerts and nightclubs and a leading performer on the Broadway musical stage and on television. Tamiris, too, was active on the Broadway stage during her career; among the shows that she choreographed were *Annie Get Your Gun, Show Boat, Up in Central Park,* and *Inside U.S.A.*

In addition to her gifts as a dancer and choreographer, Tamiris was a strong force for the promotion of modern dance. She was one of the main organizers of the First National Dance Congress, first president of the American Dance Association, and influential in having dance made part of the Federal Theater Program of the Works Progress Administration during the late 1930s.

A number of other dancers, who had been leading performers in the early period of modern dance, became choreographers and respected teachers themselves during the 1940s and 1950s. These included Jane Dudley, Sophie Maslow, and Bill Bales.

DUDLEY, MASLOW, AND BALES

Jane Dudley had been a pupil of Hanya Holm and was a featured dancer in the Graham Company; one of her best-known roles was in *Letter to the World.* Like Tamiris, much of her choreography was based on social themes; she also had a strong concern with folklore and jazz rhythms. Her best-known works included *Harmonica Breakdown, Adolescence, Short Story, American Morning, Swing Your Lady,* and *New World A-Coming.* There was much comedy and sheer animal spirit in her work. Like most of the dancers of her generation, she continued to teach, at Teachers College, Columbia University, at Bennington College, the New Dance Group in New York, and in Israel.

Sophie Maslow studied at the Neighborhood Playhouse and with Irene Lewisohn at the Manhattan Opera Ballet School. One of her best-known works was *Folksay,* done to verses from Carl Sandburg's "The People, Yes," interspersed with folk ballads and stories. She also composed *Inheritance, Partisan Journey, Champion,* and *Festival,* the last of which was later developed into a full-length work, *The Village I Knew.* All her dances are lyrical and expressive of human drives and conflicts, but are not sharply partisan as many of the earlier "social protest" dances were. She continued to choreograph major works for public festival programs in New York City, and to teach extensively.

Bill Bales, the third member of what came to be known as the Dudley-Maslow-Bales Trio, which was closely associated with the New Dance Group in New York, attended the Carnegie Tech Drama School, and studied ballet and Dalcroze eurhythmics. He danced in the Humphrey-Weidman Company, and taught on the faculty at Bennington until 1967. He has been a guest artist with Hanya Holm, and has choreographed many solo works, as well as his featured roles in the major New Dance Group presentations. Most of his choreography was based on Spanish, Mexican, and black themes. During the early and mid-1970s, Bales served as Dean of Dance at the State University College at Purchase, New York, as part of that newly established institution's strong emphasis on the performing arts.

There were many other dancers in the period prior to mid-century, including such figures as Jean Erdman, Eve Gentry, Nona Schurman, May O'Donnell, Pearl Lang, Pauline Koner, Lester Horton, Ruth Currier, Katherine Litz, Eleanor King, Talley Beatty, Katherine Dunham, Pearl Primus, Sybil Shearer, and many others. It is not possible to describe all of their careers even in brief, other than to say that in most cases they continued to teach, choreograph, and perform in one form or another throughtout the 1960s and 1970s.

MODERN DANCE AT MID-CENTURY

After half a century of development, what then was the state of modern dance in the early 1950s? First, it was clear that it was an American art. The impulses that had given birth to Mary Wigman and other European experimenters were spent, and now the United States was the scene of contemporary dance activity. Those Europeans who wished to study modern dance came here, to the studios of the major modern dancers, or to the colleges that offered specialized dance programs.

It was clear that what had begun as the creative expression of a few gifted individuals, who operated independently but were able to reach fairly large audiences through their tours and theater presentations, had changed considerably. Now there were many choreographers and many small companies throughout the country—located chiefly in the large cities where the cultural arts tended to find a sympathetic audience, and also in many university communities. Particularly during the 1930s and 1940s, modern dance had swept through colleges and universities, exciting the interest not only of physical education departments—which usually placed dance in the hands of educators who had a special interest but often a limited background in dance—but also of others in the arts.

However, the great surge of creativity and popular enthusiasm about modern dance was over. It was apparent that, although probably hundreds of thousands of college students—mostly women—had been exposed to modern dance over a period of three decades, this had not succeeded in building a large, literate, and supportive audience for modern dance. To the contrary: during the 1940s and 1950s, many performers found that it had become increasingly difficult to schedule and finance company tours throughout the country, or to have successful performances, extending beyond a day or two, in theaters in the large cities. Partly, this was the inevitable outcome of the growing costs of production. It was also due to the fact that the audience for modern dance proved to be limited—in terms of taste.

One of the problems was that, like all modern arts—modern poetry, painting, and theater—it was hard to understand, and people did not know how to receive it. Too few artists, and too few educators, had been successful in achieving a sense of how to view, or be open to, these pioneering, avant-garde forms. And, in dance, one of the great problems was its diversity. There was no single method or technique. In the hundreds of tiny groups that performed around the country (for anyone was entitled to call himself a performer, or a choreographer), the quality of both composition and performance ranged from the most abysmally weak to an extremely high level of competence. Viewing this range, too many audiences, already insecure in terms of understanding and appreciating dance, had quick reactions that rejected compositions that were to them, pretentious, confusing, or silly, or that shocked or disturbed them. No longer did the notion that one needed only to express one's feelings to make a stage work worthwhile, have any meaning—if it ever did.

McDonagh comments that many of the pioneer modern dancers thought of themselves as constituting a movement and, at times, even a "crusade." They were opposed to decorative prettiness, superficial or silly themes, ornate settings and costumes, and wary of the commercial theater. He points out that:

> The act of courage for these dancer/choreographers was to abandon commercial success in pursuit of artistic expression. (They were) brave in asserting that dance was a serious mode of expression or could be, when the prevailing theater world did not believe it to be so. The forerunners strove to demonstrate their belief to the existent audience; the new generation looked for a new audience . . .[23]

Clearly, the pioneers of the 1930s and 1940s had been successful in gaining critical and intellectual appreciation for dance as a significant art form. But their followers, after mid-century, were ready to abandon the harsh, stark tenets of the early modern dance, and to move out into a greater range of themes and theatrical approaches. Indeed, the very rationale that led to the development of modern dance was under challenge. Originally, it had been developed to provide an alternative to ballet. One of its major premises was that ballet technique was outdated, arbitrary, and uncreative, and that the artistic works of ballet companies also were archaic and meaningless in a modern world. Thus, the early modern dancers tended to avoid balletic training in their studios (although many of them had had at least a modicum of such training); they dealt with thematic materials, and used choreographic approaches that were completely unlike those of the classic ballet. In a sense, it was this freshness of modern dance, its contemporary significance, its ability to say things that were personal and immediately

[23]Don McDonagh, *op. cit.*, pp. 69–70.

meaningful to an audience, that captured its first fresh audiences—and that the audiences found lacking in ballet.

But, over the 50-year period, ballet too had changed.

It was no longer the same art form that had been tired and stereotyped at the end of the 19th century. Instead, it was now a fresh and vital art that had gained tremendous new audiences and that, indeed, owed much of its spirit and contemporary outlook to the influence of modern dance.

What were the steps that led to the revival and enrichment of ballet, and to its recapture of public interest? The first of them took place in Russia and in France, in the early part of this century.

9 Age of Innovation in Ballet

As described in earlier chapters, ballet in Europe had reached a low ebb at the end of the 19th century. Only in Russia had it retained a measure of its former grandeur, and even there, under the artistic despotism of Petipa, it had become stereotyped and lacking in inspiration. It remained for two Russians, Michel Fokine and Serge Diaghileff, to make radical reforms and to embark the ballet on an age of innovation.

MICHEL FOKINE

Michel Fokine was born in St. Petersburg in 1880; he entered the Imperial School of Ballet in 1889. Graduating nine years later, he entered the Maryinsky Theater ballet company as a soloist, instead of a member of the corps. He was a brilliant dancer, but ultimately became known as a choreographer and teacher, rather than a *premier danseur*. Fokine was much disturbed by the rigidity and sterility of Russian ballet, which he criticized in his writings. He described the nature of a typical *pas de deux* of his early years as a performer, commenting that each dance was little more than an exhibition of agility and physical virtuosity. There was little conscious choreography involved:

> We did whatever we felt we could do best. I did high jumps and Pavlova pirouettes. There was no connection whatsoever between our "number" and the ballet into which it was inserted. Neither was there any connection with the music. We began our adagio when the music began and finished when the music came to an end.[1]

[1]Michel Fokine, quoted in Agnes de Mille, *The Book of the Dance* (New York: Golden Press, 1963), p. 138.

Gradually, Fokine began to teach and to assume responsibility for choreographing student performances. In 1904, he submitted a plan for the ballet *Daphnis and Chloe,* which revealed his philosophy for the first time. It was much like that of Noverre, stressing the need for unifying ballet as a meaningful dramatic enterprise, and for fusing its major elements of dance, music, and painting. This proposal was rejected, but three years later, Fokine's first major ballet, *Le Pavillon d'Armide,* was produced featuring two brilliant young performers, Vaslav Nijinsky and Anna Pavlova. However, he had little opportunity to put his ideas for reform into practice; typically, when he attempted to have dancers playing the role of Greeks dance with bare feet, the force of tradition was so strong that he was compelled to have them wear pink tights, with toes painted on them. Shortly after, Fokine was impressed by Isadora Duncan on her visit to Russia, and when the opportunity came to travel to Paris to stage several ballets for the Russian company that was going to perform there in the summer of 1909 with Serge Diaghileff as impresario, he seized it.

It was in Paris, during the years between 1909 and 1914, that Fokine rapidly achieved success as a choreographer. In that period, he staged a number of major works, some of which are still being performed today, including: *Prince Igor* (1909); *Les Sylphides* (1909); *Carnaval* (1910); *Firebird* (1910); *Le Spectre de la Rose* (1911); *Petrouchka* (1911); and *Le Coq D'Or* (1914). It was there too that his philosophy of ballet matured. His views were fully expressed in a famous letter to *The London Times* in 1914, in which he outlined five major principles which should govern the choreography and production of ballet:

1. It was necessary to create for each dance new forms of movement, suitable to the subject matter, period, or country of the ballet, and appropriate to the music, rather than to use ready-made movements straight from the classic tradition.
2. The dramatic action of the ballet should be continuously developed by means of movement, rather than using sections of pantomime to relate the story alternating with dance numbers that had no dramatic or narrative significance.
3. The traditional gesture-language, or pantomime, which often was unintelligible to the audience and even sometimes to the dancers, should be abandoned; instead, in its place, the entire body of the dancer should be used to communicate ideas and feelings.
4. Similarly, the entire group of dancers should be used to develop the theme of the ballet and should be part of the plot, rather than having the corps de ballet provide decorative interludes that had no significance.
5. Ballet should reflect an active and equal cooperation of all the arts involved in it; music, scenery, dancing, costuming, all were crucial to a unified creative effort. Specifically, music should no longer be a series of separate and unrelated numbers, but should be a unified composition dramatically integrated with the plot.

Fokine's concern was to make the ballet a fully expressive art that mirrored life. For the period, his ideas were revolutionary, and the Paris audiences were immensely enthusiastic. In part, this was because the French ballet had become so lackluster, particularly in terms of male dancing. When the brilliant Russian dancers appeared on stage, in Fokine's colorful and dynamic ballets, using a range of movement that had never before been seen on the stage, disregarding the rigid conventions of past choreography, and dancing in a manner that involved real characterization, the audiences went wild. Fokine wrote of their excitement:

> After the Polovetzian Dances, the audience rushed forward and actually tore off the orchestra rail in the Chatelet Theater. The success was absolutely unbelievable.[2]

De Mille comments that in these early years in Paris, and in four years in England during World War I, ballet was transformed from a pretty entertainment to a major form of theater. Fokine based the choreography of his ballets on the locale and period in which they were laid. The music too was closely integrated with these elements. The style of the dances and their manner of execution were a sharp break from previous models; the classic technique was expanded to include freer and fuller arm and leg movements and a more supple back. The former rigid positions for the head and arm were now loosened, and the movement generally was more free-flowing and emotional. Costumes suited the period and plot; the old classic costumes were abandoned for these new works.

In 1912, Diaghileff replaced Fokine with Nijinsky as choreographer. Although he continued to create a few ballets for the company, Fokine left in 1914 and worked intermittently with opera-ballet companies in Copenhagen, Paris, Buenos Aires, and with his own company in New York. Fokine died in America in 1942; it was unfortunate that for over two decades, while he was at the height of his creative powers, he had not been associated with a major company of stability, for which he could have continued to choreograph his brilliant ballets.

SERGE DIAGHILEFF

Serge Diaghileff, who lived from 1872 to 1929, was born a member of the Russian nobility. He studied both law and music, became interested in ballet and opera, and was given a supervisory post at the Maryinsky Theater. Because of his independence, he found it difficult to work there, and resigned shortly. He staged art exhibitions in St. Petersburg and Paris and, in 1908, became a theatrical impresario. It was in this role that he made his great contribution to dance. In 1909, he assembled a group of the leading Russian dancers of the Imperial Ballet, and arranged to present a season in Paris, during the summer vacation. His dancers for this first season included Michel Fokine, Anna Pavlova, Tamara Karsavina, Vaslav Nijinsky, and Mikhail Mordkin; the ballets were mostly the work of Fokine.

The next summer, Diaghileff's company appeared at the Paris Opéra, and such new works or revivals as *Scheherazade, Firebird,* and *Giselle* were

[2]Michel Fokine, quoted in de Mille, *op. cit.,* p. 143.

added to the repertoire. In 1911, Nijinsky resigned from the St. Petersburg Company and Diaghileff decided to establish his company on a permanent basis, rather than have it continue as an informal offshoot of the Imperial Russian Ballet.

In 1911, the company played a season in Rome, Monte Carlo, Paris, and London; in the following year it also appeared in Berlin, Vienna, and Budapest; after that, in South America and, in 1916, in the United States. There it created a sensation and spurred American interest in the ballet. Diaghileff's company toured steadily from 1916 to 1929, during what had become an international period for ballet—but one in which increasingly the art came to be considered almost exclusively Russian. In 1923, Diaghileff signed a contract with the principality of Monaco to become the official ballet of the Monte Carlo Ballet; its name was changed to Les Ballets Russes de Monte Carlo.

During all this time, although he used different choreographers, including Fokine, Nijinsky, Massine, Nijinska, and Balanchine, as well as a host of leading dancers, the Diaghileff company was pre-eminent in world ballet. What was the gift that accounted for Diaghileff's leadership?

He had remarkable ability as a manager and organizer and, while not a dancer himself, had great artistic taste and judgment. Like Fokine, he

Vaslav Nijinsky in *Afternoon of a Faun.* Photograph by de Meyer, Paris, 1911. Reprinted with permission of the Dance Collection of the Library and Museum of the Performing Arts at Lincoln Center in New York City.

Anna Pavlova in *The Dying Swan.* Reprinted with permission of the Dance Collection of the Library and Museum of the Performing Arts at Lincoln Center in New York City.

recognized that ballet was a combination of choreography, painting, and music; he was able to get great artists in each of these areas to collaborate fully with each other.

In addition to the choreographers listed above, most of whom also were among his leading dancers, Diaghileff's stars included Tamara Karsavina, Anna Pavlova, Adolph Bolm, Alicia Markova, Anton Dolin, and Alexandra Danilova. He was part of the total revolutionary movement in modern art and knew well the many painters and composers who were working, particularly in France, during this period. Among the composers whom he used for his ballets were Stravinsky, Ravel, Glazounov, Prokofieff, Debussy, Satie, and Milhaud—a roll call of the leading musicians of his day. Similarly, among painters, such leading artists as Bakst, Benois, Derain, Picasso, Tchelitcheff, Roualt, Chirico, and Cocteau designed for his productions. Kirstein points out that since Diaghileff was not a creative artist himself, the exact role he played tended to be obscure and even mythical. However, without question, his contribution was tremendous; he influenced every aspect of art in his era, and brought together the great creative artists of his time in a "hotbed of collaboration."[3]

Gradually, through the 1920s, the great generation that had received its training and had reached stardom initially in St. Petersburg slipped away. Although the company continued to be known as Russian, it became somewhat more international in flavor and makeup. Kirstein comments that Diaghileff became known as a "purveyor of novelty," who presented the extraordinary. Gradually, the company decayed artistically; the music became increasingly trivial, the dancing more and more capricious and

[3]Lincoln Kirstein, *Dance: A Short History of Classic Theatrical Dancing* (New York: G. P. Putnam's Sons, 1935), p. 289.

fragmentary. A number of Diaghileff's leading dancers and choreographers had left the company long before he died in 1929. At his death, it dissolved completely, although attempts were made to carry on its tradition under a number of competing sponsors.

NIJINSKY AND PAVLOVA

Diaghileff's two greatest stars were Vaslav Nijinsky and Anna Pavlova; their reputations are legendary.

Nijinsky is reputed to have been the greatest male ballet dancer of all time, although his dancing career lasted for only nine years, during two of which (1914-1916) he danced little. Of Polish extraction, but born in the Ukraine in 1890, Nijinsky attended the St. Petersburg Imperial School of Ballet, where he was considered to be a brilliant performer, although weak in his general studies. Shortly after his graduation in 1908, and his debut in Fokine's *Don Juan,* he accepted Diaghileff's proposal to go to Paris for his first season there. Nijinsky was an overwhelming success in several of Fokine's ballets and, two years later, in 1911, resigned formally from the St. Petersburg Company, to become a permanent member of Diaghileff's company. There, he continued as a *premier danseur* until 1913, dancing such great roles as *Le Spectre de la Rose* and *Petrouchka.* He temporarily left the Diaghileff company because of the impresario's anger at his marriage; although he later returned to it in 1916 for a tour of the United States and performed briefly after that in South America, Nijinsky's career came to a tragic end. He was mentally ill, and was confined to sanitariums for the remainder of his life.

What was the basis of the Nijinsky legend?

First, it stemmed from his great ability as a classic dancer; he was famed for his tremendous technique, his elevation, leaps, and pirouettes. He was believed to be the greatest jumper of all time, and could accomplish an *entrechat douze* (six full crossings of the feet in mid-air). Thus, in terms of sheer dancing brilliance, he deserved the reputation.

But Nijinsky was not just a classic dancer. He explored the possibilities of movement in a way that was akin to the beginning modern dancers of the 1920s. He was a remarkable choreographer who created four works: *Afternoon of a Faun, Le Sacre du Printemps, Jeux,* and *Till Eulenspiegel.* The first two of these aroused great controversy because of their radical break with traditional movement, and what some saw as a too frank depiction of sexual behavior on the stage. Nijinsky created movement that had never been seen before on the stage:

> . . . instead of tension, extension, elevation, feet turned-out, Nijinsky used relaxation, hugged-in shivers, jerky shakes, sub-human vibrations and feet turned-in . . . the grotesque, ugly, brutal and the strong he wielded like a weapon . . .[4]

[4]*Ibid.,* p. 289.

Anna Pavlova and Vaslav Nijinsky in *Le Pavillon d'Armide,* about 1909. Reprinted with permission of the Dance Collection of the Library and Museum of the Performing Arts at Lincoln Center in New York City.

Even at his most experimental, Nijinsky did not reject the classic ballet technique; indeed, his unique choreography was based on technical skills that could be performed only by a highly trained artist. To it, he added a remarkable gift for dramatic portrayal in leading roles in *Les Orientales, Le Spectre de la Rose, Le Carnaval,* and *Petrouchka.* Finally, Philp makes the point that his magnetic performances and his personal brilliance helped to "secure for the male dancer a dignity which had not been present for generations," and drew huge audiences of non-balletomanes to see Diaghileff's touring company.[5] Thus, he made a great contribution to the world of ballet. It is difficult to predict what his total impact might have been if his career had not been so tragically concluded.

[5]Richard Philp, *New York Times,* October 26, 1975, p. 6-D.

In contrast was the role played by Anna Pavlova. Like Nijinsky, her name is legendary as the greatest female dancer in ballet history, although it is hard to measure the basis for fame, or to compare her abilities accurately with those of present-day ballerinas. She was born in 1881, studied as a girl at the Maryinsky Theater's Imperial School, and was a featured performer in St. Petersburg for ten years. With Adolph Bolm, she toured Scandinavia in 1905, thus becoming the first great Russian ballerina to perform outside her country. She joined Diaghileff in Paris in 1909, but then left him and, forming her own company with Mikhail Mordkin, toured independently throughout the world for twenty years, until her death.

To millions, Pavlova was the embodiment of ballet. Chujoy comments that she took what had been an aristocratic, imperial art, found in the theaters and opera houses of Russia and Western Europe, and gave it to the common people in towns and villages throughout America:

> She played her great art in theaters and music halls, high school auditoriums and movie houses. She made available to the people an art form that before her had belonged to a chosen few, and thus elevated the people to an understanding, appreciation and enjoyment of it.[6]

Particularly in America, Pavlova's influence was tremendous. As Elssler had done during the Golden Age of ballet, she toured the country to tumultuous acclaim, making almost annual coast-to-coast tours between 1912 and 1925. Thanks to her, a generation of Americans became exposed to ballet as worthy art. What they saw was nothing like the revolutionary choreography or dancing of Nijinsky. Instead, Pavlova was a conservative and traditional dancer. Her performances on tour were not embellished by a sumptuous corps of dancers, but featured herself and a leading male partner. Her dancing was "distinguished by its grace, airiness, and absence of visible effort. It was sincere, refined, marked by a vivid sense of style-atmosphere, and a genuine and deeply felt reverence for the poetry of movement. . . ."[7]

Other leading figures during the Diaghileff period included Leonide Massine, Bronislava Nijinska, and George Balanchine.

Massine, known both as an outstanding character dancer and as one of the leading choreographers of the 20th century, was born in Moscow in 1894. He graduated from the Moscow Imperial Ballet School, and was selected by Diaghileff in 1912 to join his company as a dancer. In 1915 he was assigned the task of ballet master, then that of choreographer to replace Nijinsky. From that time to the late 1940s Massine produced some 50 ballets for the Diaghileff Company, for the Roxy Theater in New York, Colonel de Basil's Ballet Russe de Monte Carlo, La Scala in Milan, and Ballet Theater in America.

Massine was known for two ballet styles. The first was the so-called symphonic ballet, in which he composed major works to the symphonies of Tchaikovsky, Berlioz, Beethoven, and Shostakovitch. Essentially, these were abstract dance works. His other metier involved story ballets, often with a high degree of comedy, satire, and character dancing; typical of these were

[6]Anatole Chujoy, *The Dance Encyclopedia* (New York: A. S. Barnes and Co., 1949), p. 358.

[7]Cyril Beaumont, quoted in Chujoy, *op. cit.,* p. 356.

The Good-Humored Ladies, La Boutique Fantastique, The Three-Cornered Hat, and *Capriccio Espagnol.* Throughout his work, Massine achieved a reputation for a high degree of musicianship and for great color, inventiveness, and choreographic soundness.

Bronislava Nijinska was also a leading dancer and choreographer for the Diaghileff Company. Born in Warsaw in 1891, the sister of Vaslav Nijinsky, she studied at the St. Petersburg School, joined the Maryinsky Theater, and, in 1909, went to Paris with Diaghileff. With some interruptions, she continued to choreograph for Diaghileff through the 1920s. She revived a number of works for him, and, for several years was his chief choreographer, creating such major works as *Le Renard, Le Train Bleu, Les Biches,* and *Les Noces,* the most striking. Set to Stravinsky's revolutionary music scored for pianos, percussion, and voices, the latter:

> . . .was a primitive Russian wedding ceremonial, with starkly simple scenery . . . and an unornamented, architectural use of movement, mostly by solid groups of dancers. There was a marked kinship here to her brother's use of purely invented movement for expressive purposes, though in a more ordered and less violent form . . . [the work displayed] a kind of inarticulate, archaic passion . . . [it remains] one of the outstanding modern masterpieces.[8]

During the decades after the death of Diaghileff, Nijinska continued to choreograph for the Ballets Russes de Monte Carlo, the Markova-Dolin Company, Ballet Theater, and other opera and ballet companies throughout the world.

Without question, the member of Diaghileff's choreographic team who had the greatest influence on ballet in America was George Balanchine. Born in St. Petersburg in 1904, he entered the Imperial School of Ballet at the age of ten. After graduating in 1921, having appeared in many student performances drawn from the established 19th-century Imperial repertory, he began to choreograph a number of experimental works with a small group of young dancers in what was now Leningrad. However, there was much opposition to his work, and in 1924, Balanchine was permitted to leave Russia for a tour of Germany with a small group of young artists known as the Soviet State Dancers. Traveling on to Paris, they were auditioned by Diaghileff and absorbed into his company. At the age of twenty, Balanchine became ballet master, replacing Nijinska. He served in this role for four and a half years, creating ten new works, restaging many others, and producing ballets during the opera seasons at Monte Carlo.

When Diaghileff died in 1929, the members of his company scattered. When Balanchine had joined the company, he was a young man of remarkable gifts, but immature in his judgment. Now, he had become a fully developed choreographer. Due to a severe knee injury in 1927, he was no longer able to dance in demanding roles. What was he to do? Two of his works, *Apollo* and *The Prodigal Son,* had aroused much interest, but thus far he had not achieved a major reputation.

He was invited to the Paris Opéra, to stage a new version of *Prometheus,* a two-act work to music by Beethoven. However, illness intervened; he had

[8]John Martin, *John Martin's Book of the Dance* (New York: Tudor Publishing Co., 1963), p. 57

contracted tuberculosis and could not go on. After several months, he recovered, but the Paris assignment was gone. The period that followed was a rootless one for Balanchine. He concocted minor ballets and entertainments in revues in Paris and London. He served as guest ballet master in 1930 and 1931 for the Royal Danish Ballet in Copenhagen. He acted as ballet master for a new company under the direction of René Blum in Monte Carlo. He organized another new company (Les Ballets, 1933) at the Champs-Élysées in Paris. And then he was invited by a wealthy young American, Lincoln Kirstein, to come to the United States. With the cooperation of Edward Warburg, Kirstein had plans for the ballet in America. Taper writes:

> He was not content to have some Russian . . . company come here on tour, but, rather, it was his idea to have ballet take root and prosper as a vital, indigenous art in the United States—to establish a ballet company, a ballet repertoire, and a ballet audience. Such a transplanting had succeeded only three or four times in the three hundred years since the first ballet company was chartered by Louis XIV, and each time it had taken a monarch with ample coffers to achieve it. Each time, too, it had been effected by the importation into the new country of a great ballet master from the old, who brought the art with him. . . .[9]

RUSSIAN BALLET IN AMERICA

It was not an auspicious time to begin a ballet venture in the United States. The history of ballet in this country during recent years had been fragmentary and discouraging. While there had been a number of tours by foreign companies, such as the one-year tour by the Diaghileff Company in 1916, or Nijinsky's performances in 1916 and 1917, these had not served to arouse a permanent interest. Pavlova had appeared here first with Mikhail Mordkin at the Metropolitan Opera House, in 1910, and later had toured regularly until 1925. However, the Metropolitan itself, which might well have been the sponsor of a leading ballet company, never took sufficient interest to develop native talent, and relied heavily on European stars.

Adolph Bolm, who had been one of the leading stars of the Diaghileff Company, had remained in the United States and had formed a school and company. Later he was to work with the Chicago Civic Opera, to found Chicago Allied Arts, and to choreograph in Hollywood and with the San Francisco Opera. Michel Fokine came to the United States at the invitation of the impresario, Morris Gest; he staged musicals and also founded a school and company here. A third major European dancer was Mikhail Mordkin, who had been Pavlova's partner at the Paris Opéra and in her early American tours. After serving as ballet master of the Bolshoi Theater, following the Russian Revolution, Mordkin returned to the United States in 1924. He toured the country, taught ballet in New York and Philadelphia, and formed the Mordkin Ballet (later to be assimilated into Ballet Theater) in 1937.

[9]Bernard Taper, *Balanchine* (New York: Harper and Row, 1963), p. 161.

But, in 1933, the picture was not promising. It was a time of depression in the United States—hardly a good moment to introduce an art which was usually viewed as exotic, aristocratic, and certainly costly. Instead, at a time of crisis and unrest, modern dance, which dealt with significant social themes, seemed better attuned to the times.

The first ballet company to break the ice was the Ballet Russe de Monte Carlo, for which Balanchine had choreographed in 1932. Now Leonide Massine was the choreographer. Alexandra Danilova was the leading ballerina and there were several fine young Russian ballerinas in the company. The repertoire was drawn largely from the Diaghileff period, with emphasis on works by Fokine. The 1933 season, consisting of a brief series of performances in New York and then a tour of the country, was a critical success but a financial loss. Sol Hurok, who had arranged the visit, was convinced, however, that America was ready for ballet. He brought the company back year after year, and it gradually became a widely accepted and profitable enterprise.

This was still essentially Russian ballet; it remained for Balanchine and Kirstein to provide the foundation for what was to become an American art.

Their plans were to begin a new academy, to be called the School of American Ballet, and a performing company, to be called the American Ballet. The school began on a small scale in New York City, in 1934, and the first season for the company was in March, 1935. It presented a small repertory of Balanchine works: *Serenade, Dreams, Transcendence, Alma Mater, Errante,* and *Reminiscence.* Critical reaction was mildy negative, and the comment was voiced frequently that Balanchine was not an appropriate choice, if the intent was to develop a truly American school and style of ballet. The company set out on a short-lived tour in the fall of 1935; shortly after, it disbanded as an independent performing group, and joined the Metropolitan Opera as a resident ballet company, with Balanchine as ballet master. The contract was made, but much conflict rapidly developed between Balanchine and the opera management. Critic Virgil Thomson pointed out that the clash lay in part between the Russian style that Balanchine had brought to America, ". . . dynamic, explosive, sharply precise . . . full of enormous tension and vigor," and the Franco-Italian stage movement employed by singers on the opera stage, which was slow, broad, and much softer.

A second and even more serious difficulty arose when it became clear that the Metropolitan had no intention of scheduling regular separate ballet performances, which was the custom in great opera houses in Europe. Most of Balanchine's work for the Metropolitan was mutually dissatisfying, with the exception of his choreography of a new production of Gluck's *Orpheus and Eurydice.*

In 1938, Balanchine and the Metropolitan dissolved their relationship. For several years, Balanchine turned to the Broadway stage, and choreographed the most popular musicals to appear during this era, including *On Your Toes, I Married an Angel, Babes in Arms, The Boys from Syracuse,* and a number of other hits, as well as several movies.

In this same period, in 1939, Kirstein made a second attempt at developing a performing company. This was named Ballet Caravan, and it included a number of the original dancers from the American Ballet Company, as well as others who had been trained by the School of American

Ballet. Indeed, its avowed purpose was to promote dance as an indigenous art; it presented no ballets by Balanchine, but concentrated on the works of such choreographers as William Dollar, Lew Christensen, and Eugene Loring. Christensen's *Filling Station,* and Eugene Loring's *Billy the Kid,* to music by Aaron Copland, were among the first major ballets to deal successfully with American themes.

In 1946, after a hiatus caused by World War II, Kirstein returned to the United States and, with Balanchine, formed the Ballet Society. Leon Barzin was musical director and Lew Christensen, ballet master. This membership organization gave performances of a number of Balanchine's works, including *The Spellbound Child* and *The Four Temperaments,* and later, *Symphonie Concertante* and *Symphony in C,* as well as works by Todd Bolender, Merce Cunningham, William Dollar, and Lew Christensen.

THE NEW YORK CITY BALLET

Then, in 1948, the Ballet Society joined forces with the newly established New York City Center of Music and Drama, under the title of the New York City Ballet. During the first years, the company performed in the New York City Center. Although it lacked a subsidy as such, the city's sponsorship and the deliberately low admission scale helped to build a large new audience for ballet. During the following decade, the company, under the artistic domination of Balanchine, achieved its reputation as one of the outstanding ballet companies in the world. A key factor in this growth was that the School of American Ballet had continued, during the 12 years since the demise of the original company, to train a number of outstanding young dancers, who were now ready to join the company. Among these were Tanaquil LeClercq, Jacques d'Amboise, and Edward Villella. Other principal dancers included Maria Tallchief, Nicholas Magallanes, Francisco Moncion, and Todd Bolender.

The first season was brief, consisting of only 14 performances. Artistically, it was considered successful. However, financially it was poor, because of the competition of the Ballet Russe de Monte Carlo, which had just concluded a smash four-week season at the Metropolitan Opera House, with such stars as Alicia Markova, Mia Slavenska, Agnes de Mille, Anton Dolin, Alexandra Danilova, and Frederic Franklin. In a second season, beginning in January 1949, the company was joined by Jerome Robbins and Antony Tudor as guest choreographers. The American public began to respond favorably to the new artistic directions, and financially the season was a greater success.

At the outset, however, it appeared as if the New York City Ballet would perform in the City Center only twice a year, for a total of about four or five weeks. This would mean that, even with rehearsal time, the dancers would be occupied for only thirteen weeks per year. Could many of the ranking dancers in the company remain committed under these conditions? Many of them had to go into musical shows, Ballet Theater, and other companies. However, under determined management and with the support of the City Center directors, the company continued; in the fall of 1949, attendance was larger and the deficit decreased. Then, remarkable recognition came for such a young company, when Ninette de Valois, director of the famed British Sadler's Wells Ballet, which was on its first American tour at the time, indicated that she was extremely impressed with the New York City Ballet Company. Balanchine was invited to come to London in the following spring to stage his *Ballet Imperial,* and shortly thereafter, the entire New York company was invited to perform for a season at Covent Garden.

This season, in July 1950, was under the auspices of the Arts Council of Great Britain, and was considered a quasi-official exchange visit for the Sadler's Wells Ballet season in New York in 1949. Sixty of America's leading dancers were in the company; it was the first international recognition of the United States in the field of ballet. The literary, art, and music worlds were well represented; all the London and Paris periodicals sent their leading dance critics. And the reviews were highly favorable. One critic wrote:

> . . . they danced with such vigour and athletic enthusiasm that they had the audience in this hallowed theater whistling its enthusiasm long before the end came. . . .
>
> These fresh young Americans bring no mystery or sentiment to their dancing. They are rugged, tough, and gay. The men attack feats of grace as a sport and the girls make almost a miracle of their execution of the classical routine. That is the strangest thing about their visit. They are not so much interested in the folksy style. They are pure classicists absorbed by the perfection of the old Imperial Russian Ballet.[10]

Although there was some criticism of Balanchine's revival of the Stravinsky-Fokine *Firebird,* and of Balanchine's "cold and undramatic" abstract ballet, in general the reception was highly enthusiastic. Chujoy comments that, despite some critical "coolness," the London audience was greatly impressed; indeed, much of the criticism served as excellent publicity:

> Controversial ballets like *Illuminations, Age of Anxiety, Orpheus,* and *Firebird* attracted wide attention. Technically difficult ballets, the so-called abstracts, never failed to bring out cheers. *The Prodigal Son* (with the real Rouault backdrop, which the company had had freshly painted for the London season) was probably the favorite of all. . . .[11]

The visit of Great Britain, which included a tour of other cities, was a triumph and focused international attention on the New York City Ballet. The artistic prestige of the United States was enhanced. Increasingly, leading dancers who had not formerly been with the company joined it, including Jerome Robbins, Janet Reed, Melissa Hayden, Hugh Laing, and Diana Adams. The next seasons brought widespread acclaim, and now the company was augmented by André Eglevsky and Nora Kaye. Through the 1950s, and then as it moved into its sumptuous new home, the New York State Theater in the Lincoln Center arts complex, it gradually assumed the status of being one of the world's few great ballet companies, comparable to the British Royal Ballet, the Royal Danish Ballet, the Stuttgart Ballet, and

[10]Paul Holt, quoted in Anatole Chujoy, *The New York City Ballet* (New York: Alfred A. Knopf, 1953), p. 254.

[11]Chujoy, *op. cit.,* p. 261.

the two leading Russian companies, the Bolshoi in Moscow and the Kirov in Leningrad.

Under Balanchine, the New York City Ballet has developed an enormous and brilliant repertoire; its dancers perform superbly and its productions are handsomely staged. If it has a major problem, it is that the company is so strongly dominated by Balanchine. Although, through the years, it has presented works by other leading choreographers, such as Todd Bolender, Antony Tudor, Frederick Ashton, and Jerome Robbins, and a few works by members of the company, such as Jacques d'Amboise, it has always been a showcase for Balanchine's choreography. And to some, his highly disciplined and unemotional "neo-classic" approach is too restrictive, lacking the color and variety that a great ballet company should have. De Mille gives a balanced view of Balanchine's work, commenting that, although he is highly musical himself, he demands of his dancers only that they "hear a downbeat" and stay in time with the music. He attempts to suppress all show of emotion; the dancer must be anonymous and is viewed essentially as a tool for the choreographer. Nonetheless, she finds his works deeply moving and exciting, because of the sheer inventiveness of his composition.[12]

BALLET THEATER

A second major thread that is traced through the development of ballet in the United States is that of Ballet Theater. This company has without question developed more native American performers than any other; its repertoire has been broad and diverse; it has mounted the works of all the great modern ballet choreographers; and it has presented superb ballet for over a quarter of a century to audiences throughout the United States and abroad.

Ballet Theater developed as an outgrowth of the Mordkin Ballet, which had been founded in 1937 to provide a performing outlet for the students of Mordkin's New York school. In this little company, Lucia Chase and Leon Danielian were among the leading dancers, and the program consisted chiefly of older romantic works which Mordkin had restaged. In the following year, the Mordkin Ballet was expanded by a number of leading dancers and by additions to the repertoire.

As the company began to gain an audience and a sense of artistic direction, it decided in 1939 to expand. Lucia Chase, who was not only a dancer but also an extremely wealthy patron of the ballet, and Richard Pleasant, who had become general manager of the company, determined to form a full-fledged ballet company, to be known as Ballet Theater. It was to be under Pleasant's direction, and Mordkin's role was subordinated. During the first season of the new company, four weeks in the winter of 1940, works were presented by Michel Fokine, Adolph Bolm, Anton Dolin, Antony Tudor, Agnes de Mille, Eugene Loring, and Bronislava Nijinska. The company included a considerable number of leading dancers, many of whom had been active in the Diaghileff Company in the 1920s, or in its

[12]de Mille, *op. cit.,* p. 154.

successor organizations. Following the first season in New York, which was well received by the critics, Ballet Theater toured a number of other American cities, appearing in Chicago as the official company of the Chicago Opera.

In its second year, 1941, the company displayed a new and unusual structure. Anton Dolin was choreographer-in-residence and stage manager of the Classic Wing, Eugene Loring of the American Wing, and Antony Tudor of the New English Wing. This was part of Pleasant's much broader plan, which was to develop not a single ballet company, but rather a producing organization which would perform existing works of all periods and national sources, as well as assist in the creation of new ballets from many contemporary viewpoints. Thus, Pleasant intended to develop a classical wing, a Fokine-Diaghileff Russian Wing, and contemporary American, British, black and Spanish Wings; there even was the intention of including modern dance in the company's repertoire.

Unfortunately, the plan was too ambitious and the financial hazards too great. Despite excellent reviews and enthusiastic audiences, Pleasant's plans could not be carried further and he himself was forced to resign at the end of 1941. At the end of that year, Sol Hurok undertook to book Ballet Theater. In the years that followed, the company traveled widely, performing in all of Europe, the Near East, and South America. Particularly until the 1950s, it offered a roll call of the leading dancers to have appeared on the American scene: Diana Adams, Alicia Alonso, Agnes de Mille, André Eglevsky, Melissa Hayden, Nora Kaye, Michael Kidd, John Kriza, Harold Lang, Alicia Markova, Janet Reed, Jerome Robbins, and many others. Similarly, it provided a vehicle for the most talented choreographers of the time to present their works, either for the first time, or in revival.

Among the masterpieces which became part of Ballet Theater's repertoire were the following:

Antony Tudor: *Dark Elegies, Lilca Garden, Pillar of Fire, Romeo and Juliet, Dim Lustre, Undertow.*

Michael Kidd: *On Stage.*

Agnes de Mille: *Tally-Ho, Fall River Legend, Three Virgins and a Devil, Rodeo, Black Ritual* (composed for a company of black dancers under Ballet Theater sponsorship).

David Lichine: *Helen of Troy.*

Jerome Robbins: *Fancy Free, Interplay, Facsimile.*

Frederick Ashton: *Les Patineurs.*

Financial difficulties have plagued Ballet Theater throughout its existence. The original plan to have a company in which there would be no star system, no subdivision of dancers in a complex classification of levels, but rather simply "principals" and "company," was forfeited in order to develop glamor and encourage ticket sales. Similarly, during the years in which Hurok was in charge of Ballet Theater's touring schedule, its desire to be an American company was subordinated to the need for audience appeal. Instead it was widely advertised as Russian ballet, in an effort to capitalize on the reputation that had been established by Ballet Russe in years past. The company has always suffered from the lack of clear-cut artistic direction, and, particularly during the 1950s, lost many of its leading dancers to other companies.

Nonetheless, it continued to perform throughout America and in many other countries, and has continued to make a major contribution to the world of ballet, since 1957 under the name "American Ballet Theater."

The third major development in American ballet represented the continuation, particularly during the 1930s and 1940s, of the Russian ballet tradition that Diaghileff had first brought to the United States. As described earlier, René Blum and Colonel de Basil had founded the Ballet Russe de Monte Carlo in 1932, assembling many of the leading dancers from the original Diaghileff company. At first, the company was under the direction of Balanchine, then under Leonide Massine.

The first season in New York and London, in 1933, involved chiefly works by the two Russian choreographers; it was regarded as an artistic success but a financial failure. However, Sol Hurok promoted the Ballet Russe de Monte Carlo (the title had been changed to the singular) strongly, and with each succeeding year, the tours and seasons grew longer, and the audiences fuller and more appreciative. By 1935, the Ballet Russe de Monte Carlo was booked into the Metropolitan Opera House in New York; it had become an accepted part of the city's cultural life. Among the works presented at this time were several new symphony ballets by Massine including *Les Présages, Choreartium,* and *Symphonie Fantastique.*

René Blum retired as co-director of Ballet Russe in 1936, with Colonel de Basil assuming full control. However, friction split the company and in 1938 Leonide Massine left it, returning to Europe, where he founded a new company with Blum. The history from this point is one of tangled relationships, rapidly shifting titles, and lawsuits over the use of ballets. The major company to retain the name and tradition, however, was the company which came here under Massine's direction in 1938. Among its dancers were such great stars as Alexandra Danilova, Alicia Markova, Mia Slavenska, Igor Youskevitch, André Eglevsky, Frederic Franklin, and Serge Lifar.

At the outset, the company was clearly Russian in its origin and style; those Americans who joined it often changed their names in order to sound foreign. During the late 1930s, Ballet Russe ventured into Americana with such works as Massine's *Saratoga* and *Union Pacific.* However, these were not truly in the American genre, and not until Agnes de Mille's *Rodeo* was created did the company produce a work that was really native in spirit and style. Cut off from Europe by World War II, Ballet Russe gradually became American in character, and more and more American in its membership. It lost many of its leading dancers, some to age and some to the other leading companies—Ballet Theater and the New York City Ballet. Nonetheless, it continued to be an exciting company through the 1960s, constantly on the move and bringing many American audiences colorful and well-performed ballets.

A final important development of the period prior to 1950 in the United States was that a number of American dancers and choreographers had emerged who, in turn, began to develop regional ballet companies and schools in cities other than New York. Unlike such gifted dancers as Augusta Maywood or Mary Ann Lee of the previous century, they were able to find a high quality of professional training and many opportunities for employment here in the United States. Three of the leading examples of such home-grown talent were Catherine Littlefield, Ruth Page, and Lew Christensen.

Catherine Littlefield, a recognized American choreographer and ballerina, studied first in her mother's school in Philadelphia, and then under Albertieri at the Metropolitan in New York, and under Egorova, in Paris. On her return to the United States, she danced in Broadway musicals and was for several years a *première danseuse* for the Philadelphia Grand Opera Company. In 1935, she founded the Littlefield Ballet, which later became known as the Philadelphia Ballet—the first of its kind to be organized and staffed entirely by Americans. The company toured the United States and also performed in Europe in 1937, where it was well received; it continued to be active under Littlefield's direction until 1942. She also served for several seasons as the director of the Chicago Opera Ballet.

During her years as a teacher and ballet director, Littlefield helped train a considerable number of fine young dancers, who later performed on Broadway or in the major ballet companies in New York. Among these were Joan McCracken and Zachary Solov, who danced for both the American Ballet and Ballet Theater, and who served for seven years as choreographer at the Metropolitan Opera. Littlefield herself restaged a number of classical ballets, including *The Fairy Doll* and *Daphnis and Chloe.* Her own best known work was *Barn Dance,* which became part of the repertory of Ballet Theater.

Another American-born dancer and choreographer was Ruth Page, whose career centered in Chicago, although she danced throughout the United States and on a number of international tours.

Page studied with Adolph Bolm and Cecchetti; at an early age she accompanied Anna Pavlova on a South American tour, and appeared in the Broadway show, *Music Box Revue.* She was a leading dancer for Bolm in the Chicago Opera, for Diaghileff's Ballets Russes, and was the first American prima ballerina of the Metropolitan during the late 1920s. She toured widely through the United States and the Orient with Harald Kreutzberg, and was a guest performer with the Federal Theater Project. In 1938, she formed the Page-Stone Ballet Company with Bentley Stone. Among her best known works were *Frankie and Johnny, The Bells,* and *Billy Sunday,* all choreographed during the period of 1945 to 1948, and produced by Ballet Russe.

Ruth Page has been a choreographer of opera-ballet, and has converted into ballet form such works as *Carmen, Salomé, The Barber of Seville,* and *The Merry Widow.* Since the middle 1950s, her company, titled the Ruth Page Chicago Opera Ballet, has made major annual tours, with outstanding guest artists such as George Skibine and Marjorie Tallchief.

Lew Christensen, who was born in Brigham City, Utah, in 1908, has been one of the leading American male dancers and choreographers. Like Littlefield and Page, he did much to develop regional interest in ballet—in his case, in San Francisco. Christensen came of a musical and dancing family; his brothers, Harold and William, were also distinguished dancers and teachers. He received his training with an uncle and at the School of American Ballet in New York. He danced in vaudeville and was a member of the American Ballet Company in 1934, taking the title roles of *Orpheus* and *Apollo,* in performances at the Metropolitan Opera House. He also was a soloist, choreographer, and ballet master for Ballet Caravan during the period of 1936 to 1940. It was at this time that he choreographed *Filling Station, Pocahontas,* and *Encounter*—all part of Kirstein's effort to develop young native choreographers. His choreography was marked by clean lines and a fine sense of clarity and design. Both in his choreography and in his performance, Lew Christensen had a strong gift for characterization. His most famous dancing role was that of Pat Garret, in Loring's *Billy the Kid.*

After serving as ballet master of Ballet Society in 1946-1948, and as a faculty member of the School of American Ballet, he joined the San Francisco Ballet, which had been founded by Adolph Bolm in 1933 and was therefore the oldest extant company in America. Though originally formed as an auxiliary to the Opera, the San Francisco Ballet is now an independent organization, but it continues to dance the ballets that are part of the San Francisco Opera. In 1951, Lew Christensen succeeded his brother William as director of the San Francisco Ballet, and held this post for many years. There is a close tie between this company and the New York City Ballet Company. Kirstein has served as the artistic director of the West Coast company, and Christensen has been a director of the New York City Ballet. An example of this relationship is found in one of Christensen's later choreographic works; *Con Amore,* which he created for the San Francisco company, was first danced in the New York City Ballet by the leading dancers of the San Francisco Ballet.

In addition to these dancers and choreographers who played a strong part in developing regional ballet enterprises throughout the United States, several other choreographers of major stature were attached to the major New York companies; they will be described in the following chapter.

In summation, what was the effect of the first 50 years of the 20th century, in terms of the development of ballet as a theater art? It broke through the traditional ties that had imposed artistic sterility on it in Europe and that had weakened it as an expressive theatrical form, through the radical reforms of Fokine, and the brilliant productions of Diaghileff. During the 1920s, ballet became truly an international art of high esteem.

In America, the scene was marked, beginning in 1933, by an increasing amount of performing activitiy which was to culminate in the establishment of several major companies. By 1950, there was little doubt that ballet had gained acceptance as an American art form, with native dancers, choreographers, and schools of high standards. There was now a large, vitally interested audience, both for American and for foreign companies. This did not mean that the art was now on a thoroughly solid footing. Although great progress had been made in the artistic quality of American ballet performance, and although a measure of stability had been achieved in audience support, there was still much work to be done in terms of expanding the audience and achieving a real measure of financial security for ballet schools and performing companies.

10 Ballet Today

The bright promise that shone for ballet in the United States in 1950 was not an illusion. At that time, George Amberg commented that while there had been some form of ballet in America for over a century and a half, ballet as a native form of art was barely fifteen years old. It appeared as a consequence of the stimulus provided by the Ballet Russe, and was aided by expert training in the classical idiom provided by leading Russian teachers:

> Native talent emerged and an appreciative audience has developed and been consolidated. Recent attendances throughout the country have exceeded an estimated million and a half, not counting the enormous audience of the musical comedy.[1]

And, three years later, choreographer Agnes de Mille was to say, at a luncheon celebrating her best-selling *Dance to the Piper,* that dance in America had finally come of age. It was, at last, "stimulating, indigenous, and important" to the country; it offered a career that was respectable. More men would be going into the profession, able to expect a "normal, happy life. There will be copyright laws for choreography. There will be literature for dancing, and a real school of choreography. I as a dancer rejoice in all this."[2]

If anything, the growth of ballet has exceeded the expectations that were held for it at mid-century. When the New York City Ballet offered its first season at the City Center, it was barely able to justify a two-week season. By 1955, its season had expanded to eight weeks; in the same season, Ballet Theater performed at the Metropolitan Opera House for three weeks. The Sadler's Wells Company filled the Metropolitan for five weeks, and a host

[1]George Amberg, *Ballet in America* (New York: Duell, Sloan and Pearce, 1949), p. viii.

[2]Agnes de Mille, quoted in *The New York Herald-Tribune,* January 16, 1952, p. 13.

of other companies from abroad had seasons in New York—Antonio and his *Spanish Ballet,* the *Comédie Française,* the *Azuma Kabuki Dancers,* and *Dance Theater-Berlin,* the *Yugoslav Folk Ballet,* and *Ballet Espagnol*—all just during the fall and early winter months.

All this was nothing, compared with what was to come.

By 1967, the number of indigenous and visiting ballet companies had strikingly expanded. During the months of April and May alone, in New York City, balletgoers were able to see performances by five major companies. The British Royal Ballet, starring Rudolf Nureyev and Margot Fonteyn, was to give its longest season yet in New York City, and the first by any visiting dance company at the new Metropolitan Opera House in Lincoln Center. Simultaneously, in the New York State Theater, also located in the Lincoln Center complex, the New York City Ballet Company was completing a highly successful New York season, before going on an extended six-month tour. In May, the American Ballet Theater, with guest star Erik Bruhn, moved into the New York State Theater for four weeks. During the same season, two comparatively new but highly regarded companies, the Joffrey Ballet of New York, and the National Ballet of Washington, featuring Frederic Franklin, appeared at the City Center.

All this was an indication that the audience for ballet had grown tremendously. In a sense, it reflected the national interest which had given rise to a number of other major companies—in Boston, Philadelphia, San Francisco, Houston, and other cities—as well as dozens of surprisingly competent regional ballet companies throughout the country. In the words of dance critic Clive Barnes of *The New York Times:*

> . . . within that brief period the United States has become, together with Russia and Britain, one of the major dance powers. The richness and variety of American dance are unmatched anywhere. Its possibilities—given proper financial support—are limitless.[3]

Throughout the 1970s, ballet's popularity continued to expand dramatically. The established American companies broadened their audiences, lengthened their seasons, and toured widely. Typically, when the box office opened for the American Ballet Theater's spring season in New York in 1978, $52,000 worth of tickets were sold on the first day—a record for the Metropolitan Opera House, which was hosting the company. Throughout the nation, in cities such as Boston, Philadelphia, San Francisco, Chicago, Milwaukee, Salt Lake City, Los Angeles, Atlanta, and dozens of other communities, professional ballet companies were flourishing. Glamorous foreign companies—from Holland, Denmark, Great Britain, Canada, the Soviet Union, and Germany—toured the United States regularly. Regional ballet was thriving as never before, and ballet superstars had captured new audiences for their art, through popular films and major television ballet broadcasts.

Yet, although ballet companies proliferated and audiences swelled, as part of the nation's cultural explosion, the whole financial base for the art remained fragile and insecure. More than one company was forced to curtail

[3]Clive Barnes, "Dance Critic's Credo," *The New York Times, Theater Section,* September 12, 1965.

its season, and strikes of musicians paralyzed major performing contracts. The role of government and foundations grew increasingly significant, as a means of promoting the arts in national life. Siegel summarized the trend:

> The fortunes of ballet's private benefactors became insufficient to cover its growing needs. Government and quasi-public agencies have taken over more and more of its huge deficits, with a corresponding pressure for more egalitarian artistic policies. Companies became institutions, totems. Whether they do good ballets or not seems to have little more effect on their survival than the whims of fashion and habit, politics, and civic virtue. Big ballet's role has quietly shifted from serving the artist to serving society.[4]

NEW YORK CITY BALLET

Without question, the highest ranking company in the United States, and one which rates as a coequal with the best in the world, is the New York City Ballet, directed by George Balanchine. Its early promise, described in the preceding chapter, has been amply fulfilled. It is a handsomely mounted, vigorous, and exciting company, with superb dancing skills, and impeccably directed by Balanchine. Both in its extensive home seasons at the New York

New York City Ballet in the party scene from *The Nutcracker.* Choreography by George Balanchine. Photograph by Martha Swope.

[4]Marcia B. Siegel, *At the Vanishing Point, A Critic Looks at Dance* (New York: Saturday Review Press, 1972), p. 9.

City Center (and since 1964, in the New York State Theater at Lincoln Center), and in its many tours abroad, it has been acclaimed by critics and public alike. In its season at the Bolshoi Theater in Moscow in the fall of 1962, it stunned the houses packed with Russian balletomanes with its versatility and freshness.

In a sense, however, the New York City Ballet's great strength—the brilliant direction it is given by Balanchine—is also its weakness. For a number of years, both critics and members of the public have protested that the repertoire of the company has been so dominated by Balanchine's extraordinary body of work that the works of other major choreographers have not been included on his program. The charge is really one of artistic dictatorship. But in recent years the New York City Ballet has performed Robbins's *The Cage,* Tudor's *Dim Lustre,* and a number of other works by major choreographers of the Royal Ballet or Ballet Theater, such as Ashton's *Illuminations.* Also, Balanchine has presented a number of premieres by younger choreographers, such as Edward Villella's *Narkissos,* or *La Guilande de Campra* of John Taras, or the *Irish Fantasy* and *Prologue* of Jacques d'Amboise. The New York City Ballet has even performed a specially commissioned work, *Summerspace,* by Merce Cunningham, who is primarily known as a modern dancer.

During the 1960s, there was particularly strong criticism of Balanchine's works dominating the repertory of the New York City Ballet in seasons in New York and on tour. Typically, in the opening performance of the spring 1967 season at Lincoln Center, all of the works shown (*Raymonda*

New York City Ballet in *Raymonda Variations.* Choreography by George Balanchine.

Variations, Episodes, Ragtime, and *Ballet Imperial*) were by Balanchine. A month or two before, six out of seven works shown on consecutive evenings at the State Theater were Balanchine's. The feeling has been frequently expressed that Balanchine and the management of the company arrogantly disregard the wishes of the ballet's patrons. This is coupled with a long-standing annoyance at the refusal of the company to announce in advance the names of those who will be dancing. In a sense, this represents Balanchine's unwillingness to embrace the "star system," and his belief that the dancing is more important than any single performer; his critics translate this to mean that *his* dances are more important than anything. These views were strongly expressed by Allen Hughes, then dance critic of *The New York Times,* at the time of the company's move to Lincoln Center. Hughes commented that while the New York City Ballet had certainly matured as an artistic ensemble, it had failed to grow up as a theatrical institution:

> Up to now the public has allowed the company to ignore worthy works by choreographers outside the New York City Ballet in favor of second-rate items by Mr. Balanchine and choreographers of his choice. But how long will the regular public pay to see *Western Symphony, Con Amore* and *Fanfare?* How long will it be willing to buy repetitions of pieces like these when the best works of Sir Frederick Ashton, Antony Tudor, and Agnes de Mille, to mention a few of Mr. Balanchine's contemporaries . . . are being ignored?[4]

Giving credit to Balanchine's genius as a creator, but questioning his competence as the "program chairman of our only resident ballet company," Hughes commented later (shortly before he was replaced as dance critic for the *Times*) on the unwillingness of the company to publicize the names of performers in advance. Pointing out that the principle of preeminence of works over personalities had now been firmly established, he asked when the public would be informed "who is going to dance what and when?"

> Or would this reveal too obviously the fact that very young dancers are being pushed at an inordinately fast rate while experienced dancers at the peak of their artistic accomplishments are dancing less frequently than they might be expected to?[5]

The implication of such criticism was that the New York City Ballet company had flourished since its inception under a benevolent dictatorship. During the 1970s, this situation eased somewhat; the company retained about 40 works in its repertory, including a number of ballets choreographed by Balanchine during the period from 1930 to 1950. However, there was also a substantial offering of works by such leading choreographers as Frederick Ashton, Antony Tudor, and Jerome Robbins. By the 1977–1978 season at Lincoln Center, of the 49 ballets offered during the fall–winter season, ten were choreographed by Robbins alone.

[4]Marcia B. Siegel, *At the Vanishing Point, A Critic Looks at Dance* (New York: Saturday Review Press, 1972), p. 9.

[5]Allen Hughes, *The New York Times, Theater Section,* January 26, 1964, p. 18-X.

In 1978, a number of special programs offered by the New City Ballet were devoted solely to such Robbins works as *Afternoon of a Faun, The Concert, Dances at a Gathering,* and *The Cage.* Generally considered to be the ballet world's finest American-born choreographer, Robbins has also been immensely successful on the Broadway stage, as director–choreographer of *West Side Story, Gypsy,* and *Fiddler on the Roof.* Thus, much of the criticism of George Balanchine's choreographic monopoly of the New York City Ballet's program has been muted.

Balanchine's tendency has always been to feature the ballerina; he has had a series of female protégées, and through the years has guided such performers as Patricia McBride, Allegra Kent, Kay Mazzo, and Gelsey Kirkland to stardom. Indeed, he justifies the dominance of women in ballet; in contrast to the earlier Russian period in which such stars as Nijinsky, Massine, or Lifar were featured, Balanchine frankly avows that:

> The principle of classical ballet is woman. The woman is queen . . . The man is prince consort. . . . If the woman were less important, it would not be ballet.
>
> The woman's body is more flexible, there is more technique. Why? Why is Venus the goddess of love, not a man? That's the way it is. Woman is like that. They don't have to fight, go to war. Men can be generals if they want, or doctors, or whatever. But the woman's function is to fascinate men . . .[6]

Despite this sexist view, Balanchine has continued as a leading choreographer well into his 70s. One of his unique contributions has been to emphasize the *corps de ballet.* In his company, this ensemble, which formerly was seen almost as a muted background for the featured dancers, is given great emphasis. He employs in it only dancers who have soloist capability, and he choreographs works that give the *corps* challenging and dynamic movement, equal to the action and appeal of soloists.

A frequently voiced criticism of Balanchine has been that he exerted control that extended far beyond the New York Ballet itself. For example, it has been charged that other leading companies in the United States that have received important financial assistance from foundations in recent years are closely connected to Balanchine and the New York City Ballet. Thus, the "dictatorship" is said to extend beyond the limits of this one company and its audiences.

AMERICAN BALLET THEATER

In contrast, this criticism of the New York City Ballet is the reverse of what is usually identified as the major weakness of American Ballet Theater—that throughout its history it has lacked the consistently strong guiding hand of an artistic director that is essential for any major performing company.

After its period of greatest success in the 1940s and early 1950s, the American Ballet Theater underwent a time of extreme financial difficulty,

[6]Flora Lewis, "To Balanchine, Dance is Woman," *The New York Times,* October 6, 1976, p. 45.

American Ballet Theater in *Les Noces,* with choreography by Jerome Robbins to Igor Stravinsky's dance-cantata.

with a gradual decline in the quality of its performances. Nonetheless, under the leadership of Lucia Chase, its co-director, it continued to tour widely and to perform some of the major ballet works of the modern era. Fortunately, it received substantial grants in the late 1960s from the National Council for the Arts, on a matching-funds basis. This assistance was instrumental in helping the company maintain its extremely varied and expensive repertoire. In contrast to the New York City Ballet, the American Ballet Theater has offered in recent years such works as: MacMillan's *Romeo and Juliet,* de Mille's *Fall River Legend* and *Rodeo,* Antony Tudor's *Pillar of Fire* and *Undertow,* and Robbins's *Fancy Free.* In addition, it has regularly performed such classics as *Giselle, Swan Lake, Sleeping Beauty,* and *La Fille Mal Gardée,* and has from time to time presented new, specially commissioned works.

Lacking a home of its own, American Ballet Theater has in recent years held seasons at the Lincoln Center's New York State Theater and Metropolitan Opera House, the New York City Center, and the Kennedy Center in Washington, where it has been the official company. In addition, it has toured widely both in the United States and Canada, and has had frequent seasons abroad. It has always had a reputation for having a group of internationally renowned dancers in its company; in the 1940s and 1950s, these included Alicia Alonso, John Kriza, and Mary Ellen Moylan—all at the peak of their powers. In the 1970s, Ballet Theater continued this reputation, starring among others the great Danish dancer, Erik Bruhn, such outstanding ex-Soviet artists as Rudolf Nureyev, Mikhail Baryshnikov, and Natalia

American Ballet Theater in *Helen of Troy,* choreographed by David Lichine to music by Offenbach. Photograph by Fred Fehl.

Makarova, and a number of leading American dancers, including Cynthia Gregory and Gelsey Kirkland.

Both Antony Tudor and Nora Kaye served during this period as associate artistic directors, and have continued the policy of choreographic eclecticism that has always characterized Ballet Theater. In the late 1970s, programs ranged from continuous weeks of such classics as *The Nutcracker, Giselle,* and *Swan Lake,* to programs featuring José Limón's *The Moor's Pavane,* Eliot Feld's *At Midnight,* and Twyla Tharp's *Push Comes to Shove.* Given American Ballet Theater's continuing economic crisis and lack of a solid financial base, the tendency has been to feature the Russian stars in the great classic works that provoke near-hysterical public adulation and guarantee hefty box-office receipts. Tobias comments that the company's primary goal continues to be survival, and quotes Nora Kaye:

> . . . these days you can't be involved in a ballet company without being seriously concerned about budget. Ballet Theater, like most arts institutions, has no money, and we must get some: from the government, from corporate donors, from the private sector. I'll stand on the corner with a tin cup if necessary.[7]

Despite financial adversity—which it meets in a variety of ways, including fund-raising galas in cities throughout the United States, used to match

[7]Toby Tobias, "ABT—A Turning Point," *The New York Times,* September 18, 1977, p. 15.

"challenge grants," from the National Endowment for the Arts—American Ballet Theater has continued to thrive and tour; in 1978, its company expanded to 83 members from the previous year's 75. With Lucia Chase and Oliver Smith still playing a leading role in its artistic direction, the company remains a repository of works by de Mille, Tudor, Robbins, Feld, Fokine, and other choreographers. In addition, it has sponsored a unique smaller touring company, Ballet Repertory Company, under the direction of George Englund. This group, founded with the assistance of the Touring Residency program of the National Endowment for the Arts, has toured widely, performing in many cities throughout the United States that had not seen professional ballet of high quality in many years. It has also been instrumental in developing a diversified program of training for young dancers in the Ballet Theater school, that includes Labanotation, music, jazz, modern dance, stagecraft, aesthetics, and art history.

JOFFREY BALLET AND HARKNESS BALLET

On a much smaller scale, there has always been a need for more modest ballet companies. Walter Terry comments that small-scale companies are able to tour both in the United States and abroad with relative ease; the size of the company makes it much more adaptable and flexible, in terms of both the stages and financial arrangements that exist away from the large cities.

> For years and years in America, there has always been a need for small ballet units, for inexpensive ensembles which could bring classical ballet at budget prices to towns, high school auditoriums, women's clubs. So there is nothing really new about the small-size ballet groups—what is new is what they used to dance and what they dance now. . . .[8]

In the past, Terry comments, such companies built their programs around abridged versions of the Russian classics, extracts from famous works, all sorts of *grands pas de deux,* and sometimes a novelty version of a dramatic or operatic work. Today, however, the small-scale companies are embarking on fresh, creative choreographic works that are particularly appropriate for their personnel and skills. Obviously, the huge ballet companies of the world—such as the New York City Ballet, the Royal Danish Ballet, the Royal Ballet of Britain, or the Bolshoi Ballet, do the "great old classics or the new spectacle ballets" better than the smaller groups. However, these are extremely expensive, and the larger companies are less likely to risk commissioning new works than the "small-scale" companies.

Two such companies, founded in the 1950s and 1960s, have been the Joffrey Ballet (formerly known as the City Center Joffrey Ballet), and the Harkness Ballet, sponsored by the Rebekah Harkness Foundation. Curi-

[8]Walter Terry, "The Not-So-Little Little Ballet," *The New York Herald-Tribune Magazine,* April 24, 1966, p. 40.

City Center Joffrey Ballet in the multimedia production of *Astarte,* with choreography by Robert Joffrey, score by the rock group, the Crome Syrcus, kinetic scenery by Thomas Skelton, and projected photography by Gardner Compton. Tinette Singleton and Maximiliano Zomosa are featured. Photograph by Herbert Migdoll.

ously, these two companies, each with fewer than 40 dancers, had a closely intertwined past.

Robert Joffrey, a gifted young dancer who had studied at the School of American Ballet and performed with Roland Petit's Ballets de Paris during its New York engagement, began his own school, the American Ballet Center, in New York in 1952. In 1956, he set out with six dancers in a rented station wagon, as the Robert Joffrey Ballet. They performed in 23 different locations in eleven states; after ten consecutive tours, they appeared in more than 400 cities in 48 states. The company also toured the Near and Far East

City Center Joffrey Ballet in *The Clowns,* choreographed by Gerald Arpino. Photograph by James Howell.

for the State Department, appeared at the Kirov Theater in Leningrad as part of a ten-week tour of Soviet Russia, and gave a command performance at the White House.

In 1964, the Harkness Foundation, which had given financial support to the company for two years, wished to give its name to the company. When Joffrey refused this arrangement, the Foundation set up a separate Harkness Ballet, which drew away not only many of his better dancers, but also the rights to many of the ballets that had been produced by the company. Fortunately, Joffrey was able to rebuild his company quickly, using many of the talented dancers in his Ballet School, and he was given assistance by the Ford Foundation in reestablishing the company. Since then, Joffrey has toured widely and successfully and been acclaimed by the critics for the Joffrey Ballet's seasons at the New York City Center.

In 1966, the New York City Center formally affiliated itself with the Joffrey Ballet; this young, experimental company now had a permanent home and the promise of a rich future. Joffrey's chief choreographer has been Gerald Arpino, a fresh and exciting talent whose major works included *Viva Vivaldi, Sea Shadow, Secret Places, The Clowns,* and *Trinity.*

Meanwhile, the newly named Harkness Ballet, which consisted largely of Joffrey's original dancers and repertoire, began in 1964 with the assistance of a grant of $1 million from the Harkness Foundation to be spread over a 10-year period. Its first director was George Skibine; for the first three years of its existence the Harkness Ballet toured extensively throughout the United States and in Europe. Its repertoire consisted of Skibine's *Sarabande* and *Venta Quemada,* as well as a number of works by choreographers who have been closely associated with modern dance. These have included Alvin Ailey's *Feast of Ashes,* Stuart Hodes's *The Abyss,* and John Butler's *Sebastian.*

The company was noted for its brilliant productions, with colorful and handsomely designed costumes, decor, and lighting. For a period of time, it received favorable critical reviews, but during the 1970s, it appeared to reach a point of artistic sterility, declined in reputation as a leading ballet company, and ultimately disbanded. The Harkness Foundation also established a school of ballet at Harkness House in New York City, under the direction of Patricia Wilde and with leading artist–teachers on the faculty. The elaborately remodeled and decorated mansion which housed the school also held an exhibition gallery for dance documents, art, scenery, and costume designs. It served as the base for the Harkness Training and Research Center, concerned with scientific analysis of movement in classical ballet training.

Harkness Ballet in Stuart Hodes' *The Abyss,* featuring Helgi Thomasson and Lone Isaksen.

City Center Joffrey Ballet performs in Agnes de Mille's famous work, *Rodeo,* to music by Aaron Copland. Courtesy Shubert Theater, Philadelphia.

In contrast, the Joffrey Ballet continued to be an artistically vital and successful organization, noted in particular for the variety of its choreography. Joffrey himself has not developed any original ballets for the past several years, and Gerald Arpino has provided leading artistic direction to the company, in a style that Clive Barnes characterizes as typical of the Joffrey spirit—vital, trendy, breezy, and committed to classic dance style. Uniquely, the Joffrey Ballet has ranged from reviving major works of past centuries, to serving as a repository for the great modern ballets of the twentieth century, to commissioning new ballets by the most avant-garde modern dance choreographers.

In the late 1970s, for example, the company sponsored an all-American season at the New York City Center, with 30 ballets by such American choreographers as Jerome Robbins, Agnes de Mille, Arpino, and modern dancers Twyla Tharp and Anna Sokolow. However, it has also presented revivals of Leonide Massine's *Parade, The Green Table* by Kurt Jooss, and numerous other works by Frederick Ashton, Antony Tudor, John Cranko and other leading international choreographers. Joffrey has been particularly close to George Balanchine, with such works as *Scotch Symphony, Donizetti Variations,* and *Square Dance* in his company's repertoire; in return,

Balanchine has given the younger choreographer much assistance. In contrast to the larger companies, the Joffrey Ballet emphasizes a "no-star" policy, with dancers even being listed in the program alphabetically.

Despite its success, even the Joffrey Ballet has had financial difficulties and found it necessary to cancel its 1977 spring season at the New York City Center because of an excessive operating deficit. However, it has continued to employ its dancers for rehearsals and scheduled tours, and in general has been able to maintain a high level of artistic creativity and integrity—as well as a reassuring degree of popular support.

OTHER LEADING AMERICAN BALLET COMPANIES

In addition to these New York-based companies, there are several other ballet organizations in cities throughout the United States, that have earned a high level of recognition. Among these are the San Francisco Ballet, the Boston Ballet, the Pennsylvania Ballet in Philadelphia, and a number of newer companies.

San Francisco Ballet. The early development of the San Francisco Ballet was discussed in Chapter 9. While Lew Christensen retained artistic direction of the company for over 20 years, he was joined in 1973 by Michael Smuin, former principal dancer and choreographer with American Ballet Theater, as associate director. The San Francisco Ballet performs the works of many choreographers, including a number of ballets created originally for the New York City Ballet. It has gone on a number of federally sponsored tours in the United States which, together with a repertory season of several weeks in San Francisco and a commitment to its Opera, means that the company has had regular employment for as much as forty weeks during the year. Even without foreign tours—which many companies rely on to provide more performing time and income—this has given the San Francisco Ballet dancers and staff substantial income and security during the year.

Artistically, the company is highly regarded. Clive Barnes has written:

> The impression the company gives is one of joyous youth. They are beautifully trained dancers. The men have a buoyant elegance, with big broad jumps and an attractive stylistic openness. The women have something of the same directness and power. . . . These San Franciscans are such fun. When they dance they put their hearts and muscles into it. They care. It shows.[9]

Kisselgoff points out that, in a recent visit by the San Francisco Ballet to New York, the usual East-to-West trend was reversed. The company's eclectic choreographic works have been widely applauded, ranging from full-length revivals of *Swan Lake* and *The Nutcracker,* to 20th-century classics by Ashton, Balanchine, and other leading choreographers, and newer works

[9]Clive Barnes, "Up and Coming San Franciscans," *The New York Times,* February 27, 1977, p. 15.

by its own composers, including Smuin. Like the Joffrey, the San Francisco company does not rely on a star system; instead, it has attempted to build a true ensemble company, with marked success.[10]

Boston Ballet. A much more recently formed company has been the Boston Ballet, directed by E. Virginia Williams. Originally known as the New England Civic Ballet, this company has received several major Ford Foundation grants, and has developed a strong list of subscribers and a number of bookings that have enabled it to employ its dancers regularly from October through April.

One of the major problems of new ballet companies is the task of building up a repertory for performance. Unlike the situation facing a new opera company, symphony orchestra, or drama group, there is no convenient supply of ballet works as part of a standard repertory, which may readily be performed by such fledgling ballet organizations. The problem is twofold: acquiring rights to the ballet, and also being able to mount it properly. In the case of the Boston, Philadelphia, and Washington compa-

Feld Ballet performance of Elliot Feld's work, *Half-Time,* to music by Morton Gould. Courtesy Shubert Theater, Philadelphia. Photograph by Lois Greenfield.

[10]Anna Kisselgoff, "New Vigor in San Francisco," *The New York Times,* November 19, 1978, p. 19.

nies, Balanchine has made a large number of his own ballets available and has, in some cases, arranged to have leading dancers of the New York City Ballet visit them as guest performers.

Thus, the Boston Ballet has performed Balanchine's *Symphony in C,* and *Apollo,* with Edward Villella and Patricia McBride of the New York company as guest artists. Other works presented by the Boston Ballet have included Talley Beatty's *Phoebe Snow,* David Lichine's *Graduation Ball,* August Bournonville's classic *Flower Festival at Genzano (Pas de Deux),* and new works that were specially choreographed by John Butler, Anna Sokolow, and Joyce Trisler. Over the years, the company has developed a special relationship with Agnes de Mille; in 1977, it gave a special program devoted solely to her works, including *Summer, Logger's Clog, Fall River Legend,* and *Rodeo.*

By the late 1970s, the Boston company consisted of 32 professional performers, augmented by apprentices, paid at union scale, and performing an active repertory of 30 ballets. They are accompanied by the Boston Ballet Orchestra, a professional ensemble of considerable quality. Tobias describes them as stable, with a

> . . . marked cohesiveness of style. The dancers move with delicacy and care—a physical sensitivity, and a fine sense of placement and awareness of line. Their performances are honest, understated . . . happily, with no theatrical or stylistic excesses.[11]

Pennsylvania Ballet. The Pennsylvania Ballet was founded in Philadelphia in 1962, under the direction of Barbara Linshes Weisberger, with George Balanchine as artistic consultant. After only three years, it was providing more continuous employment for its dancers than all but one United States company—the San Francisco Ballet.[12] Its Philadelphia performances are staged at the Academy of Music, and in the 1970s, it also assumed the unique position of being New York City's unofficial fourth major ballet company, by becoming the resident ballet company of the Brooklyn Academy of Music.

A small company, with only about 30 dancers, the Pennsylvania Ballet has nonetheless earned a reputation for versatility. Its repertory includes many ballets by Balanchine, important contemporary works that have been performed by other companies, and a number of original dances specifically choreographed for the Pennsylvania group itself—including works by the company's artistic director, Benjamin Harkavy, and ballets by Gene Hill Sagan, Margo Sappington, and others. The Pennsylvania Ballet had considerable funding support at the outset from the Ford Foundation, which permitted it to develop at its own pace and not be pressured into "fast money, guest-artist" promotions. The company avoids highly publicized guest artists, who tend to diminish the importance of the regular dancers, and to develop audiences with the wrong set of expectations. Weisberger comments:

[11]Toby Tobias, "E. Virginia Williams and the Boston Ballet," *Dance Magazine,* June, 1976, p. 57.

[12]Clive Barnes, *The New York Times,* March 7, 1966.

We do not oppose having guest artists, but we feel that no individual artist should come before the art. . . . We already *have* a star company—every dancer in the company is a star, at different levels.[13]

OTHER AMERICAN BALLET COMPANIES

A number of other American ballet companies have gained distinction through the years. Historically, one of the first opera companies to have a distinct ballet ensemble was the Metropolitan Opera in New York.

Metropolitan Opera. The Metropolitan management has made an effort, through the years, to strengthen its ballet component so that it would be reasonably comparable to the ballet housed in leading European opera houses. During the 1930s, as mentioned earlier, George Balanchine's and Lincoln Kirstein's American Ballet was the opera's ballet unit, and offered separate all-ballet evenings at the Metropolitan. In the early 1950s, as part of an effort to have ballet become an increasingly important part of its staged performances, Janet Collins, a leading black choreographer, assumed leadership of the dance component. Then, for several years, Zachary Solov was responsible for ballet at the opera, and succeeded in mounting exciting ballets as part of such operas as *Eugen Onegin, Samson and Delilah, Carmen, Rigoletto, La Perichole, La Traviata,* and *Faust.* Leading ballerinas of the New York City Ballet, or Ballet Theater, such as Mary Ellen Moylan, Carmen de Lavallade, Alicia Markova, and Melissa Hayden, have appeared in these productions.

In 1963, Markova became director of the Metropolitan Opera Ballet, and succeeded in strengthening its artistic quality. In the late 1970s, Norbert Vesak, a Canadian-born choreographer attached to the Royal Winnipeg Ballet, who had also worked with the San Francisco Opera Ballet, was made artistic director of the Met Ballet. One of his projects was to develop a smaller Opera Ballet Ensemble which would tour as an independent performing unit, thus providing additional employment for the dancers and additional revenue for the ballet operation. However, through the years, dancing at the Metropolitan has generally suffered from the lack of a consistent management policy that would support the building of a strong permanent company, and that would encourage separate ballet performances in the opera house as a regular feature. In general, this has been true of other opera companies throughout the United States, such as those in Chicago and San Francisco, which, although they have given a degree of support to ballet, have seen it essentially as part of the total opera complex, rather than an independent art form.

Ballet West. This company began as the Utah Civic Ballet, with many of its first dancers having been trained in the Department of Ballet of the University of Utah. With the assistance of a Ford Foundation grant, it made

[13]Mark Deitch, "New York's Fourth Major Troupe is a Pennsylvania Import," *The New York Times,* October 23, 1977, p. D-17.

the transition to professional status in the 1960s. Influenced heavily by the Christensen brothers, it tours widely throughout the West and Southwest from its home base in Salt Lake City. It has also made a successful European tour and performed on national television; Olga Maynard comments that it is regarded as the classical ballet company of the Rocky Mountain States.[14] In addition to reviving major works of the past, Ballet West is developing a body of new contemporary choreography in its repertory, under the artistic direction of Bruce Marks. It also offers an intensive summer training program in Aspen/Snowmass, Colorado, where the company gives a summer performance season.

Los Angeles Ballet. Another relatively new company, founded in the early 1970s, the Los Angeles Ballet has toured widely, with the assistance of the Dance Touring Program of the National Endowment for the Arts. However, it also provides substantial seasons in Los Angeles itself as a residential company, with financial support from the City and County of Los Angeles. Under the artistic direction of John Clifford, formerly a leading dancer with the New York City Ballet, it has a considerable number of Balanchine works in its repertoire of approximately 55 ballets.

Ohio Ballet. Founded in 1968 as an ensemble of eight part-time dancers called the Chamber Ballet, this company has expanded to 16 fully professional performers, under the artistic direction of Heinz Poll, a German-born dancer and choreographer. Its repertoire consists mostly of Poll's work, although it also includes varied ballets by Gerald Arpino, Ruthanna Boris, Paul Taylor, and other contemporary choreographers.

What is unusual about the Ohio Ballet is its relationship with the University of Akron's Dance Institute. At first, all company members were students in this program or the university itself, and many of the dancers hold Bachelor of Fine Arts degrees from it. By the late 1970s, the programs were closely integrated. Although the university gives the Ohio Ballet no direct funding, it provides rent-free space, a portion of the artistic director's salary, and services such as utilities, maintenance and storage, all valued at about $50,000 a year. In addition, the company is able to use Thomas Hall, a spectacular university theater built in 1973 at a cost of $13.9 million, for its rehearsals and performances, at the lowest possible rate. In return, Wilma Salisbury points out, the ballet company enhances the cultural image of Akron University by carrying its name on tour and in all promotional materials.[15] Clearly, the Ohio Ballet provides a model of cooperation between the university and the performing arts that other companies and universities might do well to examine.

Atlanta Ballet. A young and growing company in the southern region of the United States, the Atlanta Ballet held its first full season in 1977–1978, featuring a production of *Carmina Burana, Swan Lake Act II, The Nut-*

[14]Olga Maynard, "Ballet in Utah: A Christmas Seminar," *Dance Magazine,* November 1978, p. 26.

[15]Wilma Salisbury, "Akron's Treasure: The Ohio Ballet," *Dance Magazine,* October, 1978, pp. 50–53.

cracker, and other classic works. In addition, the company has been augmented by other Atlanta dance and musical performing groups, and has sponsored performances by premier dancers of the American Ballet and the Pennsylvania Ballet.

Numerous other ballet companies might be described, including the Houston Ballet Foundation, the Milwaukee Ballet Company (which has been featured at the Jacob's Pillow Dance Festival), the Dance Theater of Harlem, directed by Arthur Mitchell, Pittsburgh Ballet Theater, and the Hartford Ballet. To give a fuller picture of the growth of ballet in the United States, it is necessary to look also at what appears to be a uniquely American phenomenon—the development of an extensive network of highly successful regional ballet companies.

REGIONAL BALLET IN THE UNITED STATES

The term "regional ballet" is usually applied to those companies scattered throughout the United States which consist largely of nonsalaried dancers and directors, although their directors may occasionally perform professionally and may indeed have had extensive performing experience. They often are supported by organizations made up of members of the local community who are interested in the arts, and who contribute their services. They provide performance opportunities to local dancers and help to promote ballet interest in their regions of the country. They do not tour nationally, although there is often interchange among regions.

In general, two types of regional ballet companies exist: those whose members come from a single school, and those whose members may come from several schools. Invariably, they are incorporated as nonprofit organizations, and whatever income may be received through performance does not go back to the school, but goes rather to production expenses—costuming, scenery, rent for rehearsal space, and similar costs. Usually such companies require their members to pay annual dues, to sign a contract guaranteeing their commitment to the group, and to observe a rigorous schedule of classes and performances. The majority of members of regional ballet companies are between the ages of 13 and 18, although the range may include somewhat older dancers.

The regional ballet movement began with the formation of the Atlanta Civic Ballet in 1929 by a dedicated teacher and choreographer, Dorothy Alexander. Since then, the movement has swept the country. In 1955 there were 30 such companies, and by 1965, there were over 200 regional ballet groups. The growth continues steadily; in 1966, for example, the Southeastern Regional Ballet Association numbered 22 member companies. In the following year the number climbed to 25; the new groups were the City Center Ballet of Tampa, Florida; the Huntsville, Alabama, Civic Ballet; and the Savannah, Georgia, Civic Ballet.

Typically, the members of regional ballet companies are directed and taught by individuals who have received excellent training themselves and, in many cases, have performed for Ballet Theater, Ballet Russe, and the New York City Ballet. Teaching and directing is a natural outlet for such individuals, once they are past performing age, and may serve as an excellent livelihood. In addition to their efforts, many who join regional companies have been inspired by the highly polished performances of professional touring companies.

Most regional ballet companies offer a series of public performances during the year; sometimes their directors give lectures or demonstrations throughout their region, to heighten interest in ballet.

Other activities of regional ballet companies include publishing newsletters or newspapers, making scenery, and being involved with all the business aspects of scheduling performances. Often non-dancers in the community, such as lawyers, businessmen, and other professionals, are extremely helpful in filling posts or committee chairmanships having to do with publicity, fund raising, transportation, printing of programs and tickets, stage crew tasks, set design and construction, and the like. Typically, the organization chart of the Schenectady Civic Ballet in New York has a board of directors consisting of president, treasurer, secretary, producer, business manager, workshop manager, and artistic director, as well as several vice-presidents assigned specific tasks of administration.

The major problems of regional ballet companies involve raising funds (today, in addition to gate receipts, the Atlanta Civic Ballet gains support from performance fees, membership dues, and contributions from patrons or businesses); recruiting male dancers; and developing an organizational structure so that the professional choreographer-director is free from management and business responsibilities. Increasingly, the larger and more successful regional ballets throughout the country have been able to solve these difficulties.

One of the highlights each year for regional ballet companies is participation in festivals sponsored by regional ballet associations. The Southeast Regional Ballet Association was the first of these to be formed, and it has held an annual festival since 1956. Since then, four other associations have been established—the Northeast, Southwest, Southeast, Pacific and Mid-States Regional Ballet Associations.

In 1963, the National Association for Regional Ballet was founded, and in 1972, it received its first major grant from the National Endowment for the Arts. By the late 1970s, the NARB had 120 member companies; Doris Hering describes their criteria for affiliation:

> [Each member company] consists of at least 12 dancers, had been incorporated for at least one year before applying for membership, and had given at least one performance for a paying public prior to membership. A company may be admitted as a performing member or as an intern member, which means it needs to gain strength.
>
> [To promote professionalism], the NARB has a Professional Wing consisting of those companies that maintain at least 12 paid dancers under contract for 30 weeks or more and that give between 10 and 20 performances a year (theater size being a factor) in their home communities. They also maintain a minimum budget of $120,000 per year and have three people (artistic director, business manager, and technical director) under annual contract.[16]

[16]Doris Hering, "Regional Ballet is on the March," *The New York Times*, April 24, 1977, p. 10-D.

Customarily, yearly fees are paid by member companies to support annual festivals, which represent a climax for the total year's activity. In addition to socializing, master classes, rehearsals, symposiums, and workshops are held, with, of course, the main event being performances by member companies. Works are selected through adjudication by experts, and customarily the general public is admitted to gala performances, while only association members view workshop or showcase performances.

Large audiences, often numbering several thousand, usually view regional ballet festivals, particularly the gala events. In addition, such events frequently offer workshops and special classes for teachers and students. Often these are in areas other than traditional ballet technique; they may include modern dance, jazz, Oriental, and character dancing. The interchange that takes place among directors and teachers provides an important stimulus to the work they carry on in their own regions.

In addition, each year the NARB sponsors two Craft of Choreography Conferences. Past directors of choreography have included such outstanding ballet and modern dance artists and choreographers as Mary Hinkson, Pauline Koner, Glen Tetley, Birgit Cullberg, and Bella Lewitsky. Emphasis is given to dance technique and improvisation, music, lighting, costume design, and choreographic problem-solving, within a workshop setting, with lecture–demonstrations by leading experts. Each year, these 14-day conferences are carefully evaluated by the NARB Board of Directors and the National Endowment for the Arts, before plans are made for the following year's faculty and location.

The goals of regional ballet companies are varied. However, a fairly representative statement of purpose is that of the Richmond, Virginia, Ballet Impromptu:

1. To establish a regional ballet company which shall be adjudicated in festival competition.
2. To present ballet programs of the highest quality for adults and children.
3. To elevate the art of the regional performing dancer to the highest degree possible.
4. To provide a medium of expression for regional choreographers, designers, musicians, and dancers.
5. To stimulate interest and support of ballet and ballet schools.
6. To solicit, and raise funds to further these purposes.[17]

Probably the fifth purpose, that of stimulating interest and support of ballet, is of greatest importance to those concerned with the expansion of dance as a performing art today. The growth of larger, professional companies around the United States must in large measure be supported by the existence of knowledgeable and enthusiastic audiences, young and old, throughout the country. Without question, a major contribution of the regional ballet movement has been to develop such audiences—and in this effort they have been highly successful.

[17]Doris Hering, "Framework for a Regional Ballet," *Dance Magazine,* October, 1958, p. 49.

A final influence which must be commented upon is the continuing presence of a wide variety of performing groups from other lands, on American concert stages. Ever since the colonial period in this country, foreign companies have toured in American theaters. Often, with indigenous theater dance so weak, it was the glamorous importation of dancers such as Fanny Elssler or Anna Pavlova which continued to inspire American audiences and to keep ballet interest alive. Today, with a flourishing group of native companies, they are no longer needed for this purpose. However, without question, the international ballet companies that tour the United States each year serve other valuable purposes. They offer performers, works, and artistic styles that are quite different from our own companies, and so provide a basis for contrast—or a comparison of quality. In general, they are divided into two categories: those companies which have been founded in a classic ballet tradition (although their works may have a strong modern flavor), and those which are essentially rooted in folk or ethnic materials, and which may be performed either by balletically trained dancers, in carefully choreographed works, or in their original forms.

Typically, in the first group, one would include such major companies as the Leningrad Kirov Ballet and the Bolshoi Ballet of Moscow, the Royal Ballet of England, the Stuttgart Ballet of Germany, and the Royal Danish Ballet. In the second are such companies as the Hungarian National Ballet; Kolo, the Yugoslav company; the Ballet Folklorico of Mexico; the Moiseyev Dance Company of Russia; Antonio and his Ballets de Madrid; the Philippine Folk Dance company, Bayanihan; and many smaller companies or solo performers, particularly of Oriental and Eastern dance forms.

Bolshoi Ballet. For most of its history, the Bolshoi Ballet of Moscow was regarded as second to the more celebrated Maryinsky Ballet in St. Petersburg. Even today, there is a strong feeling of competition between the Bolshoi, and Leningrad's Kirov Ballet, as the Maryinsky is now called. Yet, most regard the Bolshoi as preeminent today. It is a huge company; when it came to America several years ago, it brought over 135 dancers and sent its famous ballet master, Asaf Messerer, six weeks in advance of the rest of the group to train an additional 65 American dancers for lesser roles in such giant spectacles as the full-length *Spartacus.*

It is brilliantly trained in the classical ballet technique; one critic has commented that, with their better-subsidized schools, the Russians have a tremendous advantage in the development of sheer dancing ability.[18] The general level of Russian performance is superb; the men in particular are capable of dancing with great zest and vigor—in an almost flamboyant style, and with unbelievable athleticism. The ballerinas of the Bolshoi, Galina Ulanova (as legendary for her time as Pavlova) and in more recent years, Raissa Struchkova and the magnificent Maya Plisetskaya, are among the very top rank of world dancers. The productions are splendid, and the entire effect highly theatrical.

[18]Clive Barnes, *The New York Times, Theater Section,* May 8, 1966, p. 6-X.

Yet, for years, those visitors who saw the Bolshoi perform in Moscow, or who saw it when it visited Western Europe in 1956, or embarked on its first tour to the United States in 1959, were highly critical of its choreography. Of all the nations of the world, Russia, which underwent a national revolution in 1917, has been the most determinedly conservative in its approach to the arts. This has had two effects on its ballet choreography. First, it has continued until recently to base its repertoire very heavily upon the great works of the Romantic era—such ballets as *Giselle, The Sleeping Beauty, Raymonda, Swan Lake,* and *Don Quixote.* Even when works have been choreographed in fairly recent times, they have dealt heavily with bird-maidens, gnomes, goblins, fairy princesses and godmothers, and pastoral romances.

A second preoccupation in more recent choreography has been dramatic subject matter that served the point of view of the Soviet state. Just as in Russian painting, literature, and sculpture, the ballets are expected to contribute in some way to Socialist ideology; Russians are serious about their art, and usually expect that it present a recognizable image or narrative. The leading choreographer of the Bolshoi, Yuri Grigorovich, commented that while he regarded pure classical ballet as the "highest form of dance," for him this did not mean plotless ballet:

> While I feel there can exist, must exist, dance form without subject matter, for myself I am interested in the total theatrical aspect, in a ballet theater that has a literary as well as a dance component.[19]

And, whenever possible, this literary component must be made to support Soviet doctrine. Thus, *Romeo and Juliet,* choreographed in 1946 by Lavrovsky, has been interpreted as an aspect of the class struggle; the Soviet ballet version of *Othello,* produced by Chabukiani, has similarly been seen as an example of racial conflict.

The initial impression many had of the Bolshoi's choreography was that it was ponderous, tedious, and, while technically excellent, so stodgy and traditional that it represented a throwback to the 19th century. Hering commented in 1959:

> Sometimes we felt as though we were returning to a neglected and worthy esthetic—the esthetic of realism. Sometimes that very realism seemed to be nothing more than a repository for outmoded sets, costumes and gestures . . . their reliance upon narrative mime seemed uncomfortably melodramatic . . . sometimes their approach to pure dance passages was merely athletic, with no sense of character revelation or dramatic furtherance. . . .[20]

Gradually, however, as the Bolshoi dancers and choreographers have been exposed to the performances of British and American companies—including the Jerome Robbins State Department tour of Russia in the early 1960s—they appear to have broadened their view of choreographic possibilities. While they still mount huge spectacles and present revivals of classi-

[19]Yuri Grigorovich, quoted in "The Fresh New Look of the Bolshoi," by Clive Barnes, *The New York Times,* May 15, 1966, p. D-5.

[20]Doris Hering, "First Impressions of the Bolshoi Ballet," *Dance Magazine,* June 1959, p. 38.

cal works as a major feature of their repertory, they are demonstrating a greater level of inventiveness, adventurousness, and humor. However, even fairly recently, in a review of the Bolshoi's latest version of *Spartacus,* Marcia Siegel commented that the work's rigid formalism, high speed, high intensity dancing, and mechanical use of groups of dancers led ultimately to a sense of monotony that overcame one's appreciation of the undeniably brilliant dancing.[21] Among the Bolshoi's leading performers in recent years have been Natalia Bessmerthova, Ekaterina Maximova, Ludmilla Semenyaka, Vladimir Vassiliev, Mikail Lavrovsky, and Vyachislav Gordeyev, dancers who would be in the first rank of any company in the world.

Kirov Ballet. In many ways, the Kirov Ballet in Leningrad is comparable to the Bolshoi; the dancers are equally superb and the productions equally lavish. The major difference is that the Kirov is less flamboyant and more reserved than the Bolshoi, characterized by an air of elegant style—a "pure line, musicality, and a restrained and aristocratic bearing." It has produced many of Russia's leading choreographers, including Vachtang Chabukiani, Rotislav Zakharov, and Grigorovich.

Among its leading dancers in recent years have been Natalia Dudinskaya, Irina Kolpakhova, Alla Sizova, Vladilen Semenov, Yuri Soloviev, Konstantin Sergeyev—and four of the world's outstanding performers who have all defected to the West—Rudolf Nureyev, who left in 1961, and Natalia Makarova, Mikhail Baryshnikov, and Valery Panov, who came to America in the early and mid-1970s. Their departure was evidence of the cultural isolation and sterility of the Soviet ballet. Bland points out that the Bolshoi and Kirov Ballets seek to:

> . . . shut out all foreign elements and exist entirely on their own native talent, using nothing but Russian dancers performing Russian choreography to Russian music in Russian decors. . . . (resulting in) the dissatisfaction of individual dancers, artistic conservatism and the lack of creative urge.[22]

Yet, there is little question that the Soviet ballet system has been successful in creating a number of the world's most magnificent dancers. The reason lies in the Russian system of ballet instruction. This is carried on through state-supported, controlled schools throughout the member republics of the Soviet Union. Often, those pupils who are most talented find their way to the major centers of dance, such as Moscow or Leningrad, to complete their training and to join the Soviet's top companies. Rudolf Nureyev, in his autobiography, tells of his training in the Kirov School, before he joined the company, achieved stardom, and ultimately fled to the West. It was a highly conservative establishment, in which students worked between 8 and 11 hours a day, starting early in the morning. There were usually two hours of instruction in art history and aesthetics each day, and then two hours of literature. This was followed by two hours of classical dance instruction which, in his words, was "so concentrated, so well pre-

[21]Marcia B. Siegel, *Watching the Dance Go By* (Boston: Houghton Mifflin Co., 1977), pp. 93–95.

[22]Alexander Bland, *A History of Ballet and Dance in the Western World* (New York: Praeger Book Co., 1976), p. 107.

pared, and so absorbing that one session there was worth four hours' instruction anywhere else in Europe."[23] In the afternoon, students were given two hours on the history of the ballet and the history of music, and then another two hours of dancing, this time "character" work. In addition, academic courses were also scheduled during the week in physics, chemistry, geography, and similar subjects, as well as regular lessons in fencing. In the evenings, students would often observe rehearsals of the Kirov company, or see actual performances in the theater next door.

The competition was severe and the discipline rigid. The sense of uncertainty or lack of societal approval that affects many dance students in the West (in the sense that they recognize that the career they have chosen lacks widely accepted status) never affected Nureyev. He wrote:

> The fact that ballet teaching in Russia is such a scrupulously regulated profession is, I believe, the main reason for our ballet's consistent high standard. Many European dancers (I don't know yet about the American ones) go endlessly from one studio to another in a misguided search for innovations and amplifications of their technique—and not always to teachers fully qualified for their work. The end result of amateur teachers in charge of shaping amateur dancers is that ballet gradually loses its purity and splendid traditions.
>
> How different in Russia! How severely controlled, how strongly rooted in tradition is the profession of the ballet teacher![24]

In a sense, the same conservatism that accounted for the unwillingness to venture into new choreographic directions is responsible for the rigid but productive system that creates a Nureyev—as well as a great number of other brilliant Soviet dancers. And it becomes understandable that an artist as individual as Nureyev, with extremes of temperament and deeply felt artistic conviction, would find it impossible to live under the Soviet system and would leave, first for Great Britain and ultimately to the United States.

Royal Ballet. Of all the great foreign ballet companies, perhaps the most familiar to American audiences has been the Royal Ballet, both under its present name, and as the Sadler's Wells Theater Ballet, the name under which it first came to the United States. Although it was not actually founded until just after World War II, this company had its roots in 1926 when Ninette de Valois established a ballet school in London, shortly after leaving the Diaghileff Company. For a period of years, she staged the ballets which were produced at the Old Vic Theater, and, when the new Sadler's Wells Theater was built, de Valois was asked to found a school there. She did so in 1931. The students of the Sadler's Wells Ballet School, known as the Vic-Wells Ballet, continued to dance at the Old Vic and in operas given at the Sadler's Wells. This went on into the 1940s; during the war, the company performed at the New Theater, under the worst bombing raids, and so helped to maintain the morale of Londoners.

After the war, in 1946, the company began to perform at the Covent Garden Royal Opera House, rapidly gaining in public and critical esteem.

[23]Rudolf Nureyev, "Nureyev: An Autobiography," *Dance Magazine,* May, 1966, p. 40.

[24]*Ibid.,* p. 42.

One reason underlying its success was that many of the dancers during the 1930s had performed in Marie Rambert's Ballet Club in London, which later became the Ballet Rambert. In this setting, many of the most distinguished figures in British ballet, such as Frederick Ashton and Antony Tudor, made their choreographic debuts. In it too, dozens of younger British dancers received their early professional experience.

It was the wartime service of the Sadler's Wells Theater Ballet that won for the company the affection of the British public and a later government subsidy (under the Arts Council of Great Britain) and, finally, the Royal Charter, in 1956. During the late 1940s and early 1950s, the company performed over thirty ballets by Ninette de Valois; Frederick Ashton's *Facade, Les Rendez-vous, Apparitions, Nocturne, Les Patineurs;* Robert Helpmann's *Comus, Hamlet, Miracle in the Gorbals;* a number of works by other choreographers, and classic ballets such as *Swan Lake, Giselle, Coppelia, The Nutcracker, Les Sylphides, Carnaval, Le Spectre de la Rose,* and similar works.

When, in 1951, the Sadler's Wells Theater Ballet toured the United States for the third time, it consisted of an extremely young company—the average age of the dancers was 18. A new choreographer, John Cranko, had created works that were now highlights of the repertoire: *Sea Change, Harlequin in April, The Fairy Queen,* and *Pineapple Poll.* Ashton's own works, including musical abstractions such as *Symphonic Variations* and *Scènes de Ballet,* the superb coronation ballet, *Homage to the Queen,* and *Birthday Offering,* created in celebration of the 25th anniversary of the ballet company, had become masterpieces of the British company's repertoire.

The Royal Ballet continued through the 1960s with an outstanding cast of superbly skilled dancers and an extremely diverse repertoire. Thus, in 1967, it revived Nijinska's powerful *Les Noces* (first performed four decades before by the Diaghileff ballet); it continues to have new works by Antony Tudor *(Shadowplay)* and Ashton (*The Dream,* a one-act version of Shakespeare's *A Midsummer Night's Dream*); Kenneth MacMillan's *Song of the Earth;* a new production by Ashton of *Cinderella; Paradise Lost* by Roland Petit; and many other works both classic and modern.

There is a degree of concern in Britain about the future of the Royal Ballet, in terms of its ability to maintain consistently a strong repertoire for the company. In the view of many, Sir Frederick Ashton, who succeeded Ninette de Valois as director in 1963, while a brilliant choreographer, failed to do justice to his own work, or to draw a clear-cut artistic policy for others. Ashton was succeeded by Kenneth MacMillan in 1970 as artistic director.

The dancing of the Royal Ballet has continued to be outstanding. For a number of years, the leading dancers were Rudolf Nureyev and Margot Fonteyn, both classified as guest artists, and possessing much the same glamor as Nijinsky and Pavlova in their day. Among the leading dancers in the 1960s were Svetlana Beriosova, Merle Park, Antoinette Sibley and, among the men, Anthony Dowell, David Wall, Michael Koleman, and Kenneth Mason. In the 1970s, Dowell and Sibley replaced Nureyev and Fonteyn as the Royal Ballet's leading dancers.

In the 1960s and 1970s, the Royal Ballet made a number of extensive tours of the United States. Perhaps its major effect was in the introduction of full-evening spectacle ballets. At first, Americans who were accustomed to having three short, separate works in a program, found this difficult to accept. However, after exposure to the Royal Ballet, with its full-evening *Sleeping Beauty, Swan Lake,* and *Cinderella,* as well as similar long works by the two Russian companies, the New York City Ballet and American Ballet Theater have also begun to produce full-evening works. Although a number of Ashton's works, which had dominated the company's repertoire, were dropped in the 1970s, he has continued to choreograph for it from time to time, with one of his most successful recent works the lovely *A Month in the Country.* Among other recent works performed by the Royal Ballet have been MacMillan's *Anastasia* and Jerome Robbins's *Dances at a Gathering.*

A final comment on the relationship between the British and American ballets is that it has been heavily one-sided. Thus, although the Royal Ballet had frequently been to America, British audiences had seen only one two-week season by an American company during the decade preceding 1967. This may in part be due to the narrow loyalty of the British public; undoubtedly too, it is related to the fact that the British company is subsidized. Also, Sol Hurok was extremely active in bringing foreign importations to America, whereas in Britain and Europe there has been no private impresario with comparable enthusiasm and ability.

There are, of course, other British companies of distinguished reputation. Actually, the Royal Ballet has a second company which is approximately the same size as the Covent Garden Company. This "other" Royal Ballet spends most of its time touring through the British provinces and on the Continent; it also has an occasional London season at Covent Garden.

In England, there is also the Festival Ballet which performs in the Royal Festival Hall on London's south bank. Founded by Anton Dolin and Alicia Markova in 1949, this is essentially a touring company which, like the American Ballet Theater, has had difficulty in maintaining a company of high quality and a diverse, well produced repertory of ballets. Like the American company, it has shown much improvement recently, and thus offers promise for the British ballet scene.

Royal Danish Ballet. Another internationally famous company which comes close in stature to the Russian and British companies just described is the Royal Danish Ballet. The history of this company is an ancient one. It was founded in 1748 and has been under royal patronage since that time. The school in which its young dancers are trained was founded in 1829 by August Bournonville, who was responsible for the initial development of the company, whose repertoire of classic ballets is still performed by the company, and whose system of dance training still gives the graduates of the Royal Danish Ballet School a unique character.

Since the middle of the 19th century, the Royal Danish Ballet has continued to perform such Bournonville works as *Napoli, Konservatoriet, Far from Denmark,* and *Valdemar.* While it had produced a number of outstanding dancers and excellent new works under the direction of its ballet master during the 1940s, Harald Lander, the company was not widely known. Then, after the first annual ballet festival in Copenhagen in 1950, it began to tour more widely. When it visited the United States for the first time in 1956, it received high praise from American critics. Typically, Hering wrote:

> Their pure dance passages are meticulously hewn. And their acting is a human experience. Americans are known for their realistic acting in modern works.

> But the Danes have found a way of extending this style into the traditional ballets, so that even the oldest ones like *La Sylphide* and *Napoli* (both more than a century old) emerge curiously alive and convincing. And from an acting point of view the Danes are equally at home in contemporary works like Frederick Ashton's *Romeo and Juliet* and Balanchine's *La Sonnambula.* . . .[25]

In summarizing the strengths and weaknesses of the Royal Danish Ballet, the question of its repertoire has often been raised. Chiefly, it has consisted of the Bournonville works, a number of other classic ballets, and several modern ballets drawn from choreographers of other nations. For example, in its repertoire in the middle 1960s, the Danish company included: Roland Petit's *Carmen,* Jerome Robbins's *Fanfare,* Frederick Ashton's *Romeo and Juliet,* David Lichine's *Graduation Ball,* and other works by Kenneth MacMillan, Balanchine, and other modern choreographers. Recently, several new works, including two ballets by Flemming Flindt (*The Private Lesson* and *Three Musketeers*) have been introduced into the repertoire. Also, the Danes have veered into avant-garde experimentation with such works as *Tropisms,* choreographed by Eske Holm to "serial" music, Ivo Cramer's *Catharsis,* and *Cleopatra,* by the American modern dance choreog-

Stars of the Royal Danish Ballet. Courtesy Shubert Theater, Philadelphia.

[25]Doris Hering, "The Danes: An American Debut," *Dance Magazine,* November, 1956, p. 14.

rapher, Murray Louis, both accompanied by electronic music. While the Royal Danish Ballet has a curious gift for endowing the works of other companies, periods, and national origins with a uniquely different style and manner, its problem clearly will be to establish a modern Danish repertory to accompany the Bournonville works that are its unique trademark.

In terms of dancing, the Danish dancers reflect their Bournonville heritage: it is a style that requires both stamina and strong technique. Leaps have extra bounce and spring, and the footwork is brilliant and precise. Probably the best known Danish dancer of the modern era has been Erik Bruhn, who performed with a number of major companies throughout the world. Other leading dancers have been Henning Kronstam, Niels Larsen, Peter Martins, and Helgi Tomasson among the men, and Anna Laerkesen, Viveka Segerskog, and Ruth Andersen among the women. A number of leading Danish performers have joined American companies, and the New York City Ballet has given special performances of Bournonville's choreography staged by Stanley Williams, who was formerly with the Royal Danish Ballet.

Under Flemming Flindt's direction during the late 1970s, the Danish Ballet has given seasons at New York's Metropolitan Opera House and in Washington, D.C., and has been featured in ensemble form at Jacob's Pillow in Massachusetts.

Canadian Ballet. There are three strong companies at present in Canada, including the National Ballet of Canada (the largest and most firmly established), the Royal Winnipeg Ballet (the oldest company in the country, about the size of the Joffrey Ballet), and Les Grands Ballets Canadiens from the Province of Quebec. All three companies are subsidized by the Canada Council, a program for support of the arts that is modeled after the Arts Council of Great Britain. The National Ballet, which is viewed as one of Canada's leading arts institutions, receives 38 percent of its annual budget from the government; in return, it is regarded as a "diplomatic service with a national obligation" for touring and giving performances from Halifax to Vancouver. In addition, the companies receive funding from provincial governments and are able to raise substantial contributions from private industry.

The National Ballet in particular has been heavily influenced by the Royal Ballet of Britain; it was formed after a visit of the Royal Ballet to Toronto, and was directed for a number of years by Celia Franca, formerly a dancer with the British company. Gradually, it grew in professional stature and today, under the artistic direction of Alexander Grant—also with strong Royal Ballet connections—it is regarded as an excellent company, on par with Stuttgart, Joffrey, Paris Opéra, and Dutch National Ballet. It has featured both Rudolf Nureyev and Erik Bruhn as guest artists on tour. One of its weaknesses, as Clive Barnes points out, is that it is required to tour so heavily, and it must perform before audiences with little knowledge of ballet, that strongly prefer the older, classic full-evening ballets. To be a recognized major company, it is necessary to have three things: "a classic repertory, significant 20th century revivals, and indigenous works."[26] Thus

[26]Clive Barnes, "Future Prospects for the Canadians," *The New York Times,* November 28, 1976, p. D-42.

far, at least, none of the Canadian companies have been successful in producing new choreographic works of recognized value.

Ballet in France. In France, long considered the birthplace of ballet, there has not been a major ballet company for several decades. The last one, under Diaghileff, was, of course, composed chiefly of Russian dancers. Two French choreographers of considerable promise have emerged in recent years. Roland Petit achieved fame in the late 1940s and early 1950s, choreographing a number of extremely appealing works for *Les Ballets des Champs-Élysées.* However, the critical consensus is that he never matured fully as a choreographer. While he has continued to create a number of important works for other ballet companies, Petit certainly did not succeed in developing a strong French ballet. Maurice Béjart, another dramatically forceful French choreographer, has produced several enthusiastically received modern works, and is presently attached to a Brussels company, the Ballet of the Twentieth Century. Béjart has become known for a theatrical style of choreography, often with works that resemble a sort of "pop-ballet," suited for performance in huge amphitheaters. Béjart has a special appeal for many young Americans, which Barnes explains as due to his "feeling for ritual, . . . his Orientalism, his use of beautiful bodies, his abstractly poetic themes, the sense his company gives of being more of a commune than a troupe . . ."[27]

The historic Paris Opéra Ballet has continued to produce ballet through the years, both as part of the operas themselves and as independent productions. For almost 30 years, Serge Lifar, who had been a leading dancer with Diaghileff, was director of the Opéra Ballet and choreographed many of its works. One interpretation of the failure of French ballet to achieve a greater reputation in the modern era is that the close connection between ballet and opera has tended to encourage choreographic novelty and sensationalism for its own sake—almost a frivolous and dilettantish attitude toward the production of new works.

In such a situation, ballet has not flourished as an independent art, and works of choreographers of the stature of Balanchine or Ashton have rarely been performed. In the late 1960s, George Skibine joined the Opera Ballet as a leading dancer and choreographer, and greater emphasis was put on diversifying the company's works. However, ballet at the Opéra continued to be poorly supported and viewed as an artistic "fifth wheel" through the 1970s. In 1977, Violette Verdy, a French-born ballerina and star of the New York City Ballet, was appointed as artistic director, in an attempt to upgrade the Opéra's ballet component.

OTHER EUROPEAN BALLET COMPANIES

Other companies are to be found in most of the larger European cities, as well as in many smaller ones. Typically, they are attached to the local opera house, performing during the opera season (which may last as long as 10 or 11 months) and also producing evenings of ballet performance, or

[27]Clive Barnes, "Coming to Terms with Béjart's Theatricality," *The New York Times,* April 10, 1977, p. D-9.

scheduling ballet seasons of their own. Two such companies are to be found at the Bavarian Staatsoper in Munich and La Scala in Milan. Both companies maintain schools from which dancers enter the corps de ballet. They are fairly sizable; the Munich Staatsoper has 70 dancers, and La Scala a company of 46.

Both companies perform an international repertory, including a number of classic works as well as many dances by leading foreign choreographers. When possible, they invite the choreographer himself to stage his own work. Both at such occasions and at annual Festival Weeks, major choreographers from Britain, America, and the Soviet Union have come to Munich to stage their ballets—along with outstanding guest performers.

Independent ballet companies also exist in Holland (the Dutch National Ballet and the Netherlands Dance Theater); in Germany a company which has increasingly gained international recognition, (the Stuttgart Ballet); Sweden (the Royal Swedish Ballet); the member republics of the Soviet Union; and other European and South American countries. The Australian ballet has flourished during recent years, and Israel, Cuba, Mexico, Brazil, and Venezuela have all become active in hosting touring ballet companies and developing their own dance theaters.

Increasingly, as major companies tour from country to country and as both dancers and choreographers move from company to company, the idea of unique national ballet styles tends to be less supportable. Certainly, the Russian ballet is marked by an impressive virtuosity of technique, while the Danish ballet continues to be recognized because of its firm foundation in Bournonville technique. However, although such distinctions exist, by and large, the international trend in dancing tends to blend previously marked stylistic differences from country to country. Instead, the differences that exist among companies tend to result from the influence of artistic directors and dancers. Kisselgoff writes:

> . . . style in ballet, as in any art, is a direct result of creative influence. . . . (that of) the individuals who have shaped that company. Indeed, there is no "American style" in classical ballet; the three major American companies all differ in their styles. The New York City Ballet, for example, dances the way it does because that is how George Balanchine wants it to dance. . . . similarly, the Joffrey Ballet's style was fashioned by Robert Joffrey, and American Ballet Theater's by . . . Michel Fokine and Antony Tudor . . . (and) the Royal Ballet (by) Frederick Ashton . . .[28]

INTERNATIONAL FESTIVALS AND COMPETITIONS

A relatively new influence on ballet throughout the world, reflecting the growth of popular interest in it, has been the emergence of international festivals and competitions that attract great numbers of performers and balletomanes. For example, the International Ballet Competition held in the ancient city and modern resort of Varna, Bulgaria, on the Black Sea, has

[28]Anna Kisselgoff, "There is Nothing 'National' About Ballet Styles," *The New York Times*, December 12, 1976, p. D-15.

been called the "Olympics of dance." Hundreds of dancers in separate age categories perform before a panel of jurors from 20 nations, headed by outstanding choreographers. As evidence of the quality of such competitions, winners in the past have included stars like Mikhail Baryshnikov, the Bolshoi's Ekaterina Maximova and Vladimir Vasiliev; Hungary's Ivan Nagy and Canada's Martine van Hamel; and America's Fernando Bujones, all of whom became leading dancers with major world companies.

Other important competitions are held in Moscow and Japan; the World Ballet Concours held every two years in Tokyo has the pomp and circumstance of a national event, attended by royalty and leading government figures. Contestants perform solos and *pas de deux,* with excerpts being taken both from the classical repertoire and from major contemporary ballet works. In the late 1970s, International Ballet Festivals were established in the United States, in Chicago and Jackson, Mississippi, and it seems likely that such events will continue to grow in number.

While they are a reflection of the worldwide growth of interest in ballet, they tend also to promote the growing trend toward internationalism in ballet. The nomadism of dance companies and of performers and choreographers, and the sharing of an increasingly common contemporary repertoire, has meant that a new sort of international ballet has come into being. Superstars like Baryshnikov, Makarova, Nureyev, Bruhn and others travel from country to country, doing a special performance here, or a brief season there. Often they tend to influence the style and standards of the indigenous company with whom they perform. Choreographers are commissioned to create works across national lines, often incorporating modern dance approaches and techniques. Thus, the world of ballet has continued to expand dramatically, and to achieve a new level of appeal that takes it far beyond the rather narrow, upper-class or highbrow audience of the past.

However, it has become increasingly clear that this art is one which—while it may arouse widespread interest and attendance—has great difficulty in supporting itself properly in a financial sense. It is unlike the legitimate theater, which may have as few as a handful of actors and a single set or two. Instead, a ballet company with an extensive repertoire must have a large number of dancers (Britain's Royal Ballet has about 140 dancers, and the Bolshoi in Moscow actually has over 240), plus different sets and costumes for each work that is to be performed, and an orchestra that in some cases is a full-scale symphony orchestra. Under these circumstances, even granted a full house, or a close-to-capacity audience throughout its home and touring season, ballet must operate at a considerable deficit. The alternatives of charging admission prices that are so high that much of the potential audience is excluded or of having subscription series that insure a regular, capacity attendance, are at least partially self-defeating.

In part, the problem has been met by some companies through offering special seasons or performances which highlight stars such as Nureyev or Baryshnikov; these may be specially priced and usually attract capacity audiences. However, this approach tends to undermine the artistic integrity of the company itself, which serves chiefly as a backdrop for the visiting artist, and which is pressured to offer works which the public at large will readily accept, rather than to explore new choreographic directions which may be less popular at the box office.

The alternative of having foundation grants or governmental support for specific dance projects, or of receiving grants to support special aspects of touring, training, or production, is becoming increasingly recognized as a desirable solution for the support of the performing arts. Later chapters will describe this pattern of foundation and government support for dance—both modern dance and ballet—as it has evolved in recent years.

11 Modern Dance Today

As the preceding chapter has shown, ballet has acquired an extremely broad audience in the United States since mid-century. Many professional companies and organizations have been formed throughout the country—often with major public subsidies or foundation grants—and a broad network of regional performing ballet companies has been established. A number of these companies now can assure their dancers 30 or more weeks of paid employment through the year, in addition to special tours and other performances.

Modern dance has not yet achieved this level of public acceptance and support. There are many more modern dance companies today than there were three decades ago, and there is certainly a sharply expanded number of performances, particularly in larger cities and on university campuses. Indeed dance education in American colleges has grown tremendously, with most programs giving primary emphasis to modern dance. In terms of worldwide influence, American modern dance companies have toured successfully throughout Europe, the Far East, and in other regions to enthusiastic acclaim.

However, it is clear that, when compared to ballet, interest in modern dance is relatively much narrower throughout the United States. The public—with the exception of those exposed to this aspect of dance in colleges and universities, or those who are generally interested in the arts—tends to be much less informed about modern dance than ballet. There are no companies with the stability and support of the major ballet companies, nor have any, lacking strong support from citizens' groups, been identified with the communities that support them. As a result, the status of the modern dance choreographer–performer has not improved significantly since mid-century. Although a number of choreographers or company directors have been able to gather sufficient funding from government programs assisting the arts, it is still extremely difficult to earn a livelihood in the field of modern dance unless one's income is supplemented through teaching.

Certain changes have taken place in the field itself. First, in terms of approaches to choreography, there appear to be three distinct groups active today. The first consists of those artists or companies who were active and successful before mid-century, and who have continued to maintain their companies and to develop as creative artists. The second consists of those dancer–choreographers who developed reputations since 1950, and who are continuing to move ahead in exciting new directions. The third group consists of those avant-garde experimenters who, like their counterparts in "op" or "pop" art, have developed radically new approaches, often creating works that are so improvised in nature, or so lacking in the qualities that have traditionally been considered part of dance, that they might almost be regarded as *anti*dance, or *non*-dance.

The general tenor of modern dance purpose or philosophy seems also to have changed through the years. The early modern dancers were in a sense crusaders who sought to create a new, vital, uniquely American form of dance. This purpose does not seem to exist today. Nor has the psychoanalytically oriented view of dance as a means of emotional catharsis or release continued as a primary motivation. Today, most modern dancers regard what they are doing as a disciplined art form, and not simply as a convenient means of emotional release. Other dancers, particularly the more experimental ones, seem concerned chiefly with developing new forms of movement or ways of using sound and visual effects, objects, and events from everyday life, as the basis for creating dance. In Marcia Siegel's words:

> Some of the most interesting dance of our time is classifiable as dance only because it doesn't fit anywhere else. . . . Today's experimental dancers frequently do not dance. They seldom employ music, and when they do, they don't use it as accompaniment for their dancing or non-dancing. They hardly ever dance, or non-dance, in theaters. Their structures, content, methods, and means not only exist outside the usual channels of dance production but call into question the nature of dance itself. Yet this is not a destructive revolution. . . . Experimental dance today is affirmative and challenging.[1]

Rapprochement with Ballet. What other shifts have occurred? The most marked change is that modern dancers are rarely as opposed to training in ballet technique as they were at the beginning of the modern dance period. Instead, many recognize the fundamental value of classic dance technique. In a number of other ways, the gulf that existed between modern dance and ballet has now been bridged; ballet choreography has been markedly influenced by modern dance approaches, and a number of leading modern dancers have been commissioned to design works for major ballet companies. Indeed, all contemporary ballet clearly reflects the influence of modern dance as a vital creative force.

It would be a mistake to suggest that because modern dance has not been as successful in gaining popular support and understanding as ballet,

[1]Marcia B. Siegel, *At The Vanishing Point, A Critic Looks at Dance* (New York: Saturday Review Press, 1972), p. 247.

it has failed in its mission. Any art form that is at the cutting edge of creative discovery tends to limit its audience by definition. At the same time, much of what is being done by the more experimental modern dancers today is universal in its appeal and has meaning for all those open to aesthetic experience, whether or not they have had direct background in the arts. In a sense, as a later section of this chapter will show, modern dance has become closely intertwined with a whole new philosophy of life and art, linked to the human potential movement and to a humanistic approach to culture and self-actualization.

To fully understand the modern dance scene today, it is necessary to examine each of the three major groups of contemporary dancers and choreographers, beginning with the pre-eminent figure in America modern dance, Martha Graham.

MARTHA GRAHAM

Through the 1960s and 1970s, Graham's company continued to represent a major influence among modern dancers—almost like that of George Balanchine in the professional ballet field. Graham's prestige and identity have been so well established that among audiences that would otherwise not see modern dance, she is accepted and appreciated. Through the many dancers who had been in her company for a period of years and who then became choreographers and teachers themselves, her technique and artistic viewpoint became widely disseminated. Particularly in dance education in schools and colleges, her influence has been pervasive.

What changes occurred in Graham's approach to choreography and performance through the years? In her last years of creative original work, she was concerned only with creating major dance–dramas made, in Doris Hering's words, "to last." There was a sharp contrast between the choreography designed for the rest of the company, which was more opulent, more pulsating, more swift, and that which she designed for herself, which was more fragmentary, less flowing, and less demanding.[2]

A number of her dances choreographed in the 1960s tended to be less weighty or serious than the earlier works. While not to be regarded as "fillers" or pleasant trifles, they tended to be abstract in mood or to reveal a satirical bite. Some, like *Acrobats of God,* a lively and joyful comedy piece about herself and dance, were of this category. Others, notably *Part Dream, Part Real; Circe;* and *Phaedra,* had a marked erotic quality, justified by the dramatic content of the work. Overall, her works continued to be impressively staged, superbly choreographed, and danced by a company of unmatched dancing skill and physical attractiveness.

The Graham Company continued to receive impressive financial support from varied sources. For example, in the late 1960s, a substantial grant from the Lila Acheson Wallace Foundation made possible her three-week season in New York; two new works presented at this time, *Dancing-Ground* and *Cortège of Eagles,* were financed by a grant from the National Council on

[2]Doris Hering, "What Sorrow Is There That Is Not Mine?" *Dance Magazine,* May 1967, p. 55.

Martha Graham and Company in *Clytemnestra.* Photograph by Martha Swope.

the Arts. Graham's school and company have continued to be financed through the years by the de Rothschild Foundation.

As she approached 80, Graham went through a two-year period of illness and disassociation from her work. Then, in 1972, she returned to her company, having made two major decisions—she would not perform again (although she would continue to choreograph and appear on stage as commentator), and she would help her company reconstruct her old works. In her Broadway season in the spring of 1973, for example, seven dances were revived, including the full-length *Clytemnestra,* along with two new Graham works. It was her hope to bring back a substantial number of the approximately 150 dances she had created since 1926, and to film and notate many of them as a permanent record. This policy has been continued; in 1977, for example, the company presented five major revivals: *Primitive Mysteries, Plain of Prayer, Deaths and Entrances, Phaedra,* and *Dark Meadow,* many of them carried out with former dancers from all phases and periods of Graham's career assisting in the reconstruction.

Martha Graham and Company in *The Lady of the House of Sleep.* Photograph by Martha Swope.

In the mid-1970s, the Graham company was joined by Rudolf Nureyev as guest artist, performing in such works as *The Scarlet Letter, Lucifer,* and *Appalachian Spring.* It was a surprising combination, which Clive Barnes described as:

> . . . unthinkable and marvelous, this unexpected conjunction of Russia's leading dancer and dance's leading prophetess.[3]

At the same time, it was apparent that, excellent as past Graham dancers might have been, the new crop was marked by an unmatched level of technical brilliance. In comparison to the earlier dancers, however, they were dramatically less passionate. Graham herself has commented on this change; when asked to comment on young dancers today, she revealed her own aesthetic view:

> Young dancers are much more facile than I've ever seen . . . (but have) very little depth. . . . The language of the human being, the inner language, is being neglected. They don't have to look deeply *because* they can do so much physically. . . . They are well-trained bodies but not well trained in their adjustment to life, or in recognition of their mission . . .

[3]Clive Barnes, "Nureyev Shines With Graham," *The New York Times,* December 28, 1975, p. 20.

Dancers today don't go into the meaning of things. . . . people must feel your completeness and not just physical virtuosity.[4]

Looking over the body of her work from the perspective of the late 1970s, it is apparent that one of Martha Graham's major contributions was to celebrate women in dance. In the late 1960s, Hering commented:

. . . the women Miss Graham has chosen to portray have more and more been the super-heroines of Bible and mythology—Jocasta, Medea, Judith, Phaedra, Clytemnestra, Hecuba—all women whose conflicts are big and whose wills are equal to them.[5]

Yet, Graham's initial motivation was not to mythologize women as super-beings. In a number of her earlier works in particular, she showed women as hedged in, neurotic when unable to submit to male dominance or societal tradition, and sometimes even reduced, in Siegel's words, to "simpering dolls." But, Siegel goes on to say, Graham has managed to make her female protagonists human, rather than one-dimensional. Almost all of our understanding of the world's past and of human culture has been transmitted to us through the eyes of men, and with men seen as the key forces. Siegel writes of Graham as a pre-eminently gifted feminist:

Her dances redo history through a female mind. . . . I doubt if there's ever been as concerted an effort as Martha Graham's to present a more balanced perspective. . . . The dignity and power of Graham's women emanate from her sense that women do have an independent existence, as rich psychically and reactively as that of men . . .[6]

Yet, it obviously would be a mistake to think of Graham only as a great woman dancer and choreographer. Within the history of dance as a major aspect of human culture, she stands equal to any great figure of the past or present, as a manager and as a creative artist.

JOSÉ LIMÓN

A second major figure whose reputation was established long before mid-century and who continued to perform, choreograph and teach was José Limón. Though lacking the stability afforded by a major school and permanently established company, he had a number of important affiliations through the years. He was a director of the Juilliard Dance Theater, where his company performed both his own works and those by Doris Humphrey. He continued to be head of the faculty and a leading performer at the Connecticut College of the Dance in New London where, summer after summer, many of his new works received their premieres.

[4]Interview with Martha Graham, *The New York Times,* May 15, 1977, p. D-15.

[5]Hering, *op. cit.,* p. 55.

[6]Marcia B. Siegel, *Watching the Dance Go By* (Boston: Houghton Mifflin Co., 1977), p. 205.

Through the years, the Limón Company carried out a number of highly successful tours of Europe, the Orient, and Latin America, under State Department sponsorship. In 1964, when the New York State Council on the Arts agreed to underwrite two performances of the American Dance Theater at Lincoln Center in New York, José Limón acted as artistic director, bringing together the works of Donald McKayle, Anna Sokolow, and Doris Humphrey on a single program, and performing in a premiere of his own *A Choreographic Offering.*

However, it was difficult for Limón to discover a consistent audience for his works. In 1966, for example, his dance company was able to arrange only one appearance in New York City, at the Brooklyn Academy of Music, where he performed two of his most recent works, *A Choreographic Offering* and *Missa Brevis.* Clive Barnes commented on this occasion that the inability of the Limón company to have more than a "meager one-night stand" in New York City, despite its distinguished reputation, was "scandalous."[7]

Although no longer in his prime as a dancer in the later years of his career, Limón continued to be an impressive and moving figure. His choreography was consistently serene and powerful; unfortunately, there was too little opportunity for it to be seen during his lifetime. After his death in 1972, it was expected this his company would dissolve. However, under

José Limón and Lucas Hoving in *The Traitor.* Photograph by Matthew Wysocki.

[7]Clive Barnes "A Master's One-Night Stand," *The New York Times,* February 14, 1966, p. 33.

the artistic direction of Ruth Currier, later succeeded by Carla Maxwell, the José Limón Company has continued to perform. The present company gives primary emphasis to Limón's dances, but also shows the work of Doris Humphrey, Pauline Koner, and Lucas Hoving (all of whom had been closely linked to Limón); more recently, it has also presented works by Murray Louis and Kurt Jooss. Both on tour with the assistance of the U.S. State Department, and in regular seasons at the Roundabout Theater and the City Center in New York, the Limón Company represents the first major modern dance group to survive the death of its founder.

MERCE CUNNINGHAM

Another dancer-choreographer whose career has bridged the past quarter-century is Merce Cunningham. During the years from 1940 to 1945, he was a soloist with the Martha Graham Company, creating such roles as the Acrobat in *Every Soul Is a Circus,* the Christ Figure in *El Penitente,* March in *Letter to the World,* and the Revivalist in *Appalachian Spring.* While with Graham, he also studied ballet at the School of American Ballet where, during the late 1940s, he taught a class in modern dance.

Since the 1940s, Cunningham has been extremely successful as a choreographer with his own company. He has used the works of a number of

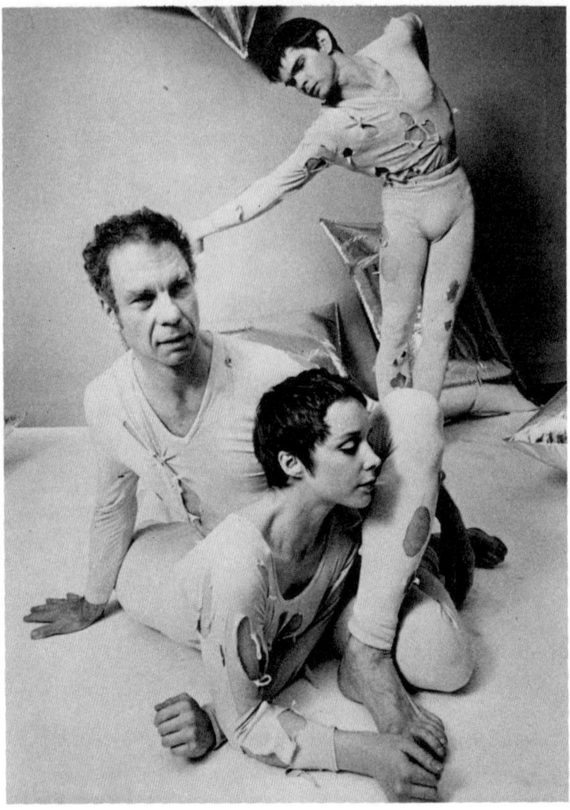

Merce Cunningham, Barbara Lloyd, and Albert Reid in *Riverwind,* with décor by Andy Warhol. Photograph by Jack Mitchell.

contemporary composers, but has collaborated most intensively with the avant-garde pianist-composer, John Cage. His work has varied greatly, and invariably stirs up a strong audience reaction. He is known for his experiments with "choreography by chance," as illustrated in a 1953 work titled *Suite by Chance.* For this long dance in four movements, a large series of charts was made. One gave body movements, phrases, and positions; another chart gave numbered lengths of time; and another gave directions in space. These charts, which defined the physical limits within which the continuity would take place, were not made by chance. But from them, the actual continuity was determined as by a lottery:

> . . . a sequence of movements for a single dancer was determined by means of chance from the numbered movements in the chart; space, direction and lengths of time were found in the other charts. At important structural points in the music, the number of dancers on stage, exits and entrances, unison or individual movements of dancers were all decided by tossing coins. . . .[8]

In another work during the same period, titled *Solo Suite in Time and Space,* with music by John Cage, spots or slight imperfections on sheets of white paper (seen by holding the paper up in front of a bright light) were numbered. From these chance arrangements came the space and lengths of time of each dance. Spots on other sheets of paper, similarly numbered, gave the sequence of the movement. In another work, *Solo,* chance movements were attached to other chance movements; thus, a found-by-chance leg or torso movement would be added to a found-by-chance arm or head movement.

Often, his choreography has been jarring and unpleasant:

> The sound score by Gordon Mumma relentlessly blares the hideous noises of our modern life. . . . For *Place* sets us down in one spot and shows us with pitiless inexorability the shrinking of the world until there is no space left. There is only this tiny plot of ground into which the dancers huddle. Cunningham is sometimes in sole possession of it, but the others crowd in and he is reduced to cringing in a corner. They inch their way into a vacant place but, with foot in midair, they find that the space is no longer free. Only the air is still without boundary and they flail their arms, creating an illusion of freedom in which to move. . . .[9]

Consistently, Cunningham has been a gadfly; in Don McDonagh's words, intent on "baffling the unwary," or "deriving some personal satisfaction from practicing a unique audiovisual torture technique."[10] At one point, when presenting four programs at the Brooklyn Academy of Music as a "resident" company, he deliberately scheduled all four programs as "events," with hour-and-a-half-long dances, with whole dances, parts of dances, and excerpts thrown together in no particular order and without an intermission. The audience staged a near-riot. Twelve years later, in 1974,

[8]Remy Charlip, "Composing by Chance," *Dance Magazine,* January 1954, p. 19.

[9]"Merce Cunningham Dance Company," *Dance News,* January 19, 1967, p. 9.

[10]Don McDonagh, *The Rise and Fall and Rise of Modern Dance* (New York: Mentor, New American Library, 1970), p. 53.

when Cunningham had become a respected elder statesman of the dance world, a Boston Ballet performance of *Winterbranch,* with lighting by Robert Rauschenberg that left the dancers dancing mostly in the dark but beamed a blinding white light directly at the audience, caused half the audience to respond by leaving the theater.

Cunningham has continued to choreograph in an equally experimental vein through the years. He has toured internationally with much acclaim, and has performed at major foreign festivals. In recent years, his works appear to be more carefully pre-structured than during the "chance" period, although they still are often jarring to audiences.

Cunningham has a great range of moods; in *How to Pass, Kick, Fall, and Run,* his dancers caper about in the gayest of spirits. In general, his choreography is an imaginative, no-holds-barred commentary on life, visually exciting, and often highly demanding of the audience. His own dancing and that of his company are of an extremely high caliber.

Of all modern dance choreographers, Cunningham probably comes closest to ballet in his movement approach. His dancers have typically had extensive ballet training, and his movement vocabulary makes use of the complicated and articulate footwork of ballet combined with an upright, open torso, and expressive arm and hand gestures. It is always clear to the audience that if what the dancers are doing does not *look* like dance as it is popularly conceived, at least it is by the choreographer's choice, rather than the performers' inability to dance.

Just as Cunningham was a featured dancer with the Graham Company early in his career, so today a number of members of his company have become well-known choreographers in their own right. Probably more than any other established artist, he has influenced the young generation of avant-garde performers in their movement experimentation. Anna Kisselgoff sums it up: "Above all, Cunningham has given both dancers and audiences a radical new vision of what a dance performance can be."[11]

Among the numerous modern dance choreographers who have become widely known and successful since 1950, several names stand out: Alwin Nikolais, Paul Taylor, Alvin Ailey, Murray Louis, Anna Sokolow, and Erick Hawkins.

ALWIN NIKOLAIS

Alwin Nikolais, who for a number of years was director of the Henry Street Playhouse Dance Company in New York City, is an accomplished musician who worked closely with Hanya Holm for a number of years, and who composes his own musical scores, which are usually electronic. He has, since the late 1950s, become noted for a new kind of dance theater which is almost completely abstract in terms of dramatic content, but which represents a unique and imaginative fusing of sound, color, light, bizarre props, shapes, and movement, to create a remarkably theatrical set of illusions on the stage.

[11]Anna Kisselgoff, *The New York Times,* January 16, 1977, pp. D-1, D-8.

Imago, dance theater-piece by Alwin Nikolais. Photographs by Robert Sosenko.

The first of his works to be widely seen was *Totem,* choreographed in 1960. This is a full-evening work, consisting of 15 episodes, in which abstract props seem to extend the performers' bodies. In one episode, *Shadow Totem,* dancers appear to be headless; in another, *Banshee,* dancers create a weird effect as they wave lights about under their huge, shapeless costumes; in still another, titled *Clowns,* figures clad in felt of bright color move heavily, their feet and arms suggesting bells. It is a work that has been described as deriving from "mysticism, fetishism and fanaticism." Choreographer-designer Nikolais has said of it:

> Ritual and ceremony are like a formula in that certain ingredients, proportioned and mixed, cause a magical result. *Totem* comprises a number of such imagined rituals and ceremonies. I can conceive ritual in the growth of a flower, the kaleidoscopic interplay of geometrical design, the intermingling of people, the flickering of colored lights. Some of *Totem* is fun and foolish ritual, some macabre, and some frightening. To me it shows some of the fanciful moods of nature as it transpires through some of its earthly instruments, including man.[12]

A color film has been made of *Totem;* in addition, it has been seen widely throughout the United States, and was performed in 1962 at the Festival of Two Worlds in Spoleto, Italy.

A second major work of Nikolais's has been *Imago,* a full-evening dance theater piece premiered in 1963. It consists of 12 episodes involving solos, small groups, or the entire Alwin Nikolais Dance Company. Choreography, lighting, and costumes are by Nikolais, and he created the electronic score in collaboration with James Seawright. *Imago* has been variously described by critics as "weird," "fantastic," and "delightful." Like *Totem,* it combines dance movement, color, lighting, and electronic music. Its ten dancers are depersonalized through remarkable costuming, the use of white makeup, and stylized headdresses. It contains both humor and menace, as well as sequences of great visual beauty.

Other important works of Nikolais have included *Sanctum* (1964), *Galaxy* (commissioned by the John Simon Guggenheim Foundation in 1965), and *Vaudeville of the Elements,* first performed in New York in 1966, and described as a "shifting science-fiction world."

Works created in the late 1970s include: *Gallery,* based on the idea of a moving shooting gallery, with multimasked, hydralike figures; *Castings,* a variation on his many works using dancers encased in stretch fabric; and *Sanctum,* often considered his most dancelike work.

As he became increasingly successful, Nikolais moved from the tiny Henry Street Playhouse to larger halls in New York, such as the Brooklyn Academy of Music, the City Center, and the Beacon Theater, where he had fuller scope for his environmental works. As much as any other dance choreographer, Nikolais has succeeded in reaching both an audience of dancers and dance enthusiasts (including those influential in the other modern arts) and the public at large. In addition to several appearances on national television programs, he has appeared at several international festi-

[12]Alwin Nikolais, quoted in *Dance Magazine,* February 1962, p. 43.

vals, has had his color films shown around the world, and has received a number of commissions for choreography from various universities and foundations.

The single major criticism that is frequently made of Nikolais's work is that it is dehumanized, impersonal—simply a visual and auditory design in which the performers are not dancers as such, but rather movable props, and in which man is not the concern of the dance. To this, he has replied eloquently, pointing out that all the arts have today become freed from the need to portray literal subject matter, and are able to directly translate the "abstract elements that characterize and underline an art object:"

> I look upon this polygamy of motion, shape, color, and sound as the basic art of the theater. To me, the art of drama is one thing; the art of theater is another. In the latter, a magical panorama of things, sounds, colors, shapes, lights, illusions, and events happen before your eyes and your ears. I find my needs cannot be wholly satisfied by one art. I like to mix my magics. We are now in a new period of modern dance, and it is a period of new freedom.[13]

Nikolais goes on to comment that, while the early modern dance explored the human psyche and was almost a form of psychological drama, today character is no longer dominant. In his view, dance figures speak through motion, shape, time, and space. He points out that man's ability to communicate in nonverbal ways, and to sense meaning beyond literal and materialistic language or visual symbols, is his greatest distinction from the lower animals. Finally, he defends his work against the charge that it is cold, unemotional, and dehumanized by claiming that it is the very reverse; that it has the power to depict man to himself, as no literal image could.

Siegel agrees, commenting that it is wrong to think of Nikolais's work as reducing human beings to robots dancing in a chromeplated, computerized laboratory. His mechanical and technological devices are a creative means, not an end in themselves; and his ideas are always founded in the human experience. She writes:

> He sees man not as a heroic figure struggling to realize some personal truth, but as a creature who exists as only one part of an environment no less complex than himself.[14]

Among Nikolais's leading dancers have been Gladys Bailin, Bill Frank, Phyllis Lamhut, and Murray Louis.

MURRAY LOUIS

Of these, Louis in particular has emerged as a remarkable choreographer-dancer in his own right. Performing first at the Henry Street Playhouse with a small company drawn primarily from the parent group, Louis has now

[13]Alwin Nikolais, "No Man from Mars," in Selma Jeanne Cohen, ed., *The Modern Dance: Seven Statements of Belief* (Middletown, Connecticut: Wesleyan University Press, 1966), pp. 63–64.

[14]Siegel, *op cit.,* p. 214.

appeared in other dance series and in tours of the major cities in the United States. He is widely regarded as a brilliant dancer and a highly creative choreographer whose stage works display a great range of inventive movement, humor, pathos, a suggestion of mimetic meaning, remarkable sensitivity, and choreographic authority. The mood is often mysterious and, while dramatic relationships may be suggested, the overall characteristic of Louis's work is abstraction.

Among his better known works have been *Interims,* to music by Lucas Foss; *Chimera,* a solo which offers what seems to be a pop-art parody of electronic music; *Concerto,* a much-praised and much-abused interpretation of a Bach Brandenburg Concerto; *Illume,* danced to a score by Toshiro Mayuzumi, suggesting strange creatures of the sea; *Facets,* a duet with Gladys Bailin; and *Calligraph for Martyrs,* an impressive piece which reaches great heights of emotion. He has shared programs at the Brooklyn Academy with Alwin Nikolais, and has also choreographed works in the mid- and late 1970s for major international ballet companies. While his choreography has undoubtedly been influenced by Nikolais, Murray Louis makes much less use of elaborate sets, props and visual effects, and is much more directly concerned with the recognizable and comparatively unadorned dancer.

PAUL TAYLOR

Among the most successful American dancer-choreographers, in terms of having reached a broad international audience in recent years, has been Paul Taylor. Originally a painter, Taylor danced first with Merce Cunningham and then with Martha Graham. Since 1956, when he formed his own small company—now consisting of eleven dancers—he has choreographed many works, has toured widely, and has earned a reputation as one of the world's leading modern dance choreographers. The Paul Taylor Dance Company appeared at the 1960 Spoleto Festival, toured Italy in 1961, danced at the Festival of Nations in Paris in 1962 where Taylor received an international critics' award as best choreographer, and performed in 1963 in performances in Mexico sponsored by the Mexican Government. In 1964, he toured throughout the United States and then through Europe (Italy, France, Belgium, Holland, England, Iceland). In the following years, he has continued to travel widely. In 1967, the company toured the Near and Far East, including Egypt, Korea, and Japan; it was Taylor's fourth tour under the auspices of the U.S. State Department. Taylor comments himself:

> Most places overseas are hungry for our kind of thing. European ballet seems somewhat outdated, and audiences have begun to look to American dance. They're receptive to new work and they seem to have a marvelous time with us. . . .[15]

Taylor's success is heavily due to the dancing that his company offers. He is unpretentious about his own work, and has written amusingly on the

[15]Paul Taylor, quoted in "Have Troupe, Will Travel," *The New York Times,* July 3, 1966, p. 16-D.

Paul Taylor and Company in *Orbs.* Photograph by Jack Mitchell.

theme, "Down with choreographers!" Nonetheless, his work is painstakingly developed and permits his excellent dancers to show their strengths in well-mounted pieces. It is both complex and simple, serene and exciting, stylish and witty. Taylor is not afraid to repeat himself to build an effect, and sometimes deliberately limits the amount of invention in his dances, repeating and changing basic movement patterns, and setting them to music with contrasting tempi, in order to develop them fully. His vocabulary of movement tends to be extremely simple; instead of formal dance movement, he often makes use of such ordinary movements as walking, running, falling, or standing. However, he combines and recombines these in a variety of interesting ways often setting them to music with contrasting tempi. McDonagh describes Taylor's dance posture as "modified balletic with free swinging arms for gestural comment."[16] It has also been noted that Taylor's work is orderly and musical, at a time when other modern dance choreographers are moving away from dependence on music.

For the most part, his work is abstract although the viewer may perceive dramatic content if he wishes to do so. Taylor seems almost to represent a blending of Martha Graham and Balanchine; his work is authoritative, almost classic, and yet refreshingly new, with emphasis placed on dance first and foremost. Among his dances have been *Party Mix,* a parody on party-

[16]McDonagh, *op cit.,* p. 205.

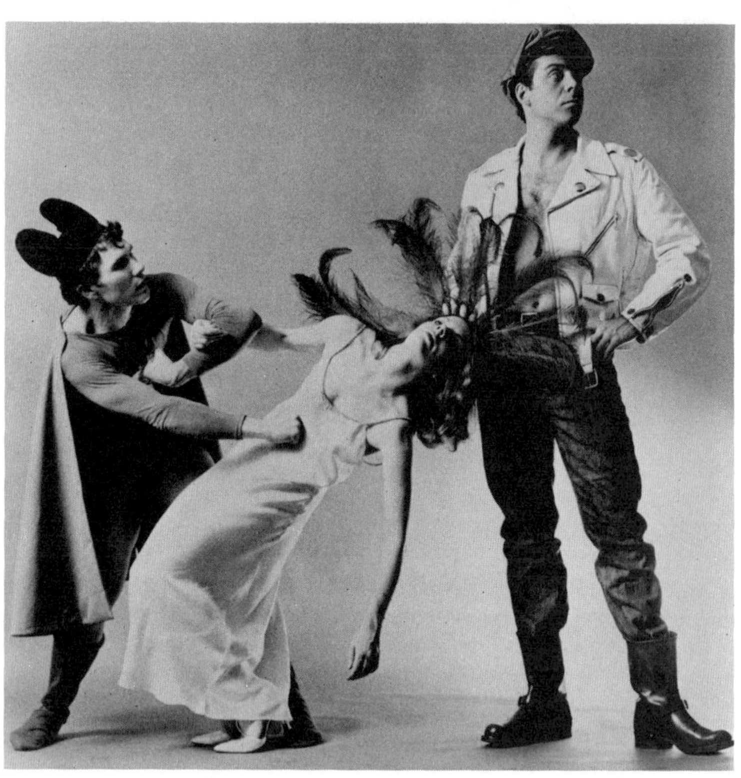

Paul Taylor with Dan Wagoner and Molly Reinhart in *From Sea to Shining Sea.* Photograph by Jack Mitchell.

going; *Scudorama,* concerned with the grim life of cities; *Aureole,* a bouncing, poetically musical work to a setting by Handel; *From Sea to Shining Sea,* a satirical appraisal of American culture; and *Orbs,* an examination of man and the universe, which was premiered in New York in 1966, and was hailed by critics and the public as a masterpiece of choreography. His work during the 1970s has included *American Genesis,* an evening-length historical piece reviewing American dance idioms from colonial times to the present; *Runes,* a serious work concerned with human rituals; and *Sports and Follies,* a spoof on athletic competition, games and cheerleaders. Taylor has choreographed for major ballet companies, and has featured Rudolf Nureyev as a guest artist with his own company.

Despite his increased success and public acceptance in the 1970s, Taylor has had difficulty in maintaining his company on a sound financial base. For years, he found it necessary to tour abroad in order to support his company, and in 1976, steps were taken to dissolve the group until an emergency grant from the National Endowment for the Arts made it possible to continue. Of the earlier period, Taylor commented:

> We're homebodies and we like to perform our work for American audiences. And for dancers, the constant traveling is disruptive and exhausting. But it's

financially impossible to put on a big-city show in the United States. The expenses always exceed what we take in at the box office. Actually, we're very lucky to be one of the few companies that can exist by performing abroad.[17]

ALVIN AILEY

Another American dancer-choreographer who has enjoyed remarkable success both abroad and in the United States is Alvin Ailey. Originally trained as a dancer by Lester Horton on the West Coast, Ailey has assembled a company of strong dancers who perform both his own works and those of a number of other modern choreographers. One of the highlights of the Alvin Ailey Dance Theater is that it was the first black company to be sent abroad by the President's International Exchange Program, administered by ANTA under the auspices of the U.S. State Department. During this 1962 tour, the company presented sixty performances for 146,791 people in twenty-five cities in ten countries—Australia, Burma, Viet Nam, Malaya, Indonesia, the Philippines, Hong Kong, Formosa, Japan, and Korea. Rich praise was heaped upon them; in Hong Kong the dance critic wrote:

> These dancers spin, jackknife, twist, swivel, leap, prance, ripple, flutter, slide, contract, recoil, spring, shiver and quake in a way that makes any other dancing look jaded, wooden and stiff.[18]

One important effect of this tour was that it conveyed an understanding of creative dance in America to large groups of artists and intellectuals throughout the East, as well as a more varied and positive view of the role of the American black. Edwin Reischauer, American Ambassador to Japan commented:

> In many fields of art and culture we of the United States have much to learn from the culture of Japan, but in other fields—and here I would especially single out the field of modern dance—we believe that we have something of value to contribute. . . . In the entire range of the performing arts, I know of no art form more uniquely American than the music of the American Negro. This music, and the dances which derive from it . . . have about them something of the originality of expression and the vitality that I like to think of as characteristic to the United States.[19]

Actually, the Ailey company does not perform works that are restricted to black themes or musical sources. In the Far Eastern tour, for example, the following works were performed: John Butler's drama of New England, *Letter to a Lady;* Glen Tetley's *Mountain Way Chant,* an archaic ritual of the Navajo Indian with music by Carlos Chavez; and *Hermit Songs,* a series of solo dances by Ailey, set to ancient poems written by Irish monks, to music

[17]Taylor, *op. cit.,* p. 16-D.

[18]Arthur Todd, "Two Way Passage for Dance," *Dance Magazine,* July 1962, p. 39.

[19]Edwin Reischauer, quoted in "Two Way Passage for Dance," *op. cit.,* p. 39.

Alvin Ailey with Carmen de Lavallade in *Roots of the Blues.* Photograph by Jack Mitchell.

by Samuel Barber. Only in the final 40-minute section of the two-hour program were black materials used exclusively. This section included one of Ailey's major works, *Revelations,* a deeply felt work based on the black experience in America—full of anger, compassion and, ultimately, a moving spirit of celebration. Other pieces choreographed by Ailey included *Roots of the Blues,* a duet with Carmen de Lavallade, with three jazz musicians and folk singer Brother John Sellers on stage; and *Fix Me Jesus,* a starkly effective study. Among the most popular works performed by the Ailey Dance Company have been *Congo Tango Palace* and *The Road of the Phoebe Snow,* both by Talley Beatty; *Caravan,* by Louis Falco; and *Rainbow Round My Shoulder,* by Donald McKayle.

Since then , the Ailey company has continued to offer works, not only by himself, but by a wide variety of other choreographers, young and old, white and black, men and women. On this policy, he has commented:

> I think it's much more important in a program of dance to see many people's ideas, rather than just one person's. This also keeps the public interested; the catholicity of what we do keeps the audiences coming, to see lots of different kinds of work.[20]

The style and music of the Ailey company also are eclectic; he blends ballet, modern dance, and jazz dancing into a dynamic and appealing stage

[20]Richard Philp, "Twenty Years Later: The Alvin Ailey American Dance Theater," *Dance Magazine,* October, 1978, p. 73.

presentation that makes an immediate impact on the audience. He has made much use of both traditional black music, and more recently composed popular songs. Stability was gained by the company when it moved in 1972 to the New York City Center as a home base. The Ailey company has grown from 7 to 27 dancers and by the late 1970s it had an active repertoire of 28 works, along with two junior companies and a large, active dance school.

In recent years, the Ailey Company has toured the United States frequently, and has also performed in a number of European countries, including a spectacularly successful visit to Russia. It is clear that, far from being a choreographer who deals only with folk materials—in this case dance and music of the American black—Alvin Ailey must be recognized as a major creative artist of our time. Like Paul Taylor, he has been a superb ambassador for America abroad, as well as for dance itself, in his own land.

ANNA SOKOLOW

One of the most unusual choreographers of the present day, in terms of her background and the scope of her professional efforts, is Anna Sokolow. Sokolow spans the period from Martha Graham's early days at the Neighborhood Playhouse on the lower East Side, through the present. She has taught movement to actors and choreography to ballet dancers; her works today are performed in foreign lands and by a number of American companies, both modern dance and ballet.

Sokolow performed in the Graham company during the 1930s; she also appeared in workers' clubs with her Dance Unit, performing works with anti-Fascist themes and other themes of social significance. She worked and performed in Russia in the mid-1930s, and in 1939 was invited to Mexico by the Fine Arts Ministry to appear for a six-week season with a company she had formed there years before. She remained in Mexico, teaching young Mexican dancers, who called themselves "Las Sokolovas" and who later became the nucleus of a large group called "La Paloma Azul." From this group came several leading Mexican choreographers, including Raquel Gutierrez and Ana Mérida. For nine years after this, Anna Sokolow commuted between New York and Mexico City. There, the largest and most impressive theater was hers and she choreographed a number of important works, with the collaboration of Mexico's leading composers and designers. Mexican themes have since pervaded a number of her works, such as *Mexican Retablo* and *Lament for the Death of a Bullfighter.*

Drawn back to New York City as a center for her creative work, Sokolow was again involved in another land when, in 1953, she went to Israel, to teach movement to the Inbal group, a company of Yemenite dancers that has since toured the world with great success. Over a period of years, she then divided her activities between Israel and the United States, spending between four and six months in Israel each year, staging theater works. In the early 1960s, she served as director-teacher-choreographer for the Lyric Theater there, a unique form of experimental theater:

> It is in the truest sense of the word a dance theater fusing dance and drama. . . . Essentially, I want to experiment with the spoken word and movement as I have done with Kafka's *Metamorphosis.* Kafkaesque images particularly lend themselves to the style of dance theatre I conceive.[21]

Since that time, Anna Sokolow has become extremely active once again in the United States. She teaches the actors of the Lincoln Center Repertory Theater dramatic movement, just as years before she taught choreography to ballet students in New York's School of American Ballet. This crossing of traditional lines is typical of Sokolow's career. In 1967, the National Ballet of Washington performed the Broadway premiere of her work, *Night,* a grim and ominous study to electronic music by Luciano Berio. At the same time, her jazz ballet *Opus 65* was being performed by the City Center Joffrey Ballet, in New York. Her work *Rooms* was performed by the Alvin Ailey Company and the Netherlands Dance Theater.

In these works, as in others which she performs with her own company, such as *Dreams, Déserts, Lyric Suite,* or *Time +7,* Sokolow shows a deep concern with modern man's existential state. Her view of life is a bleak and painful one, and her dances are bitter, frightening, tragic—and yet somehow compassionate and moving. The choreography of *Night* is described as:

> [a] madhouse delirium of weird night-shapes . . . and compulsive night fears . . . terrified and lost, full of half formulated gestures and dances either shaking with tension or limp with despair. . . .[22]

In *Dreams,* there is the shattering imagery of humans imprisoned in an imaginary concentration camp; people running hopelessly in place; falling, despairing; an unbearable message of misery. In *Déserts,* a world of mystery and loneliness is exposed. It begins and ends with the same image: a dozen individuals are seated on the floor, heads bowed, their postures defenseless and exhausted.

> When they move, it is with the frantic quality of people under attack by invisible assailants; they writhe; they spin feverishly; their eyeballs bulge with the pressure of panic. They jump straight into the air, then fall, their arms flailing against bodies which burn with a thousand itches. It is as if each is experiencing a personal inferno, unreachable and unrelievable.[23]

During the 1970s, Sokolow continued to choreograph for Contemporary Dance System, a performing company affiliated with the Juilliard School of Music and Dance in New York City, and to teach and choreograph as guest artist for many small companies throughout the country. Although the bleak and alienated spirit of many of her works seems to be more attuned to an earlier era than to this later period, she continues to be clearly recognized as a major creative figure in the world of contemporary dance.

[21]Walter Sorell, "We Work Toward Freedom," *Dance Magazine,* January, 1964, p. 53.

[22]Clive Barnes, "A Sombre 'Night' Unfolds," *The New York Times,* May 7, 1966, p. 8.

[23]Jacqueline Maskey, "Anna Sokolow Dance Company," *Dance Magazine,* May, 1967, p. 36.

Another gifted and original choreographer today is Erick Hawkins, a leading dancer with the Graham Company for a number of years. Working to music composed by Lucia Dlugoszewski, musical director of the Hawkins Dance Company, he has performed with a small group of dancers in the major modern dance series, has toured the college circuit for decades, with much success, and has taught as a guest artist in public schools. Through lectures, discussions and printed materials, he seeks to broaden the audience's understanding of his art. Hawkins's work is highly experimental and abstract, and stresses the use of unusual music or "choreographic sound," created during the performance, on sculpturally designed instruments. Indeed, the totality of dance, music, and stage design has always been a key element in his choreography; whether the music is performed by symphony orchestra, chamber music groups, or Dlugoszewski, it is critical to his work, and he insists on it being "live," rather than played on tapes, records, or electronic devices.

Hawkins is also unique in that he has deeply probed the roots of dance in a variety of ethnic cultures; he has studied the Greeks, the ritual dances of Southwestern American Indians, and Oriental religion and aesthetics.

Erick Hawkins (right) with Nancy Meehan and James Tyler in *Early Floating.* Photograph by Jack Mitchell.

Among his best-known works have been *Early Floating, Geography of Noon, Naked Leopard,* and *Lord of Persia.* In the 1970s, he explored his own roots, with a series of dances dealing with the American heritage, including *Plains Daybreak, Parson Weems and the Cherry Tree,* and *Hurrah,* all dealing with aspects of American history.

OTHER LEADING CHOREOGRAPHERS

A number of other modern dancers who continued or developed successful careers as choreographers during the period after mid-century include Glen Tetley, Daniel Nagrin and Donald McKayle.

Tetley is particularly noteworthy for having successfully bridged the gap between modern dance and ballet. He had extensive ballet training with Margaret Craske and Antony Tudor, but also studied and performed with Martha Graham and Hanya Holm; he has frequently appeared with his own company as part of modern dance series. He has also been a soloist with American Ballet Theater, and has choreographed works for that company. He choreographed for the Netherlands Dance Theater, resident company of The Hague, eventually becoming its co-director. After John Cranko's death in 1973, he briefly held the post of artistic director for the Stuttgart Ballet, and during the 1970s also mounted works for the Hamburg State Opera Ballet and the British Royal Ballet.

Regarded as an extremely inventive and subtle choreographer and performer, Tetley's works include *Ricercare,* created for the American Ballet Theater; *Pierrot Lunaire,* danced by the Netherlands Company; and *The Mythical Hunters,* commissioned for the *Batsheva Company* of Israel. Among his later works are a new dance to Stravinsky's *Le Sacre du Printemps,* and *Mutations,* a highly publicized nude ballet danced by the Netherlands Dance Theater.

Daniel Nagrin, for many years co-director of the Tamiris-Nagrin Dance Company with his wife Helen Tamiris, studied dance with Martha Graham, Hanya Holm, and Anna Sokolow. In 1946, he was given the lead dance role in *Annie Get Your Gun,* choreographed by Tamiris; he continued to perform on Broadway, receiving the Donaldson Award for Best Male Dancer in 1955 for his performance in *Plain and Fancy.* His dance style is rooted in jazz, which always has been an important element of his choreography.

At the age of 40, Nagrin presented his first solo concert; two of his most acclaimed works were *Spanish Dance,* and *Pelopennesian War,* a commentary on the social and political aspects of the human condition: In 1970 Nagrin organized an improvisational dance company, the Workgroup, and during the 1970s continued to tour the United States, Europe, and the Pacific as a solo performer, teacher, and lecturer. An extremely intense and vigorous dancer, Nagrin is known for such other works as *A Gratitude; Not Me, But Him;* and *Indeterminate Figure*—a view of man whose commanding self-image is contradicted by his irrepressible foibles and weaknesses of character.

A leading black dancer, who has performed with the Martha Graham Company, the New Dance Group, the Anna Sokolow Dance Theater, and the New York City Center Opera Ballet, is Donald McKayle. He has appeared on Broadway in a number of musicals, and has choreographed several successful shows, including *Golden Boy,* as well as many television productions. On the concert stage, his best known early works were *District Storyville, Rainbow Round My Shoulder,* and *Games,* based on such themes as Southern chain gangs, jazz in a New Orleans brothel years ago, and street games played in the urban ghetto. His later work, such as *Barrio* or *Songs of the Disinherited,* is a less literal treatment of the black experience and more fully concerned with movement exploration as such.

McKayle has been guest choreographer at the Festival of Two Worlds in Spoleto, Italy, has taught and performed in Israel, and had his work performed in the 1970s by the Inner City Repertory Dance Company of Los Angeles.

Other dancers active during this period included Pauline Koner, Pearl Lang, Katherine Litz, Paul Sanasardo, Sybil Shearer, Bertram Ross, Ruth Currier, Stuart Hodes, Lucas Hoving, Helen McGehee, and May O'Donnell. In many cases, they had been leading dancers with one or more of the companies or choreographers described earlier, and have since ventured into independent careers heading their own performing groups. Often this role has been combined with teaching on the college level, or in independent dance schools and studios. To do full justice to them, as well as to many other active choreographers around the country, is not possible within the confines of this chapter.

THE NEW EXPERIMENTALISTS

Finally, a group of new, younger choreographers emerged, chiefly during the 1960s and 1970s, who might best be described as the new experimentalists—or far avant-garde. In many ways, these individuals differed from their predecessors. Their performances, or presentations, often had little that was dancelike about them; they tended to be improvised, or to consist of movements drawn from daily life, put together in casual or unstructured ways. They performed in impromptu settings—in lofts, remodeled warehouses, church basements, streets, and parks—rather than in proscenium theaters or concert halls. Usually, their costumes were casual; often, they consisted of jeans and T-shirts or exercise clothes, and frequently they were shed as the dance continued. Instead of formal music used as accompaniment, the dancers performed in silence, or to the spoken word, or to other sounds of nature, or improvised noises made on musical instruments.

With this non-dance, or antidance approach, they tended to appeal to new kinds of audiences—people not necessarily interested in or knowledgeable about the arts, but open to new kinds of human expression. Similar things were happening in the other arts, and the modern dance experimentalists were part of an important new trend. Often the groups were fluid in nature; sometimes they formed communelike organizations which made it possible for different individuals to organize and present concerts through a mutual-assistance plan. The impact of the choreographer was minimized to a degree. Instead of the companies being known by the name of the director–choreographer, they had such titles as *Acme Dance Co.* (James Cunningham), *The Farm* (Deborah Hay), *Grand Union* (Yvonne Rainer), and *The House* (Meredith Monk), reminiscent of the titles of rock bands.

In considering the work of these groups, it must be recognized first that experimentalism has always flourished in modern dance, as in all contemporary art. The essence of modern dance is that it challenges old traditions and must represent a seeking for the new, rather than a replaying of old tunes.

The notion of dance being abstract—in the sense of not having a literal message—is not at all shocking or controversial. While historically ballet represented a form of drama in that it told recognizable stories, most of the choreography of George Balanchine (to select the most solidly entrenched choreographer in that field) has been completely non-literal. Similarly, the fields of painting and sculpture have been dominated by abstractionists in recent years. What if dance movement is not familiar to the audience (as the ballet *danse d'ecole* would be), or does not fit its expectation in other ways? Throughout the history of dance, new techniques and movements have constantly been developed by innovative performers and choreographers.

In terms of having dancers disguised as objects, or making use of properties that tend to make the dance something of an engineering phenomenon—these too have counterparts in history (such as the lighting and staging techniques of Loie Fuller) and in the other arts, with the recent example of "op art" that makes use of objects that are moved by magnetism and built-in motors. Even the sound that is used to accompany avant-garde dance is paralleled by what is happening widely in the music field itself—the use of "fixed" instruments, electronic sound, or even silence as a form of "sound."

The real stumbling block for many audiences or dance critics appeared in the realm of dances that were essentially "happenings," during the late 1960s and early 1970s. One writer defined the term as follows:

> A Happening is simply anything that happens to more than one person in a sort of half-planned, half-spontaneous way. It is an experience shared, and each individual takes from it what he will. Sometimes there are performers and an audience; sometimes the audience are themselves the participants; sometimes there are participants and no audience. A Happening usually consists of several Events which are totally unrelated—a kaleidoscope of impressions, as it were. Performers do not portray characters in specific environments; they are always themselves in precisely the environment in which the Happening is taking place.[24]

Examples of possible happenings:

A butterfly is let loose in a theater. The audience watches. When the butterfly flies out the window, the performance is over, or;

Several musicians appear before an audience and sit in perfect silence. The audience listens to the incidental sounds of traffic, coughing, or;

A mass mural is painted in the park, by having a hundred feet of heavy paper put up and dozens of children and adults splash it with poster paint.

[24]Jerome Rockwood, "What's Happening," Letter to the Editor, *The New York Times*, January 16, 1966, p. X-7.

There is something intriguing about all this, but a good part of it has to do just with the novelty of the situation, and with humans involved in an informal process of self-discovery and social contact. How much it relates to art is another question—and the degree to which it represents leg-pulling on the part of the "happening" planner, is a moot point.

When a dance "happening" was staged, it usually involved a degree of preplanning and structure. Thus, in one work, a solo dancer moved around the stage in a dance of five sections. For each section, the audience was asked to participate in a different way. In the first, they rattled paper. In the next, they shouted out numbers at random. In another, they scraped their feet on the floor or cleared their throats. Presumably, the dance was influenced by the sounds they made. After a period of time, the dance was over.

In another dance on the same program, a jazz musician played a series of unconnected, spontaneous phrases on a horn; the sounds were evocative, original, and drew forth a series of vocal sounds from the dancer who sat next to him for the first part of the work. Finally, the dancer began to move about the floor, as the musician explored the possibilities of his instrument with short bursts of sound. The dancer's movement had no strict beginning or end; it seemed to be a cross-section of unrelated gestures and locomotor movement, chosen at random and stopped abruptly.

All of this, as indicated, has a base in the other arts—particularly in trends in the graphic and plastic arts. There, the surrealist, abstract expressionist, and action schools of painting prepared the way, through the 1960s, for the "pop" and "op" movements. Characteristic of the latter are that they frequently are based on, or make use of, commonplace objects. Sometimes these may be "found" objects which most would regard as little more than junk. Thus, in a museum one may find on display a crushed automobile, a toilet seat, the replica of the inside of a grimy diner, or the plaster cast of a man driving a car. When it is not the actual object itself, it may be the photographlike painting of it, as in the painting of giant soup cans, comic strips, or posters. Sometimes it may represent a carefully worked-out abstract design to create visual illusions, or may be based on mechanical contrivances which supply motion to the art object, as in a motor-driven mobile.

Over a period of time, a number of leading choreographers have reflected these approaches. In Merce Cunningham's "chance" dances, the idea of improvisation, based on certain stimuli being chosen at random, results in what might almost be called "found" movement. In Nikolais's choreography, one finds a strong resemblance to "op art." In almost all of the avant-garde works, there is a tendency to avoid literal thematic material, and also to avoid the appearance of dance that is organized, fitted to instrumental musical accompaniment, and consistently danced in the same way.

To illustrate the point further, it may be helpful to describe more fully the work of one of the major experimenters in avant-garde dance, Ann Halprin. Her company, the Dancers' Workshop of San Francisco, performed an extensive piece titled *Parades and Changes* in New York, in 1967. Hering describes their work as intended to be fluid and semi-improvisational, yet quite intense in mood. The curtain was raised as the audience assembled; the dancers, dressed in trousers and skirts, moved down the aisles and lined up neatly on stage. Then they turned to face the audience and began to disrobe.

> . . . one's interest shifted to the cleverly timed device of having some dancers dressing while others were undressing; by having some dancers suddenly contemplate each other or give the impression that they were competing over each other. All of this was understated, almost ritualistic. Endless carpets of brown wrapping paper were stretched across the stage. The dancers, by now all nude, became entangled in the paper. Some punched at it furiously. Some crawled or stood beneath it. . . . By degrees all gathered up huge armfuls of the paper and began jumping into the pit. . . .[25]

At a later point, the company, dressed now in white, crawled down the aisles, ran down, descended from rope ladders which were attached from the balcony, or just stood and swayed epileptically. They trembled, shouted at the audience and flopped to the floor, now and then rearing up like a "mass of beached fish." The dancers embraced wildly but sexlessly. They stamped on little platforms, yelled like jungle beasts, laughed hysterically, threw themselves about with no concern for their physical safety.

In another series of experiments in California, Halprin's dancers joined together with a group of architects exploring the possibility of "kinetic environments." The purpose of this collaboration was to enable members of each group to become aware of the nature and possibilities of the other art. As part of it, they constructed a driftwood village on the beach, each person or small team developing environments that suited their needs. Another involved a "tower and paper event" in which dancers "told stories" either physically or verbally, and the architects designed and immediately put up light-and-paper constructions based on the repeated telling of the story in different locations. Anderson recounts a major event which illustrates the approach to developing the "kinetic environment." It took place in Union Square in San Francisco, and was designed to constitute simultaneously a dance composition, an architectural investigation, an exploration of how environment affects man and man affects environment, and finally, a "theater event." At noon on a July day, 40 young people entered the square. They sat about, ate lunch, casually napped, or fed pigeons. At three o'clock chimes from a nearby building struck the hour.

> The 40 young people immediately stopped whatever they were doing and solemnly rose to their feet, as though for a ceremony in church. Each person scanned the square, attempting to establish eye contact with at least 20 other people from the group. That done, they slowly began walking to the center of the square. As though they were magnets or modern-day Pied Pipers, their simple act of walking to a common meeting-point drew a crowd of curious followers behind them. Now in the center where all the paths converged, each of the 40 inflated a balloon and either let it fly off into the air or gave it to a child. Then the 40 mysterious strangers walked away.[26]

[25]Doris Hering, "Dancer's Workshop of San Francisco in 'Parades and Changes,' " *Dance Magazine,* June 1967, p. 37.

[26]Jack Anderson, "Dancer's and Architects Build Kinetic Environment," *Dance Magazine,* November 1966, p. 52.

The purpose of all this is difficult to assess, as are the outcomes. A comparatively small audience gets to view such works, although occasionally a mass audience may be attracted, as in the case of an unusual production which was given in a New York City armory during the fall of 1966. This program, which combined the arts of music, painting, and dance with a total controlled environment that made use of high-powered sound and lighting equipment, was in effect a nine-day "happening" that drew many thousands as spectators and semiparticipants. Ultimately, it was revealed as a somewhat boring sequence of pretentious but meaningless large-scale episodes to which the audience reacted, in a generally good-natured way, by walking out in large numbers.

To give a fuller picture of work being done by avant-garde dancers today, it is helpful to examine several of the leading performers and choreographers. In some cases they have functioned primarily as individuals; in others as parts of cooperative producing groups. As an example of the latter, one group in New York City is the Dance Theater Workshop; among those who have shown choreographic work as part of this structure have been Jeff Duncan, Jack Moore, Judith Willis, Gus Solomons, Elizabeth Keen, Judith Dunn, and Bill Dixon. Others who have developed strong reputations in recent years as highly experimental choreographers include: Trisha Brown, James Cunningham, Laura Dean, Douglass Dunn, Viola Farber, Meredith Monk, Steve Paxton, Rudy Perez, Yvonne Rainer, and Twyla Tharp. While it is not possible to review them all in full detail, several are described in the section that follows.

TRISHA BROWN

Trisha Brown's essential focus has been on improvisation and the use of human figures within a massive environment of structures and planes. Improvisation was typically used as a means of having dancers work together to develop a dance structure and jointly create a group work before performing it. In the more contemporary sense, it involves dancers actually creating new movement solutions or relationships while in the process of performing before an audience.

The group of dancers is given a problem, and then, based on an awareness of each other's movement styles and responding to signals, moves ahead to develop a choreographic solution to it. The problem may relate to a relationship or other situation within the group, a prop, costumes, or movement phrase; as the dancers explore it over time, they develop a facility for dealing with it in an entertaining and creative way. In one dance called *Sticks* (part of a larger work titled *Line Up*), five women lie on their backs in a head-to-toe line, with long sticks lined up above and parallel to their bodies. Maintaining contact with the sticks in a straight line, they crawl out from under them, step over them, and get under them again from the other side. In another piece from the same work, titled *Mistitled (5'Clacker)*, they repetitively run forward and back from a starting line, with more steps each time, to the accompaniment of a tape of a wooden stick hitting a glass at ten second intervals.

In another series of works presented by the Trisha Brown group, dancers stood on the roofs of 15 buildings, relaying movement in a steady stream to the one member of a group in a position to see all of them. One of Brown's best-known pieces consisted of having dancers walk vertically up and down the walls of the Whitney Museum of American Art, assisted by suction-soled shoes and cables attached to an overhead trolley. Siegel comments about her work:

> Brown has a special quality of plainness and unexcitability that always makes her work seem extraordinary to me. . . . Brown's work is concerned first with the subjective experience of the dancer, then with the vicarious experience of the audience. Presentation, or how it looks as a theatrical show, comes pretty low in her priorities. . . .[27]

LAURA DEAN

Laura Dean's work is characterized by simple dance structures (often geometrical in nature), and minimal movement elements, such as stepping, kicking, clapping, jumping or turning, performed to a steady, driving rhythm set by the choreographer. In *Circle Dance,* for example, performed in the mid-1970s, ten performers, dressed in simple white pants and shirts, moved in four concentric circles for 35 minutes. There was no variation, except for occasional reversals of direction. At the end of the dance, each performer broke away, into five minutes of rapid spinning. In *Jumping Dance,* 12 people arranged in a three-by-four pattern, jumped steadily in unison, grunting "ha" as they landed, until exhausted.

One critic has called Dean's work "overly possessed by the rudimentary;" another describes it as "extremely monotonous." Yet, somehow, it radiates a sense of vitality and clockwork precision; a single new gesture or change of direction carries a strong impact. Toby Tobias sums up the audience's typical reaction as one of disarmed pleasure:

> Drawn into the work by its hypnotic qualities, they are . . . seduced by the forthright simplicity and the vigor of Miss Dean's compositions into seeing exactly what she intends them to see: the freshness and enormous interest of the simple elements of dancing.[28]

Beyond this, like Trisha Brown, Laura Dean is also deeply concerned about the dancers themselves; she sees the work as a means of unifying the group, strengthening its sense of kinship and minimizing its differences.[29] In this sense, much avant-garde dance has been influenced by the encounter group movement of the 1960s and early 1970s, in the sense that such groups used movement, touching, and varied other forms of physical contact and sensing each other, as ways to heighten their own self-awareness, increasing their potential for self-actualization. Clearly, such experiences, carried on by non-dancers, had a strong influence on the dance experimentalists who

[27]Siegel, *Watching the Dance Go By,* p. 298.

[28]Toby Tobias, "Step, Kick, Jump—Back-to-Basics Dance," *New York Times,* November 6, 1977, p. 6.

[29]Siegel, *op cit.,* p. 304.

moved into the special orientation to movement called "contact improvisation." For them, workshops in group movement exploration and interpersonal contact contributed directly to performances before audiences; sometimes the two were indistinguishable.

MEREDITH MONK

Another uniquely different avant-garde creator and performer is Meredith Monk. Although she began her career as a dancer and is customarily reviewed by dance critics, her work is a unique blend of music, dance and theater, which she herself has described as opera-epics, theater cantatas, non-verbal opera, visual poetry, image dance, and mosaic theater.

Her pieces are not improvised on the spot; instead, they are carefully structured and staged, with elaborate musical accompaniment, often with extensive trappings or in planned environments. For example, in a major work, *Juice,* sections of the dance were presented along the spiraling ramp of New York's Guggenheim Museum, with spectators taking an elevator to the top and walking down along the ramp to view the exhibits. At other points, the costumed dancers surged up to the top of the ramp to perform, or down to the lower level, to chant and dance, as the audience watched

"The Rally," a section from Meredith Monk's *Quarry.*

from the ramp. Much of Monk's work has a mystical, symbolic, and childlike quality. In another piece, *Education of the Girlchild,* several dancers perform what appear to be a series of rites, visions, and morality plays; at one point, Monk is dressed as an old crone by the others and left to sit alone and immobile on a cloth-shrouded throne during intermission, while the audience mills around her. In a later section of the work, Monk does a 45-minute solo, retracing the stages of life back to childhood. In these and other pieces, Monk uses music which consists of singing, chanting, her own creation of non-literal, yelplike sounds, and simple but evocative keyboard music. Her movement consists, in John Rockwell's words, of "quick stylizations of natural motion, funny, oddly flowing, puppetlike jerkiness and sudden ritual poses."[30]

Critical reaction to Monk's work has been mixed. Clive Barnes, certainly an extremely influential commentator on dance through the 1960s and 1970s, dismissed her as "mildly tedious" and later as "a disgrace to the name of dancing." Yet other critics have called her "spectacularly original" or "the most significant intermedia artist of our time," and audiences, particularly the young, tend to be fascinated by Meredith Monk.

STEVE PAXTON

For years a leading dancer in the Merce Cunningham company, Steve Paxton has been deeply concerned with discovering the sources of dance movement. He has used varied devices to suggest movement forms and sequences, and has, like other avant-garde choreographers, sought to develop performers as people, rather than technicians. To facilitate this, he has simplified movement to the basic actions of walking, standing, turning and jumping, and has at times used non-dancers because they were more natural and personal in their approach to movement than dancers. Indeed, he has incorporated animals such as dogs and chickens in his work, seeking to express the casual untidiness of everyday life. Once, after a duet with a chicken, he commented, "The performance was bad but we had a good rehearsal."

In his attempt to help audiences view dance in new ways, Paxton has used nudity as a choreographic element—a vogue that became accepted on the Broadway stage with *Oh, Calcutta, Hair,* and in the much more radical presentations of the Environmental Theater Company directed by Richard Schechner.

At one point, when invited to perform in a dance series sponsored by New York University, he notified the directors of the series that his concert included having 42 nude redheaded people walking across the stage of the theater. When the university ruled that it would not permit this, he canceled his scheduled performance; however, since there was no way of notifying the prospective audience of the change, he substituted a piece titled *Intravenous Lecture.* This consisted of Paxton's delivering a lecture on performing situations and sponsors, while having a doctor plunge a needle in his arm and

[30]John Rockwell, *The New York Times,* March 28, 1976, p. D-8.

having an unidentified liquid dripped into his vein for 20 minutes—as a bitter protest against the university's action. Siegel asks:

> Why do college administrators fail to see that the difference between art and pornography turns on something besides the amount of human flesh exposed? And why, having exercised their right of uncomprehending censorship, are they surprised when the artist doesn't spew out his anger . . . around the debating table, but instead restates the issue in a harsher and more obscene way than anyone had intended?[31]

TWYLA THARP

Twyla Tharp is inexhaustible in invention and dynamic performance. The dances she creates are rich in musicality, underlying structure, and a casual, loose-jointed, quickly shifting energy which often presents a nonchalant, meandering view of the dancer. Born in Indiana, her family moved to California when she was a young child, and she remained there until attending Barnard College. While a student in New York, she studied a great deal of dance. Upon graduating in 1963, with a degree in art history, she joined Paul Taylor's Company for two years. In the mid-1960s she began to choreograph extensively, completing 22 works between 1965 and 1970.

The *Bix Pieces* was premiered in 1971 and has become one of the best-known of her works. A group of dances interspersed with dialogue appears casually serious, yet as an extremely personal statement. The dances have a strong relation to music by Bix Beiderbeck, Joseph Haydn, and Thelonius Monk; she conveys her ideas and reactions in a variety of dance styles. Another popular work, *Sue's Leg,* was premiered in 1974 as a 25-minute dance, choreographed to music by Fats Waller.

In addition to continued extensive choreography for her company, Tharp also has created dances for Joffrey Ballet Company and American Ballet Theater; and her *Push Comes to Shove,* choreographed for Mikhail Baryshnikov, was hailed by ballet and modern supporters alike. In the late 1970's, she choreographed a dance for Olympic medalist John Curry, contributing to the broadening concept of "ice-dancing." She has been the recipient of numerous awards, including the respected Guggenheim Fellowship, which she received twice.

PLACES FOR EXPERIMENTAL DANCE

One of the differences between modern dance and ballet has to do with the places where dance is performed. Although the major modern dance companies tend to perform in concert halls or theaters, with a traditional orientation toward the use of the stage and seated audience, many of the more experimental dancers tend to think in entirely different terms, for both aesthetic and economic reasons. A major influence was brought to bear by

[31]Siegel, *At the Vanishing Point,* p. 266.

a number of modern playwrights, such as Sam Sheppard, or producing companies, like the Environmental Theater, which had entirely new and revolutionary concepts of staging. Richard Schechner writes:

> The first scenic principle of environmental theater is to create and use whole spaces. Literally spheres of spaces, spaces within spaces, spaces which contain, or envelop, or relate, or touch all the areas where the audience is and/or the performers perform. All the spaces are actively involved in all the aspects of the performance. . . . And the theater itself is part of larger environments outside the theater. These larger out-of-the-theater spaces are the life of the city; and also temporal-historical spaces—modalities of time/space.[32]

Often, in the work of such companies, huge interior spaces are redesigned to permit a fluid use of different kinds of space and to permit the actors or dancers to become involved with the audience, and conversely the audience with the performers. Environmental theater is concerned with the fullness of space and the varied ways in which space can be transformed, articulated, and animated. Performer training involves exercises that help the group members become aware of space as a force, and their relationship

Dance, choreographed by Lucinda Childs to music by Philip Glass. Courtesy of Performing Artservices, Inc. Photographed by Lois Greenfield.

[32]Richard Schechner, *Environmental Theater* (New York: Hawthorn Books, 1973), p. 2.

with it. They offer "means by which people communicate with space and with each other through space; ways of locating centers of energy and boundaries, areas of inter-penetration, exchange, and isolation, 'auras' and 'lines of energy.'"[33]

Experimental dancers, as described in the previous pages, have pursued this approach. Numerous other examples might be cited. McDonagh, for example, comments that Twyla Tharp's main purpose in choreography "is to throw lines of movement across and through space and thereby establish a zone of human mastery over the real estate that is our environment."[34]

Loft Dance. An inevitable outcome of this concern with controlled space, as well as of the economics of modern dance performance, resulted in a growing number of experimental modern dancers developing remodeled loft, garage, or warehouse areas where they lived, rehearsed, choreographed, and performed for audiences. Often living in run-down industrial and manufacturing areas, side by side with other artists, such arrangements made it unnecessary to rent space in expensive theaters or concert halls, and provided an intimate setting for informal dance presentations. Often, too, since rehearsal space was also performance space, the line between groups improvising and creating dances, and presenting them, tended to disappear. Audiences came to see process, as well as product, and in many cases became involved in the work themselves. At the same time, the works tended to be so casual, informal, and modest in presentation that the dance critics ignored them and, without public attention, they came to constitute a sort of "dance underground." In some measure, this tendency has been counteracted by the fusion of loft choreographers in special festivals, bringing together a variety of performing groups and attracting larger audiences and public attention.

MODERN DANCE COOPERATIVES

Historically, a number of smaller halls have been made available in large cities for modern dance. In New York, for example, the 92nd Street Y.M. and Y.W.H.A. for years provided a setting for a wide variety of modern dance companies to perform. In the same city, the Judson Memorial Church in Greenwich Village and Riverside Church, near Columbia University, have been centers of experimental modern dance activity. On a larger scale, the Brooklyn Academy of Music and New York City Center have hosted many dance groups.

A more recent development has involved a number of avant-garde choreographers and small companies joining together in cooperative producing groups with their own rehearsal and performing halls. In New York City, one of the first such organizations was the Dance Theater Workshop, headed by David White, which has sought to assist small modern dance

[33]*Ibid.,* p. 12.

[34]McDonagh, *op cit.,* p. 100.

David Gordon/Pick Up Company in *What Happened?* Photograph by Lois Greenfield.

companies since the mid-1960s with problems of promotion, scheduling, rehearsal and performance space, publicity, and similar administrative concerns. Operating at first in a loft in the Chelsea area of Manhattan, the workshop encouraged member groups to exchange services with each other on a volunteer basis. Often choreographers danced in each other's works, and assisted with lighting, staging, and other technical production tasks. Now known as the American Theater Laboratory, and operating in a larger facility leased from Jerome Robbins, the center presents a forty-five-week performance season, with assistance from the National Endowment for the Arts and other non-profit foundations, and is a vital center of creative dance activity.

Similarly, in the mid-1970s, a modern dance cooperative known as the Dance Umbrella was formed, to provide a permanent and economically viable performing space for dance in New York. Twelve established groups, including the Viola Farber, Cliff Keuter, James Cunningham, Lar Lubovitch, Merce Cunningham, Kathryn Posin, Elizabeth Keen, Dan Wagoner, Margaret Beals, and Kazuko Hirabayashi dance companies, joined together to sponsor separate dance evenings for each of the groups during the 1975–1976 season, at the Roundabout Theater in New York. The theater itself, with a large stage and 300-seat hall, provided such services as box office and administrative services, technical functions and equipment; a subscription series relieved many of the companies of the need to actively promote their own performances. With funding by the National Endowment for the Arts Dance Panel, the New York State Council on the Arts, and grants by the Mellon and Ford Foundations, the Dance Umbrella concept has flourished, projecting a clearer and more forceful professional image of modern dance than the companies' separate seasons would have done individually.[35]

Although New York City has tended to be the center of modern dance activity in the United States, obviously there are flourishing centers of performance in many other locations throughout the country and in Canada. Among the most active sponsors of new choreography and performing groups are the colleges and universities; many of them host special dance workshops, institutes, student groups, and dance series in which leading companies perform on tour.

MODERN DANCE IN OTHER CITIES

In the San Francisco Bay Area of California, for example, modern dancers have forged a solid organizational foundation for mutual support and sharing. Numerous dance groups cooperate in sponsoring professional-level classes and workshops, sharing rehearsal and performing space, and promoting each others' efforts. A considerable number of groups involved in contact improvisation, such as Mangrove, Metropolitan Quartet, Reunion, and West Wing, make up the Bay Area Contact Coalition. The San Francisco Dancers' Workshop, led by Ann Halprin, has encouraged creative development in modern dance, and sponsored year-long series of free concerts for the public at large, in cooperation with the San Francisco Museum of Modern Art. Other groups, including the San Francisco Bay Area Dance Coalition, have joined in efforts to hold dance film festivals, establish an archives system for the performing arts, and assist performing groups with legal and other administrative needs. A non-profit corporation, Performing Arts Services, Inc., was recently established to help modern dance and other performing arts companies in the Bay Area promote attendance, and make low-cost tickets available to a wider segment of the general public.

The Colorado Contemporary Dance is a recently formed non-profit organization of volunteers in Denver, established to heighten awareness of modern dance and develop enthusiastic dance audiences. Recently, it began a well-received performance series of professional companies, including the Alwin Nikolais Dance Theater, the Utah Repertory Dance Company, the Pilobolus Company, and others.

The Philadelphia Dance Alliance has recently organized major festivals of that city's modern dance and ballet companies, with emphasis on representation by newer contemporary dance choreographers and groups, and by the area's numerous college dance programs. They have sponsored annual choreographic workshops by artists such as Anna Sokolow and annual series of master classes by leading dancers and teachers.

[35]Bruce Bordelon, "Umbrella: New Concept in American Dance Management," *Dance Magazine,* May, 1976, pp. 29–30.

Foot Rules, choreographed by Douglass Dunn. Courtesy of Performing Artservices, Inc. Photograph by Nathaniel Tileston.

Winnipeg's Contemporary Dancers is promoting modern dance influence throughout Western Canada, with a repertory subscription series and extensive touring funded by the Canada Council. Because of the shortage of trained dancers in the region, auditions are held in Winnipeg, Toronto, Montreal, and occasionally in New York.

The Bureau for Cultural Affairs in Atlanta, Georgia, has actively promoted modern dance festivals and performances by a large number of local and regional contemporary dance groups. In addition, the Metropolitan Atlanta Dance Coalition, a cooperative effort of local modern dance companies, has been formed to assist its members as an information clearinghouse, to publish a dance newsletter, and conduct seminars on grant strategies and proposal-writing.

The Utah Repertory Dance Theater, a democratically-run modern dance collective established originally by Virginia Tanner, has toured widely, sponsored a number of dance workshops in collaboration with colleges in the Rocky Mountain region, and offered regional summer dance festivals in Salt Lake City.

The Detroit Metropolitan Dance Project, in cooperation with the Michigan Dance Association, has sponsored statewide conferences to ex-

Trisha Brown Dance Company in *Glacial Decoy,* with visual presentation and costumes by Robert Rauschenberg. Courtesy of Performing Artservices, Inc. Photograph by Babette Mangolte.

plore varied aspects of dance aesthetics, criticism, management, and production.

Numerous other examples might be cited of local or state organizations being formed to assist modern dance, or to join the efforts of smaller, struggling companies in collaborative productions, seasons, or other promotional efforts. Obviously, there is a tremendous amount of ferment in this field and, unlike ballet, where large companies with a relative degree of establishment support are able to capture major elements of public support, modern dancers are exploring new organizational approaches to supporting themselves financially and reaching new audiences.

Such coalitions as those mentioned have typically sponsored professional concert series, regional dance festivals, dance event calendars, master classes, and choreographic workshops, have served as resource centers for the dance community, and have encouraged expansion of dance awareness in the public at large.

STANDARDS AND AUDIENCE EXPECTATIONS

Earlier in this chapter, it was pointed out that many newer avant-garde artists are relatively unconcerned about attracting and pleasing large and consistent audiences. Instead, they are content to dance for themselves, or for small numbers of sympathetic dance enthusiasts. However, the majority of modern dancers and choreographers do not share this view. Instead, their intention is to make an aesthetic statement that will *reach* an audience and make a significant impact. In this regard, there is a marked difference between modern dance and ballet.

One of the most serious problems of modern dance is that, both in colleges and in the community, it is widely assumed that anyone can become a choreographer. As a consequence, many individuals with comparatively little training, skill, or talent have established themselves as choreographers and have presented works through which audiences have judged the field of modern dance. Often audiences have lacked criteria by which to do this, or any sense of perspective, or knowledge of other modern art forms. The result has frequently been that the product is poor and the audience response negative. The temptation of avant-garde dance is that it creates a situation in which there are even fewer standards—in fact, none—which an audience or choreographer can apply. Thus, how intelligently can it be judged by a spectator? How many uncomfortable questions can a choreographer ask himself?

The premises on which avant-garde dance are based sacrifice certain strengths inherent in a more traditional approach to choreography. Self-expression, naive as it may be, at least provides an impulse for the composer and the possibility of meaningful communication with an audience. The selection of thematic material which is dramatic, or which is perceptibly concerned with social content or psychological insights, again offers the possibility of holding an audience, or providing the piece with structure. The use of music which has its own form, mood, rhythms, and aesthetic content, lends another kind of strength to dance. The approach to choreography which values the application of traditional principles of artistic construction—balance, contrast, sequence, climax, dynamics—offers a system in which the composer may learn a craft, and through which he may be judged.

Much avant-garde dance tends to lack these elements. It stands or falls strictly on the basis of superficial and transitory audience appeal. And, based on many of the works that have been presented thus far, many of the most experimental pieces have little to offer, once the novelty of freedom in "no-holds-barred" improvisation, or the surprise of seeing dancers in customarily hidden activity, or states of dress (or undress) has passed away.

This, of course, represents a personal judgment. Each artist, as well as each spectator, must make his own decisions in matters of artistic taste. However, many teachers and choreographers fear that if the avant-garde approach to choreography assumes dominance in the modern dance field, it will have serious consequences. If an increasing number of choreographers—particularly those who lack real conviction in this area, or whose basic skills are limited—adopt this approach because it is fashionable and they feel it is easy and cannot be judged with rigor, the risk is that modern dance will come increasingly to be judged as a strange and mysterious "put on." Instead of being regarded as a significant art form, it will be threatened, even more than in the recent past, with rejection or disinterest. Therefore, it would appear that an atmosphere somehow must be maintained—both in dance academies and in colleges where beginning choreography is done—that permits young artists to critically evaluate the trend, to see it in comparison to other styles of choreography, and if they wish, to reject it, rather than accept it blindly.

However, it must be strongly affirmed that a movement like this *must* exist if modern dance, like any other art, is to be healthy. It represents the cutting edge of creativity in dance, and it is entirely possible that a decade or two from now, when entirely new possibilities for creative dance have been discovered, what is being done today will appear incredibly traditional and outmoded.

CHANGING RELATIONSHIP WITH BALLET

Finally, it is necessary to examine the changing relationship between modern dance and ballet. Obviously, during the early decades of modern dance's development, there was much hostility between the two. Modern dancers for the most part rejected ballet strenuously, as a foreign, decadent, and mechanical art form. They saw it as meaningless in terms of meeting the contemporary concerns of people. In their view, it was so committed to an obsolete movement vocabulary, and to themes of a distant past, that it no longer was significant to those who wished to view dance as part of the contemporary cultural scene.

Margaret H'Doubler, the leading pioneer of modern dance in higher education, wrote in this vein:

> The ballet is a form of theater dance that continues to be popular in the more urban centers of this country, although as an art form it has never taken root in American soil. Its earliest importations were taught by foreign dance masters, and in essence they were dances of an aristocratic Europe. . . . As a theater art, dance should inspire and thrill, and cause man to think and feel. If ballet were denied its spectacular settings, costumes and orchestra, and were forced to rely upon its movements for conveyance of meaning, it is doubtful if it would carry as much significance as drama or dance. Both the technique and the themes seem to have lost touch with life, with common human impulses from which all the arts spring.[36]

On the other hand, Lincoln Kirstein, writing in the mid-1930s, characterized the way in which many of the proponents of ballet thought about modern dance. He described those who create "in spite of and outside tradition" as almost invariably suffering from lack of information, competence, or accomplishment. Ultimately, he saw what they created as becoming a rigid "school of formulated dilettantism."[37]

Even more critically, the English ballet critic Arnold Haskell wrote about an early stage of what was to become modern dance:

[36]Margaret H'Doubler, *Dance: A Creative Art Experience* (New York: F. S. Crofts and Co., 1940), p. 38.

[37]Lincoln Kirstein, *Dance: A Short History of Classic Theatrical Dancing* (New York: G. P. Putnam's Sons, 1935), p. 305.

> Dancing that gets its inspiration from ancient Greece is also popular today, and doubtless it is of distinct benefit as physical education. So is hockey. (Both have a thickening effect on the ankles.) Its artistic pedigree will not bear close examination. . . . The dancing rebels do provide one fine ingredient—thought. There is a close parallel here with the unlicensed medical practitioner.[38]

Thus there was a mutual hostility between modern dancers and ballet performers; it extended to audiences, teachers, and choreographers. Most modern dancers, although they might have had a degree of ballet training in their youth, regarded it as a separate and unrelated art, and one in which they had little interest—certainly one which had no part in their own systems of technical training. Most ballet dancers and choreographers saw modern dance as a somewhat obscure cult of enthusiasts who concealed with mystic statements of purpose their lack of ability to really dance. Or, in contrast, they viewed it, as Haskell did, as a fairly vigorous but certainly not artistic form of physical education.

However, even in the early years there were some exceptions. Ted Shawn, who had had ballet training himself, regarded it as a valuable ingredient in the development of a dancer:

> So much has been said and written against the ballet that I feel it is wise to emphasize some of its positive virtues. Nothing has ever taken its place for disciplinary training. There is no technique in any other style of dancing that is so valuable for producing exactitude, precision, sense of form, and sense of line. I do not think that it should be used as the sole type of training, just as I would not advocate in an academic curriculum that a student should have nothing but mathematics. . . . It must be taught wisely and with discrimination. . . .[39]

On the other hand, an increasing number of ballet choreographers came to be influenced by the approach of the leading modern dance composers. In a number of cases, their works became hardly distinguishable from modern dance itself. Kurt Jooss, in Germany during the 1920s and 1930s, was strongly influenced by the work of Mary Wigman and Rudolf von Laban; many of his important ballet works, including the famous *The Green Table,* clearly show the influence of the early modern dance. Respect began to grow steadily for the major modern dance choreographers who emerged in America during the 1930s. Thus, in England, which has never had a strong modern dance movement, in spite of Laban's influence there, Susan Lester comments, "The principal pioneers in Modern Dance are a force which has made a formidable impression on the course of theatrical stage dancing. . . ."[40]

> In Britain, all too little is known, and less is appreciated, about dancing in this genre, despite the presence of the Ballets Jooss between 1933 and 1947. The

[38] Arnold Haskell, *Ballet* (Harmondsworth, Middlesex, England: Pergamon Books, 1951), p. 45.

[39] Ted Shawn, *Dance We Must* (London: Dennis Dobson, Ltd., 1946), p. 88.

[40] Susan Lester, *Ballet Here and Now* (London: Dennis Dobson, Ltd., 1961), p. 25.

visit of Martha Graham and her company from the U.S.A. in 1954 was a significant introduction to Britain of a unique form, combining highly trained artists, an artistic director and principal choreographer of great ability, and intensely theatrical ballets with finely conceived modern musical scores and décors. The chief barrier between Graham and her public in Britain has been unfamiliarity with her medium and hence, some prejudice and a general hesitation in acceptance.[41]

Others were to follow Graham; by the middle 1960s, the companies of Merce Cunningham, Alvin Ailey, and Paul Taylor all enjoyed extended seasons in Great Britain. In 1964, Francis Mason, Deputy Cultural Attaché, of the United States Embassy in London, described their great success:

> ... audiences were fervent, faithful, and articulate.... If there ever was a prejudice here against dance that is not strictly ballet, it is now strictly on the wane.[42]

Both in the United States and abroad, the barrier between modern dance and ballet has been breached in two ways.

First, modern dancers have increasingly recognized the value of ballet training. More and more they are incorporating fundamental ballet terms, positions, and movements into their systems of modern dance training. It is becoming increasingly necessary for a skilled modern dancer to take separate classes in ballet as part of his training. This is reflected both in the schools that serve professional modern dance companies, and in the programs that are devoted to dance as a performing art in American colleges and universities.

Ballet, on the other hand, has been chiefly influenced by modern dance in terms of choreographic ideas and approaches. Many of the great contemporary ballet choreographers, including Tudor, de Mille, Robbins, and Ashton, have selected the kinds of themes that modern dance broke new ground exploring—in symbolic works involving psychological insights of human behavior. They have also clearly been influenced by the leading modern dancers in terms of their use of dancers and dance groups, in their selection of music and decor, and in their extension of the range of dance movement. In a number of contemporary ballet works, the movement is indistinguishable from what one might find on the modern dance concert stage.

As a consequence of this breakdown of the barriers between the two forms, there has in recent years been a widespread use of modern dance choreographers to develop works for major ballet companies. One of the frequently noted problems of the ballet world is its lack of gifted young choreographers. Thus, company directors have felt free to cross the line. American Ballet Theater has premiered new works by Glen Tetley, known as a modern dance choreographer. The Harkness Ballet has included in its repertory dances by such moderns as Alvin Ailey, Stuart Hodes, and Donald McKayle. The Joffrey Ballet presents works by Anna Sokolow and Norman

[41] *Ibid.,* p. 26.

[42] Francis Mason, "London Likes American Dancer," *The New York Times,* December 27, 1964, p. X-19.

Walker. Martha Graham and Balanchine collaborated on a two-part work, *Episodes,* with music by Anton Webern; it was performed by the New York City Ballet at the City Center as part of the regular 1959 season. Other examples are numerous. In 1966, Merce Cunningham created a new work, *Summerspace,* on commission for the New York City Ballet. John Butler, whose primary background is in modern dance, has composed many works for the Harkness Ballet, the Netherlands Dance Theater, the Pennsylvania Ballet, and the Metropolitan Opera Ballet, as well as numerous nationwide television dance programs. James Waring, a highly experimental and creative choreographer, merged the two forms so fully in both his teaching and composition, that it was not possible to definitely identify him with either modern dance or ballet. McDonagh wrote:

> (Waring) never believed in the distinctions that people drew between the performance of modern dances and ballets and thought that the generic name, ballet, should be applied to both forms of serious theater dancing. At one point, he referred to his own works as "choreographies" so as not to skew them into one camp or the other . . .[43]

Indeed, just as modern dance technique has been influenced by ballet, the strength and vitality of modern dance has influenced much of contemporary ballet movement. As a result, much of the work of such choreographers as Glen Tetley, John Butler, Gerald Arpino, Norman Walker, and John Cranko is really a synthesis of both forms, and not clearly distinguishable as either.

Yet, will the difference between the two forms break down completely? It seems unlikely. There will be, for the foreseeable future, a group of modern dancers and choreographers who will reject ballet training, or at least be unwilling to accept it as a primary source of technique. They will be determined to pursue such irrevocably experimental directions that they will continue to be recognizable as modern dancers. On the other hand, certain companies will continue to base their repertory very heavily on classic dances of the Romantic period, or on modern works which have a strong classic flavor about them; these companies will be easily identifiable as ballet companies. Somewhere in a middle group, there will probably be an increasing number of modern dance companies that look very much as if they were performing ballet—and vice versa.

This process of cross-fertilization is undoubtedly a good thing for theater dance in America. It does not, for the immediate future, however, serve to solve the pressing problems of professional dance companies—particularly those of modern dance artists. For them, as suggested earlier, there continues to be a minimal degree of support and acceptance by the public at large.

Many proposals have been made to improve this situation. Some suggest that the solution is the establishment of modern dance repertory companies, which will perform the great works of the outstanding American choreographers and thus ensure their continued availability, as well as pro-

[43]Don McDonagh, "Keeping James Waring's Choreography Alive," *The New York Times,* March 6, 1977, p. D-16.

vide the field with a sense of tradition, which it has lacked when compared to ballet. Others feel that the primary need is to develop more theaters specifically designed for and available to modern dance companies. Still others believe that the heart of the problem lies in the need for the American public to become more fully attuned to *all* forms of contemporary art. As far as dance is concerned, they feel that this can only be done by bringing high-quality dance programs to "grass roots" regions of the country, and by strengthening the role of colleges and universities in this field.

Without question, the heart of the matter, for both modern dance and ballet, lies in audience readiness for dance, and in the approaches that may be used to bring dance more effectively before the public. The roles of educational institutions, and of government and foundation programs in the arts, are explored in the chapters that follow.

12 Ethnic, Folk, Ballroom, and Jazz Dance

The preceding chapters have dealt in detail with the artistic or theatrical forms of dance that are most familiar to the Western world—ballet and modern dance.

In addition to these, there are several other important forms of dance which involve great numbers of enthusiasts around the world, as skilled performers, spectators, or recreational participants. These forms are *ethnic, folk, ballroom,* and *jazz* dance. While related to each other, each has a distinct character and function in society.

ETHNIC DANCE

Ethnic dance is the term used to describe the traditional dances performed by the people in a given nation or region, as part of the society's cultural heritage. Anatol Joukowsky stresses the unchanging quality of true ethnic dance:

> Ethnic dance is one done by the people in the original place, in living form, today or yesterday. It is transferred or transported to a new place without any change and is performed as it was originally. The music is done without adaptation. . . . Like the museum piece, ethnic dance . . . transfers the culture and knowledge of a people to present and future generations.[1]

Often ethnic dances have close ties to national history, social custom, religion, or other cultural elements. The term itself is derived from the Greek *ethnos,* meaning *people,* suggesting that ethnic dances are those of the common people. This is not necessarily the case, since ethnic dances may

[1]Anatol M. Joukowsky, *The Teaching of Ethnic Dance* (New York: J. Lowell Pratt and Co., 1965), p. 1.

also be difficult or complex dances which are presented by a group of highly skilled performers to large audiences. Typically, Indian classical dancing requires many years of intensive training to perform well, and is quite different from peasant dancing which is much simpler in technique and style.

We tend also to apply the term *ethnic* to the dance of non-Western cultures in Asia, Africa, or Latin America. These dance forms tend to be somewhat less familiar to us and more exotic than the traditional dances of Western nations; in addition, they are generally more closely attached to their original cultural sources or ceremonial functions. However, the authentic dances of Spain, Yugoslavia, or other European nations which have retained a peasant way of life in rural areas and have treasured their historic customs often are also referred to as ethnic dances.

Among the most unique and interesting ethnic dance traditions are those of Indonesia, Japan, India, and Spain, each of which are briefly described in the following pages.

Indonesian Dance. Dance is an integral part of life throughout the Indonesian archipelago, and particularly on the island of Bali. According to Beryl de Zoete and Walter Spies, it accompanies every stage of life from infancy to the grave, and is an essential element in an endless series of public and private festivals, temple services, and processions:

> . . . it is as members of age groups that unmarried boys and girls perform ceremonial dances of offering and dedication in the temple, where also old women renew the religious dances of their youth.[2]

In non-religious dances, people of every age, caste, or occupation may perform, and most dancers or actors (the same word applies to both) have other occupations as craftsmen, agricultural workers, or fishermen. Only for a few highly skilled dancers or teachers does dance become an exclusive way of life. The Balinese people themselves are physically extremely graceful and sensitive; their daily movement appears to have an almost choreographic quality. In addition, music pervades the atmosphere, with even the youngest children sitting between their fathers' knees in the *gamelan* orchestra, or learning the melodies and complicated rhythms of the gongs, drums, cymbals, and other percussive instruments at an extremely early age.

Dance itself appears everywhere, not only in temples or other religious ceremonials, but throughout the Balinese village. De Zoete and Spies write:

> . . . wherever there is a space to dance, to mount a play, there is the Balinese stage. It may be the village street, the graveyard, the temple-court, the ground outside the temple, the courtyard of a Balinese house. . . . Its floor is the bare earth . . . its roof the sky or an overhanging tree . . .[3]

Dances are of many traditional types and may be carried on as dramatic spectacles for extended periods of time, while villagers sit in the audience

[2]Beryl de Zoete and Walter Spies, *Dance and Drama in Bali* (New York: Thomas Yoseloff, 1958), p. 7.

[3]*Ibid.*, p. 11.

and at the same time eat, drink, chat, or play with their children. Many dances are performed in spectacular costumes and masks, often of monkeys, birds, or other animals. Other dances, such as the *Pentjak,* are warlike spectacles, dramatic plays, known as *Legong,* or sung dance-dramas called *Ardja.* Perhaps the most spectacular Balinese dances are the so-called trance dances, in which performers go into an apparent state of hypnosis or religious possession, handling red-hot coals, or striking themselves with the Malay kris (a long, sharp dagger) so forcefully that the weapon may bend against their chests, but apparently does not wound them. From time to time, troupes of highly skilled Balinese dancers tour the world and are acclaimed by sophisticated dance audiences and critics for the remarkable virtuosity of their performance. When this happens, obviously, the dance has been removed from its natural setting and is presented in a concert-art form; yet it gives a vivid impression of the unique quality, grace, and mood of Indonesian dance.

Japanese Dance. Somewhat more formalized in its style, presentation, and organization is the ethnic dance art of Japan. This may be described under several categories: the theatrical, classic dance known as *Bugaku,* the famous *Kabuki* dance-theater, or such peasant dances as the *Bon* dances, linked to countryside festivals and celebrations.[4]

Dance in Japan has an ancient and well-documented history. *Gagaku* is the term used to describe noble or elegant music, stemming from a period from the 9th to 10th century A.D. which drew elements from many Asian nations and cultures and was established as a traditional form of entertainment in the Imperial Japanese household. *Gagaku* incorporated both music and dance of both sacred and secular origin, as part of Buddhist services and at Shinto shrines and as entertainment at the Imperial Court. A dance performance in *Gagaku* is known as *Bugaku. Bugaku* dance is relatively simple and symmetrical, lacking in rapid or complex movement and with dramatic elements subordinated to pure dance form. Extremely subtle in its impact, and generally done in old court costumes, *Bugaku* is not a dead art. New dances continue to be composed within the traditional style for presentation at major ceremonies or national events, such as the marriage of a crown prince.

In contrast, the *Kabuki* dance theater is a relatively new form of dance art, having originated during the 19th century. However, it was clearly influenced by older and more traditional elements of the Japanese theater. Much of its content, in terms of dramatic themes, costuming and other conventions of dance, is descended from ancient sources. However, *Kabuki* also continues to change, as new plays are created to fit contemporary themes. *Kabuki* blends music, acting, and dance in a highly stylized performance. Men enact all the roles, both male and female. Many of the poses and movements are influenced by an earlier period of puppet theater, and the performers wear extremely heavy make-up which gives them a fixed facial expression, like puppets. *Kabuki* is performed in several styles or types: the *Kyogen Zyoruri,* which is related to the puppet drama and has much

[4]See Gladys Michaelis, "The Kabuki—A Dance-Drama Art Form of Japan," *Dance Magazine,* May 1977, pp. 83–86.

dramatic content; dances drawn from the traditional *Noh* drama, which are performed only at special times of the year; so-called "transfiguration" dances, in which there is little story or plot, but in which dancers change roles and characters; comic *Zyoruri* dances; and others.

In addition, dances are also characterized by the style and range of movement. *Odori* is a form of stage dance marked by swift movements of the feet and lower part of the body, while *Mai* involves movement of the upper half of the body, including the head, arms, and shoulders, and *Shosa* dance is generally mimetic and realistic imitative movement. Like the dance of Bali, Japanese stage dance is deeply rooted in cultural tradition and may be difficult for Westerners to understand and appreciate. Nevertheless, outstanding *Kabuki* or *Bugaku* companies occasionally visit the United States and are generally well-received as emissaries of a unique and fascinating dance tradition.

Indian Dance. Indian dance represents probably the most varied and highly developed ethnic dance form of the Orient. There are several major schools of Indian dance, related to the varied regions and ethnic or religious sub-groups of this nation, with the predominant form being Hindu dance. Since the Hindus believe that the universe was created by Lord Shiva, a dancing god, dance is intricately attached to their religion and is found in many ceremonies, rituals, and in varied temple decorations and carvings. In India, dance has been highly developed as a form of communication, with stylized movements and gestures of many parts of the body—hands, fingers, arms, eyes, nose, mouth, head, and neck, among others—being used to convey literal meaning. While the upper part of the body is the most active in dance, there are also definite foot positions and movements both on the ground and in the air.[5]

Bharata Natya is one of the major Hindu dance styles or schools of Southern India, and is believed to date back as far as 1500 B.C. It is practiced by temple dancers and originated in and around Madras, where it was found as part of the royal court. *Bharata Natya* programs, with both dancers and musicians on stage, continue without pause for three hours or more, and range from abstract, lyric dances to more literally expressive or pantomimic works. *Kathakali* is a separate dance form (actually a dance–drama) which originated at a much later time in the region of Malabar, and is used to illustrate the broad range of Hindu literature. Costumes and make-up are highly stylized, and facial expressions, body movements, and gesture language of the hands, known as *hasta mudras,* all help to tell the story.

Dances of the North tend to be less ornate and structured. *Kathak* dance, for example, was originally done by Brahmin priests known as Kathaks, who used dance movement to illustrate religious fables or anecdotes of the gods. Today it is performed by both men and women as a form of entertainment, and is marked by heavy, rhythmic beating of feet on the ground, chanting of syllables by the dancer to the drummer to convey rhythms, and pantomimic episodes drawn from religious lore. *Manipuri* dance represents still another important dance form of the Northeast re-

[5]La Meri, "Hindu Dance," in Anatole Chujoy and P. W. Manchester, eds., *The Dance Encyclopedia* (New York: Simon and Schuster, 1967), p. 456.

gion; it also deals with religious themes, has relatively little gesture language, and tends to be more flowing and quiet than other Indian dance styles.

Because of its highly stylized movements and the great range of dance vocabulary and dance episodes or stories, Indian dance requires intensive training over many years for the individual who seeks to refine professional performance technique and style.

Spanish Dance. Spanish dance is one of the most exciting and varied of ethnic dance forms. It has traditionally been a highly popular form of stage dance, with many touring companies and star dancers who perform in night clubs and theaters around the world. Spaniards have a deep love for their native dances; for them it is almost a cult.[6] Within the nation's 49 regions, there are over 100 accepted, unchanging, traditional dances, of several major styles. The mood of Spanish dance ranges widely from the fiery, explosive flamenco to quieter, subtler, and even languorous dance styles which are somewhat Oriental in their flavor. Typically, Spanish dancing is accompanied by the guitar and singing, although it may also be performed to the orchestral music of leading Spanish composers. It represents both a popular, even peasant, art form which is seen everywhere—at village festivals, processionals, and varied social events—and, in more developed presentations, a dance art that approaches ballet in its technical demands and virtuosity.

Historically, a number of popular Spanish dances have come into being throughout the centuries—each one arousing a great wave of national interest, and then becoming part of the body of national dance. Examples of these have been the *Fandango, Bolero, Zarabanda, Chacona,* and *Seguidillas.* Some dances were typically found in the popular lyric theater, while others are attached to the major regions of Spain, such as Andalucia, Catalonia, or the region surrounding Seville. La Meri points out that one major classification of Spanish dance is the "school dance;" this includes such dances as the courtly *Pavane,* still performed within the repertoire of leading Spanish dances. A distinctly different style is the flamenco, a flirtatious, fiery dance of gypsy origin, using castanets, much heel work on the floor, and staccato, explosive guitar playing and singing.

Spanish dancing has typically been done to the music of such composers as de Falla, Granados, and Albeniz, and has been a popular element in operas like *Carmen* or folk ballets like *The Three-Cornered Hat.* It has also been an important element in the repertoires of such early ballerinas as Taglioni or Fanny Elssler; in more recent years, leading Spanish dance idols have been Argentina, Argentinita, Pilar Lopez, José Greco, or Rosario and Antonio, who have toured extensively with their own companies of dancers, singers and musicians, to popular acclaim. Within the past two decades, Spanish dance has undergone something of an ebb in popularity, as far as public interest is concerned. In part, this is due to changing modes of popular entertainment. The kinds of night clubs or theaters that featured Spanish dance and similar forms of musical entertainment have declined sharply, possibly because of the growth of television as a form of home-

[6]La Meri, *Spanish Dancing* (New York: A. S. Barnes and Co., 1948), p. 1.

based amusement. Walter Terry also believes that the emphasis on flamenco dancing as the most spectacular and exciting of all Spanish dance forms (to the exclusion of numerous other regional or classical dances which lend variety and interest to the art) has tended to limit its appeal to audiences.[7] However, there is no question that it will persist as an important national dance art, and that, as companies continue to present Spanish dance, it will grow again in popularity.

FOLK DANCE

The term *folk dance* is often used interchangeably with *ethnic dance,* and indeed may be used to describe the same kinds of traditional national dances. In a scholarly analysis of European folk dance, Joan Lawson shows clearly how the historical development, geography, social customs, religion, and occupations found in various regions of Europe have directly influenced the folk dances that emerged through the centuries.[8]

Today the term folk dance tends to be applied to dances of somewhat recent origin, or dances of the people which are related more closely to social customs and recreational events than to ancient religious and ceremonial sources. Typically, many dances which are called folk dances today tend to be based on such ballroom dance steps as the waltz, schottische, mazurka, and polka, and thus to be of relatively recent origin and to have little or no ritual or other cultural significance. Joukowsky also suggests that what we call folk dances today seem to be ethnic dances which have undergone change through the years, and lost their original character and authentic forms.

Finally, most of the dances which are called folk dances today are of European or Middle-East origin, while ethnic dances, as shown earlier, tend to come from other parts of the world. Folk dancing is particularly popular as a recreational pastime in the United States. Since World War II, there has been a thriving international folk dance movement, with thousands of clubs or community groups that practice traditional dances of many nations. Dances from the Balkan countries, such as Rumania, Bulgaria, and Yugoslavia, along with Greek, Israeli, and other Middle-Eastern dances, are performed in many college and university dance groups, often with native instructors conducting workshops. In school and college physical education programs, folk dances tend to be drawn from older collections of dances which were published several decades ago by Elizabeth Burchenal and other authorities in this field.

It would be inaccurate to say that *all* folk dance is historically authentic and performed today just as it was centuries ago. The very nature of the folk process, in which dances, songs, or stories are changed as they are passed along from teacher to teacher or performer to performer, means that the cultural heritage inevitably is transformed over time. Sometimes dances of the common people are deliberately stylized for performance, or put to-

[7]Walter Terry, cited in Lois Draegin, "Spanish Dance in America: Fanning the Spanish Fever," *Dance Magazine,* April, 1978, p. 66.

[8]Joan Lawson, *European Folk Dance* (London: Sir Isaac Pitman, Ltd., 1955), Chapter 1.

Members of Dobré Folk Ensemble of the University of Oregon, directed by Linda Hearn and Jerry Duke, perform Bulgarian dance suite.

gether in new forms in published collections or phonograph record descriptions. Not infrequently, new dances are created by folk leaders. If these are widely accepted and continue to be performed over a period of time, eventually they come to be regarded as folk dances.

For example, an organization that is highly regarded within the folk arts field is the Country Dance and Song Society of America. Early in this century, a leading British folklorist, Cecil Sharp, revived interest in the traditional Morris, sword, country, and court dances of England, and explored the lingering heritage of English dancing in the American Appalachian Mountain region. He established an English folk dance and song society; its American counterpart was formed by an outstanding English teacher of folk dancing who came to the United States, May Gadd. Today, the Society has dozens of branches throughout the United States which offer courses, workshops, festivals, publications, and leader-training courses in traditional English and American country dancing and music. Yet, even this organization, which greatly values authentic presentation of old materials, does not hesitate to include newer American square dances, contra dances, mixers, and English dances as well, in its repertoire.

Perhaps the most interesting example of how a literature of folk dance may deliberately be created is found in the young nation of Israel. Here, when Jews came together from all over the world, after Israel was declared a nation, it became necessary to weld a new, unified culture, based on many old traditions. Dance was seen as one of the ways of doing this; Judith Ingber writes:

> The dance creators took their inspiration from the rich characteristics of the various communities outside of Israel in the Diaspora; from the traditions and rituals of Judaism; from the colorful life-styles of those who had continued to live in Israel. . . . The folk dance creators forged all these factors in their individual yet Jewish experience, creating dances that spoke to the kibbutzim, the villages, the cities, and the immigrants. The dances gathered a swift momentum and the result has been a spirited dance, Mid-Eastern yet reflective of the experience of the Diaspora.[9]

The new Israeli folk dances had many roots: the traditional dances of North African or Oriental Jews who settled Israel, or the exciting Slavic dances of Russia or Poland, from which many other pioneers came. Often dances were created to celebrate first harvests or the discovery of water wells in the desert; typically, too, dances were choreographed for national festivals or to commemorate historical events or major festivals of Biblical times. Eventually, a great number of dances were created, of which many have survived to the present day and continue to be performed by international folk dance groups around the world.

Square and Country Dancing. Although people of many nations have brought their folk arts to the United States—immigrants from the British Isles, Scandinavia, Italy, Germany, Poland, and a host of other countries—the one uniquely American form of folk dance is the square dance.

This form is descended from the quadrille, a four-sided set dance performed as a type of social or ballroom dance throughout the Western world during the 19th century. It also was influenced by the movement patterns and steps of English and other European folk dances; in American cities and rural areas, these tended to be combined into a form of lively, robust, informal dance which emphasized a playlike, humorous spirit and was marked by the role of the caller. Traditionally, the square dance caller either chants, sings, or "prompts" the dances, and may improvise the sequence of the action, to challenge the dancers or catch them unawares. His humor and ingenious "patter" calling tends to make square dancing a rhythmic, highly entertaining activity.

Square dancing died out in interest during the early decades of this century, and then was revived by Lloyd Shaw in Colorado and by a number of other callers and teachers after World War II. It became extremely popular, with millions of dancers and thousands of clubs, particularly in small towns and suburban areas, taking up this new hobby. Square dancing appeared on television and in the movies and attracted widespread interest; however, as the fad spread, it became highly competitive. Companies published square dance books and magazines, and manufactured records of new

[9]Judith B. Ingber, "The Roots of Israeli Folk Dance," *Dance Perspectives No. 59,* Autumn 1974.

dances, costumes, loudspeaker systems, and other forms of square dance paraphernalia. The movement itself became extremely complex, with high-level callers constantly creating new dances and movements to the point that square dance clubs required that dancers take extended beginners' courses before being considered for membership. This overemphasis on complicated dancing—which often resembled close-order drills more than dancing—resulted in the movement narrowing down to a much smaller number of enthusiasts doing extremely advanced dances in tightly knit, exclusive square dance clubs.

More recently, there has been a new wave of interest in traditional square dancing, particularly among college students. Today, there are hundreds of square dance groups in university towns; students and faculty members dance to live fiddle and banjo music, practice informal clogging and relaxed, easy-going, traditional square, circle, and line dances of authentic regional backgrounds. In this sense, country dance interest is closely tied to a revival of interest in folk music. John Wilson writes of folk music festivals throughout the United States and Canada with swelling attendance, in which emphasis is placed on authentic styles rather than the synthetic music created during the folk music boom of the 1960s. Dancing plays an important part in these folk events. There is less emphasis on the words of the songs, and more on the danceable rhythms of British and Irish-inspired melodies; often dancers do impulsive solo clogging or other improvised dancing, along with structured set dances.[10]

BALLROOM DANCING

This represents a purely social form of dance, originally done in the royal court or by polite society, and today practiced as a popular, recreational form of activity. In past generations, it tended to include such set or group dances as cotillions, quadrilles, contra dances, or circle progressive dances, which are today regarded as part of the country dance movement. In contrast, ballroom dancing today is generally enjoyed by couples, and includes both the foxtrot, waltz, jitterbug, or Latin-American dances which have been popular for the past few decades and the newer disco dances, such as the "hustle" and the "chase," which represent an offshot of rock-and-roll dancing.

Ballroom dancing is truly international in scope; the same dances tend to be done in discotheques, night clubs, adult resorts, and as part of social recreation in similar settings around the world. It is performed to popular music of the present day, in which the music determines the type of dance that is to be done. Each Latin-American dance, for example, such as the tango, cha-cha-cha, merengue, or samba, is done to a particular rhythm. The recent disco dance craze has emerged as a $4-billion-a-year industry, with immense sales of records, "mod" clothing, and with thousands of popular dance halls or discotheques, catering primarily to young people, and offer-

[10]John S. Wilson, "Today's Folk Music: It Goes to Your Feet," *The New York Times*, September 7, 1975, p. D-1.

ing non-stop, recorded music of the latest hits, skillfully blended to create a hypnotic, exciting effect on the dancers—often in a highly stylized setting, with dramatic strobe lighting effects.[11] The movement itself, as seen in such hit films as *Saturday Night Fever,* is a blend of older dance forms, with elements of rock-and-roll, Latin dance movement, and the jitterbug, and much sexually expressive movement.

Overall, social dancing is certainly the most popular dance form in terms of public awareness and direct participation. Many thousands of dance teachers are employed in commercial dance studios in cities and towns throughout the country, either as part of large chains or as independent enterprises. In some cases, such studios provide instruction only in ballroom dancing. In many others, however, several forms of dance are offered, including tap dance, ballet, jazz dance, children's creative dance, and ballroom dancing—each catering to a somewhat different audience, and each with specially skilled teachers. There also are high-level ballroom dance contests, in which amateur enthusiasts compete for regional, national, and even international awards, very much like major ice-skating competitions.[12]

JAZZ DANCE

A final dance form which is linked to the other kinds of dance that have just been described is *jazz dance.* It evolved in the early part of the 20th century as a natural accompaniment to jazz music—a highly syncopated, rhythmic, and uniquely American form of popular music. Jazz got its start in the South, particularly in New Orleans, and was first played by small black bands which provided music for funeral marches, parades, honkey-tonks, and brothels. The nation first became fully aware of it during the 1920s, when, as part of the new freedom and vibrancy in national life after World War I, a period known as the "Jazz Age," dances like the black bottom, bunny hug, Charleston and varsity drag became widely popular. Jazz moved North and gave rise to the era of "swing" music, with large bands, both white and black, that played popular music heavily influenced by the rhythm and style of the earlier jazz pioneers. Swing represented a watered-down, popularized form of jazz; a smaller and more specialized group of musicians continued to perform what was often called Dixieland music, closer to the original jazz in spirit, and appealing to a much smaller group of jazz aficionados.

Jazz dance itself emerged as a hybrid form during this period. It took many of the movements that had been created as part of the popular new dances of the 1920s, and combined them with elements of primitive African dance, as well as other steps or movements that were used in the musical

[11]"Now Eggheads Begin to Study Disco Craze," *Philadelphia Inquirer,* October 20, 1978, p. 7-B.

[12]Ann Kolson, "They Dance for the Glory and the Joy," *Philadelphia Inquirer,* February 9, 1979, Weekend, p. 3.

stage dance. All these were blended into a varied and eclectic form of theater dance. As performers and choreographers like Katherine Dunham and Pearl Primus did research on authentic African, Caribbean, or Afro-American dance rituals or steps, elements of their dance were adapted and used in jazz dance. However, although heavily influenced by black sources, jazz has become a popular movement art which is used as an important area of dance training for those who seek to become professional stage or television dancers, regardless of race.

As a dance form, jazz has an exciting, vibrant and dynamic quality that makes it a natural for popular stage performances. Students of jazz learn to use their bodies in new ways, with a fluid and almost primitive movement quality. In describing a class for performers of the American Dance Machine, a company devoted to exploring past jazz traditions and presenting them for modern audiences, John Gruen comments that much of the movement resembles ritualistic steps and gestures out of deepest Africa, with vigorous, rhythmic movement of the torso and pelvis, carried on to an insistent, staccato rhythm:

> For an hour-and-a-half, the on-going dance movements are carefully dissected and analyzed. Head, neck, shoulders, torso, arms, hips, and pelvis are given difficult and highly specialized isolated movements. When the group is ready, the movements are all put together, and, two by two, the dancers execute a perfectly coordinated variation that translates into an exhilarating '60s frug.[13]

The same company has reconstructed and performed such other historic dances as the Charleston or tango of the 1920s, a Lindy or rumba of the 1940s, a 1950s jitterbug or samba, and numerous other popular dances which have been part of the continuing social dance tradition. Other teachers or choreographers do not concern themselves with specific dances of the past, but simply use jazz dance steps and movements as a key element in dance training and performance. Among the leading choreographers who have used jazz in this way have been Jerome Robbins, Jack Cole, Michael Kidd, and Bob Fosse.

Each of the dance forms described in this chapter continues to play an important role within the overall dance scene in the United States. Ethnic dance, for example, comprises hundreds of stage performances in major cities each year. In a review of a single recent season in New York City, Linda Small describes performances by a leading Scottish group, the Regimental Band of Her Majesty's Grenadier Guards and the Pipes, Drums, and Dancers of Her Majesty's Scots Guards, appearing in honor of the Silver Jubilee of Queen Elizabeth II; the Yatran Ukrainian Dance Company; the Soviet Georgian Dancers; the Ballet Nacional Festivales de España, Spain's official representative company formed to preserve historic dances of the 19th century bolera school and neo-classical dance; the Mariano Parra Spanish Dance Company; the Ibrahim Farrach Near East Dance Group; the Dancers and Musicians of Bali and Penca and Topeng Babakan of West Java; and

[13]John Gruen, "American Dance Machine: The Era of Reconstruction," *Dance Magazine*, February 1978, p. 48.

numerous other performing groups, including Indian and Japanese dance companies.[14]

In addition to being part of popular cultural entertainment, ethnic, folk, ballroom, and jazz dance are important elements in the broad spectrum of dance education in American schools and colleges today. Their role will be described more fully in Chapter 14.

[14]Linda Small, "Reflections on a Season of Ethnic Dance," *Dance Magazine,* April 1978, p. 79.

13 Dance and the Goals of Contemporary Education

The preceding chapters have described the historical development and present role of dance as a cultural form in American society. This development has been marked by the increasing inclusion of dance as a medium of education in American schools and colleges. On all levels—elementary, secondary, and in higher education—some form of dance instruction is today being provided. What is the contemporary rationale for such programs, and what are the actual practices? These questions are considered in this chapter and in the one that follows.

First, it is helpful to review the history of dance in education earlier in this century. As described in Chapter 7, the most popular forms of educational dance were aesthetic and gymnastic dance, tap and clog, folk and national dance. By the 1920s, the natural rhythmic expression identified with Bird Larson, the so-called natural dance that was taught by Gertrude Colby, and the creative dance introduced by Margaret H'Doubler in Wisconsin, became widely influential.

Colby's early teaching was at the Speyer Demonstration School of Columbia University's Teachers College. During the period between 1913 and 1916 she had developed a movement program which incorporated the educational views promoted by John Dewey—those of encouraging the uniqueness of each child and the integration of the various aspects within the curriculum. She experimented with natural, expressive, and rhythmic movement, providing a dance program which could exist within an educational framework.

Bird Larson, originally a student of Colby at Teachers College, became a leading figure in the growth of dance education. In 1914 she initiated the first dance courses at Barnard College, modeling the curriculum on Colby's program at Speyer. Larson expanded the expressive and natural components of natural dance, and in her natural rhythmic expression also included a solid foundation of technical control, based on extensive understanding of anatomy, kinesiology, and physiology. Of Larson's work, Speisman wrote:

> There were no impersonal, arbitrary movement standards to be accomplished; the child determined for himself his movement goals, he understood his range of movement possibilities, and he gained a thorough understanding of the science of movement as it was initiated in the torso of his body.[1]

Margaret H'Doubler had studied with Colby and Larson at Teachers College, after which she returned to her faculty position at the University of Wisconsin. In 1919 she offered the first dance course there, and in 1926 the nation's first dance degree program on the college level was established. H'Doubler continued teaching at the University until 1954, and during her forty years as a professional dance educator taught hundreds of teachers, clarified the educational principles underlying dance in education, and organized Orchesis, a college dance club which developed many chapters throughout the United States.

The forms of dance which evolved through the work of these pioneers became the basis of modern dance in education during the early 1930s. By this time, many women physical educators had developed a considerable interest in dance education. The National Society of Directors of Physical Education for Women devoted an entire meeting to dance at its national convention in Boston in 1930. In 1931, the American Physical Education Association (later to become the American Association for Health, Physical Education, and Recreation) established a separate Section on Dance. This became a leading force in promoting dance education throughout the United States; it sponsored major dance events and workshops, issued publications, provided advisory services, and stimulated research. Its first chairperson was May O'Donnell, and other leaders included Martha Hill, Dorothy La Salle, Mary Jo Shelley, and Ruth Murray.

A number of women's colleges or women's physical education departments in larger universities, including Smith, Vassar, Wellesley, Barnard, New York University, and the University of Michigan, sponsored symposiums on dance education during the 1930s. Increasingly, professional dance artists were drawn into educational programs and workshops:

> In the . . . 1930s the concert dance artists and their groups were on tour in specific areas and at times on transcontinental trek. At this time it was possible for an interested person in almost any part of the United States to [become] familiar with the repertory of a number of renowned dance artists. Into almost every state came the top American dancers to appear in concert, to give lecture-demonstrations, to spend a day or two on a college campus, or to present a program at a national or district association convention.
>
> One could see Martha Graham in solo performance or with her group; Doris Humphrey and Charles Weidman in duo, or with their company, which then included José Limón; Hanya Holm and company; Ruth St. Denis and Ted Shawn; and a bit later, Ted Shawn and his group of men. From Germany came

[1]For a chronology of these events, see the *Journal of Health and Physical Education* for the period between 1930 and 1940.

Mary Wigman in solo concert, to return the following year with her company, and Harald Kreutzberg with his partner, Yvonne Georgi.[2]

Gradually, dance emerged as a distinct and important focus of educational concerns at a growing number of colleges and universities.

In the summer of 1934 the Bennington School of the Dance was established at Bennington College in Vermont; Martha Hill, director of dance at New York University, was made director of programs and Mary Josephine Shelley, dance promotor and physical education teacher at New College, Teachers College, Columbia University, became administrative director. Graham, Holm, Humphrey, Weidman, and Louis Horst were among those who presented the new, mysterious modern dance to students between the years 1934 and 1942. In 1936 Margaret Lloyd wrote:

> The Bennington Festival of the Bennington School of the Dance is unlike any other summer festival in Europe or America. It is the only one devoted exclusively to the dance and to the dance in its newest, experimental forms. It is a festival that is making rather than commemorating art . . . I think it can truthfully be said that the Bennington School of Dance has gathered the modern dance up in its conglomerate arms and swept it several paces forward.[3]

In 1948, a new Summer School of the Dance was begun at Connecticut College in New London, providing a vital impetus to dance in education (see page 259). Across the Atlantic, Rudolf von Laban succeeded in introducing educational dance into the British school system, and many Americans were influenced by his philosophy and teaching approach.

Increasingly, dance education in American schools and colleges turned to the emerging field of professional dance for assistance; its content became more and more oriented toward developing dance as an artistic experience. In time, physical educators became concerned about the rapidly growing number of programs that emphasized dance as a performing art. It was apparent that many colleges had become involved in what was described as a "competitive marathon" of demonstrations, concerts, and other events designed to bring favorable publicity to their departments—just as competitive sports had increased in emphasis as part of men's programs. It was clear too that the original stress on individual creativity and freedom of expression that had been found in natural dance was giving way to much greater emphasis on the teaching of dance technique as a formal discipline.

By the end of the 1930s, the professional point of view toward modern dance had become highly influential in educational dance circles. This posed a problem. Were the goals and needs of college or secondary school students the same as those of aspiring dance artists? Should the teaching techniques used by dance educators be the same as those who taught in professional studios?

In 1937, Eugene C. Howe summarized what he considered to be the "most recent event of major importance in physical education"—the ex-

[2]Barbara Page Beiswanger, "National Section on Dance, Its First Ten Years," *Journal of Health, Physical Education, and Recreation,* May–June 1960, p. 23.

[3]Margaret Lloyd, quoted in Tom Rorek, "The Connecticut College American Dance Festival," *Dance Perspectives No. 50,* Summer, 1972, p. 10.

traordinary rise of the modern dance—and asked some searching questions about the relationship between the two fields:

> It can hardly be denied that the recent adoption by the profession of the leading concert dancers, critics, and counselors as *professors extraordinaire* has been a truly remarkable phenomenon. The dance of the 1920s in physical education, though the seed came from the world of art, grew up *in* and *for* physical education; the dance of the 1930s in physical education is for and by the concert artist in that he now virtually heads up this activity in a field foreign to his primary interests and about the nature of whose objectives he may, quite naturally and justifiably, be assumed to have no detailed and comprehensive understanding. The situation obviously has possibilities for both good and evil.[4]

He went on to suggest that serious difficulties might develop in the years ahead, in terms of the compatibility of dance, as a serious art form, with physical education as a sponsoring department, in American schools and colleges. Before this could happen, however, World War II forced a hiatus on all kinds of educational innovation and growth. The grim necessity was to win the war, and education went on an "austerity" basis. Dance, where it continued to be offered in secondary schools or colleges, was frequently given a body-conditioning emphasis, in accord with the national concern about "physical fitness." In community life, dance was widely used as a form of social recreation (folk and square dancing became popular in service centers and community clubs during this period). But in schools and colleges, dance education underwent a "holding action."

World War II ended the Bennington epoch, but its vision of dance as a vital force in American education remained in the energy and planning drive of Martha Hill. As a result, the Connecticut College Summer Dance Program was established, with Ruth Bloomer, a former Bennington student and teacher of dance at Connecticut, and Martha Hill as co-directors. By 1950 choreographers-in-residence at New London included José Limón, Jane Dudley, Sophie Maslow, William Bales, Merce Cunningham, Katherine Litz, and Pearl Primus. Pre-classic and modern dance forms were taught by Louis Horst, and Doris Humphrey guided students through intermediate and advanced composition. Those first years of the school also premiered works such as Limón's *The Moor's Pavane* and Humphrey's *Night Spell* and *Ruins and Visions.*

By 1957, a short decade since the founding of the Connecticut College American Dance Festival, 60 works had been premiered and 189 dances had been performed. In the summer of 1957, more than 150 summer students attended, representing 30 states and seven foreign countries. In 1965 the enrollment was limited to 250 of the most promising and competent applicants. The summer program in 1969 had 319 students, and employed a full-time faculty of 35. Until 1977, the Connecticut College American Dance Festival continued as a combined center of dance education and performance. In 1978, the Festival moved to Duke University in Durham, North Carolina, where in addition to the summer school program with leading

[4]E. C. Howe, "What Business Has Modern Dance in Physical Education?" *Journal of Health and Physical Education,* March, 1937, p. 132.

dancer/choreographers, it has sponsored an annual Critics Conference, directed by *Village Voice* dance critic Deborah Jowitt; an annual Dance Television Workshop; Dance Therapy Workshops; an annual Dance Educators' Weekend; and an annual community outreach program.

However, throughout this period of rapid expansion of activity after World War II, it was necessary for dance educators to come seriously to grips with the important question of identifying their basic objectives. What was the theoretical rationale for dance in education? At a time of considerable ferment in educational philosophy, this became a critical issue.

RATIONALE FOR DANCE IN EDUCATION

Certainly, it was not an entirely new question. During the earlier periods of its history, dance had been supported in very specific terms as an activity area within physical education intended to achieve certain outcomes important to that field. Also, it had been praised for its cultural and aesthetic values. Frederick Rogers wrote in 1941:

> . . .our major thesis is that dance, earliest of the arts and pedagogies, should become once more a basic educational technique, because it may serve, and probably more rapidly than any other single kind of pupil activity teachers now utilize, to transform children into more healthy, graceful, sensitive, courteous, courageous, cooperative, cultured, and charitable citizens. The classic Greeks knew this, and made practice conform to knowledge, as have more ancient and primitive peoples everywhere. But contemporary English and American pedagogy, beclouded by heritages of asceticism, scholasticism, and puritanism, has, until very recently, ignored or even proscribed dancing in schools.[5]

Similarly, Margaret H'Doubler had suggested that if every child, throughout his entire educational experience, were able to take dance as a creative art, "the enrichment of his adult life might reach beyond any results we now can contemplate." She wrote persuasively about the great social value of dance as a vitalizing experience within human society:

> This element has proven to be an enduring and vitally important power in the cultural life of all ages. It is for us today to rediscover this power and seek its influence.[6]

H'Doubler had a vision of dance education as a liberating and civilizing force that would contribute to a healthy philosophy of life and an integrated sense of self for all. She commented that while it was not expected that all students would experience dance to its fullest extent as a form of personal artistic expression,

[5]Frederick Rand Rogers, *Dance: A Basic Educational Technique* (New York: The Macmillan Co., 1941), p. viii.

[6]Margaret H'Doubler, *Dance: A Creative Art Experience* (New York: F. S. Crofts and Co., 1940), p. xii.

> . . . every child has a right to know how to achieve control of his body in order that he may use it to the limit of his ability for the expression of his own reactions to life. Even if he can never carry his efforts far enough to realize dance in its highest forms, he may experience the sheer joy of the rhythmic sense of free, controlled, and expressive movement, and through this know an addition to life to which every human being is entitled.[7]

In the late 1940s it became evident, however, that this sort of statement of purpose, inspiring though it might be to dance educators, would not hold much currency in the marketplace of educational philosophy and curriculum development. There were many other special subjects in the curriculum, all of whose adherents were equally convinced of the merit of what they were teaching. Why were the writings of dance enthusiasts to be considered of any greater value than theirs?

The need to develop a more convincing and objective rationale for dance as an important element in modern education became increasingly apparent as a number of highly regarded critics launched a vigorous attack on the pervasive influence of "progressive educationists" on the American educational system, during the 1950s and early 1960s. Paul Woodring, Arthur Bestor, H. G. Rickover, and others argued that American education had become soft, wasteful, and ineffective in terms of bringing about true learning. Specifically, they were critical of curricula that had proliferated far beyond the "three Rs" to include a host of activities that Rickover, for example, described as having ". . . little resemblance to traditional programs and intellectual disciplines but . . . making the school a sort of gigantic social-service agency aimed not at education but adjustment."[8] In his view, not more than 25 percent of what was taught in schools could now be described as "serious learning."

The major fire of the critics was directed against nonacademic courses and school experiences related to "social adjustment." Thus, Woodring characterized the period of the 1930s and 1940s in these terms:

> The high schools tried in a hundred ways to keep the student interested: easier courses, more "practical" courses, more varied offerings, individual guidance, dances, parties, and other social activities supervised by the school, including extensive athletic programs and allowing high school credit for everything from social dancing to camping and fishing.[9]

It was proposed that greater stress be placed upon the fundamental academic disciplines, such as the sciences and social sciences, mathematics, and the language arts. The fine and performing arts—particularly when approached as "doing" fields—were regarded as secondary in importance.

In the face of these attacks, and their influence on the attitudes of the taxpaying public and on school administrators, many educators in essentially nonacademic fields found themselves under extreme pressure.

For one, many educators had accepted the goal of "social adjustment" as a primary objective. To illustrate, in one of the leading educational dance

[7] *Ibid.,* p. 66.

[8] H. G. Rickover, *Education and Freedom* (New York: E. P. Dutton and Co., 1960), p. 197.

[9] Paul Woodring, *A Fourth of a Nation* (New York: McGraw-Hill Book Co., 1957), p. 3.

texts of the time, Ruth Radir justified dance because it gave students group experiences in democratic living:

> Dance fulfills its function in the curricula of democracy's schools only if group work is so conducted that it is a little laboratory in democratic living. Students, working in groups, should be, in effect, self-directing, with the teacher acting only as a guide in helping them solve the problems of construction . . . [they] talk them over . . . to clarify meaning and find its essence . . . work in groups to objectify their idea in a movement theme, and then build this theme into a dance. In this group composition there is a constant interchange of ideas, opportunity to lead, and to follow, and a kind of informal majority rule . . . the core of the learning experience in a democracy. . . . [10]

By the late 1950s, this emphasis on the life-adjustment goals of education was decidedly out of style.

Similarly, those who had sought to pursue dance primarily as an aesthetic experience also were experiencing difficulty. For, following the first Russian Sputnik and the disclosure of the advanced level of Soviet education in mathematics, science, and engineering, there was a "crash" program of strengthening these areas of education. By default, the arts necessarily received less support and attention. Greater academic pressure in the schools meant that many students who might formerly have been involved in school music, theater, or dance activities, now found it difficult to fit them into their schedules.

Physical educators recognized that two of the goals they had professed during the preceding decades ("social adjustment" and "education for leisure") were no longer supported by the educational profession at large. Instead, they seized upon recent research findings that demonstrated the poor physical fitness of American youth, as a basis for embarking upon crash programs of testing and conditioning for fitness. Surely in a period of continuing national emergency, the fitness of youth was an important concern; and so it proved to be.

But dance educators could not accept this as a focal point for their efforts. Instead, if anything, those who were leaders in the field pressed even more strongly for the recognition of dance as an area separate from physical education, and one which was essentially an art form. In so doing, they were supported not only by their own conviction of what dance education should be, but also by the growing swell of conviction about the importance of the arts in national life, during the late 1950s and early 1960s.

The growth of public interest and involvement in the arts provided justification for pressing for a fuller place for the performing arts at the educational table. In terms of verbal support at least, many school administrators supported this cause. The American Association of School Administrators adopted the following resolution at its annual conference in 1959:

> The American Association of School Administrators commends the president, the Executive Committee, and the staff for selecting the *Creative Arts* as the general theme for the 1959 convention. We believe in a well-balanced school

[10]Ruth Radir, *Modern Dance for the Youth of America* (New York: A. S. Barnes and Co., 1944), p. 4.

curriculum in which music, drama, painting, poetry, sculpture, architecture, and the like are included side by side with other important subjects such as mathematics, history, and science. It is important that pupils, as a part of general education, learn to appreciate, to understand, to create, and to criticize with discrimination those products of the mind, the voice, the hand, and the body which give dignity to the person and exalt the spirit of man.[11]

Nor was support for the arts lacking among many of the leading educational philosophers of the period. In a sharp rejoinder to the mid-century critics of modern education, Sidney Hook wrote:

> An unfailing mark of philistinism in education is reference to the study of art and music as "the frills and fads" of schooling. Insofar as those who speak this way are not tone-deaf or color-blind, they are themselves products of a narrow education, unaware of the profound experiences which are uniquely bound up with the trained perception of color and form. . . . A sufficient justification for making some study of art and music required in modern education is that it provides an unfailing source of delight in personal experience, a certain grace in living, and a variety of dimensions of meaning by which to interpret the world around us.[12]

Increasingly there was recognition of the need for educational experiences which would provide a sense of personal involvement, to counteract the growing tendency toward depersonalization in a mechanized society dominated by the mass media of communication. Philip Phenix commented that in wide areas of modern life, significant personal relatedness had disappeared from view:

> People feel isolated and estranged from nature, from themselves, from one another, and from the ultimate sources of their being. The depersonalization and collectivization of life is far advanced. . . . Another cause of meaninglessness in the contemporary world is the growing mechanization and depersonalization of life. Man has become assimilated to the machine, and in the process has lost his identity as a person. He has merged with the mass in the anonymity of impersonal organization.[13]

Within this climate, there was increasing need for education to provide experiences which would help students become aware of their own uniqueness, and that would help them become capable of making meaningful personal judgments within all areas of life. If it is anything at all—for either the doer or the audience—art represents a profoundly individual kind of experience. Thus, there developed support for the arts as a form of highly personalized creative experience. Although there is no single accepted definition of creativity, one influential view today is that it is heavily based on "divergent" thinking and exploration. As contrasted with "convergent" (which means moving toward a single correct solution or answer), "diver-

[11]Resolution adopted by the American Association of School Administrators, Atlantic City, New Jersey, February 1959.

[12]Sidney Hook, *Education for Modern Man* (New York: Alfred A. Knopf, 1963), p. 154.

[13]Philip M. Phenix, *Realms of Meaning, A Philosophy of the Curriculum for General Education* (New York: McGraw-Hill Book Co., 1964), p. 34.

gent" involves searching around, changing directions, not necessarily flying in the face of convention, but often coming out with unconventional solutions and answers. It is felt that creative people are more likely to excel in divergent thinking and activity, and that the kind of educational experience which is open-ended (that is, which has no single solution or desired response) is likely to lead to creative growth. Creativity is believed to be fostered in education when students are permitted or encouraged to exhibit spontaneity and individuality; when they are not regimented or repressed by imposed restraints or required conformity; when they have the freedom to initiate purposeful behavior, to communicate freely, and to make their own choices of activity or learning experiences.

Most educators in the arts—including dance educators—believe that their position in education today is strengthened because of the current need for creative development of students. But this is only one aspect of a total rationale supporting dance in the curriculum. Viewed broadly, how are educators to define the overall values and educational objectives of dance in the curriculum?

GOVERNING PHILOSOPHY OF EDUCATION

In the United States, educational philosophers have developed two prevailing orientations, broadly described as "traditionalist" and "experimentalist." The traditionalist position has generally been concerned with the development of the intellect; all other values related to morality, civic or social development, creative involvement, or preprofessional career training have been viewed as secondary. This philosophical approach has obviously stressed the fundamental academic skills, and has been generally resistant to the presentation of art experiences as personal creative involvement within the curriculum.

In contrast, the view of the experimentalist is that education must serve to meet the needs of modern man, by helping him adjust to his environment and indeed helping him remodel or reshape it. Within this broad philosophy, human nature is seen as differing widely; since this is so, and since the needs of people change according to geographical and social settings, no one scheme of education can apply universally. John Dewey, who was the most influential of modern experimentalist philosophers, held that the study of the past must be made relevant to the needs and demands of the present; that the curriculum must be broad and of great variety, respecting individual needs, interests, and capacities; and that the study of society is at the heart of the school's effort.

Stated succinctly, Dewey's view of education was:

> Education is that reconstruction of experience which adds to the meaning of experience, and which increases ability to direct the course of subsequent experience.[14]

Throughout the period between the 1930s and the 1950s, the view of education as a dynamic process of change that both improved society and

[14]John Dewey, *Democracy and Education* (New York: The Macmillan Co., 1938), pp. 89–90.

enabled individuals to live most effectively within society was established. In several influential policy statements on the goals of American education, the role of well-integrated citizens within democratic society was defined in detail. It encompassed the following areas of needed competence: membership in a family, in an economic system, and in a community. The well-educated person was described as one who was able to fulfill responsibilities of citizenship within his own community and in the nation at large. He should have the necessary skills to function adequately in an economic sense, both as a producer and as a consumer. He should be able to relate effectively to others, and to develop a constructive and happy family life. As part of this, he is expected to have a working command of the basic skills imparted by education—reading, writing, and arithmetic, as well as an understanding of the cultural heritage of the past. Finally, the well-educated citizen is expected to have an intelligent, inquiring mind and to be—so far as his capabilities permit—a creative individual.

During this period, dance was generally conceived of as a skill or activity area within physical education. As such, it was expected to contribute to the widely cited goals of *organic development, neuromuscular development, interpretive development,* and *personal-social development.* None of these goals implied any great stress on creative or aesthetic expression. Nor, in the great majority of situations in which dance was taught, was it really approached as an art form. The capabilities of most teachers, and the size and degree of motivation of their classes, generally did not encourage or sustain attempts to develop dance programs of technical or artistic merit.

Over the past two decades, no new philosophy of education has emerged. To the extent that there has been a continuing emphasis on the basic academic disciplines, the stress has been on a rather utilitarian approach to meeting the practical needs of the individual and society. With an increasing number of students completing high school and going on to some form of higher education, a strong effort was made to help this larger population achieve more advanced levels of vocational competence and understanding. For a time, there was a "downward thrust" of courses, with more rigorous instructional programs (particularly in mathematics, science, and foreign languages) being introduced in the junior high school and elementary school.

Yet, it has been understood that the mere acquisition of presently available knowledge, or skills that are currently required, will not be enough to prepare American youth for useful and productive lives in the years ahead. Farsighted educators recognize that students must be prepared for a lifelong learning process:

> The student must learn to learn, for he will need to grow intellectually during his entire lifetime in order to avoid obsolescence. Less emphasis should be placed upon high school as a preparation for college and more attention given to the development of an open-ended attitude toward the students' needs and aspirations in a learning society. It has been stated that half of what a graduate engineer studies today will be obsolete in ten years; half of what he will need to know is not yet known by anyone. The total amount of all knowledge will double in the next 15 years.[15]

[15]Lloyd S. Michaels, "The High School's Changing Tasks," in *The Challenge of Curricular Change* (New York: College Entrance Examination Board, 1966), p. 15.

Beginning in the late 1960s, many students, including the most gifted, began to question and reject the values that were being imposed on them. The increasing specialization of learning in particular disciplines and their subfields had resulted in an "academic pressure cooker," which many students resisted. There was a widespread demand for a relaxation of rigid academic standards, particularly in secondary schools and colleges. In the former, many school systems provided enriched elective programs or "alternative" programs; in the colleges, many institutions relaxed their curriculum requirements, in some cases giving students considerable flexibility in planning their course programs. Increasingly, courses concerned with humanistic lifestyles, ethnic history and identification, women's needs, and similar contemporary interests were introduced into the curriculum. More and more students sought relevance in their education, and genuine and significant forms of personal commitment.

What does all this have to do with the arts?

Clearly, one way for secondary school and college students to achieve a more meaningful personal involvement in life is through participation in the creative arts. Increasingly, educational authorities spoke out in recognition of the contribution of the arts to total education. C. Robert Pace, for example, suggested that there was a need for another kind of learning—one which is essentially non-verbal, creative, and open. He urged that we give fuller emphasis to:

> . . .the languages of movement and form, of color, and sequence, and sound, the languages of direct expression and feeling. Throughout history these have been powerful and significant avenues by which man has expressed his knowledge, his aspirations, his beliefs, his insights, and his wisdom. Are these still foreign languages to many of our students? Is the capacity to translate them, to understand their meaning, and to communicate through them teachable? If we must require competence in two languages for graduation from college, why not the languages of painting and sculpture, of drama and dance or of music?[16]

One major stumbling block preventing a fuller acceptance of the arts within American education has been the sharp distinction made between art and science in the public mind—in an era in which science is viewed as increasingly essential to our survival. Pointing out that basic differences between science and art are widely assumed, Harold Taylor notes that scientists are seen as rational, objective, abstract, concerned with the intellect, and with reducing everything to a formula, while artists, on the other hand, are seen as temperamental, subjective, irrational, and chiefly concerned with the expression of the emotions.[17] He goes on to say:

> One of the most unfortunate results of this misunderstanding of the nature of the intellect is that the practice of the arts and the creative arts themselves are too often excluded from the regular curriculum of school and college or given

[16]C. Robert Pace, in Lawrence F. Dennis and Joseph F. Kauffman, eds., *The College and the Student* (Washington, D.C.: American Council on Education, 1966), p. 99.

[17]Harold Taylor, *Art and the Intellect* (New York: Museum of Modern Art, 1960), p. 9.

such a minor role in the educational process that they are unable to make the intellectual contribution of which they are supremely capable.[18]

There appears to be increasing awareness today that the barrier that has been erected between science and art is a false one. J. Bronowski contends that there exists a single creative activity, which is displayed alike in the arts and in the sciences:

> It is wrong to think of science as a mechanical record of facts, and it is wrong to think of the arts as remote and private fancies. What makes each human, what makes them universal is the stamp of the creative mind. I found the act of creation to lie in the discovery of a hidden likeness. The scientist or the artist takes two facts or experiences which are separate; he finds in them a likeness which had not been seen before; and he creates a unity by showing the likeness.[19]

More and more, the dichotomy between "the two cultures" is being challenged by thoughtful educators and philosophers. Taylor suggests that there is a need to recognize that dance, music, painting, design, and sculpture are all forms of knowledge even though they do not express themselves in words. Further, he protests against adding "more blocks of science and mathematics while we allow the arts and the humanities to languish," by asking:

> Do we not need scientists and engineers who combine with knowledge and skill of a practical kind a sensitivity to human values, a sense of social responsibility, an understanding and appreciation of the arts? The widest sweep of imagination, the deepest level of intuition, the greatest command of insight are as necessary to the true scientist as to the poet or to the philosopher.[20]

The needs to educate feeling, to inculcate sensitivity, to provide a testing-ground for values and personal growth and change, are all related to the search for educational experiences which can counter the stultifying effect of the "high-pressure knowledge industry" of the present. While certainly no definitive statement of this viewpoint has been widely accepted by American educators, it represents an area of conviction which increasingly is influencing the shaping of curriculum—particularly on the college level. It is within this philosophical context that all forms of creative and artistic experience in education, including dance, find their support.

VALUES OF DANCE IN EDUCATION

Meanwhile, what of the specific area of the curriculum to which dance has traditionally been attached over the past several decades—physical education? What shifts have occurred in this field, particularly in its philosophical undergirding?

[18] *Ibid.,* p. 11.

[19] J. Bronowski, *Science and Human Values* (New York: Harper and Bros., 1956), p. 56.

[20] Taylor, *op. cit.,* p. 27.

Following the period in which primary emphasis was given to achieving physical fitness as a goal of physical education, there was a pronounced shift toward identifying physical education as an academic discipline. Increasingly, physical education departments in colleges and universities became concerned with gathering a comprehensive and integrated knowledge of the motor behavior and capabilities of human beings. Franklin Henry described the field in these terms:

> There is indeed a scholarly field of knowledge basic to physical education. It is constituted of certain portions of such diverse fields as anatomy, physics and physiology, cultural anthropology, history and sociology, as well as psychology. The focus of attention is on the study of man as an individual, engaging in the motor performances required by his daily life and in other motor performances yielding aesthetic values or serving as expressions of his physical and competitive nature. . . . [21]

Far from being concerned solely with sports and games, as popularly conceived, physical educators in the 1960s and 1970s saw all of the following as important aspects of their discipline: kinesiology and body mechanics; the physiology of exercise, training, and environment; neuromotor coordination, the kinesthetic senses, motor learning, and transfers; emotional and personality factors in physical performance, and the relation of all of these to human development; the functional status of the individual and an ability to engage in motor activity; and the history and sociology of sports and related physical activities.

As this concept of physical education as an academic discipline gained currency, dance educators were compelled to examine *their* essential values and purposes. Although an impressive number of dance departments in colleges and universities had become independent of physical education and were housed in programs or departments of the performing arts—often linked to drama, music, or liberal arts—the majority were still part of physical education programs and regarded as an area within that broader field.

However, dance obviously has a character and identity of its own, and cannot simply be regarded as another sport, or a form of gymnastics. Its long history as an independent art in human society, and the unique roles that it plays in cultures throughout the world mean that it must be examined and understood in its own right.

Essentially, six main areas of purpose of dance in education may be identified.

1. *Movement Education.* As indicated earlier, movement education has become an important thrust of physical education, particularly on the elementary level. What is the special contribution to be made by dance in this area? Elizabeth Hayes suggests that its particular appeal lies in the satisfaction or enjoyment that it provides the participant; it is pleasure in the kinesthetic sensation of movement that impels the dancer to move as he does.

> The key to its distinction lies in that the dancer's immediate concern is not with lifting weights, transporting himself through water, balancing on skates or skis,

[21]Franklin Henry, "Physical Education as an Academic Discipline," *Journal of Health, Physical Education and Recreation,* September 1964, p. 32.

or winning a game, but rather with movement per se—movement that has consciously been given form and rhythmic structure to provide physical, emotional or aesthetic satisfaction. If dance happens also to promote good physical condition or otherwise contribute to the welfare of the dancer, so much the better; but the derivation of such benefits is not the essential reason for the existence of dance.[22]

As indicated, movement education has been given particular emphasis on the elementary level, where it has been seen as a vital element in the overall personality development of the child. Research by Kephart and others has shown the child's motor performance to be closely linked to emotional development, intellectual, and cognitive functioning, and indeed all aspects of personal growth. Obviously, dance provides a medium for experimentation and creative performance in movement that is rich with potential. Gladys Andrews Fleming writes:

> *Movement is not dance, but all dance involves movement.* Children must be able to move easily and readily in order to effectively compose dances. They require time to perfect movement skills necessary to make their bodies do what their emotions dictate. . . .
>
> Movement experiences can be initiated and presented in such a way that children are anxious to respond to new and more complex situations. This involves thinking about movement of the self rather than just about the self and "how I look." Dance that is based on movement is not concerned with developing movement in a vacuum but rather with developing, inventing, and controlling movement simultaneously with thinking, sensing, responding, feeling, and inquiring. . . . The development of the imagination is ignited and creativity is uncorked as inventiveness and selection of movement are used abundantly.[23]

Although movement education is usually thought of primarily as a needed experience for young children, it also may have important values for people of all ages. Psychologists have noted that we tend to become more fixed and less expressive as we grow older; surely, at all age levels, there is need for vitalizing and creative movement experience. Dance, as a pleasurable and even exciting form of physical activity, offers a unique alternative to other forms of physical exercise in which adults may participate. So-called "aerobic dancing," which places primary emphasis on fitness outcomes, has become a popular adult activity in many community recreation programs. Increasing numbers of adults today are taking studio courses in ballet—not because they hope seriously to become ballet dancers, but because of its fitness value and the refreshment of spirit that it offers. Even among retired adults in senior centers, more and more dance is being offered today as a pleasurable form of exercise.

The tremendous growth of interest in jogging, running, and all forms of sports and outdoor activity that has marked the past decade is evidence of the search by Americans for a more dynamic and active life style. Movement education that leads to fuller participation in dance of all kinds and

[22]Elizabeth R. Hayes, *An Introduction to the Teaching of Dance* (New York: Ronald Press Co., 1964), p. 3.

[23]Gladys Andrews Fleming, "Helping Children Discover Dance," *Journal of Physical Education and Recreation,* October, 1971, pp. 38–39.

at all age levels, makes an important contribution to this trend. Many physical educators have made the case that dance should be regarded as an integral part of the total educational experience concerned with movement, and not as a narrowly-conceived, performance-oriented art. Ulrich writes:

> It will also be necessary for the new band of dance educators to acknowledge the artistry and expression found in gymnastics, sport, and aquatics. The dancers' world can not be apart from these movement forms; it must be a part of the whole world of human movement.[24]

2. *Development of Personal Creativity.* Dance, like all the arts, offers the opportunity for teaching and learning that is designed to enhance and encourage the personal creativity of students. Through the posing of compositional problems, as well as tasks related to performance and staging, the student is encouraged to produce imaginative and inventive thinking and movement solutions. Uniquely, of course, he does not make use of other tools or symbols in doing so. His body is the instrument with which he works, and movement constitutes the vocabulary; thus the creative expression is a particularly free and open one, unhampered by the need to translate meaning. Such experience, at any age, makes a vital contribution to the growth of the individual. Taylor writes:

> The essence of the modern movement in education is the idea of creativity and its liberating effects on the individual. The modern movement is in fact a fundamental shift in attitude toward life itself. It refuses to accept the conventional forms in which life is presented to us and looks for fresh ways of interpreting facts, for new forms of art, of architecture, of scientific discovery, of literature, of science. . . .[25]

Creative modern dance in particular may be taught as a problem-solving experience, in which students seek solutions to assigned movement tasks involving the elements of energy, time and space, or combinations of movement directions, levels, or uses of different parts of the body. Such experiences, Ellen Moore writes, enhance the learner's creative development, and enrich technical development, which may otherwise become a dry or boring routine.[26]

3. *Aesthetic Experience.* At the same time as it develops creativity, dance provides an aesthetic opportunity for students. They are helped to become open to aesthetic experience, both in terms of being able to respond fully and sensitively to artistic stimuli, and also in terms of being willing and increasingly able to express themselves through creative media. The purpose of such experience is not narrowly confined to specially gifted individuals. Robert Henri, the art critic, wrote several decades ago:

[24]Celeste Ulrich, "Education for a Dynamic Life Style," *Journal of Physical Education and Recreation,* May 1977, p. 48.

[25]Harold Taylor, "Individualism and the Liberal Tradition," in Willis D. Weatherford, Jr., ed., *The Goals of Higher Education* (Cambridge, Mass.: Harvard University Press, 1960), p. 12.

[26]Ellen Moore, "Dance Technique Through Problem-Solving," *Journal of Physical Education and Recreation,* January 1974, p. 53.

> Art, when really understood, is the province of every human being. . . . When the artist is alive in any person . . . he becomes an inventive, searching, daring, self-expressive creature. He becomes interesting to other people. The world would stagnate without him—and the world would be beautiful with him. He does not have to be a painter or a sculptor to be an artist. He can work in any medium.[27]

The uniqueness, of course, of dance as a form of aesthetic experience is that the dancer's body, intellect, and emotions are all *directly* involved in a unified expressive experience. Unlike other art forms, in which the poem, painting, or piece of sculpture may exist as a product *apart* from its creator, the dancer in action *is* the work of art. A second remarkable aspect of dance is that its presentation lends itself to a fusion of all the arts. It may involve music, literary expression, sculptural design, or painting (in both costumes and sets), and other forms of artistic expression used either as the inspiration or accompaniment for dance, or as an integral part of the dance work itself. Thus, its potential for aesthetic growth is almost unlimited.

4. *Intercultural and Integrative Experience.* Dance provides a rich medium for exploring the customs, attitudes, history, and living circumstances of people of other lands. Through the study of folk and ethnic dance, carried on under skilled instructors or sometimes as field assignments, students may venture deep into ethnology and anthropology. On the elementary school level, where the unit-study approach makes use of various forms of educational experience that focus on a single problem or theme, dance is frequently one of the key forms of activity. Similarly, in terms of the integration of various subject areas, dance has strong links with such fields as the fine and graphic arts, music, the language arts, and theater. In many secondary school programs, and in some courses in the humanities on the college level, all of these art fields may be linked in interdepartmental courses which stress the common elements among the arts.

Intercultural experience of this kind may go far beyond merely learning facts about the people of other lands and their customs, or linking dance in a practical way with other forms of expressive activity. Often, dance may provide a medium in which the spirit and philosophy of people of other lands may be meaningfully experienced. Sondra Fraleigh, for example, points out that in the Western world we have sought to integrate the arts into the general fabric of life in a "self-conscious" way, and that, in so doing, we have focused on competition, speed, and productivity—typical characteristics of the Western way of life.[28] Alienation, materialism, mechanical dominance and technological display have influenced much of our creative dance, and dance expression often tends to be remote from our inner lives. In contrast, Fraleigh suggests that Eastern dance represents a more unifying and humanizing force, stemming as it does from a deep philosophy based on man's essential "oneness" in harmony with nature. Instead of being active, athletic and outgoing, as in the Western world, Eastern dance leads to a fuller sense of unity and internal harmony and self-awareness.

[27]Robert Henri, *The Art Spirit* (Philadelphia, Pa.: J. B. Lippincott Co., 1923), p. 5.

[28]Sondra Fraleigh, "Humanizing Dance Education: Eastern Acquisitions," *Journal of Physical Education and Recreation,* May 1975, pp. 51–52.

When fully understood and intelligently presented, then, dance may provide a valuable medium for transmitting in-depth awareness of the philosophy and lifestyle of other peoples of the world.

5. *Social Involvement.* Recognizing that "social-adjustment" and "life-adjustment" have become archaic terms in today's educational glossary, it is clear that many of the most serious concerns of adults about young people over the past decade have had to do with their social behavior. The problems have ranged from a spirit of rebellion against traditional societal values in such areas as work-orientation, sexual behavior, or the use of drugs, to a sense of alienation on the part of many young people. While such problems declined somewhat during the 1970s, they still represent a significant concern of educators on all levels.

It is important to recognize that dance provides a unique opportunity for meaningful group involvement. More than most other kinds of academic experience, it encourages intense, positive social interaction and interpersonal relationships in small working groups. The range of social participation in dance activities, and the necessity for both providing and accepting critical judgment, is rarely equalled in other courses or student activities. In those forms of dance which are specifically recreational, such as folk, square, and social dancing (found in many school and college instructional programs), there is the opportunity for constructive and relaxed social involvement for students.

At the same time, dance may provide a medium through which participants may examine their own values and come to grips with new ideas and challenges. Edrie Ferdun, for example, suggests that many of our most stereotypic views—in such areas as appropriate sexual identification and behavior, bodily display and attitudes toward pleasure, or worthy forms of achievement in life—may be reexamined as part of the process of dance involvement.[29] While dance can operate within a multitude of social frameworks, it has the potential for establishing its own values and contributing to each individual's potential for the fullest possible self-actualization in society.

6. *Carry-over Values.* Clearly, a major purpose of education today must be to prepare for the enjoyable and enriching use of future leisure. Dance—as well as experiences in the other arts—must be viewed as such preparation. Through it, students may gain favorable attitudes and performing skills for active participation after graduation in modern dance or ballet, or recreational dance forms as hobby interests that combine physical, social, and creative values. In other cases, through their school or college dance experience, students may gain an interest and awareness of dance as a performing art that will help them become part of the growing audience for theater dance throughout the country.

Without question, one of the major reasons for the tremendous growth of interest in the arts in society has been the expansion of leisure during the past several decades. It is essential, therefore, that school and college programs in the arts help to equip students to use their present and future leisure most creatively and constructively. Dance, because of its var-

[29]Edrie Ferdun, "Dance Power," *Journal of Physical Education and Recreation,* April 1975, p. 35.

ied values—aesthetic, physical, social, and intellectual—is uniquely useful in this regard, and may be enjoyed at any age.

These, then are regarded as the primary values of dance education. They may be stated somewhat differently. For example, in a policy statement on *Dance as Education* formulated through a National Dance Association Project on *Issues and Concerns in Dance Education,* sponsored by the Alliance for Arts Education with funding from the Office of Education of the U.S. Department of Health, Education and Welfare, the following justifications for dance within the curriculum were cited: a) dance is basic education, intensifying and clarifying the human experience; b) dance reinforces all learning, relating to and enhancing other academic areas; c) dance provides an alternative to the usual modes of education and is valuable in reaching children who may not respond to more formal modes of teaching; d) dance promotes self- and social awareness, helping students confront and understand themselves and cooperate effectively with others; e) dance promotes good health and may be of particular value to students with physical or mental disabilities; and f) dance promotes fuller understanding of one's own culture, and that of other peoples.[30]

It would be a mistake to assume that dance has been fully accepted on all levels of education, and that it is always taught, particularly on elementary and secondary levels, by instructors who are well trained within this art field. Bruce King makes a convincing case that education has not yet fully committed itself to supporting the varied creative arts fields, and that it is particularly necessary to train and require certification for dance specialists and to provide an adequate core of competence in movement education for all elementary school teachers.[31] The American Council for the Arts in Education has concluded, in a comprehensive report titled *Coming to Our Senses: The Significance of the Arts for American Education,* that a massive contradiction exists concerning the arts in our national life. On the one hand, popular interest in the arts has grown tremendously over the past 15 years. On the other hand, arts education lacks adequate support, and when budgetary priorities compel cutting educational programs, teachers in such fields as music and fine arts tend to lose their jobs on a wholesale basis.[32]

Given this paradox, exactly what *is* the state of dance education in the United States today? The following chapter outlines actual practices and programs on all three levels of education: elementary, secondary, and college. It shows the remarkable diversity of offerings in the dance, ranging from non-existent or totally inadequate, to curricula of extremely high quality.

[30]Charles B. Fowler and Araminta Little, *Dance as Education* (Washington, D.C.: National Dance Association and Alliance for Arts Education, 1977), pp. 10–13.

[31]Bruce King, "Will Education Discover Dance?" *Dance Magazine,* March 1978, pp. 56–58.

[32]David Rockefeller, Chairman, *Coming to Our Senses: The Significance of the Arts for American Education* (New York: McGraw-Hill and the Arts, Education and Americans Panel, 1977), p. 46.

14 Current Practices in Dance Education

Instruction and guidance in dance is provided in a wide variety of settings in the United States today. First, it is part of general education, in the sense that the elementary and secondary schools of the nation, as well as colleges and universities of all types, often provide some form of dance education. Second, dance is offered in a variety of professional or specialized settings, in thousands of privately owned studios, academies, conservatories, or schools attached to ballet companies or other performing groups. Third, a number of community organizations or associations of dance professionals sponsor classes in dance, including teachers' workshops and conferences.

This chapter will examine each of these forms of dance education—with primary emphasis given to dance in general education.

DANCE INSTRUCTION IN SCHOOLS AND COLLEGES

Dance instruction is provided on all three levels of American education today, although practices obviously vary from school system to school system, or college to college.

In elementary grades, dance is generally taught by classroom teachers or, in the upper elementary grades, by physical education teachers. In junior and senior high schools, it is usually the responsibility of physical education teachers and is provided most frequently for girl students. In higher education, it continues to be taught primarily as an area of activity within women's physical education departments, although in a growing number of colleges, it is offered through a separate department of dance, or a dance program within a department of theater arts or music. On each level, it is characterized by a distinct set of practices and by goals appropriate to the age level of those being served.

OVERVIEW OF OFFERINGS

How widespread are offerings in dance education on each level?

No recent, comprehensive study of dance education in the United States has been completed, although a number of directories of dance in higher education have been compiled. During the 1960s, a graduate student at Teachers College, Columbia University, in cooperation with one of the authors, carried out a nationwide study of such practices. Questionnaires were sent to a randomly selected sample of 510 institutions (204 junior and senior high schools and 306 junior and senior colleges), with the only stratification being that each state was represented by at least four colleges or universities, and that an attempt was made to avoid sending questionnaires to obviously religious institutions, or all-male schools or colleges.

Several findings from this survey are reported in this chapter; in addition, a smaller survey, conducted in 1979, yielded information specifically on college dance programs. Table 14–1, drawn from the first survey, shows the percentage of institutions on each level that reported offering dance as part of their curricula.

This survey showed that a majority of the institutions that responded on each level offered some form of dance instruction. It should be noted that the highest percentage of instruction in dance (82.4 percent) was found in senior colleges, and the lowest (58.6 percent) in junior colleges.

Practices in dance education are now examined for each level in turn, beginning with elementary school programs.

DANCE IN ELEMENTARY EDUCATION

Dance in elementary education is generally regarded as having important physical, social, and creative values that contribute significantly to the development of children in their most formative years. It is recognized that children have a hunger for movement that must be satisfied if their proper biological development is to be achieved, and that motor learning provides an important avenue for personal growth that is related to all forms of development and school achievement. Don Radler and Newell Kephart write:

> The primary process is *motor development.* This is the basis upon which is built the child's ability to control his body. . . .In addition to being the result of an order from the brain, each movement made by the developing child, is in itself, an experience which contributes to the basic store of information held by the brain. In other words, movements are not only output; they are input as well.[1]

It is believed that control and mastery of the body's movement relate to emotional as well as physical and mental development. Ruth Murray comments that control of one's body means the beginning of self-control in general. In bringing his own body under control, the child begins to

[1]Don C. Radler and Newell C. Kephart, *Success Through Play* (New York: Harper & Row, 1960), p. 23.

Table 14–1

Does your institution offer instruction in dance as part of the curriculum?

Level	*Yes*	*No*	*Number Responding*
Junior High School	23 (63.9%)	13 (36.1%)	36
Senior High School	62 (62.0%)	38 (38.0%)	100
Junior College	17 (58.6%)	12 (41.4%)	29
Senior College	108 (82.4%)	23 (17.6%)	131
Totals:	210 (70.6%)	86 (29.4%)	296

understand himself better, and to have confidence in his ability to direct his own actions and to control his environment meaningfully.[2]

It is important that, through creative rhythmic experiences, children explore their movement capabilities and gradually improve in terms of physical strength, flexibility, body balance, endurance, and coordination. Furthermore, dance should be a pleasurable, happy experience, in which children are able to express themselves creatively in free and spontaneous movement, as well as in guided or structured movement experiences.

What forms of dance are actually offered in elementary schools? The 1977 report of the Arts, Education, and Americans Panel gives the following brief description of typical programs on this level:

> An elementary school dance program usually consists of dancing games, folk, and square dances. Activities such as gymnastics and calisthenics are often included as part of the dance program.
>
> Fundamental movement, rhythm games and activities, and folk dance are common at the kindergarten through third grade level.
>
> Rhythmic activities (for example, skipping rope), and folk and square dance are common at the fourth through sixth grade level.
>
> Movement exercises with an emphasis on problem solving can be found in some schools. . . . There is greater acceptance for creative movement as a separate subject, and increased use of the movement specialist.
>
> Dance is becoming part of interrelated arts and interdisciplinary approaches.[3]

In a more detailed analysis, two physical education authorities, Arthur Miller and Virginia Whitcomb, have suggested that there should be three components to the dance education offering in elementary schools:

> *Movement Fundamentals and Variations.* This consists of the necessary tools for dance, including such fundamental locomotor and non-locomotor skills as walking, running, hopping, jumping, leaping, galloping, skipping, bending, pushing, twisting, falling—or combinations

[2]Ruth Murray, *Dance in Elementary Education* (New York: Harper & Row, Publishers, 1960), p. 23.

[3]David Rockefeller, Chairman, *Coming to Our Senses: The Significance of the Arts for American Education* (New York: McGraw-Hill and the Arts, Education and Americans Panel, 1977), p. 74.

of these—all learned and practiced in various rhythms, tempos, and floor patterns or groupings.

Creative Rhythms and Dance. This extends the fundamental movements into creative expression, by having children create dance movement or actual dance, through response to such stimuli as music, percussion accompaniment, stories, songs, pictures, poems, suggestions for pantomime (i.e., sports movements, work movements, familiar characters), moods, colors, textures, etc. On the simplest level, it may involve children moving freely to such stimuli; on more advanced levels, it may involve individual or group compositions that represent more thoughtful and extended solutions to dance problems. In some cases, dance compositions may actually become class projects, for presentation at assemblies or other programs.

Folk Dance. This includes singing games and folk dances of America and other lands, performed in various formations: circles, lines, squares, threesomes, and as mixers and icebreakers. Often the same skills which are learned as part of dance fundamentals are essential to correct performance of folk dances and singing games; similarly, the movements and patterns of such structured dances may be used by children to create their own dance compositions. Thus, all three forms of dance experience are interrelated.[4]

Ruth Murray, whose text, *Dance in Elementary Education,* continues to be one of the most authoritative in this field, has suggested that there are four major categories of experience: *creative movement and movement skills, rhythmic skills* (related primarily to musical understandings and rhythmic competence), the development of *original individual or group dances,* and *learning dances,* such as singing games, play parties, folk and square dances. She suggests that the emphasis in each of these categories should vary, according to the age level of children being taught:[5]

Murray's breakdown has the following implications. First, she does not separate creative movement and the learning of movement skills, as Miller and Whitcomb do. Instead, it is obviously her view that the fundamental skills of movement may be learned in a creative way. Second, she suggests that greatest emphasis be given to this category of dance experience with younger children. Making individual dances (and later, group compositions)

Table 14–2

Suggested percentage of involvement

Age Levels	*5–7*	*8–10*	*11–13*
Creative Movement and Movement Skills	50%	30%	25%
Rhythmic Skills	20%	20%	15%
Making Individual Dances	20%	30%	20%
Learning Structured Dances	10%	20%	40%

[4]Arthur G. Miller and Virginia Whitcomb, *Physical Education in the Elementary School Curriculum,* 3rd ed. (Englewood Cliffs, New Jersey: Prentice-Hall, 1969), pp. 228–279.

[5]Murray, *op. cit.,* p. 15.

is at its peak during the middle elementary years, and increasing emphasis is given to the learning and performance of structured dances with each succeeding age level.

The final point reflects the fact that older children are more capable (in terms of their physical skills, ability to perform complex tasks, attention span, and social attitudes) of learning folk and square dances. It also suggests that the emphasis on free creative response that is appropriate for young children is no longer as suitable for those in the preadolescent period. It is true that creative movement experiences can be made increasingly difficult and advanced, to add progression to learning and provide challenge to the experience. Creative movement can be related in a more complex way to problems of space, force, musical meter and dynamics, level and direction of movement, mood, and dramatic content. Often other classroom learnings, such as the language arts or the social or physical sciences, may be related to problems of group composition, as part of "core" or unit studies. Often, it may be integrated with the language arts, or with other elements of instruction, such as geometric shapes.[6]

In the hands of gifted teachers, children in the middle elementary grades are often able to develop group compositions of surprisingly high quality—as well as to maintain a high level of interest and personal growth. A basic problem at this point is that children, as they move into the upper elementary grades, become increasingly uncomfortable about moving freely or spontaneously. Often, they may feel too big, too awkward, too silly—or they are aware that there is an actual technique involved in dancing skillfully, which they have not mastered. Just as creative writing may become frustrating for them if they do not possess the necessary vocabulary and knowledge of grammar, so, in dance, they may feel limited by the lack of an adequate movement vocabulary.

Many children—particularly girls—may have begun to study ballet or modern dance in classes outside of school. What is being done in school in the form of "creative rhythmic movement" may appear simple and childish to them. With boys, if the teacher is not ingenious in introducing masculine and physically challenging themes and forms of dance, an attitude of resistance may quickly be built up.

For all these reasons, it is important that instruction in elementary school dance activities be highly knowledgeable. The teacher of the upper elementary age level should be able to demonstrate and lead children through sequences of warm-ups, stretches, bends, swaying movements, and exercises for different parts of the body, for flexibility, strength, and coordination. In addition, he or she should have a broad awareness of the purpose of dance in education, a knowledge of musical structure, and the ability to work sensitively and creatively with children. Perhaps the most significant responsibility of the teacher is to guide the dance experiences of the children in ways which stimulate the creative process, develop an understanding of aesthetics, and provide enrichment for the children's movement capabilities.

[6]Helen V. Wagner, "A Dance Lesson Based on Geometric Shapes," *Journal of Physical Education and Recreation,* January 1975, p. 67, and Gertrude Blanchard, "Alphabet Dance," *Journal of Physical Education and Recreation,* February 1975, p. 65.

The question must be asked—who teaches dance in the elementary school and how widespread are such programs? When one reads texts in this area and sees impressive photographs of children moving freely and imaginatively, the impression is given that such programs are widely found. The reality is that they are rare, and that actual instruction of dance and creative rhythmic movement in elementary schools often is stereotyped and limited.

In the lower elementary grades, it is usually the classroom teacher who is responsible for "rhythms," as the activity is often termed. This teacher is expected to be competent in a wide range of learning skills—with the priority usually given to the more academic skills of arithmetic and reading instruction. She may have had a course or two in physical activities for the elementary school. Usually, this will have placed emphasis on the use of traditional singing games and simple folk dances, as well as other forms of physical activities such as group games, lead-up ball games, self-testing activities, etc. Thus, the dance program in the lower elementary grades tends to consist heavily of structured dances—singing games, play parties, and folk dances.

As far as fundamental movement skills and creative expression are concerned, most teachers in the elementary grades who provide such activities tend to use phonograph records which have different rhythmic sequences (and sometimes verbal instruction or songs which provide cues for movement) on them. Occasionally, in the lower elementary grades, the classroom teacher may be helped by a music or physical education specialist; such special teachers, however, rarely work directly with children in the lower grades. In general, dance on this level, when taught by classroom teachers, tends to consist primarily of structured dance forms, such as singing games and simple folk dances. Creative movement, when it is attempted, (in part because of the lack of musical accompanists) is usually handled in a stereotyped and limited fashion.

What of the middle and upper elementary grades?

It is usually at about the fourth grade level that curriculum specialists in the fields of art, music, physical education, and sometimes science are introduced to elementary school classes. A common practice is for such specialists to work with individual classes once or twice a week, and have the classroom teacher take responsibility for other teaching sessions. The specialist is also expected to provide consultation assistance to classroom teachers and, in many schools, to offer in-service training sessions for teachers.

At this point, in many elementary schools, one finds the separation of boys and girls in physical education classes. When this occurs, the boys are usually assigned a male teacher, and the girls a female teacher. The boys' program then focuses on active games and sports, tumbling, gymnastics, conditioning exercises, and similar activities. If they have any involvement at all in dance, it usually consists of special coeducational classes (usually in folk and square dancing), often under the direction of the woman physical education instructor. More frequently, boys have no involvement at all in creative dance forms, after the third or fourth grade, unlike the English approach to movement education which was heavily influenced by the work of Rudolf Laban, and in which both boys and girls participate extensively in creative movement experiences throughout the grades. Thus, it is understandable that many American boys quickly gain a stereotyped view of dance as a feminine activity.

For girls, dance activitiy in the upper elementary grades tends to consist of recreational dance forms and, in some cases, creative or modern dance. It is usually taught by the physical education instructor, and too often tends to be approached as an exercise or drill, devoid of true creative meaning or expressive content. In most cases, physical education instructors on the elementary level are generalists, and have a somewhat limited background in modern dance, which prevents them from offering the solid technical content that children who are approaching the teen years are capable of absorbing.

In a limited number of communities or state educational systems, a greater priority is given to dance education. There is a strong effort to have classroom teachers become more highly skilled, through preservice and in-service training, and to prepare physical educators more effectively in dance. Often, at physical education conferences, elementary school dancing programs of very high caliber are seen.

In some communities which have received special funding through federal grants, unusual dance programs have been initiated on the elementary level. In Richmond, Virginia, for example, an interdisciplinary program of arts and humanities has given strong emphasis to dance, both as a form of movement education, and in its relation to other arts, including drama, music, painting, and poetry. Thousands of children have attended citywide performances of Arthur Mitchell's Dance Theater of Harlem; the Duquesne University Tamburitzans; the Richmond Ballet; Ezibu Muntu, an African dance group from Virginia Commonwealth University; and the Virginia Dance Theater, from Madison College. Funding for enriched instruction in dance and the related arts was provided by a grant under the Elementary and Secondary Education Act, the Virginia Commission of Arts and Humanities, and the Richmond Public Schools, along with voluntary assistance from professional dancers and teachers in the community at large.

While a number of such programs have been highly successful, it must be generalized that in only a very small proportion of public elementary schools do children receive a meaningful educational dance experience. Although a number of physical educators have argued strongly that dance is an integral part of physical education, a careful review of current texts used in the professional preparation of physical educators indicates a contradictory point of view. For example, in the latest editions of two leading textbooks, *Methods and Materials in Secondary School Physical Education* by Charles Bucher and Constance Koenig and *An Introduction to Physical Education* by John Nixon and Ann Jewett, the word "dance" does not even appear in the index, other than in a single reference to "dance therapy."[7]

In a number of other texts, dance does not emerge as a unique educational experience, but is subsumed under other forms of physical education activity. Victor Dauer and Robert Pangrazi include dancelike activities in a number of separate chapters on "movement education," "creative play,"

[7]Charles A. Bucher and Constance R. Koenig, *Methods and Materials in Secondary School Physical Education* (St. Louis: C. V. Mosby, 1978), and John E. Nixon and Ann E. Jewett, *An Introduction to Physical Education* (Philadelphia: W. B. Saunders, 1974).

and "rhythmic activities." In the latter case, activities include "singing movement songs," "folk dance and other dance activities," "Lummi Sticks," "games using rhythmic background," "rope jumping to music," and "movement sequences to music."[8] Nowhere is there reference to dance as a meaningful and unified creative and aesthetic experience. In contrast, in several recent textbooks, such as *The New Physical Education for Elementary School Children* by Elsie Carter Burton, movement education is highlighted as the most important recent development in American physical education.

Attributing this development largely to the influence of Rudolf Laban in England, Burton presents the following definition of movement education:

> . . . that phase of the total education program which has as its contribution the development of effective, efficient, and expressive movement responses in a thinking, feeling, and sharing human being. . . .
>
> Emphasis is placed on *self-* and *body awareness, basic skill development, creative satisfaction, and a sense of total involvement in the learning experience*. . . . Exploration is the principal teaching method employed in movement education . . . a 'child-centered' approach or method of teaching which allows for individuality, creativity, spontaneity, and self-discovery.[9]

In some applications of Laban's approach, movement education may be closely linked to dance education as such, with emphasis being placed on using movement to further aesthetic awareness, or to promote personal expression or communication. Movement exploration may lead to the actual creation of individual or group dances by children. Indeed, in a discussion of educational dance based on Laban's work, Kate Barrett identified a progressive sequence of themes which are inherent in movement education as well: (1) awareness of the body; (2) awareness of weight and time; (3) awareness of space; (4) awareness of the flow of movement; (5) awareness of adaptation to partners and small groups; (6) awareness of the body; and (7) awareness of the basic effort actions.[10] These represent an introductory sequence which Laban called "movement themes" in his book, *Modern Educational Dance.*

It is clear that in most cases, elementary school physical education does *not* provide a meaningful degree of dance education. However, this does not mean that children of this age cannot experience dance as a form of artistic expression. Often those who have a special interest in this field receive training in dance by attending private dance schools or studios. More and more summer camps specializing in dance have been established in recent years. In a growing number of communities, the school system has begun to cooperate with other agencies or groups interested in providing special instruction in dance. For example, a Parent-Teachers Association may join

[8]Victor P. Dauer and Robert P. Pangrazi, *Dynamic Physical Education for Elementary School Children* (Minneapolis: Burgess, 1976).

[9]Elsie Carter Burton, *The New Physical Education for Elementary School Children* (Boston: Houghton-Mifflin Co., 1977), p. 11.

[10]Kate R. Barrett, in Bette J. Logsdon et al, *Physical Education for Children* (Philadelphia: Lea and Febiger, 1977), p. 125.

forces with a community arts association, local dance council, or municipal recreation department, to co-sponsor an afternoon series of dance classes.

However, such programs, while they often are conducted by highly skilled teachers, tend to serve only those children who are well motivated toward dance to begin with, and whose parents are able and willing to pay the necessary fees.

What accounts for this somewhat negative picture of practices in elementary school dance education? One may blame the obvious shortages that exist in many school systems—the lack of adequate physical education staffs, facilities, and programs, or the limited training of classroom teachers. However, more to the point is the lack of understanding of teachers, school administrators, and parents about the importance of creative experience in general—and dance in particular—during the formative years of childhood. Without such understanding it is extremely difficult to develop and support a rich program of dance and creative rhythmic movement in the elementary grades.

DANCE EDUCATION IN SECONDARY SCHOOLS

In public secondary schools throughout the United States, dance is almost invariably taught in departments of physical education. A typical statement of its purposes in secondary education would include the following objectives:

1. To develop a perception of rhythm for greater efficiency and pleasure in the performance of all motor skills.
2. To develop a knowledge of the fundamentals of music and other accompaniments as they relate to dance.
3. To develop an awareness and appreciation of dance as presented in concert and theater.
4. To develop a vocabulary of movement and a knowledge of the factors which influence movement.
5. To develop strength, endurance, flexibility, and coordination.
6. To develop a feeling of pride in the body as an instrument of expression, not only in dance, but in life situations as well.
7. To provide greater enjoyment of dance as a recreational activity both in school and later in adult life.
8. To provide satisfactory socializing experiences through the use of group activity.

However, the reality of what is offered in physical education programs often is at variance with such objectives. Again, it is helpful to turn to the texts of physical education authorities to illustrate the point. In a report published by the Center for Applied Research in Education during the mid-1960s, based on a major study of physical education in secondary schools, Karl Bookwalter wrote:

> It is expected that the fundamentals of the dance will have been developed at the elementary school level. This must be kept in mind in teaching the various types of dance in the secondary schools. Indian dancing, and folk and square dancing are particularly valuable in the junior high schools. Social, square, and modern dancing are most suitable in the senior high school. There is a dearth of dance or rhythm instruction in boys' programs. Beginning with the ninth grade, some coeducational dance instruction is possible and desirable. Men and women instructors must share that duty.[11]

Although one finds a measure of support for dance in physical education in this statement, the view that creative dance has no place in the junior high school (usually grades seven through eight, or seven through nine), and that, at most, boys may be given some coeducational dance instruction in the later grades, indicates that it is very faint support indeed. The author's reference to Indian dancing as a staple of the junior high school curriculum is a curious one and may reflect the lack of current information on the part of many physical educators in the area of dance. It is doubtful whether one percent of junior high schools offer instruction in "Indian dancing," or, indeed (even if this were perceived as having important educational value) whether their teachers have received training in this field. In terms of the time that should be allotted to "rhythms," the Bookwalter study recommended:

> Athletic sports should be allotted, collectively, 30 to 32 percent of the boys' class instruction time, and 21 to 24 percent of the girls' time in junior and senior high school.
>
> Rhythmic activities (dance) should be allotted from 5 to 8 percent for boys and from 16 to 18 percent for girls, in junior and senior high school.
>
> Formal gymnastic activities should be allotted from 27 to 28 percent for boys, and from 21 to 25 percent for girls, in junior and senior high school.[12]

In another text on secondary school physical education, the authors suggest that the following types of dance be offered: "social dancing, folk dancing, rhythms, gymnastic dancing, square dancing, tap dancing, and modern dancing."[13] Gymnastic and tap dancing, as the historical review of dance education in this text points out, were popular during the first three decades of this century, and have since largely been eliminated in American schools. What is even more striking is the glaring omission of any reference to dance as an art form—specifically the lack of recommended courses in modern dance or ballet. In terms of actual practices, the Teachers College, Columbia University survey mentioned earlier found that secondary schools offered the following kinds of dance activities:

[11]Karl W. Bookwalter, *Physical Education in the Secondary Schools* (Washington, D.C.: The Center for Applied Research in Education, 1964), p. 52.

[12]*Ibid.*, pp. 53–55.

[13]Charles A. Bucher, Constance R. Koenig, and Milton Barnhard, *Methods and Materials for Secondary School Physical Education* (St. Louis: C. V. Mosby Co., 1965), pp. 192–193.

Table 14–3

Which forms of dance are taught in your curriculum?

Type of Dance	*Number of Schools Offering It*	*Percentage of Responding Schools*
Modern Dance	44	70.9%
Square Dance	44	70.9%
Folk Dance	43	69.3%
Ballroom Dance	17	27.4%
Tap Dance	2	3.2%
Hawaiian Dance	2	3.2%
Ballet, Ethnic Dance, and Eurhythmics	1 each	1.6% each

In a more recent survey of secondary schools sponsored by the National Dance Association, Nancy Schuman reported the following findings:

Modern dance is the most widely found form of dance.

Students are typically required to enroll in dance classes, and receive credit for them.

Dance is offered at several skill levels, but advanced classes are rarely provided.

Dance units are relatively brief, consisting of classes meeting twice a week, for three or four week units once a year, as a typical pattern.

Phonograph records are the most frequently found form of accompaniment for all forms of dance.

Classes tend to be large, sometimes extending up into the hundreds, and with few male students enrolled.

Teachers are generally trained in physical education, with some course work in dance; they express a strong need for workshop experiences in such areas as composition and dance technique.

Most respondents indicate that there are few dance programs or other resources in their communities.[14]

Based on such reports, a more detailed picture of dance in the secondary school may be drawn:

1. Dance is viewed as a comparatively minor "skills" area within the majority of physical education programs. Little attention is paid to it as a medium for achieving creative or aesthetic growth. Invariably it is offered within the girls' physical education department.

2. Girls participate in both modern dance and recreational dance forms. Modern dance, when taught, tends to be treated as a technique "drill" or as a form of physical conditioning exercise. Partly because of the size of physical education classes, and partly because of the lack

[14]Nancy Schuman, "Secondary School Commission Report," *Spotlight on Dance,* May 1976.

of adequate accompaniment, many classes offer no improvisation or other creative dance activities. While curriculum guides often recommend a certain number of periods during the year for boys in square, folk, and ballroom dancing, in many schools they do not take part in any instructional dance activity.

3. A number of secondary schools have modern dance clubs, in which particularly interested students may obtain more advanced instruction in modern dance, and may be involved in performance. Often this represents a much more demanding and challenging experience in dance as a performing art than is provided in classes. Very rarely (and usually through the special effort of the dance teacher and department chairman or school principal) boys may be involved in the modern dance club—or a special club may be established for them.

4. Sometimes secondary schools may sponsor clubs in recreational dance forms (folk, square, or round dancing). In a few cases, such clubs have developed into performing groups which have toured the country giving performances. In such schools, dance has become a very popular activity for boys.

5. Just as in elementary schools, there are no special teachers of dance. Instead, in order to teach dance in secondary school, one must meet state certification requirements as a physical educator. As a minimum requirement, this usually means that a teacher has had two or three courses in modern dance and recreational dance forms as part of her undergraduate professional preparation.

6. Often the teacher of physical education in the secondary schools regards dance as a subject of minor responsibility. Only rarely, on this level, is a teacher hired as a full-time dance specialist (with physical education credentials, of course). Usually this happens in large urban high schools, where there are several women teachers in the girls' physical education department, and it is possible to assign teachers to different specialized areas in the curriculum.

To state, as Bookwalter does, that the fundamentals of dance may be assumed to have been taught at the elementary level, is not an accurate reflection of existing conditions. All too often, junior and senior high school students lack all but the most cursory information about dance. Typical teacher responses to the Teachers College study cited earlier, with respect to student attitudes about dance, were:

> Among the girls, modern or creative dance has to be taught and developed. Many dislike it because of little or no knowledge of it and lack of experience in performing it. TV and movies have helped somewhat but there is still much more to be done before this type of dance can be widely accepted in this locality. (High School, Delaware.)

> I was wondering if you could give me some information as to how to get girls in junior and senior high school motivated in learning modern dance. (High School, West Virginia.)

The point should be made that in some areas of the country, there is a considerable amount of dance interest. In states like Michigan and California, enthusiastic leadership and support by physical educators appear to have resulted in a fairly high level of dance activity in the schools. In such areas, professional organizations hold conferences and meetings, and provide in-service training classes for teachers. Dance festivals are held, and high school students and teachers attend concerts by leading companies at nearby colleges, sometimes taking part in dance clinics and workshops.

In a number of situations, teachers have been successful in involving boys in modern dance activities. At Washington Park High School in Racine, Wisconsin, an all-boys' modern dance club, composed of members of the school's athletic teams, gave impressive performances. In a large coeducational high school in New York City, with many students belonging to racial minorities, boys have participated in a coeducational modern dance program, both in actual dance classes and in an annual school festival. In Novato High School, Novato, California, considerable success has been met in involving boys in recreational dance classes.

In some cases, special administrative arrangements have been made to enrich dance programs in the secondary school. For example, in Portland, Oregon, a performing arts "magnet" school, Jefferson High, has developed a strong dance curriculum and has also been assigned the task of sending special dance courses in ballet, tap, modern dance, or jazz to several selected middle schools around the city. Jefferson's dance department has been able to employ a number of dance specialists as instructors, and has had a number of dancers-in-residence, including Walter Nicks, during the late 1970s.[15]

Sometimes secondary school dance programs are strengthened by input from nearby colleges with dance majors. Jefferson Junior High School in Champaign, Illinois, has had a cooperative arrangement with the Dance Department of the University of Illinois, under which junior or senior dance majors at the University regularly work at the junior high school, as part of a "methods" course. Such experiences have a two-way effect; the college dance program focused heavily on dance as a theater experience, but exposure to the active dance program in the Junior High School showed many college students the value of folk, ethnic, jazz, and social dance forms as well. Jo Ann Busch and Bonnie Schmidt write:

> ... these cooperative efforts are enriching the professional and personal growth of all who are involved. The public school students are participating in more broadly based dance experience than previously possible, the university students have a greater understanding of how they can translate their studies and training into meaningful experiences, (the junior high school teacher) has a continual updating of her own education, and (the college dance educator advisor) is keeping in touch with the needs of the public school faculty and students while opening new doors for her students.[16]

Often it is necessary to provide forms of dance to which secondary students can respond directly and easily. Too often, dance programs in the

[15]See Mindy Aloff, "Dance Growing in Oregon Public Schools," *Dance Magazine,* November 1978, p. 33.

[16]Jo Ann Busch and Bonnie Schmidt, "Everybody Teaches, Everybody Learns," *Journal of Physical Education and Recreation,* February 1976, pp. 55–56.

secondary school lack strong administrative support simply because students themselves are not interested in or attached to dance. Jazz dance can be of special value in overcoming such prejudices or lack of interest. Jean Sabatine writes:

> . . . jazz dance (stimulates) and (broadens) the students' interest in dance. Students identify with jazz. It draws from their jazz and rock music, and they can use their rock dance as a source of movement. Students find jazz movement human, natural, and realistic. In this dance form they see a certain power and vitality, and in the choreography a chance for contemporary themes. The male student finds, in jazz, an opportunity to move in a masculine manner. There is nothing ethereal, bloodless, or sexless in jazz. Some students respect jazz as the only native American concert dance form.[17]

In a few cases, entire school systems have developed strong support for dance as an educational medium. In Salt Lake City, for example, the influence of the University of Utah, with its outstanding program of teacher-training in dance (preparing certified dance education majors with a fine arts degree) is strongly felt. Eighteen high schools in Salt Lake City have full-time dance teachers, some with as many as three. Dance classes, which can be substituted for physical education, are extremely popular; in recent years boys have shown growing interest in dance, and in several high schools there are all-male or coeducational classes. Examples of special programs may be cited:

> At East High School in Salt Lake City, a large weekly lecture class covers the history and theory of dance and presents films and special guests. Modular scheduling allows a studio period of 1½ hours twice a week; at Cottonwood High School studio periods are three times a week. At Olympus High the Dance Production class meets daily from 1:45 to 4:00, which gives sufficient practice time for those dancers who are participating in musicals, concerts, and lecture demonstrations outside of school hours.[18]

In other schools, special arrangements may be made to enable specially gifted students to pursue their dance interest more fully. The Nassau County, New York, Board of Cooperative Educational Services operates a Cultural Arts Center for 44 school districts. Through this, talented public high school students may spend half a day in their home schools doing academic studies, and the other half at the Center doing intensive work in music, drama, dance, or art. The daily instruction given by a small group of specialists who are certified teachers is augmented by part-time instructors who are respected performing artists. In another situation, the Teaneck, New Jersey, High School has permitted a talented student to spend her mornings taking regular academic courses at the high school and her afternoons taking classes at the School of American Ballet in New York City —for academic credit.[19]

[17]Jean Sabatine, "Jazz Dance in the Secondary Schools," *Journal of Health, Physical Education and Recreation,* February 1972, pp. 69–70.

[18]Rockefeller, *op. cit.,* p. 109.

[19]*Ibid.,* p. 111.

DANCE IN SPECIAL SECONDARY SCHOOLS

While other examples of successful secondary school dance programs could be cited, it should be stressed that they are the exception, rather than the rule. All too few school systems have given strong support to the performing arts in general, or dance in particular, in secondary education. A final direction that some school systems have taken lies in the establishment of special schools oriented toward developing professional skills in the performing arts. For several years there have been, in a number of American cities, such schools, offering advanced programs in music, art, theater, or dance, along with a solid academic study component.

The first public secondary school to have initiated a curriculum to provide professional preparation in the performing arts was the High School of Performing Arts in New York City. Founded in 1947, this public school was designed to provide talented boys and girls in New York City with the opportunity to specialize intensively in music, drama, or dance, and at the same time to obtain an academic education of high quality. The premise for its existence was that New York City, as a major artistic and cultural center and, in effect, the "entertainment capital" of the nation, offered a considerable amount of employment to professionals in the theater arts, the concert field, television, radio, and night club fields. However, any student who wished to have an intensive professional development in

Two students in High School of Performing Arts ballet class. Photograph by Victoria Beller.

his high school years found it almost impossible to also obtain a rounded academic education at the same time. John Martin commented in *The New York Times:*

> Professional dance education . . . has always had to be obtained in spare time and chiefly after the normal high school years have been completed. Since dancing is a profession demanding youth, this means just that many years lost out of the income producing career. The advantage of getting the professional training along with a standard high school education can hardly be overestimated.[20]

Competition to enter the High School of Performing Arts is vigorous. Only one of four applicants can be admitted, and the most talented of those who apply are selected through auditions in music, drama, or dance—rather than through academic ability. Among those who have served on the audition board for dance have been Martha Graham, Doris Humphrey, Hanya Holm, Agnes de Mille, and John Martin. The curriculum itself is a difficult and exhaustive one, with the first half of the day devoted to academic studies and the afternoons to work in the performing arts.

The approach to instruction is extremely realistic and practical; the attempt is made to equip students with real skills and knowledge that will make them as professionally competent as possible upon graduation. Many graduates have already achieved success in the performing arts. Several of those actually attending the school are members of Actor's Equity; some have performed in summer stock, danced in musical shows on Broadway, played with major symphony orchestras, or performed in concerts. In dance, a number of graduates have joined the New York City Ballet, or leading modern dance companies, or performed on television.

The dance curriculum includes both theory and practice in the broad range of ballet, modern dance, musical comedy, and other theater dance forms, as well as various types of ethnological dance—African, Spanish, and Oriental. During the first year or two, dance majors are encouraged to explore all forms of dance. In later years, they specialize in one of the major areas of dance performance, concentrating on technique, composition, and nonpublic performance. During the fourth year of study, students take part in public performances, which are of an extremely high caliber.

A number of outstanding dancers have been employed as teachers of dance by the High School of Performing Arts. The New York Board of Education has made it possible for noncertified teachers to be employed by the school, in order to insure a high caliber of professional instruction. The director of the dance department has maintained a flexibility in assignments that permits members of the faculty to take part in concert tours, and then to return to their responsibilities at the school.

A high percentage—approximately 70 percent—of those who graduate from Performing Arts go on to college. This, coupled with the professional success of a number of graduates, suggests that thus far the school

[20]John Martin, "The Dance: Training," *The New York Times,* November 2, 1947; see also David Boroff, "High School with a Flair," *Dance Magazine,* February 1962, pp. 29-33.

has lived up to its initially stated purposes, and that it is possible to meet both academic and professional needs on the secondary level in public education.

Other examples of public high schools devoted to the arts include the Western High School of Performing Arts in Washington, D.C. and the Houston, Texas, High School for the Performing and Visual Arts, both established during the 1970s. Community support for such experimental curricula tends to be strong; in Houston, this has been encouraged by the fact that groups from the High School for the Performing and Visual Arts gave more than 100 performances in varied community settings during a recent school year.

Another example of a professionally oriented secondary school offering high-level instruction in the performing arts is the North Carolina School of the Arts, in Winston-Salem. This school was established by an act of the North Carolina Legislature in 1963, and is open by audition to junior high school, high school, and college students throughout the nation who are considered to have outstanding talent in music, drama, or dance. Professional training in the arts constitutes the major emphasis of the course of study, supplemented by an intensive academic curriculum. The thirty-acre campus includes dormitories, dance studios, rehearsal halls, theater, and classrooms; it has served students from over thirty states, plus such foreign countries as Bolivia, Brazil, Japan, Mexico, and Hungary. For a number of years, Pauline Koner, formerly a leading performer, choreographer, teacher, and guest soloist with the José Limón Company, directed modern dance instruction at the School. Ballet students worked under the direction of Robert Lindgren, formerly a featured artist with Ballet Theater, the Ballet Russe de Monte Carlo and the New York City Ballet, and his wife, Sonia Tyven. Today, Lindgren serves as dean of the entire program. In addition to a range of courses dealing with modern dance, ballet, choreography and production, students take courses in repertory, mime and acting for dancers, and have the opportunity to perform with the North Carolina Dance Theater.

Ballet performance by students of North Carolina School of the Arts. Photograph by Phil Barringer.

On the secondary level, a number of private schools also offer a combined program of academic study with professional-level training in dance. For example, the National Academy of Arts, in Champaign, Illinois, has a fully accredited college-preparatory academic program for grades seven through twelve, combined with intensive study in dance. Each year, the Academy conducts national competitive scholarship auditions in 15 cities throughout the United States; its graduates today dance professionally in numerous leading companies, including Alvin Ailey, American Ballet Theater, Boston Ballet, Elliot Feld Ballet, Pennsylvania Ballet, and Robert Joffrey Ballet.

It is possible that such schools as the High School of Performing Arts in New York City and the North Carolina School of the Arts may be the forerunners of a trend toward providing professional education in the arts in tuition-free public secondary schools. Similarly, schools like the National Academy of Arts offer opportunities for students who are financially able to attend private institutions or who are extremely talented and able to win scholarships. However, such programs do not begin to deal with the major problem of providing high quality education in dance for all students—rather than just the gifted or affluent. The solution to that need is not yet in sight.

DANCE IN COLLEGES AND UNIVERSITIES

Through the years, a number of surveys have gathered information about dance programs in higher education. They support the view that the major portion of growth in dance education in the United States in recent years has taken place on the college and university level.

During the 1940s, Walter Terry carried out surveys of college dance programs which were reported in his book, *Invitation to the Dance* and in his column in the *New York Herald-Tribune.* Based on his analysis of courses offered, nature of sponsoring departments, and background of dance instructors, Terry concluded that dance in higher education was expanding rapidly.

Other periodic surveys of dance in higher education have since been carried out by *Dance Magazine.* The number of college and university dance programs identified in its surveys has risen steadily, from 59 such programs in the mid-1950s to 99 in the mid-1960s. More recently, the *Dance Directory of Programs of Professional Preparation in American Colleges and Universities* published by the National Dance Association, a member association of the American Alliance for Health, Physical Education, and Recreation and Dance, listed 218 institutions in which dance was part of a degree-granting program. In its tenth edition (1978) the *Dance Directory* gave details of programs ranging from the baccalaureate through the master's degree and doctorate, under the following three headings:

> *Dance Education:* a major curriculum in dance designed to prepare teachers of dance.
>
> *Performing Arts:* a major curriculum in dance designed to prepare performing dance artists.

Kathryn Karipides and Kelly Holt, of Dance Training Program at Case Western Reserve University, Cleveland, Ohio.

Dance Concentration: a selection of dance courses required in professional preparation for a major in a related field, such as Physical Education or Fine Arts.[21]

Thus the number of dance curricula in American colleges and universities has grown steadily in recent years. This is particularly true of programs emphasizing the performing arts; a growing number of college dance curricula have moved away from an administrative base in departments of physical education, and have either gained an independent identity, or have become part of departments or schools concerned with other performing arts, such as music or theater. In increasing numbers, new departments of dance and drama have been established in such institutions. This is illustrated in a survey carried out in 1979 by the authors of this text. Using a listing of 165 college and university programs drawn from the *Dance Magazine Directory* or mentioned in that publication's columns on dance educa-

[21] *Dance Directory: Programs of Professional Preparation in American Colleges and Universities* (Washington, D.C.: National Dance Association, American Alliance for Health, Physical Education and Recreation, 1978).

Woman the Pioneer, choreographed by Virginia Tanner, performed by Brigham Young University dance company, Provo, Utah.

tion, they requested information having to do with such elements as administrative location, numbers of students and faculty members, types of courses offered, when programs were established, affiliation with dance performing companies, and similar concerns. The following information was obtained.

FINDINGS OF 1979 COLLEGE AND UNIVERSITY DANCE SURVEY

Replies were received from 95 institutions (a 57.5 percent return) in 33 states and Canada. The states with the greatest number of programs and thus presumably the highest level of interest in dance in higher education

Table 14-4

When was your program established?

1977–1979	3	1956–1958	1
1974–1976	11	1953–1955	1
1971–1973	9	1950–1952	2
1968–1970	23	1947–1949	2
1965–1967	12	1944–1946	0
1962–1964	6	1941–1943	1
1959–1961	1	Before 1940	5
		N/R	18

were: California (14 institutions replied), Michigan (12), New York (8), and Ohio (8). The titles of responding programs tended to vary greatly, with the largest single group being *Department* or *Program of Dance* (50), but with substantial numbers of others involving *Dance Education, Dance in Theater Arts,* or *Dance Concentration in Physical Education.* The greatest number of dance curricula were housed administratively in departments or schools of physical education, with many others, as indicated earlier, in departments connected to other arts areas.

When asked when their programs were established, respondents indicated that the greatest period of growth was from the mid-1960s through the early 1970s.

Student dance company at Randolph-Macon Woman's College, Lynchburg, Virginia. Photograph by Aubrey Wiley.

Table 14–5
Number of undergraduate majors

Number of Majors	*Number of Programs*
Over 200	3
151–200	2
101–150	5
81–100	8
61–80	8
41–60	4
21–40	21
1–20	17
0	20
N/R	7

Of the programs surveyed, 46 indicated that they offered degrees in dance as a major field. The number of undergraduate major students varied greatly from program to program (see Table 14-5).

The number of graduate dance majors tended to be much smaller, with 51 programs reporting that they had no graduate majors, and the largest number of programs, 23, reporting that they had fewer than ten. The number of faculty members also tended to be low in many departments, with 48 programs indicating that they had one, two or three full-time instructors. 27 programs had five or more full-time faculty members in dance.

COURSES OFFERED IN COLLEGE DANCE PROGRAMS

The survey gave a clear picture of the variety of courses offered within the responding dance programs. Among the most widely found courses were those in modern dance and ballet, on several levels of skill, dance choreography, and production. However, a wide range of other types of courses were found, including many in recreational dance forms and teaching methods (see Table 14-6).

In addition to these findings, the study also revealed that a substantial number of college dance programs sponsored summer workshops (58), often with well-known performing artists or choreographers in featured roles. Similarly, 56 programs reported that they were affiliated with performing companies (either their own or in some cases professional or semi-professional groups within their regions) which gave their students and staff the opportunity for becoming actively involved in dance production, touring, and problems of arts events management.

PROFILES OF DANCE CURRICULA IN HIGHER EDUCATION

To give a more extensive picture of the offerings of individual college or university dance programs, Table 14-7 shows capsule profiles of 11 leading curricula, taken from the 1979 study carried out by the authors, and

Table 14–6

Courses offered in dance programs*

Types of Courses	*Frequency*	*Types of Courses*	*Frequency*
Modern Dance		Dance Teaching Methods	56
Elementary	88	Music for Dance	52
Intermediate	88	Movement Fundamentals	50
Advanced	76	Jazz/Musical Comedy Dance	47
Ballet		Folk Dance	46
Elementary	74	Dance Notation	40
Intermediate	66	Square/Country Dance	37
Advanced	55	Ballroom Dance	35
Choreography		Ethnic Dance	34
Elementary	74	Effort-Shape	26
Intermediate	76	Dance Therapy	27
Advanced	63	Dance Research Methods	22
Dance Production	68	Improvisation	6
Dance History/Philosophy	63	Dance for Children	3

* Additional scattered references to: Adagio, Anatomy for Dancers, Character Dance, Lighting Design and Stagecraft, Repertory, Rhythmic Analysis, Sacred Dance, Special Ethnic Forms, Tap Dance, Anatomy, and Kinesiology for Dance.

the National Dance Association's 1978 *Dance Directory.* These are followed by descriptions of a number of other programs which show the range of individual emphasis found in higher education curricula.

Examining these profiles, certain differences are apparent between the programs of the private colleges and the public (usually state-supported) colleges and universities. As a rule, private colleges tend to be smaller in enrollment, and to give primary emphasis to dance as a performing art. In contrast, the public institutions have larger enrollments, and have traditionally located dance within departments or divisions of health, physical education, and recreation. More recently, a considerable number of state universities have developed dance curricula which have two degree options —one in dance as a performing art, and the other in dance education. Usually, in the latter programs, in order to become certified physical education teachers with a dance specialization, students must take courses in anatomy, kinesiology, motor learning and performance, and other courses in physical education principles and methods.

Of the individual colleges listed, Butler University and Juilliard are excellent examples of private institutions with an extremely professional approach to the preparation of dance performers. Their curricula emphasize both modern dance and ballet, and offer extensive experience in performance and production. Stephens College and Mills College are more typically liberal arts institutions with a performing arts orientation, but without the strong professional emphasis in the other programs described. None of these departments offer a wide range of courses in other forms of dance, such as folk, square, or ethnic dance. Brigham Young University, although a private institution (actually, it is under the sponsorship of the Mormon Church), is very similar to the larger state universities in its pro-

Modern dance performance at University of Michigan, Ann Arbor, Michigan. Photograph by Linda Alaniz.

gram; it has a strong physical education emphasis, and also provides opportunity for advanced study and performance in recreational and folk forms of dance.

Of the state universities, Ohio State University, the University of Wisconsin, and the University of Illinois, along with Texas Woman's University, have traditionally offered strong modern dance programs, to which ballet has been added in recent years. In these programs, as in the curricula of Arizona State University and the University of Maryland, students may choose between a performing arts option, and a teacher-certification, dance-education option.

Of all the programs described, the University of California at Los Angeles has the strongest graduate curriculum, both in terms of numbers of students, and the variety of course options (see page 307). On the graduate level at U.C.L.A., students may major in an interdisciplinary degree program with other ethnic arts areas, or may concentrate in historical research, dance therapy, or choreography and performance.

DANCE IN SEPARATE DEPARTMENTS

Although several of the programs described in Table 14-7 offered students the choice of performing arts or dance education majors, generally these were offered as degree options, or choices, within a single department. Not infrequently, students in such separate options study together in many core courses in dance, thus supporting the overall program. In a few col-

Table 14–7

Dance education in U.S. colleges

	1. Butler University Indianapolis, Indiana	*2. Mills College Oakland, California*	*3. Stephens College Columbia, Missouri*
Enrollment	Over 4,500	1,000	1,700
Type of Institution	Private, Coeducational	Private, Women; Coeducational	Private, Women's
Department Sponsoring Dance	Dance Department in College of Music	Dance Department	Dance Department
Dance Degrees	B.A., B.F.A., M.A., Performing Dance Major	B.A. in Fine Arts; Performing Dance, Dance Education ; M.A., M.F.A.	B.A., B.F.A., Performing Dance Major, Concentration, Dance Education
Courses Offered*			
Modern Dance			
Elementary	X	X	X
Intermediate	X	X	X
Advanced	X	X	X
Ballet			
Elementary	X	X	X
Intermediate	X	X	X
Advanced	X	–	X
Choreography	X	X	X
Production	X	X	–
Performing Group	X	X	X
Stagecraft	X	X	–
Other Forms			
Folk	–	–	–
Square	–	–	–
Ballroom	–	–	–
Ethnic	–	–	X
Tap	–	–	–
Jazz/Musical Comedy	–	–	–
Dance History/ Philosophy	X	X	X
Dance Teaching Methods	X	X	–
Dance Practice Teaching	X	X	–
Music for Dance	X	X	X
Dance Therapy	–	X	–
Labanotation	–	X	X
Number of Dance Majors			
Undergraduate	100	35	80
Graduate	12	35	–

* Courses listed here include only undergraduate courses.

Table 14–7 (cont.)

	4. *Juilliard School New York, New York*	5. *Ohio State University Columbus, Ohio*	6. *University of Illinois Urbana, Illinois*	7. *Brigham Young University Provo, Utah*
Enrollment	Under 1,000	51,000	35,000	Over 20,000
Type of Institution	Private, Coeducational	State, Coeducational	State, Coeducational	Private, Coeducational
Department Sponsoring Dance	Dance Division	Department of Dance	Department of Dance, Fine and Applied Arts	Dance Division, Department of Women's Physical Education
Dance Degrees	B.F.A., Performing Arts	B.S., B.F.A., M.A., Performing Arts, Dance Education	B.A., B.F.A., M.A., Performing Arts, Dance Education	B.A., Performing Arts, Dance Education
Courses Offered				
Modern Dance				
Elementary	X	X	X	X
Intermediate	X	X	X	X
Advanced	X	X	X	X
Ballet				
Elementary	X	X	X	X
Intermediate	X	X	X	X
Advanced	X	X	X	X
Choreography	X	X	X	X
Production	X	X	X	X
Performing Group	X	X	X	X
Stagecraft	X	–	–	–
Other Forms				
Folk	–	X	X	X
Square	–	–	–	X
Ballroom	–	–	–	X
Ethnic	–	X	X	X
Tap	–	–	–	X
Jazz/Musical Comedy	–	X	X	X
Dance History/ Philosophy	X	X	X	X
Dance Teaching Methods	–	X	X	X
Dance Practice Teaching	–	X	X	X
Music for Dance	X	X	X	X
Dance Therapy	–	–	–	–
Labanotation	X	X	X	–
Number of Dance Majors				
Undergraduate	70	98	100	150
Graduate	–	26	12	3

Table 14–7 (cont.)

	8. *Texas Woman's University Denton, Texas*	9. *University of California at Los Angeles Los Angeles, California*	10. *Arizona State University Tempe, Arizona*	11. *University of Maryland College Park, Maryland*
Enrollment	8,700	Over 30,000	37,000	38,000
Type of Institution	State, Women	State, Coeducational	State, Coeducational	State, Coeducational
Department Sponsoring Dance	Department of Dance, College of HPER	Dance Department, Interdisciplinary with Ethnic Arts	Dance Program in HPER Department	Dance Department
Dance Degrees	B.A., B.S., M.A., Ph.D., Performing Arts, Dance Education	B.A., M.A.,Therapy, Ethnology, Choreography	B.A., B.F.A., Dance Education Performance, Choreography	B.A., B.S., Performing Arts, Dance Education
Courses Offered				
Modern Dance				
Elementary	X	X	X	X
Intermediate	X	X	X	X
Advanced	X	X	X	X
Ballet				
Elementary	X	X	X	X
Intermediate	X	X	X	X
Advanced	X	X	X	X
Choreography	X	X	X	X
Production	X	X	X	X
Performing Group	X	X	X	X
Stagecraft	–	X	–	–
Other Forms				
Folk	X	X	X	–
Square	X	–	X	–
Ballroom	X	–	X	–
Ethnic	X	X	X	X
Tap	–	–	–	–
Jazz/Musical Comedy	X	–	X	X
Dance History/ Philosophy	X	X	X	X
Dance Teaching Methods	X	X	X	X
Dance Practice Teaching	X	X	X	X
Music for Dance	X	X	X	X
Dance Therapy	–	X	–	X
Labanotation	X	X	X	X
Number of Dance Majors				
Undergraduate	60	100	130	120
Graduate	30	75	4	–

leges, the trend for dance educators to seek independent departmental status *outside* the physical education department has actually resulted in two separate majors which are in *different* departments. Examples of such institutions follow:

The University of Indiana, at Bloomington, offers two completely separate dance majors. The physical education department sponsors an undergraduate Dance Education major, which emphasizes modern and recreational dance forms and teaching methods. In the same institution, there is a ballet department in the School of Music, which places primary emphasis on the development of performing skills; students in this program very frequently take part in the school's operatic performances.

The University of Oklahoma, at Norman, Oklahoma, offers an Educational Dance major and minor, in the physical education department, which stresses modern dance, folk dance, and teaching methods. Also at the University of Oklahoma there is a dance department in the School of Drama,

Performance by dance company at Texas Woman's University, Denton, Texas. Photograph by Buddy Myers.

which provides courses in ballet and modern dance, production, and stagecraft.

Perhaps the most interesting example of such separate departments was found for a number of years at the University of Utah, in Salt Lake City. There, Professor Elizabeth Hayes was in charge of a strong modern dance program within the department of physical education, assisted by such specialists as Virginia Tanner, known for outstanding work in children's dance. At the same time, there was a strong ballet program with an attached ballet theater company in the College of Fine Arts, under the direction of William Christensen and Gordon Paxman. Relationships between the two departments were good. Eventually, the modern dance educators sought their independence from physical education; in this case, they joined the ballet program in a separate department of ballet and modern dance, in the College of Fine Arts. Although the physical education department wished to retain service classes (classes used to fulfill part of the physical education requirement in general education) in modern dance, all these were assigned as a teaching responsibility to the new department. Folk, square, and social dancing continued to be offered by the physical education department.

There was considerable resistance to this move on the part of physical education administrators at the University of Utah. Thus, although the new department continued to offer a teacher education program in dance with the full support of the University's College of Education, the Utah State Office of Education refused to approve state accreditation for dance as an

University of Utah Dance Company in *Sculpture Garden,* choreographed by Joan Woodbury. Dancers are Edd Pelsmaeker, Robert Beswick, and Rich Rowsell.

area distinct from physical education. Professor Hayes commented that "the result has . . . meant that the best prepared teachers of dance are now prohibited from teaching . . . in all-dance positions in existence at many of our major high schools." Since then, however, the certification policy has changed, and dance specialists are employed in many secondary schools in Utah (see page 287).

Such moves for separation of dance programs which have traditionally been housed in departments of physical education have become increasingly common. In some cases, when they have become part of new, well equipped arts centers, supported by the wave of popularity of the arts in general, there has been little difficulty. In other situations, there has been conflict about the use of facilities, granting of permission to students to take performing arts dance courses to meet physical education requirements, and, most important, the need to establish dance as a separate, accredited area of instruction in the public schools.[22] The trend toward separate status for dance in higher education is discussed further in the final chapter of this text.

SUMMER DANCE PROGRAMS

One of the most interesting developments in dance in higher education has been the rapid proliferation of special summer programs and workshops throughout the country—usually offered for college credit. The University of Connecticut's Summer Dance Festival represented an outstanding program of this type for many years (see page 259), as did the Colorado College's summer dance program, which stressed the work of Hanya Holm. The Perry-Mansfield School of Theater and Dance in Steamboat Springs, Colorado, and the Jacob's Pillow School of Dance at Lee, Massachusetts (both of which made college credit available through affiliated institutions) are two other outstanding programs which many college students attend during the summer.

Each year, more and more colleges have established new summer dance workshops, usually with a number of well known performers teaching and performing, and sometimes with a full series of dance events for public viewing on the weekends. Over the past ten years, for example, the dance program at San Francisco State University has featured such artist-teachers as Jean Leon Destiné, Jean Erdman, Paul Sanasardo, Alvin Ailey, Talley Beatty, Rudy Perez, and Thelma Hill. Alwin Nikolais and Murray Louis have taken part in summer dance workshops at the University of Utah, and Paul Taylor, Ethel Winter, and Audrey Keane have been on the summer staff of Adelphi University in New York. The University of Oregon, the University of Pittsburgh, Texas Christian University, Southern Methodist University, the University of Washington, the University of Southern California, the University of California at Santa Cruz, the University of Georgia, the Uni-

[22]At a meeting of college dance educators at the annual conference of the American Alliance for Health, Physical Education and Recreation in New Orleans in March, 1979, strong support was given to establishing dance as an independent curriculum area in college, or linking it with fine arts or theater programs.

The Texas Christian University Ballet Company, with Zac Ward, Barbara Macklen, and Julie Rigler, in *Aurora.*

versity of Washington—these and many others have initiated special summer offerings with intensified dance courses and performances. In many cases, students from other colleges attend them to gain additional dance experience; they may also be attended by high school students with special approval, or by college graduates who are currently teaching and wish to improve their dance skills and understandings.

In some cases, other forms of dance may be featured. For example, the Dance Program of Colorado State University at Fort Collins annually features summer workshops in American Folk Dance and Elementary School Dance Rhythm Methods in cooperation with the Lloyd Shaw Foundation (Lloyd Shaw was a leading collector and teacher of traditional American square dances of the West and Southwest).

SPECIAL EMPHASES

Obviously, different departments or programs of dance tend to have somewhat specialized emphases. In New York City, for example, the Teachers College, Columbia University dance programs has for years stressed work in Effort-Shape and Labanotation, and has worked closely with followers of Rudolf von Laban in exploring movement concepts and their applications to acting, sports, work patterns, gesture, physical and dance therapy,

Boston Conservatory Dance Theater presentation of *Sleeping Beauty.*

psychology, and anthropology. Texas Christian University was one of the first institutions to offer a strong curriculum in ballet as a major field; today it boasts that there is a much higher level of community interest and support for ballet in Fort Worth, its home city, than elsewhere in the Southwestern region, because of this emphasis. Brigham Young University, in Provo, Utah, gives major emphasis to recreational and ethnic forms of dance; its International and American Folk Dance Groups have regularly toured the United States, Canada, and Europe. Other performing groups at Brigham Young include a touring and performing Ballroom Dance Team with 450 members, a Theater Ballet Company, Orchesis (a modern dance group), and the Cougarettes, a "pep and precision-dance drill team." In the Dance Program at the State University of New York at Brockport, in addition to the more familiar dance options, students may also elect to complete requirements in an Interdisciplinary Arts for Children option, or an Interdisciplinary Program in African Dance.

Many other colleges and universities have developed similar specializations which illustrate the broad range of possibilities in dance performance and dance education, as well as its linkage to other art forms or scholarly and academic disciplines.

VISITING ARTISTS AND COMMUNITY DANCE PROGRAMS

In addition to employing guest artists during summer workshops, many college and university dance programs today sponsor leading dancers and choreographers during the regular academic year, for master classes, workshops, or extended residencies. For example, at Randolph-Macon College in Lynchburg, Virginia, Helen McGehee is director of a Visiting Artists program which has brought leading artists from the Martha Graham, José Limón and Anna Sokolow Companies, and the London School of Contemporary Dance. These guest instructors have given workshops and master classes, taught sections of repertory works, and performed in concerts. In addition, during the last several years, the Lynchburg community has sponsored two professional dance companies a year who give lecture-demonstrations, classes, and performances, through the National Endowment Touring Program.

The University of Montana at Missoula has hosted the Alvin Ailey Repertory Ensemble, the Nikolais Dance Theater, Steve Paxton and the Grand Union Company, and numerous other individual performers or groups, as visiting artists. In addition, it has cooperation with the Cecchetti Council of America in sponsoring workshops in the Cecchetti ballet instruction method for the Rocky Mountain and Northwest regions of the United States, and maintains an active children's theater–dance company, the Magic Movers, which gives frequent community performances.

Towson State University in Maryland sponsors a University Dance Company which gives as many as 30 lecture-demonstrations or performances and residencies each year in schools and colleges throughout its region. The Towson State Company's work is enhanced by professional choreographers, such as Gus Giordano, William Hug, and Jo Rowan, and it has sponsored residencies by the Ohio Ballet, José Limón Company, and Pilobolus Dance Theater, among others. The schools mentioned here are only a few of the many college dance programs which make extensive use of visiting artists, and which provide performing dance and educational workshops to their surrounding communities and regions.

COOPERATIVE COLLEGE PROGRAMS

In some cases, neighboring colleges are joining together to share their resources or to cooperate in sponsoring dance events or special programs. For example, through a Five-College Dance Department which links dance curricula at the University of Massachusetts, Smith College, Mount Holyoke, Hampshire and Amherst, it has been possible to sponsor courses in dance notation and effort shape with adequate enrollment to justify these classes. In addition, the cooperation approach makes it possible to offer three levels of dance history courses, and to sponsor various other seminars taught according to the needs of dance majors on the five campuses. Similarly, in Westchester County, New York, the Manhattanville College Dance Program is able to make regular use of excellent performance facilities in a recently

The "Tamburitzans," a touring folk dance and music company from Duquesne University, in performance.

built Performing Arts Center at the State University College at Purchase. In many other regions, colleges have joined together to co-sponsor similar events, programs, or sharing of facilities.

GRADUATE DEGREE PROGRAMS IN DANCE

In the examination of college and university dance curricula presented earlier, brief references were made to graduate curricula, although specific examples of courses were not given. In general, graduate degree programs tend to focus on more theoretical and highly specialized aspects of dance education than undergraduate curricula.

For example, the University of North Carolina at Greensboro offers a Master of Fine Arts degree in dance with a 36-point requirement, including a written Comprehensive Examination, and a Master's Thesis. Core courses include work in choreography on several levels, and students may elect other courses which survey contemporary dance, dance criticism, dance education, anthropological aspects of dance, dance notation, and music for dance.

The extensive graduate dance curriculum at U.C.L.A. offers separate specializations on the Master of Arts level in the following areas: Choreography, Dance Criticism, Dance Ethnology, Dance Kinesiology, Dance Performance, Dance Therapy, and Dance Teaching. To provide a single example

Students practice videotape techniques as part of classes and rehearsals at Mills College, Oakland, California. Photograph by Dennis Geaney.

of course content within these specializations, the Dance Therapy option offers courses in movement dynamics and personality growth, dance in rehabilitation, seminar in movement therapy, and directed study or research in a hospital or clinic, along with related courses in the behavioral sciences.

Some dance curricula do continue to provide a strong emphasis on performance on the graduate level, much as a department of theater or music might stress advanced creative work. For example, the Department of Dance at the University of Michigan offers a Master of Fine Arts degree in dance which includes numerous courses in modern dance, ballet, ethnic and jazz dance technique, along with dance repertory, choreography, production, cultural concepts of dance, and dance education. Primary emphasis is given at the University of Michigan to developing strong performers and choreographers in contemporary dance, and graduate students are required to take 54 credits, or 48 credits plus a thesis.

It is apparent that the lack of uniformity that characterizes undergraduate dance programs is even more evident on the graduate level. Traditionally, graduate study has had such purposes as refining the specialized professional competence of individuals who have had a broad and unspecialized undergraduate program; or of extending the professional competence of students who have already had some degree of undergraduate specialization and are seeking advanced work in their discipline.

The general trend in graduate programs in teachers colleges or schools of education has been to focus on advanced studies and research of a theoretical nature—rather than offer a curriculum which focuses on the continued development of performance skills or the specific teaching competence of the individual. Such programs may be administered through physical education departments, and graduate students are academically advised into courses in physiology and kinesiology, motor learning and performance, or psychological and sociological aspects of human movement as reflected in dance and sport. Although the graduate student may continue to choreograph and perform, in such programs the curricular progression does not include specific technique courses, or provide performance environments within the structure.

In contrast, a number of other institutions, including New York University, Sarah Lawrence College, Smith College, and Temple University, continue to support the validity of having technique and performance courses on the graduate level. A growing number of those who study on the graduate level are interested in performing careers, and such programs encourage more advanced levels of technique and increased choreographic understandings, as well as an expanded view of dance as a creative and expressive medium within society. Additionally, graduate programs which emphasize continued involvement in dance as a performing art are of tremendous benefit to dance artist-educators who have had inadequate preparation in terms of their own performing and choreographic skills. They need experiences which provide more intensive study not only in the techniques of dance, but also in the making of dances and in the verbal articulation necessary to convey their ideas and perceptions to future students.

It becomes increasingly apparent that scholarly investigations of dance as an art form and as an important aspect of cultural life in general need to be encouraged. Over the past ten years, there has been considerable growth of interest in dance research in relation to the social and behavioral sciences. Dance history in particular has been the subject of a number of major, well-attended conferences (see page 338), and there has also been increased interest in dance ethnology research and seminars in dance criticism. Without question, this trend will help promote acceptance of dance as a worthy academic discipline within the university setting.

Traditionally, the arts have often been regarded as less "serious" or "worthy" of scholarly interest than the humanities in general, or the social and physical sciences. To the degree that dance aesthetics and criticism are refined and developed as academic disciplines, dance will gain respect as a serious aspect of university life. It is also important that dance curricula not be dominated solely by professional dancers, active or retired, who are skilled in teaching and directing techniques and performance, but who may not be prepared to organize and direct a college or university dance program. There is an important place also in dance education for the talents of those who have earned academic degrees, and for the courses they offer. The selection of faculty members must be sensitive to the need to provide

Example of use of dance in therapeutic programs: special ballet class for women who have had mastectomies is offered at University of Santa Clara, Santa Clara, California.

balanced forms of expertise appropriate to the philosophical and applied aspects of each dance curriculum.

It would seem that any graduate curriculum in the field of dance, essentially a performing art, which provides courses *only* in "aesthetics," "principles," "studies," or "research" is reverting to an earlier day when the fine arts could only be presented in college in the form of "history" or "art appreciation." Instead, there should be recognition of dance as a field of disciplinary study, involving the creator, the performer, and the theorist (researcher, critic, or historian). Dance performance and choreography, dance education, dance therapy, and the aesthetics and criticism of dance each have a unique role within the parameters of graduate study in dance and must in time emerge as refined subdisciplines within the total field.

OTHER SOURCES OF DANCE EDUCATION

Another important phase of dance education in the United States is in those private schools, studios, or academies which are devoted exclusively to the performing arts or to dance itself, and which are not part of public school systems, or degree-granting institutions. These may be operated for profit or may be noncommercial; in either case, since it is their major purpose to develop a high level of performing skill in dance, it is here that large numbers of young people receive professional training in the dance arts. In some cases, they may be attended on a part-time basis by students who are attending regular schools or colleges at the same time. In other cases, their students attend on a full-time basis.

Examples have already been given of the major ballet companies which operate their own schools, from which they draw many of their most talented young dancers. In addition, many of the lesser known ballet companies throughout the country maintain or are affiliated with ballet academies in their own communities. There are many other independent schools or studios in which ballet and modern dance are taught; *Dance Magazine* lists hundreds of these in its regularly published directory of schools, colleges, studios, and conservatories. Often, private ballet schools are directed by well-known, retired performing artists; similarly, many of the leading modern dancers, such as Martha Graham or Hanya Holm have had their own schools of dance for many years, in which they present their own techniques, and which serve as a means of employment, through teaching, for the company members.

In addition to these, there are many arts centers, community centers, performing arts organizations, YWCAs and YM-YWHAs, and similar sponsoring groups throughout the country, which offer a high level of dance instruction. Often, they are connected to civic arts councils or dance alliances, and in some cases they are directly sponsored by public (municipal, township, or county) recreation departments. Occasionally, independent dance schools may be linked administratively to nearby colleges or universities, with an interchange of staff and facilities.

Numerous examples of such community-based programs may be cited. To suggest a few, the Walker Art Center, in Minneapolis, Minnesota, offers a variety of dance courses and has sponsored major summer dance workshops. The Salt Lake City Children's Dance Theater has been directed by Virginia Tanner for a number of years, as part of the Conservatory of Creative Dance which is linked to the McCune School of Music and Art of Brigham Young University. In Cleveland, a famous settlement, Karamu House, has for years offered a variety of courses in all the arts and has been the center of outstanding dance instruction and performance. Similar centers for dance instruction may be found in many other cities throughout the country.

Similarly, there has been an increasing number of special summer workshops in dance which, unlike those listed earlier, do not provide college credit. One of the leading ones has been the annual Interlochen, Michigan, National Music Camp, which offers a high level of instruction in ballet and modern dance. Others include the Mt. Pinnacle Dance Camp in Hendersonville, North Carolina; the Southern Vermont Art Center in Manchester, Vermont; Stonegate Music and Arts Camp in Long Lake, New York; and many other such camps in New England and throughout the country, some of which are devoted to all the performing arts and some exclusively to dance. In the area of recreational dance, annual summer dance camps are held in square, folk, and country dancing in many states. Among the best known programs of this type have been the folk dance camp of the College of the Pacific, in Stockton, California; the Maine Folk Dance Camp conducted by Michael and Mary Ann Herman; the Pinewoods Camp in country dancing and folk music sponsored by the Country Dance and Song Society of America in Plymouth, Massachusetts.

Such private schools, studios, academies and special summer camps and workshops do much to develop highly skilled professional performers in dance, as well as to provide creative and artistic satisfaction to young people and adults alike who are interested in dance on a nonprofessional basis. Together with the schools and colleges described earlier in this chapter, a remarkable range of diversified dance education opportunities exists throughout the United States.

15

Dance as an Art Form: Problems and Prospects

The future of dance education is obviously closely linked to that of dance as an art form in the United States. Therefore, it is necessary to examine realistically the current status of "concert" or "theater" dance in American life, and its success in reaching a broader audience than in past years, if one is to understand the potential role of dance as an important form of education.

Following World War II, there was an unusual and dramatic growth of public interest and involvement in the arts in the United States. Documented by Alvin Toffler in *The Culture Consumers,* this growth was marked by the following: greatly increased attendance at art museums; development of a large number of cultural centers throughout the country; increased purchase of books and phonograph records; the establishment of numerous national, regional, and local organizations to promote the arts; and most important, a dramatic growth in the performing arts. The term that was generally attached to this social phenomenon was the "cultural explosion;" specific examples of the growth of participation in music, dance, theater, and other art activities are cited in Chapter 1.

With respect to dance, it was noted, for example, that within a few months in the late 1960s, there were at least 425 performances of ballet, modern, or ethnic dance in New York City, including programs by the New York City Ballet, the Manhattan Festival Ballet, the Martha Graham Dance Company, the City Center Joffrey Ballet, and American Ballet Theater, with additional performances by companies such as Ballets Africains, the Pennsylvania Ballet, the National Ballet, the Royal Ballet, the San Francisco Dancers' Workshop, and Ballet Folklórico de Mexico. In diversity of companies as well as in total number of performances, this far exceeded the dance events of previous seasons.

The steady growth of regional ballet companies and the remarkable growth of dance in colleges and universities discussed in previous chapters was also an important aspect of the "cultural explosion" within the performing arts. Further convincing evidence of artistic expansion was found in the development of cultural centers throughout the United States. A survey conducted by *Arts Management* documented this trend vividly, describing projects in cities throughout the country that involved theaters, museums, concert halls, and other arts centers with a planned expenditure of about $375 million. These did not include the many elaborate arts complexes being constructed by colleges and universities, which held enormous potential for cultural activities within their communities and regions.

Thus, the case for the "cultural explosion" was widely documented. What brought it about? Gertrude Lippincott outlined a number of key factors: (1) an increase in the amount of . . . leisure time, (2) an increase in family and personal income, (3) an emphasis on urban living which promotes a climate for the arts, (4) America's continuing (growth) as a consumer . . . society, (5) the great stress laid on creativity in education and in daily living, (6) the tax-exempt status of many art objects and gifts presented by individuals and corporations to museums, educational institutions, etc., (7) the financially profitable state of the arts for many dealers and artists, particularly painters, (8) the financially profitable investment possibilities of the arts, and (9) the status symbol syndrome of owning works of art.[1]

Perhaps more important than any of these has been a change in American attitudes about art. In the past, it was often viewed as an activity suited only for the highly gifted, or as an outlet only for the wealthy or intellectually minded person. In either case, involvement in the fine and performing arts was perceived as an "elite" activity—not attractive to, or suitable for, the mass of people in society. A second factor was that, until fairly recently, many Americans had the view that any aesthetic product of this country was second-rate, in comparison to the work of Europeans. This was linked to an attitude that art was just not too important, that it was only a peripheral concern of life, and certainly did not justify the serious attention of government, industry, foundations, or educational institutions. In effect, these attitudes were a logical outcome of our history. We have long been a nation that valued material accomplishment highly and aesthetic and cultural achievement on a much lower scale. In effect, we have had an inferiority complex about our capacity in the field of art. Our Puritan heritage has had much to do with this negative attitude.

Since World War II, these attitudes have changed very widely. No longer is art viewed as the exclusive province of a comparatively few, wealthy patrons. Toffler suggests that a new middle class of well-educated, professionally or technically trained persons, young and intelligent, and numbering between 30 and 45 million, is now the backbone of artistic support and involvement. They crowd museums, flock to concerts, support drama and ballet, study music, perform in the little theater, join cultural organizations, and spread the base of support of the arts in community life.[2]

[1]Gertrude Lippincott, "The Cultural Explosion and Its Implications for Dance," *Journal of Health, Physical Education and Recreation,* January 1965, pp. 83-84.

[2]Alvin Toffler, *The Culture Consumers* (New York: St. Martin's Press, 1964), pp. 26–27.

John D. Rockefeller III, president of the Lincoln Center for the Performing Arts, gave his view of the change in public attitudes, seeing the growth of popular interest and participation in the arts as:

> . . . another evidence of our national maturity, a natural and predictable deepening of interest in artistic matters. The people want art and are making it for themselves in a characteristically American way. They are taking what is at hand, working hard to improve it, and meanwhile enjoying it immensely. . . . A basic cause of this increased interest in the arts is man's need and desire for what I can only call creative fulfillment. It is a need for positive self-expression; a need for modern man to assert, or to reassert, his individuality. . . . It is a clear call that we accept the arts as a new community responsibility, that we place them alongside our already accepted responsibilities for the health, welfare, and education of our community. . . . [3]

However, there also has been considerable evidence that the overall national picture has not been as positive as these statements would suggest. Two critical studies, conducted during the 1960s, suggested that the cultural boom of the post-World War II period had been considerably exaggerated in the public's awareness.

CRITICAL STUDIES OF THE PERFORMING ARTS

Two Princeton University economics professors, William J. Baumol and William G. Bowen, spent several years studying the performing arts in America under a grant of the Twentieth Century Fund. Their report, *Performing Arts: The Economic Dilemma,* did much to dispute the view that there had been a widespread increase of actual attendance at artistic events, or that the "explosion" had truly cut across class and geographical lines to reach new audiences and grass roots regions of the country. They concluded that the cultural explosion:

> . . . is shown to be an extremely spotty affair, with some levels of activity increasing, some declining, and the overall result amounting best to a small and patchy pattern of growth. . . . In sum, this analysis of the record entitles us to conclude neither that this nation has entered a great cultural renaissance nor that it is lost in an artistic wilderness. Rather, as is so often the case, one is forced to a comparatively colorless in-between position—that over the course of the last decade and a half, the overall progress of professional activity in the living arts has amounted to little more than a continuation of past trends.[4]

The Twentieth Century Fund report arrived at the following specific findings:

[3]John D. Rockefeller III, in Joseph Prendergast, "The National Cultural Center," *Recreation Magazine,* October 1960, pp. 363–364.

[4]William J. Baumol and William G. Bowen, *Performing Arts: The Economic Dilemma* (New York: The Twentieth Century Fund, 1966), pp. 67–69.

Although there had been an "air of excitement and growth" that augured well for the future, there had been in reality no sharp increase in the attendance statistics at professional performing arts events. To illustrate, Americans spent $127 million on admissions in 1929, and $433 million in 1963, which, based on analysis of price levels and income, indicated a 25 percent decline in expenditure—from 15 cents to 11 cents of each $100 of disposable personal income. Undoubtedly, television, which brings professional entertainment into the home, had had much to do with this. Nor had the growth of interest in the arts been as widespread as suggested. New York City alone accounted for nearly 40 percent of all admissions to classical music performances in the most recent year recorded, and over one-half of all admissions to the professional theater.

The audience for the performing arts, concluded Baumol and Bowen, was still drawn from an extremely narrow segment of the population, consisting chiefly of well-educated, professional people in their late youth and early middle age, amounting to no more than five million individuals, about four percent of the population.

The economic dilemma of the performing arts received the major portion of Baumol and Bowen's concern. They pointed out that while salaries in music, drama, and dance had risen markedly, this was compensated for by the high level of unemployment or partial employment through the year in these fields. Thus, of 49 male professional occupations ranked by income in a recent census, actors were 34, musicians and music teachers 40, and dancers and dancing teachers 48. With the "salary levels of performers in many organizations . . . still scandalously low," Baumol and Bowen described the performer's lot as being a "nightmare world." Finally, they dealt in considerable detail with the actual situation of the major companies, orchestras, and theaters in the country. Cutting through the impressive figures about the growth of performing groups (which they identified chiefly as amateur) they concluded:

> In no case is the number of professional organizations very large; they range [in 1965] from about 60 metropolitan and major orchestras and 40 to 50 permanent theatrical groups to perhaps 7 opera companies and a slightly larger number of dance groups. In number of performers they vary from a dance company of 6 to an orchestra with over 100 musicians and grand opera with a cast of over 200.[5]

The economic structure of the performing arts makes it clear that they cannot support themselves directly through admissions alone. Taking grand opera as the most obvious example, when one considers that the cast includes leading and supporting singers, members of the chorus, ballet dancers, extras, and musicians (totalling between 200 and 300) who must perform in halls that usually have a capacity of less than 4,000 persons, one realizes that the maximal audience is 20 persons per performer. "It is as though a two-person cast in a Broadway play were to try to run night after night before an audience of 40!"

In varying measure, each of the performing arts has been faced with similar economic hazards. Even Lincoln Center for the Performing Arts,

[5] *Ibid.*, p. 32.

widely recognized as the most professional and prestigious of all cultural organizations in the country (and which includes the Metropolitan Opera, the New York Philharmonic, the City Center of Music and Drama, the Library and Museum of the Performing Arts, the Lincoln Center Repertory Theater and the Music Theater of Lincoln Center) has consistently operated at a multimillion dollar annual deficit.

The Twentieth Century Fund report came to a single major conclusion: that the performing arts in America—theater, opera, music, and dance—could not live by box office alone. Instead, government and foundation support was essential to their healthy growth and, indeed, survival.

Another report issued in the 1960s, *The Performing Arts: Problems and Prospects,* published by the Rockefeller Brothers Fund, was somewhat more positive about the "cultural explosion" in general. It confirmed that a marked expansion of the performing arts had taken place and concluded that the potential for the successful development of the performing arts was tremendous:

> There are millions of Americans who have never seen a live professional performance of any kind. There are untold numbers who might, with opportunity and training, become first-rate performing artists. There are electronic devices, still in a relatively early stage of development, to bring performances to vast audiences at modest expense. And the material resources to do all these things are available if we choose to do them.[6]

The Rockefeller Panel Report also made a significant comment—that almost all the expansion in the arts had been amateur. For example, it was shown that the professional commercial theater had declined sharply in recent years; that, of the large number of symphony orchestras, only 54 were composed predominantly of professional musicians; that only five or six dance companies met high professional standards and had a real degree of institutional stability; that, of the 754 opera groups, only 35 to 40 were fully professional, with not more than ten companies providing performances for more than 15 days in the year.

The Rockefeller Panel Report stressed that amateur production in the arts played a vital role in developing an appreciative audience for music, drama, and dance, as well as a first opportunity for many young artists to gain valuable experience in performance. If it were not for such amateur or semiprofessional companies, many communities far from the great urban centers would have no opportunity at all to view live performing arts. Clearly, through amateur participation, there has been a vital change in America's entire cultural landscape—a new spirit of interest and involvement. It meant that we no longer accepted the elitist position that, if standards of excellence were to be maintained, culture must remain the property of a privileged few. Nonetheless, the report argued strongly that:

> . . . it is on the professional performing artists and arts organizations that ultimate responsibility for the highest levels of creative output and quality rests. Some of these organizations, particularly the orchestras, are expanding

[6]Rockefeller Panel Report, *The Performing Arts: Problems and Prospects* (New York: McGraw-Hill Co., 1965), p. 11.

rapidly, some are actually in declining health, others are just barely holding their own, and others are growing at a rate much slower than might be. In general, there has been no significant improvement in the basic health of the professional arts organizations. There is much to be done.[7]

THE STATUS OF DANCE PERFORMANCE

Exactly how did professional dance fit into this picture? What did the Twentieth Century Fund and the Rockefeller Report say of this art, in terms of its health and prospects for the future?

In general, they commented that it suffered from the same difficulties as all the performing arts: problems in finding regular employment and maintaining an adequate standard of living for the performer; with few exceptions, a lack of opportunities for first-class training throughout the country; the need for more theaters designed for dance and available to dance companies for seasons of the appropriate length; a lack of strong and stable sponsoring organizations, combined with a dependence on "crisis financing;" and, finally, insufficient long-range planning and research.

The Rockefeller Report concluded that from the point of view of finance, administration, and organization, the professional dance world was "close to chaos." Not more than five or six dance companies, it stated, had both a national reputation and a reasonably stable organizational structure; in addition, there were perhaps a "dozen leading dancers, who scrape together companies, get up programs on shoestring budgets, and hope for a modest performance or two in New York, followed by a short and usually equally unprofitable road season."[8] If not for wealthy patrons such as Lincoln Kirstein, Lucia Chase, Ruth Page, and the B. de Rothschild and Rebekah Harkness Foundations, it would have been all but impossible for a number of the major dance organizations—chiefly ballet but also modern dance—to have continued to function. For a number of companies, such as the Alvin Ailey, Paul Taylor, and José Limón groups, it was absolutely necessary that they tour widely in order to find audiences and more or less sustained employment for their dancers. In addition, the Twentieth Century Fund study also pointed out that the largest and most enthusiastic audiences tended to flock to performances by glamorous foreign groups/troupes like the Bolshoi, Royal Ballet, Royal Danish Ballet, and other visiting companies. Only the New York City Ballet's audience compared favorably with those of the foreign companies.

Both studies presented a picture of dance as an area of artistic activity with considerable potential for the future, but one which would require the combined support of government, foundations, and universities in order to operate on a stronger base. The Rockefeller Report stressed the need to consider and plan for all the performing arts, as part of a total master plan for support and encouragement. It envisioned a situation in which a number of recognized major companies and organizations within each of the performing arts would provide their artists—as most do not now—with 12

[7] *Ibid.,* p. 15.

[8] *Ibid.,* p. 43.

months of employment, and the public with year-round performances of high quality. Such a program, embracing 50 permanent theater companies, 50 symphony orchestras, six regional opera companies, six regional choral groups, and six regional dance companies, in addition to the two major resident companies then in existence (New York City Ballet and San Francisco Ballet) would require a substantial annual subsidy.

GOVERNMENT SUPPORT OF THE ARTS

How promising were the prospects of such support for dance? In many ways, the United States has lagged far behind other nations in regarding the arts as worthy of significant government subsidy.

In England, for example, the Arts Council of Great Britain has been extremely effective since World War II in providing annual grants to support opera, ballet, and theater. In France, there are two national theaters (the Opéra Comique and the Comédie Française) which receive subsidies amounting to several millions of dollars annually, granted by the national Ministry of Beaux Arts. In the provinces, opera is subsidized locally, and there are many national festivals which also receive governmental support. In Germany, each state has a separate ministry of culture; in fairly large cities, theater and opera are in separate houses and performances are given every night of the week for eleven months of the year. Music and theater personnel are, in effect, on government salaries year-round, with pension rights, just as other civil employees are. Government support of the arts is also extended to great annual festivals such as the Bayreuth Festival.

In Italy, the famous La Scala Opera House in Milan is supported by municipal and state funds; such national festivals as the one at Spoleto each year are supported by the Italian government. In Austria, the government aids such undertakings as the Vienna State Opera, the Vienna Philharmonic, and the Salzburg Festival. In the Netherlands, the government sponsors a number of major orchestras, such as the Amsterdam Concertgebouw, theaters, and festivals. In Eastern Europe, the countries in the Soviet bloc all operate networks of performing arts schools, playhouses or concert halls, and companies, as a routine governmental responsibility.

In the United States, the first large-scale effort on the part of the federal government to assist the performing arts came during the depression of the 1930s. It was prompted not so much by a recognition of the special need of the arts as it was part of a total effort to provide employment during a period of national emergency. Thus, in the mid- and late 1930s, the Federal Theater included a dance unit which helped to promote a nationwide program of dance participation and performance—chiefly modern dance, although some ballet and ethnic dance were involved.

The Federal Dance Theater, founded in January, 1936, which included Doris Humphrey, Charles Weidman, and Helen Tamiris among its supervisors, sponsored many performances and tours which reflected the view of dance as part of "people's theater." Typically much of the choreography was concerned either with American folklore or with socially liberal and minority-group themes. Before long, along with the Federal Theater itself, dancers and dance came under political scrutiny and attack. The Dies Committee on Unamerican Activities in 1938 attacked the Federal Theater, charging that it had many employees who were either members of the Communist Party or sympathetic to it. Ultimately, the entire program of support for the arts was discontinued, and no further comprehensive effort to assist the performing arts or provide employment in them was undertaken for many years by the federal government.

This experience illustrated the fears shared by many individuals with respect to support of the arts by a national government.

In their view, there are grave risks of government attempting to use the arts as a means of propaganda (and so perverting their essential purposes), or curbing creativity by withholding support or terminating grants. It is feared that even if the attempt to control is not overt, some artists may, in their desire to retain support, unconsciously yield to a form of artistic censorship to avoid giving offense to the establishment. It is also thought inevitable that those who are assigned to positions of control in whatever government agency is responsible for distributing funds will favor certain individuals or companies or schools of artistic belief—thus, in effect, permitting their own taste to dominate what should be a free marketplace.

For these and other reasons, there has been hesitation, on the part of many legislators and many professionals in the arts, to support a full-fledged program of government support of the arts. It would seem that, in estimating the likelihood of censorship and control of the arts as an outcome of government subsidy, one would have to examine first the nature of the government that provides the aid, and second the kind of structure that is established to channel and direct it. In the Soviet Union and Communist China, it appears quite clear that the arts are made to serve as handmaidens of the national ideology. So, too, however, are newspapers, radio and television, youth organizations, workers' unions, and many other organizations or cultural bodies. On the other hand, in Great Britain and other Western nations, there appears to be widespread agreement that the nonpolitical structure that has been established to administer art subsidy programs has not attempted to influence or curb artistic output. Inevitably, choices for support must be made, and the tendency is to channel the major funds to large, established national companies. Undoubtedly, the problem becomes more difficult when a government attempts to distribute funds more widely, among less well established artists and companies.

Apart from the question of whether government should subsidize the arts (in terms of potential dangers in this relationship) there is the even more basic question of *why* it should do so.

Some have made the point that if the arts cannot justify themselves through attendance and ticket sales, as commercial motion pictures, or stage shows, or ice shows, or the circus, or rodeo, or rock-and-roll shows do, then they have no right to ask for support. They imply that government has no obligation to support one level of cultural taste in preference to another, which of course is the basis for such subsidy.

The answer to this, of course, is that government is in a position to support whatever it considers important in national or community life. The provision of parks, health services, sanitation, police, and education are all usually mandated by law—but only because those who make the laws perceive these as essential functions of government, which are not likely to be adequately provided in other ways. Throughout the history of the Western world, music, drama, painting, dance, and architecture have all been strongly supported in European countries. Today, it has become increasingly evident that the arts are essential to the fullest and richest life in both the community and the nation, that they express the highest ideals of a society, and provide a vital and necessary dimension of human existence.

In the United States during the 1940s and 1950s, there were a number of specific programs assisting the arts on a limited basis. For example, a number of dance companies, including those headed by José Limón, Martha Graham, Alvin Ailey, Ballet Caravan, and Ballet Theater, have made "goodwill tours" of Europe, South America, and the Orient, with funding assistance by the U.S. State Department. Such grants by no means represented full-fledged subsidies. Emphasis was placed on assisting only those companies that were able to attract large audiences in the countries visited; State Department funds were used to supplement the tour's income and to make it possible. In general, dance missions were highly regarded, as presenting a true cultural image of the United States and achieving—as an essentially non-verbal art form with universal human appeal—ready acceptance from widely varying audiences. During the 1960s, such programs were administered under the President's International Program for Cultural Presentations, with a Dance Panel screening and recommending the programs to be selected for support. In addition, a number of Fulbright grants and other International Exchange scholarship programs were awarded to dance scholars and artists for study or work abroad.

RENEWED FEDERAL SUPPORT OF THE ARTS

A broader program of federal support of the arts aimed at assisting domestic performance—rather than foreign tours—was initiated in 1964 when the National Arts and Cultural Development Act established a National Council on the Arts within the Executive Office of the President. A year later, the Arts and Humanities Act of 1965 established a National Foundation on the Arts and Humanities, with separate endowment programs and advisory bodies for the arts and the humanities. The National Council on the Arts was identified as the advisory body for the National Endowment for the Arts, and made responsible for providing funds (chiefly on a matching-grant basis) to non-profit organizations and to state and other public organizations and individuals for the following:

> . . . To assist artistic and cultural productions which give "emphasis to American creativity" and encourage professional excellence; to help make available artistic programs of high merit in areas of the country which otherwise would be culturally barren; to encourage and assist individual artists; to promote a general appreciation and understanding of the arts; and to provide assistance for relevant projects related to surveys, research and planning in the arts.[9]

[9]"National Foundation on the Arts and Humanities Act of 1965," *Health, Education and Welfare Indicator* (Washington, D.C.: U.S. Government Printing Office, November 1965), pp. 4–5.

Secondary school students in dance curriculum project demonstrate approaches to instruction and choreography. Photograph by George Dolan.

The Arts and Humanities Act of 1965 appropriated funds amounting to $21 million for each of the three fiscal years from 1966 through 1968. Its general goals were to:

Develop a larger, more informed audience;

Help meet the needs of the "new leisure;"

Decentralize the arts in the United States;

Encourage the state arts council movement (by November 1965 more than half the 50 states had developed state art agencies);

Alleviate the financial crisis in the arts and humanities by providing federal grants;

Stimulate private funding for the arts (through the matching-grant arrangement, and private assistance to state councils on the arts);

Help solve the problem of the scarcity of well-prepared teachers in the arts and humanities.[10]

Through this Act, the Commissioner of Education of the United States Department of Health, Education, and Welfare was empowered to make grants and loans to strengthen instruction and establish teacher-training institutes in the arts and humanities. Among varied programs initiated under this federal act to support and expand dance activities throughout the United States during the 1960s were the following:

[10] *Ibid.*, p. 7.

Substantial grants amounting to hundreds of thousands of dollars to such groups as the Martha Graham Dance Company or the American Ballet Theater, to make possible the choreography of new works, support tours, or meet annual deficits;

Curriculum-development grants to improve instruction in dance (including analysis of its historical and cultural backgrounds, Labanotation techniques, and varied new teaching aids) which were field-tested in varied regions of the United States and supported by the U.S. Office of Education.

The use of professional artists and their companies to perform in elementary and secondary schools, giving concerts, lecture-demonstrations, and workshops, in order to encourage school systems to enrich their offerings in dance—particularly modern dance—as part of the regular school curriculum.

Recognizing that one of the primary needs within the dance community was to have a permanent service organization which would encourage dancers and choreographers to work together in common causes, the National Endowment for the Arts funded, in June 1966, a planning meeting to help establish such an organization. During a three-day session, 150 delegates from ballet and modern dance companies from coast to coast met in New York City and planned an organization, tentatively to be called the American Dance League. Its purpose, modeled on the American Symphony Orchestra League, would be to help disseminate news and exchange information, advise in business and administrative matters, help member companies in their appeals for financial support, and attempt to increase audience support for the dance. Later in 1966 the organization was formally launched, assisted by a modest $11,000 from the National Endowment on the Arts, with promise of additional funds to be granted on a matching basis. Titled the Association of American Dance Companies, it was intended to serve as an umbrella organization, bringing together such other groups as the North American Association of Ballet Companies, the National Association for Regional Ballet, the Foundation for American Dance, and the American Dance Guild, in the overall advancement of dance as a performing art on the national scene. One of its first actions was to establish seminars on the theme of dance administration and support, in order to help alleviate problems associated with management and funding which have crippled so many dance companies. In addition, a number of states established councils on the arts in this period, which began to provide substantial support to dance companies and schools—along with performing companies in music, theater, opera, and other art forms.

A number of other programs sponsored by the federal government were directed specifically at the need to strengthen the arts in education. Under Title III of the Elementary and Secondary Education Act of 1965, for example, a special program entitled PACE—Projects to Advance Creativity in Education—millions of dollars were allocated to promote the arts and humanities. Live Lincoln Center productions of music, drama, and dance were brought into New York City schools, for example, and many after school and Saturday creative arts centers were established to serve disadvantaged and specially gifted children in cities throughout the United States.

ECONOMIC SURVIVAL IN THE 1970s

What has the picture been, with respect to the economic status of the performing arts, during the 1970s? In many ways, as described in Chapter 1, it has been extremely positive. Thousands of new music, dance and drama organizations have been established, and new millions of enthusiasts have joined their audiences—not only in the major cities of the country, but throughout smaller communities and less populated areas as well.

Yet in many ways, the picture has continued to be a bleak one. In 1973, at the final hearing for the triennial reauthorization for the National Endowment for the Arts and the National Endowment for the Humanities, national arts leaders testified before Congress that the arts in America, despite unparalleled growth in audience and earned income, were facing a serious financial crisis. W. McNeil Lowry, Vice President for the Arts and Humanities for the Ford Foundation and Goldwin A. McLellan, President of the Business Committee for the Arts, stated that funding for the country's

Example of national convention of major dance organization: Eugene Loring conducts ballet workshop at annual conference of Dance Masters of America. Photograph by Romaine. Photography, San Francisco, California.

theater, opera, dance, and symphony organizations alone had risen from $93 million to $159 million per year, over a recent six-year period. However, with escalating costs and expanding performance schedules, it would be necessary for private patrons, national foundations, and the government to increase grants to the arts substantially if many organizations were going to survive.

In 1976, the Association of American Dance Companies concluded its 10th annual conference with a warning that the preceding decade of expansion in the dance field might well be followed by a severe "financial squeeze." Rising costs based on inflation and, in some cases, an oversaturation of dance activity, presented many performing groups with the need to be more selective in their programming and to develop new forms of financial support. A year later, arts critic Harold C. Schonberg wrote in *The New York Times:*

> Inflation is killing off arts organizations left and right, and our biggest organizations—opera houses, museums, drama and dance groups, name it—are in desperate trouble, all of them, with an ever-widening gap between income and expenses.[11]

The problem, which was nationwide, was illustrated dramatically in 1977 in New York City, when the orchestra of the New York City Ballet walked out in a labor contract dispute that closed down more than half of the month-long run of *The Nutcracker,* the company's most popular, money-making work. The strike, which finally led to the cancellation of the company's entire winter season, resulted from the demand of the musicians for pay parity with other major Lincoln Center orchestras, and was only one example of the mounting financial pressures that threatened even the most successful and prestigious of dance organizations. Typically, the City Ballet's annual budget at this time was $7.4 million, with a projected operating deficit of $2.9 million.

As another example of mounting financial costs of dance production, Alwin Nikolais reported that when his company and the Murray Louis Company performed for a four-week season at the Lyceum Theater in New York City in the mid-1970s, although the house was sold out, they lost $75,000. Similarly, Martha Graham lost $125,000 in a three-week run on Broadway. A major problem of professional performance arises from demands made by stagehands' and musicians' unions. (For example, in a later season, Nikolais was faced by union demands that he hire 24 musicians for a Broadway season,) despite the fact that he uses electronic music and had no need for live musicians at all. As a result, the season was canceled. "What a great idea," said Nikolais. "Perhaps I should pay a dozen dancers not to dance."[12]

A final vivid example of the economic difficulty facing dance, even in the nation's most arts-oriented metropolitan area, was found in the closing

[11]Harold C. Schonberg, "A Bright Idea to Help Fund the Arts," *The New York Times,* April 3, 1977, p. 2-1.

[12]Alwin Nikolais, "Why Do I Go Through the Torture of New York?" *The New York Times,* August 1, 1976, p. 6-D.

of the Harkness Theater in the Lincoln Center area in 1977. The Harkness had been opened in April, 1974, to fanfare hailing it as "the first and only major theater in the United States specifically designed for the presentation of dance." Its closing three years later followed continued financial losses —due primarily to the small demand for dance and drama at the Harkness, caused by the poor state of the economy in general, as well as high operating costs and real estate taxes. This clearly demonstrated the harsh economics underlying the professional performing arts.

Only the fact that many companies in smaller cities and towns operate in university theaters or publicly subsidized arts centers, with largely volunteer dancers, musicians, and support personnel, makes it possible for them to survive economically. Even the ballet and modern dance companies described in Chapters 10 and 11 which are relatively stable in their operations must rely constantly on fundraising drives and other forms of special subsidies.

EXPANDED GOVERNMENT FUNDING OF THE ARTS

The unique and most hopeful aspect of the 1970s, however, was the sharply expanded level of Federal funding of the arts, chiefly through the National Endowment for the Arts program. As indicated in Chapter 1, this has risen steadily from $2.5 million in 1966, its first year, to $123.5 million in 1978.

Expanding more fully during the 1970s, the National Endowment for the Arts grants program has included several units which help support and promote dance. Among these have been:

Coordinated Residency Touring Program. Under this program, sponsors of dance company residencies received, through their state arts councils, as much as one-third of the fee of the companies participating in the program. This program has enabled many schools and communities to sponsor professional companies for concerts as well as workshops in dance technique, improvisation, and choreography for periods generally ranging from a few days to a week. In many cases, state arts councils have either matched NEA grants, or contributed lesser sums to the residency. In other cases, several local institutions or dance groups have formed a coalition to share the cost of such projects.

Choreography Fellowships and Production Grants. There have been several categories for these grants, some including individual choreographers, and others directed to companies. Dancers and choreographers working with community organizations or educational institutions have been encouraged to apply under this category.

Artists-in-the-Schools Program. This program, jointly supported by the U.S. Department of Health, Education and Welfare and the National Endowment for the Arts, represents an exciting and innovative effort to bring the arts to elementary and secondary schools throughout the country. With respect to dance, it "was developed to use the best American dance artists, who are also exceptional and inspirational teachers, to bring to our public

Nevada Dance Theater, affiliated with University of Nevada at Las Vegas, performs *Slavonic Dances,* choreographed by Vassili Sulich.

schools the discovery of dance as an art form and the experience of movement as a method of learning."[13] Dance artists and companies typically went to schools or groups of schools for a period of two to four weeks, to teach children directly, or work with teachers and parents, and perform in concerts. In 1976–1977, for example, the National Endowment for the Arts awarded grants totalling $3.7 million to enable some 2,000 artists to work with almost one million school children in 7,500 schools. Specifically, almost half a million dollars was assigned to supporting dance projects in the schools. In such states as Massachusetts, Arizona, Illinois, Minnesota, and Ohio, dance received funding exceeding that given to other categories of the arts.

Grants to Arts Institutions. In addition, numerous cultural institutions throughout the United States have received direct subsidies from NEA to

[13]Elvi Moore, "Spotlight on Dance: Funds for Dance," *Journal of Health, Physical Education and Recreation,* October 1973, p. 73.

Maryland Dance Theater, in residence at Department of Dance, University of Maryland, performs *Nocturne*, by Bertram Ross.

support their programs, on a "challenge grant" basis. Under this system, federal funds must be matched, $3 for each $1 granted. In 1977–1978, $27 million was awarded to 75 arts organizations, including museums, opera associations, ballet companies, and other groups, in 23 states and the District of Columbia. Among the leading recipients was the New York City Ballet, which received $1 million to support its program.

A number of other federal programs have also assisted the arts. The National Endowment for the Humanities has assisted research projects in the arts, primarily those concerned with historical and theoretical studies and criticism of major significance. The Arts and Humanities Program of the National Institute of Education of the U.S. Department of Health, Education, and Welfare, has centralized all federal research grants in education, including those in the performing arts.

Throughout the 1970s, the Dance Touring Program of the National Endowment for the Arts continued to expand; by 1975–1976, it had become the primary income source for many dance companies. As described earlier,

Zero Moving Dance Company, affiliated with Temple University Dance Department, Philadelphia, Pennsylvania.

funds were not assigned directly to the companies, but instead to such sponsors as community arts councils, local school systems or colleges, civic concert groups, theaters, museums, and recreation and park departments which in turn employed dance companies. Guidelines for the program have required that companies demonstrate sound management practices and have presented at least 15 professional performances, with dancers being paid appropriate union minimums, during the previous year. Increasingly, the effort has been to educate and cultivate dance audiences, and in a number of cases, to provide environments for intensive choreographic work and performance experience. Bruce Bordelon writes:

> Beginning in the 1977–78 season, qualifying sponsors can receive up to one half a company's residency costs and fees for residencies lasting more than two weeks. The longer residency will enable a company to choreograph, rehearse, and otherwise conduct its normal activities in another community, in addition to offering its standard residency activities. These grants are to cover costs directly related to the residency, such as publicity, theater rental, and production assistance . . .[14]

In the late 1970s, the basis for subsidizing the dance touring program was restructured, with a limited number of companies chosen to divide $2.5 million in grants. Approval of companies and their subsequent listing in the Dance Touring Program Directory, which made them eligible for residency

[14]Bruce Bordelon, "Dance Funding: Money and Management in Our Liveliest Art," *Dance Magazine,* June 1976, p. 87.

grants, shifted from purely quantitative criteria to a panel process in which companies were selected on qualitative measures as well.[15] Many dancers, choreographers and company managers protested this approach, which they charged represented a federal endorsement of certain companies and rejection of others. Partly as a reaction to this change, the Association of American Dance Companies produced a comprehensive listing of all the dance companies available for touring, or with active touring programs.

CETA SUPPORT OF THE ARTS

Another development in the late 1970s was the expansion of the federal Comprehensive Employment and Training Act (CETA) of the U.S. Department of Labor. In the most ambitious employment program operated by the federal government since the Federal Art Project and Works Progress Administration of the 1930s, a plan was set in motion to employ thousands of artists in communities throughout the nation, at salaries of $10,000 a year with additional fringe benefits. Hundreds of dancers have been employed; typically, the Association of American Dance Companies, various state councils on the arts and specific professional groups, such as the Bella Lewitsky Dance Company and the California Ballet Company among numerous other organizations, have been able to employ dancers and choreographers under the CETA residency and income guidelines. In dance programs affiliated with the Association of American Dance Companies, dancers are expected to spend 25 percent of a 35-hour work week in community service activities, and equal time in preparation for these activities. The rest of their salaried time may be spent in working with a resident dance company, which is expected to provide at least two free performances a year as a contribution to the community.

Bordelon explains that a major purpose of CETA funding is to expose citizens and neighborhoods in urban communities that have traditionally lacked access to cultural resources, to fuller arts experiences. Programs reach all ages, communities, and ethnic groups

> . . . through projects sponsored by organizations such as museums, existing arts organizations, block associations, settlement houses, correctional institutions, drug abuse and community centers, nursing homes, hospitals, and senior citizen centers.[16]

By spring 1978, over 6,500 artists were employed in CETA-supported community cultural activities, with the expectation that the number would rise to 10,000 by 1980. Clearly, this has represented a major opportunity to expand employment in the arts, traditionally an area of great weakness, and to provide support to dance within its various frameworks.

[15]Lois Draegin, "NEA's Dance Touring Program Restructured—What's to Come?," *Dance Magazine,* November 1978, p. 4.

[16]Bruce Bordelon, "Dance Funding: Money and Management in Our Liveliest Art," *Dance Magazine,* March 1978, p. 41; see also *Dance News,* January 1978, p. 2.

ROLE OF STATE ARTS COUNCILS

Another important factor in providing financial support and stability to dance organizations within the past two decades has been the emergence of active arts councils on the state level throughout the United States. Initially, a number of states, including particularly Illinois, Missouri, North Carolina, and New York, developed thriving state arts councils with the help of matching funds provided by the National Endowment for the Arts.

To illustrate, in 1962, its first year of operation, the New York State Arts Council sponsored professional theater, opera, ballet, and art in more than 50 communities. Although audiences reached 90 percent capacity, the Council needed to subsidize the programs, due to the low admissions charged. Since then, the Council has developed a broad program of assisting schools, colleges and universities throughout the state in developing instructional programs in the performing arts. These programs include lecture-demonstrations, symposia, seminars, master classes, workshops, and performances before student audiences. Among numerous other examples of the work of state arts councils during this early period, was the New Jersey Council, from which the Garden State Ballet received a $15,000 grant in 1967 to extend its educational program throughout the state; over 35,000 school children viewed live ballet as a result of this venture. During the first full year of the Connecticut Arts Commission, ten pilot programs were initiated, including film festivals, technical assistance to theaters and museums, and touring groups and master classes in music and dance. Without question, as state arts councils accepted expanded responsibility for such ventures, with the help of the National Endowment for the Arts, grass roots audiences have become increasingly knowledgeable and receptive to the performing arts.

During the 1970s, state arts councils have provided important leadership to channel federal grants to appropriate community arts organizations. Most frequently they have established panels for screening dance companies to determine eligibility for various federal dance programs; in turn, the panels have developed criteria to include a consistent level of artistic performance, responsible management procedures, fiscal responsibility and strong ties to community organizations. In many cases, special emphasis has been given to serving ethnic minority communities, such as blacks, Hispanics, Asian, native American, and European. In some cases, state arts councils may offer technical assistance to companies to solve problems of fundraising, promotion, audience development, programming, community relations, accounting, budgeting, and legal affairs. Often they maintain close ties with school systems and help to channel leading arts organizations into school and college residency programs.

SUPPORT BY FOUNDATIONS

Particularly during the 1950s and 1960s, when government subsidies were extremely limited, financial support of the performing arts by private foundations played a highly significant role. Typically, the American Ballet

Theater, which has produced more diversified works than any other American company and has spawned many brilliant choreographers and teachers, has survived largely through the generosity of a single patron, Lucia Chase. Similarly, Martha Graham, through the years, has been assisted heavily by the gifts of a single individual, administered through the B. de Rothschild Foundation.

Through the years, the largest single contributor to the arts has been the Ford Foundation. During the period from 1957 to 1964, it gave $30 million to Lincoln Center and the National Cultural Center, and approximately $30 million more for other purposes, including theater ($8.6 million), opera ($6.2 million), and dance ($8 million) with a later grant of $85 million to American symphony orchestras.

The major Ford contribution to dance consisted of $7,756,750 given in 1963 to eight ballet organizations. The New York City Ballet and its affiliated School of American Ballet, both administered by George Balanchine and Lincoln Kirstein, were given control of $5,925,000, or more than 75 percent of the allotment, to strengthen the company and school over a ten-year period and to use in programs bringing ballet to communities and schools in the New York region. The remaining millions went in varying amounts to the San Francisco Ballet, the Pennsylvania Ballet of Philadelphia, the Utah Ballet in Salt Lake City, the Houston Ballet, and the Boston Ballet.

Other major foundations which have given substantially to the performing arts during the past two decades have been the Rockefeller Foundation, William Hale Harkness Foundation, the Avalon Foundation, the A. W. Mellon Educational and Charitable Trust, the E. and A. E. Mayer Foundation, and the Old Dominion Foundation. However, it is clear that the performing arts have received comparatively little, on an overall basis, both from foundations and from large corporations that are in a position, through tax-exempted gifts, to offer meaningful support:

> The available data . . . indicate that civic and cultural activities together received 5.3 percent of corporate giving in 1962, and this category clearly includes considerably more then the performing arts alone. Estimates of the portion going to the performing arts range from about 3 to 4 percent of the total of $580 million given by the corporations in 1964—somewhere between $17 and $23 million, with the lower of these figures the more plausible. Roughly half of the nation's large corporations give something to the arts, but most of them give very little; about half of those contributing allocate less than 1 percent of their total donations to this purpose.[17]

If concert dance is to flourish in the years ahead, it will be necessary for both government, large foundations, and corporations that are capable of providing adequate assistance to do so. This is particularly true of modern dance, which has been greatly neglected in the funding just described. More and more, professional organizations are providing workshops, seminars, and publications to assist performing arts companies in the area of

[17]Baumol and Bowen, *op. cit.,* p. 333.

financial management, and particularly in the strategies of obtaining government or foundation grants. In general, it is best not to plead dire poverty, but to demonstrate a record of success and recognition that justifies a level of increased support. The process of identifying appropriate foundations or government-sponsored funding programs, and of preparing effective proposals for grants, is a complicated and sophisticated one, and is critical to successful business management in the performing arts today.

RISK FACTOR IN ART SUBSIDIES

It should be pointed out that, while such funding programs have been a critical factor in the expansion of dance as a performing art throughout the United States, they are not an unmixed blessing. Obviously, any process of selection of performers, choreographers or companies for support admits the possibility of exclusion for reasons not entirely based on artistic merit —such as association with cliques, personal alliances or enmities, or political influence. The risk of pressure on the artist is considerable, often encouraging choreography or performance which submits to "acceptable" or traditional models, thus supporting a "play-it-safe" attitude by those who hope to meet the established standards in order to receive greatly needed funding.

There has been for years a sharp disagreement between those who would restrict grants to a limited number of leading arts institutions and others who would support a broader base of performance. At the time when President Carter selected his new "cultural chieftains," Joseph Duffey as director of the National Endowment for the Humanities and Livingston Biddle Jr. as director of the National Endowment for the Arts, many critics and cultural impresarios feared that his appointments signaled a

> . . . major change in policy—from funding "elitist" institutions such as the Metropolitan Opera to a more "populist" approach that would spread Federal money to local dance troupes or even handicraft classes. As Federal funding for the NEH and NEA has grown—from $11.6 million in 1969 to $178 million last year—grass-roots groups have successfully competed for the money. The Frog Hollow Craft Association in Vermont, for example, has gotten $10,500 from the NEA, and the New Jersey Prisoners' Art Colony won $2,500.[18]

While the goal of such funding problems is, in Biddle's words, "to make the best quality art available to the greatest number of people," clearly this can be done in a number of ways, and unwise grant policies may be highly destructive to entirely legitimate arts enterprises. Apart from this, actual repression of free artistic expression, particularly at times of social or economic upheaval and consequent political tension, is an ever-present danger. Walter Goodman points out that totalitarian rulers well recognize the power of art to shape people's minds. The Athenian philosopher Plato, for example, was determined:

[18]"Culture: Populism vs Elitism," *Newsweek Magazine,* October 21, 1977, p. 39.

> . . . that his ideal society would not be undermined by the perverted display of "vice and intemperance and meanness and indecency." Musicians, sculptors, architects who did not express "the image of good in their works" would simply be prevented from practicing; better to expel them than allow them to corrupt the young.[19]

Even without the fear of such repression, the system of allocating grants tends to be a complicated one, far removed from the actual wishes of the people who are served. Some writers have suggested that the present method of assigning funds, as evolved by the National Endowments for the Arts and for the Humanities, is anything but sensitive to the will of the people, and should be much more fully linked to popular interest and support of the arts.

Beyond this, the mere existence of government subsidies has had important implications for performing arts organizations. Marcia Siegel points out that during its early years, dance survived as an independent institution, without outside means of support, except for a limited number of private benefactors, chiefly for a few leading ballet companies. When government subsidies began to appear in significant amounts, the effect at first appeared to be highly positive—"rewards for the deserving, security for the homeless, and access to a once-indifferent public." Even when funding agencies began to discriminate more carefully in their selection of dance companies for aid, it fell short of direct government control of artistic content. However, Siegel comments that arts funding gradually linked itself into the industry of arts consumerism, with dance companies' success in attracting grants increasingly based on their popular appeal, ability to sell tickets, and overall budget:

> Subsidy did not stimulate new artists, it encouraged safe ones. Novelty was more important than innovation. The star system flourished. In addition to putting our large ballet and dance companies into an almost unassailably prominent position in the public view, government funding has created a middle echelon of management and production organizations at every level of dance activity.[20]

In many cases, rather than make the kinds of difficult choices which are involved in dealing directly with choreographers and performing groups, funding agencies have preferred to assist festivals, touring programs, or other centralized booking agencies which in turn make the actual selections of groups to perform. Often, the most popular companies and not necessarily the most artistically creative ones are favored. Clearly, while government subsidy has played a critical role in supporting a considerable expansion of dance interest and performance, its growth presents problems that need to be addressed on the national scene.

[19]Walter Goodman, "The Artists and the Politician—Natural Antagonists," *The New York Times,* April 24, 1977, p. 2-1.

[20]Marcia B. Siegel, *Watching the Dance Go By* (Boston: Houghton Mifflin Co., 1977), p. xii.

Another key factor which has been critical in the promotion of all the performing arts, including dance, has been the establishment of a number of national and regional organizations working in this field. In addition to the National Association of Regional Ballet Companies and the Association of American Dance Companies, both mentioned earlier, a number of others have continued to play a critical role in the development of quality dance programs and in the increased awareness of dance as a significant art form.

One such organization was the National Council of the Arts in Education, a federation of national associations concerned with the arts at all educational levels, and now known as the Assembly of National Arts Education Associations. It supports general education in the arts in elementary and secondary schools, in preprofessional and professional education, and in teacher education. Members of the constituent organizations are active as both teachers and practitioners in the arts; they include actors, dancers, musicians, painters, and sculptors, as well as composers, museum curators, art critics, historians, and researchers. Member organizations include many national groups concerned with theater, music, art education, ethnomusicology, architecture, and dance. The dance-connected organizations are the American Dance Guild (formerly the Dance Teachers Guild) and the National Dance Association. Founded in 1958, the Assembly exists to:

Define educational goals for the arts;

Disseminate views of the artistic community on questions of national importance;

Stimulate research and development in art education;

Keep membership abreast of legislative activity affecting the arts, and develop informed opinion on pending legislation;

Provide contact among artists, art educators, school administrators, government officials;

Promote understanding of the arts and their place in education;

Discover new sources of support for the arts.

Since 1962, there has been sponsorship of important annual conferences at universities throughout the country, dealing with the development of the arts in education and in community life. One of the key organizations in such efforts has been the National Dance Association. Originally a Section of the American Association for Health, Physical Education and Recreation, it was elevated to Division status in 1965. When AAHPER was restructured in 1974, as the American Alliance for Health, Physical Education and Recreation, the Dance Division became the National Dance Association. At the 1979 national convention of the Alliance, its Representative Assembly voted to add the name Dance to its title, making it the American Alliance for Health, Physical Education, Recreation, and Dance, thus giving full recognition to dance as an essential element in education.

Today, the National Dance Association is the largest dance education organization in the country, with a membership exceeding 3,000 teachers, students, community leaders, and performers. One of its primary goals is to provide leadership at a national level in order to encourage high quality programs, materials, and methods of dance. Its structure includes a framework of national, district, and state officers, with a target of reaching every school and college throughout the United States. The NDA national office in Reston, Virginia serves as an active liaison to more than 40 groups, including government agencies, foundations, and other educational associations, as well as providing informed legislative representation. NDA is represented on the Board of Directors for the Alliance for Arts Education and the National Committee, Arts for the Handicapped. The organization also participates at the semi-annual meeting of the Assembly of National Arts Education Organizations.

As a member association of the American Alliance for Health, Physical Education, Recreation, and Dance, NDA is able to use the Alliance's publications department and public information services, in promoting dance by reaching nearly 50,000 readers through the *Dance Dynamics* insert in AAHPERD's professional magazine, *Journal of Physical Education and Recreation,* as well as through the *Dance Information* column and feature articles in the AAHPERD monthly newspaper, *Update.* In addition, *Spotlight on Dance,* the NDA newsletter, is published four times a year and includes information about functions, policies, and procedures of the organization, and occasional articles of timely interest. *Focus on Dance* is a scholarly monograph in design, including technical and esoteric articles.

Commissions on children's dance, elementary, and secondary dance in education, dance in higher education and dance therapy, work with the publications unit to prepare selected bibliographies, conference reports, records for dance, guides for curriculum building and program planning, career information, and creative films. The commissions also promote the growth of dance through workshops, seminars, and informational services. An organization which has grown tremendously during the past decade, the National Dance Association represents a liaison with hundreds of interested teachers and thousands of students throughout the country, providing a national center for the accumulation of resources and the dissemination of materials relevant to dance education in the United States.

The American Dance Guild, founded in 1956 in New York City as the Dance Teachers Guild, is an organization designed to meet the needs of creative teachers of dance throughout the country. Its goals are to improve instruction in dance, to develop increased community awareness of dance and a higher level of aesthetic taste ("to combat the impact of commercialism and its corruption of taste through techniques of parent education"), and to further the progress of dance through support from a number of levels: community, state, and federal governments.

Among its specific objectives, the American Dance Guild seeks:

1. To promote the highest standards in the study, education, and performance of the art of dance;
2. To serve the needs of dance artists (dancers, choreographers, teachers, students) through all phases of their development and career;
3. To disseminate information and strengthen communication within the field;

4. To disseminate information on dance and the needs of dance artists to other organizations and agencies and to the public at large.

The Guild, whose initial membership was primarily in the Northeast region of the country, has greatly spread its membership and range of influence. Grants from the New York State Council on the Arts and the National Endowment for the Arts have been major factors in its development and expansion. By the late 1970s it had members in 50 states, two territories, and seven foreign countries. It publishes a newspaper, sponsors workshops through local chapters, provides a placement bureau, publishes a scholarly quarterly magazine, *Dance Scope,* and holds annual conferences of high quality, which attract hundreds of dance teachers who are concerned both with enhancing their own competence and with strengthening the entire field of dance education.

In contrast to the American Dance Guild, which is essentially concerned with the teaching of creative dance on a noncommercial level (usually through small community-sponsored nonprofit organizations), there are a number of large, powerful organizations which represent commercial dancing teachers throughout the United States. The distinction is that the commercial teachers operate on a profit basis, running large-scale enterprises in private studios which may either be part of national chains or independently owned. Such studios tend to stress not modern or creative dance, but rather ballet and ballroom dancing for children and adults, modern jazz, and tap dance, as well as other forms which are associated with performing dance on a "popular" and often nonaesthetic level.

Organizations of this type include the Dance Masters of America, formed in 1884 as the American National Association, Masters of Dancing and renamed in 1926, a professional organization for certified dance teachers which holds large-scale regional and national conventions each year. The curriculum of such conventions includes: "ballet, tap, jazz, baby work, children's work, modern, acrobatic, baton, and ballroom dance." Faculty include such leading dancers and choreographers as Robert Joffrey, Leon Danielian, Violette Verdy, Matt Mattox, and other leading dancers—including many who are known as performers or choreographers for movies and television. In terms of levels of taste, the members of the Dance Masters of America are closely attuned to what people generally are inclined to accept as dance. Their studios and business operations tend to be large, flourishing enterprises which emphasize the development of technique and showmanship.

The Dance Educators of America, Inc., is a similar organization, consisting of "qualified dance teachers," who are essentially connected with private and commercial studios and whose orientation is dance instruction or performance on a popular level. There are numerous local and state chapters of the Dance Masters of America and Dance Educators of America, as well as of the American Society of Teachers of Dancing and a variety of similar organizations. Dance Caravan, U.S.A., operates a major tour each summer throughout cities in the United States, offering performing arts courses for both teachers and students, staffed by popular and highly-skilled specialists. Most of these organizations, both national and regional, are affiliated with the National Council of Dance Teacher Organizations, with offices in Elmira, New York.

In contrast to these groups, the organizations that are concerned with promoting dance as a creative, aesthetic activity on a noncommercial basis tend to be much smaller and to operate within a narrower range of influence. Nonetheless, they are attuned to both the interests of government, which seeks to promote dance essentially as an art form (in order to raise the level of popular culture) and to the role played by colleges and universities, which have the same concern.

RESEARCH IN DANCE

In addition to organizations dedicated to the growth of dance in education and the continued development of dance educators, a considerable number of scholars have undertaken collective efforts to promote the field of dance research. The Congress on Research in Dance first met formally in April, 1965, in New York City, and until 1967 operated as an ad hoc committee on dance research. In May of that year it was decided that CORD should become an organization of interdisciplinary fields committed to achieving a fuller understanding of dance through research. Its purposes include:

1. To encourage research in all aspects of dance, including related fields;
2. To foster the exchange of ideas, resources, and research methods in dance and related areas through publications, conferences, symposia, workshops, panel discussions, institutes, and other media;
3. To promote the accessibility of research materials.

By 1979, 11 *Dance Research Annuals* had been published, including issues dealing with research problems and possibilities, dance therapy investigations, reviews of anthropological studies of dance, and psychological analysis of dance. The overall interest in dance scholarship escalated markedly during the 1970s. In February, 1979, a Dance History Conference was held at the Lincoln Center for the Performing Arts' Dance Collection Library and Barnard College; over 200 persons interested in the pursuit of dance history attended, and interest in forming an organization with dance history as a focal point became apparent.

The proliferation of active membership in dance organizations, both of an educational-service and a research nature, is further example of the steady growth of interest in dance which has marked the past two decades.

DANCE AND THE MASS MEDIA

Another extremely important factor in the growing popularity of dance as an art form in the United States, has been the development of major television series or "specials" which have brought ballet and modern dance to huge new audiences. For example, in 1976, the Public Broadcasting Service broadcast a "Dance in America" series, with a $1.5 million grant from the National Endowment for the Arts, the Corporation for Public

Broadcasting, and the Exxon Corporation. Among the programs featured in this outstanding series was an hour-long introduction to the City Center Joffrey Ballet—consisting of an informal, "talk-show" approach to meeting the choreographer and performers, along with one full-length ballet and several excerpts from others. Other programs in the series presented Twyla Tharp and her avant-garde dance company, Martha Graham and a number of her outstanding works, and the New York City Ballet.

Numerous other presentations of modern dance and ballet on television have included Alwin Nikolais and his company; the American Ballet Theater's production of Tchaikovsky's *The Nutcracker;* a "Live from Lincoln Center" broadcast of the New York City Ballet's *Coppelia;* a one-hour ABC-TV special of *Ben Vereen—His Roots,* highlighting dancing by this outstanding Broadway star; and a one-hour performance by Mikhail Baryshnikov and Gelsey Kirkland in several ballet works, in the Public Broadcasting Service series, *In Performance at Wolf Trap.*

The benefits of such dance exposure on national television networks are obvious—they help to acquaint new millions with dance as a performing art, and to introduce outstanding companies and dancers to regions that might otherwise never have the opportunity to view them. At the same time, they impose some risks. By bringing top professional companies into such areas, they may in a sense undermine the efforts of smaller, more struggling companies that are able to dance and perform on a much more rudimentary level. The sheer impact of television's availability, ease and professionalism, may serve to discourage live local performance; one of the effects of phonographs becoming widely available in the society was to provide much less employment for musicians in restaurants or night clubs that had formerly employed small orchestras.

Another hazard of television dance performance is that it always involves a distortion of the art itself. The camera is selective, showing distance shots here, close-ups there, and in specially filmed performances, often creating an entirely new work that may not reflect the choreographer's original intentions. In some cases, the television director may choose to superimpose figures on each other, to use slow motion, to repeat some sequences and exclude others and, in short, to create a dance for television viewing that is markedly different from what the audience of the live performance sees. Even the physical conditions under which dancers must perform in television studios are often dangerous or ill-suited to their best efforts. Nonetheless, Merrill Brockway, producer of the "Dance in America" series, comments that his primary aim was always to preserve the original vision of the choreographer. Finally, the extent to which such efforts reach huge new audiences is impressive:

> The series could not have come at a better time. Dance is America's fastest growing performance art. (Some 11 million people saw live dance performances in 1975—an astonishing increase of about 10 million over the previous decade.) WNET estimates that between four and five million viewers will see the first hour of "Dance in America." That, in itself, is reason for applause.[21]

[21]Wallace White, "Videodance—It May Be a Whole New Art Form," *The New York Times,* January 18, 1976, p. D-10.

Similarly, dance has made an increasingly strong impact on the public through the musical theater and in movies. Since the 1940s, such works as *Oklahoma, Carrousel, Brigadoon,* and *West Side Story* have had dance of high quality—choreographed by such artists as Agnes de Mille and Jerome Robbins—as integral parts of their story lines and stage appeal. In a number of cases, choreographers like Michael Kidd and Bob Fosse have gone on to become extremely successful directors of musical productions themselves, and have created plots based on dance as the primary ingredient. Popular musicals of the late 1970s, *A Chorus Line,* and *Dancin',* illustrate this trend.

Similarly, in the popular film world, such works as *The Turning Point* have had immense success. Featuring Mikhail Baryshnikov, Leslie Browne, Alexandra Danilova, and nearly the entire company of American Ballet Theater, and directed by a former dancer and choreographer, Herbert Ross, with Nora Kaye, a well-known and successful dancer, this film fanned the nation's interest in ballet.

Based in part on its popularity, plans were immediately begun for a full-length feature film of the life of Vaslav Nijinsky. Undoubtedly, as dancers become increasingly better known, more and more films will be made which will bring the history and tradition of this performing art to the viewing public.

Similarly, there has been steady progress in the production of films which, while not geared for popular audiences in first-run theaters, present the serious work of leading choreographers and in some cases begin to build up a lasting record of their major works. It has always been a tragic flaw of dance that it is ephemeral; unlike painting, sculpture, or even music (in which sophisticated notation has made it possible to preserve great artistic creations), dance has tended to disappear, once performed. While leading ballet companies have preserved their outstanding choreographic works and performing traditions, largely on an apprenticeship, person-to-person basis, many great modern dance creations have disappeared. More recently, works have been recorded by experts using the Labanotation system of movement notation or have been revived by former members of a company. However, the increased number of films that have been made during the past several years to create a lasting heritage of theater dance probably offers the best solution to maintaining a historical record which is both accurate and accessible.

Some films are taken directly from television performances. For example, the film *Dance in America: Martha Graham Dance Company,* was taken directly from the *Dance in America* TV series. Other films have been created to serve as educational media; a recently produced series of five 30-minute color/sound films by Murray Louis, titled *Dance As an Art Form,* presents and explores such key dance concepts as "body as an instrument," "motion," "space," "time," and "shape." Still other films have been revived and made available in recent years, from existing footage, to show the work of leading dance pioneers—among them Mary Wigman, Ruth St. Denis, Ted Shawn, Harold Kreutzberg, and others. More and more, it seems likely that the work of today's choreographers and companies will be preserved through film, for future generations to enjoy.

Without question, then, dance as a performing art has reached a new level of popular support and interest today in the United States, as it has throughout the Western world. Although the problems of economics and financial support continue to exist, there is far more widespread activity in dance as a performing art today than ever was the case in past decades. For the first time, there is a broad awareness of the arts in general in community life, and growing acceptance of them in the nation's leisure, both as a form of participation and audience involvement. Similarly, there is increased recognition of the need for support from every corner of community life—from businesses and foundations, from government on various levels, from professional arts organizations, from colleges and universities, and from the artists themselves.

Indeed, for the first time, sophisticated techniques of managing the arts are being explored, and in cities throughout the country, efforts are made to involve large businesses in their support as part of their civic and cultural responsibility.[22] Professional arts managers are being trained at a number of leading universities, and the National Endowment for the Arts supports an internship program leading directly to careers in this field, and encompassing such elements as fund-raising, programming, budgeting, public relations, law and the arts, and knowledge of state and federal legislative bodies as they relate to the arts.[23]

It is clearly a time of ferment and growth. If the promise of the 1960s and 1970s is realized, theater dance, along with the other performing arts, stands at the threshold of a new era of much expanded participation and performance. What is needed above all is the establishment of solidly based organizations connected to centers for performance. The kinds of business expertise and arrangements for financial subsidy of the sort described earlier must, along with new kinds of performing cooperatives, be linked to the growth of the individual artist and the establishment of an increasing number of artistically sound ballet and modern dance companies.

Within this framework, the role of educational institutions will be extremely important—in terms both of stimulating general understanding and support of dance and of providing direct experience in dance as an art form to a much broader segment of the American public than ever before. The following chapter, therefore, is concerned with the critical task of improving and expanding programs of dance education in the nation's schools and colleges.

[22]See, for example, Luisa Kreisberg, "Department Stores Market the Arts," *The New York Times,* November 27, 1977, p. 11–1.

[23]Thomas P. Murphy, "Internships and the Professionalization of Arts Administration," *Performing Arts Review,* Vol. 7 #1, 1977, pp. 328–347.

16 Dance Education: The Years Ahead

To fully understand the way dance is regarded in American education and to suggest policies that will help it flourish in our schools and colleges in the years ahead, one must examine its present role and image in the society at large.

For, unlike many subjects in the curriculum which are somewhat isolated from direct experience in community life, dance is widely encountered in many forms outside the schools. Indeed, a great deal of dance education is provided outside the formal educational structure of the nation. Therefore, students, parents, and educators all have certain attitudes about dance which are based on their contact with it in community life; these in turn influence their attitudes about it as a form of curricular experience. And, because dance has not, within the United States, been typically regarded as a basic educational discipline or subject, it is important that these attitudes be knowledgeable and favorable.

PUBLIC ATTITUDES ABOUT DANCE

What are the widely held attitudes about dance in community life? While they may vary according to region, community, or socioeconomic status, certain generalized views may be identified.

First, for those persons in community life who have an established interest in culture and the arts, dance is regarded as an important theatrical form. While the audience for ballet and modern dance still consists of a relatively small proportion of the total population, it *has* grown remarkably over the past two decades, and represents a literate, prosperous, and influential segment of society. Once a stepchild among the arts, now dance is given full standing in programs of government support and as an important element in aesthetic education. Despite the reservations cited in earlier chapters, this recognition appears likely to become even stronger in the years ahead.

Secondly, dance continues to be an important ingredient in popular entertainment. On television, in movies, and on the musical stage, the quality of dancing has grown immeasurably. Years ago, dancing in Broadway shows or in touring companies tended to offer little more than a lineup of attractive but comparatively untrained and untalented "hoofers." Today, few dancers are hired for musical shows, movies, or television programs who have not had extensive training in ballet, modern dance, jazz, ethnic, and tap dance. Thanks to the work of such leading choreographers as George Balanchine, Agnes de Mille, Jerome Robbins, Michael Kidd, Bob Fosse, and Gower Champion, public taste with respect to dance in popular entertainment has become increasingly sophisticated. It is not at all uncommon to have the choreographer become responsible for staging the entire work, rather than have him assigned to stage a few numbers, as a minor aspect of the overall production.

Another important aspect of dance in community life is based on its widespread acceptance as a form of recreational and social activity. In the 1930s, sociologists Robert and Helen Lynd found dance to be one of the leading recreational activities in Middletown; similarly, the Neumeyers wrote, "Social dancing is one of the most common leisure pursuits, especially among young people. . . ."[1]

Today, while the forms of social dancing have changed, with rock-and-roll or discotheque dancing becoming the preoccupation of most adolescents and young adults, and the more traditional forms of ballroom dancing being enjoyed by other segments of the population, the basic activity remains a highly popular form of recreation in the society at large. In hotels, resorts, night clubs, community recreation programs, schools and colleges, and a host of other settings for social recreation, social dancing flourishes. The teaching of dance in commercial studios has expanded to the level of a major enterprise in cities and towns throughout the United States. Other forms of recreational dance, such as square, round, and folk dancing, have also increased in popularity. In many smaller towns and suburban areas, particularly in the Far West, Midwest, and Southwest, many clubs of avid square and round dancers pursue this hobby, wearing special costumes, constantly learning newly choreographed dances, and attending numerous festivals and workshops. In large cities and particularly in university settings, folk dancing appeals to individuals with cosmopolitan or international interests.

Numerous other examples of the growth of public interest in dance may be cited. For example, there is an increasing awareness of the value of dance as therapeutic activity. Although this function of dance is historically ancient, today it is finding new and varied applications. Interesting dance experiments are being carried out with the deaf, with inmates of penal institutions, with blind children, with the retarded, and, most commonly, with the mentally ill. Marian Chace of St. Elizabeth's Hospital in Washing-

[1]Martin and Esther Neumeyer, *Leisure and Recreation* (New York: A. S. Barnes and Co., 1936), pp. 94–95.

ton, D.C., has been viewed as the leading worker in the latter field, and more recently a number of other dance educators and rehabilitation specialists have contributed much to its growing body of knowledge. Since the mid-1960s, the American Dance Therapy Association has promoted public awareness of this field, encouraged specialized graduate programs of professional education in it, and sponsored various workshops and conferences to explore its values. In addition, a number of mental hospitals have conducted experimental programs in dance therapy.[2] The concept of dance as treatment not only for the psychotic or severely neurotic patient, but also for those in a more normal range of mental health, who are suffering from a degree of stress or disability, is being explored. In a number of nursing homes throughout the nation, so-called "psychomotor therapy" intended to help restore disoriented, older patients to a degree of reality in their daily living is heavily based on modified dance movements.[3] "Aerobic" dancing has evolved as a form of enjoyable exercise being used in many fitness programs for both men and women.[4]

Another unusual aspect of dance in community life has been the emphasis given it in a number of special urban antipoverty programs for disadvantaged youth—particularly those from racial minority backgrounds. Typically, the HARYOU-ACT antipoverty program in New York City's Harlem had a strong program in the performing arts, including a dance group that specialized in Afro-American and jazz dance forms. In similar programs in other cities, theater and dance activities have had considerable appeal for black and other minority group teen-agers and young adults. In some cases, talented youth have been motivated toward serious study in dance as a performing art through initial involvement in such antipoverty recreation and cultural programs.

These, then, are the most important aspects of dance in community life that illustrate positive attitudes held by the public at large. Without question, dance's image has improved markedly in recent years, and it is firmly established as a significant aesthetic, cultural, and recreational activity. On the other hand, there also exist attitudes of a somewhat negative nature which diminish the possibility of dance becoming fully accepted as an educational discipline. Only with the decrease of these misconceptions and misrepresentations will dance be able to accept a place of prominence and stability within the American educational system.

NEGATIVE PUBLIC ATTITUDES ABOUT DANCE

Moral Disapproval. The first of these has to do with a continuing degree of suspicion about dance as immoral or sinful. Although it is commonplace today to say that the centuries-old Puritan disapproval of dance has now

[2]See "Dance Therapy as a Career," *Journal of Physical Education and Recreation,* May 1977, p. 38, and Claire Schmais, "What is Dance Therapy," *Journal of Physical Education and Recreation,* January 1976, p. 39.

[3]Linda Ruth Schoenfeld, "The Psychomotor Approach in Nursing Homes," *Dance Magazine,* October 1977, p. 82.

[4]Lois Ellfeldt, "Aerobic Dance," *Journal of Physical Education and Recreation,* May 1977, p. 45.

died out, it would be false to assume that it has disappeared completely. A number of schools and colleges, particularly those in rural areas of the country or those which are affiliated with fundamentalist Protestant sects, still prohibit any form of dancing—as instruction, entertainment, or recreation. To a degree, these attitudes are a throwback to the old Calvinist teachings, or the fire-and-brimstone religious revivalism of the 19th century. But they continue to be fanned anew. A tract that is still published by a religious publishing firm in the South describes ballroom dancing in these terms:

> . . .I flatly charge that modern social dancing is fundamentally sinful and evil. I charge that dancing's charm is based entirely on sex appeal. I charge that dancing is the most advanced and most insidious of the maneuvers preliminary to sex betrayal. . . . The dance has been the downward step for many. . . . [5]

Such condemnatory attitudes stem not only from the traditional religious prohibition of dance, but also from the settings in which dance has been found in the past and present centuries. Herbert Asbury described the so-called dance-houses in the French Quarter of old New Orleans:

> Except that there were no formal programs of entertainment, the dancehouses of Gallatin Street were operated in much the same fashion as the concert-saloons—the main attractions were women, liquor, and dancing. But they were infinitely lower in the scale of depravity. . . . [6]

During the 1920s and 1930s, so-called taxi-dance halls were established in many American cities, to meet the need for feminine companionship of homeless or lonesome men crowded into rooming house districts of larger cities. Often, during the Depression, both the patrons and girls were exploited economically; many taxi-dance halls became fronts for prostitution. Even during the 1960s, there was an investigation of commercial dance halls in New York City, in which the Commissioner of Licenses found that ballrooms had provided hostesses for "lewd, obscene, and immoral dancing, and acts and conduct offensive to public decency." In one case, the operators of a dance hall were prosecuted for running a commercialized vice ring.

The very fact that ballroom dancing permits young people to embrace and move about the floor rhythmically together shocks many who are religiously conservative. The frankly sexual movement of many of the more recent rock-and-roll or discotheque dancing continues to offend others, and the linkage of dance with nudity or prurient commercial entertainment is the basis for other objections. Nor has criticism been limited to this form of dance performance. One of Martha Graham's major works, *Phaedra,* was sharply attacked as salacious and immoral by a New York Congresswoman who had seen it performed in Germany on a government-supported tour; the legislator proceeded to demand that the government impose censorship on ballets and films sent abroad in cultural exchange programs.

[5] *The Modern Dance,* Pilgrim Tract Society, Randleman, North Carolina, n.d.

[6] Herbert Asbury, *The French Quarter* (New York: Alfred A. Knopf, 1936), p.244.

While such episodes may be viewed as having minor importance, and do not reflect on the true worth of dance as an aesthetic or recreational activity, they contribute to a vague aura of sinfulness that clings to dance and which compels some school or college administrators to hesitate to provide dance instruction—because *some* students or parents may find it objectionable.

Dance as a Feminine Activity. Even more harmful, in terms of community and educational attitudes about dance, is the popular concept of it as a feminine activity. Certainly, this stereotype is a factor which prevents many educators from requiring or strongly supporting dance as an activity for boys and young men in schools and colleges. What accounts for this attitude?

First, one must recognize that in all cultures, certain roles or occupations are assigned on the basis of sex affiliation. Margaret Mead, the anthropologist, also points out that we ascribe a set of stereotyped personality traits to each sex. Historically, it was assumed that men were strong, aggressive and emotionally stoical, while women were believed to be more passive, gentle, emotional, and aesthetic in nature. While these views have been strongly challenged in recent years, they are still all too prevalent. Based on this orientation, certain activities within the arts—particularly dance—are seen as essentially more feminine than masculine. How did this prejudice come into being in the Western world? Surely history tells us that throughout the ages man has always led in dance. José Limón wrote:

> The male of the human species has always been a dancer. Whether as a savage or civilized man, whether warrior, monarch, hunter, priest, philosopher, or tiller of the soil, the atavistic urge to dance was in him and he gave it full expression. . . . [7]

The roots of the feminine stereotype of dance lie in the past. During the early history of ballet, when boys and young men dressed as women to play feminine roles in the French court, the sexual identification of the male dancer was clearly weakened. Later, during the 19th century, when the ballerina was glorified and the male dancer denigrated, dance as a profession lost its appeal for many men—except as choreographers, ballet masters, or producers. Marcia Siegel comments that for 200 years, ballet has been a woman's art; through this period:

> . . . the ballet stage has been inhabited by beautiful females with uncanny skills of speed, balance, accuracy, and elevation—women whose virtuosity gave tangible support to their stage roles as princesses or leaders, often endowed with supernatural powers. Countless ballet heroes have fallen helplessly in love with these splendid creatures. . . . the ballerina is what you go to the ballet to see. A male dancer hoping for stardom in this world learns to incline his head and step backward with regal deference.[8]

[7]José Limón, "The Virile Dancer," in Walter Sorell, *The Dance Has Many Faces* (New York: World Publishing Company, 1951), p. 192.

[8]Marcia B. Siegel, *Watching the Dance Go By* (Boston: Houghton Mifflin Co., 1977), pp. 103–104.

That this feminine image continues to be influential even today, despite the emergence of great male performers as popular idols, including Nureyev and Baryshnikov, is demonstrated by George Balanchine's characterization of "ballet as woman" (see page 173).

So it was that, by the time the Golden Age of ballet in Europe had run its course, few men were willing to embark on a career in which they could find little prestige or economic reward. Dance became a field in which the female performer was pre-eminent, although men continued to be the leading teachers, choreographers, and impresarios.

In modern times, other factors have contributed to the stereotype. Because dance, as all the stage arts, has been a competitive and economically precarious field, many young men who had the intention of marrying and raising families hesitated to enter it or, in some cases, were forced to leave it because of economic pressures. In contrast, the unmarried male dancer or homosexual dancer with fewer ties or responsibilities, has been better able to withstand the economic stresses and the demands of touring and performance. Thus, the homosexual has existed in disproportionate numbers in the field; this has tended to discourage acceptance and support of dance from more conservative advocates of arts education and elicits concern and often rejection from parents of school-age children.

It is worth comment that the stereotype has not attached itself to men in the more commercial phases of dance; performers like Fred Astaire, Ray Bolger, and Bill Robinson have not suffered from it. What is there about ballet in particular that arouses prejudice? Some of the adverse reputation undoubtedly has been due to the reaction of the untutored and artistically unsophisticated American to the very appearance of ballet. The exaggerated and flamboyant gestures, the walk which was perceived as mincing, the tight-fitting and revealing costume of the male dancer—all these aroused disapproval and suspicion of this ornate, aristocratic and graceful art.

In addition, the view of dance as an essentially feminine activity has been strengthened by the way it has been presented in schools and colleges. During the late 1800s, when aesthetic dance was developed for women and gymnastic dance for men, the male role was defined as vigorous, strong, and essentially nonartistic. As sports became increasingly important in the program of physical education for boys and men, they tended to displace dance activity. The fact that, almost invariably in secondary schools and often in colleges, physical education classes were divided into separate departments, with men teaching classes for boys and men, and women teaching girls and women, made it extremely difficult to involve males in dance programs. Sports were inevitably regarded as the most appropriate and prestigious activity for males, while dance was considered the most suitable movement domain for females. When boys entered private studios, they usually were placed in classes in which girls represented the majority. Instruction characteristically had been dominated by women, and too often the sports-oriented boy rebelled. In more recent years, female dominance in dance teaching has begun to diminish, providing expanded models for movement performance and role association with which many male dance students can more readily identify.

Historically, a reversed phenomenon has also been apparent, in the traditional exclusion of women from the area of active team sports; within recent years, this has undergone dramatic change. Today, as a result of the feminist movement and federal legislation requiring equal opportunity for girls and women in school and college sports, they have become increasingly active in a wide range of sports competition.

Many dancers and dance educators have striven to overcome the prejudice against males in dance. Ted Shawn, through his all-male touring group, his teaching and writing, was one of the early dance pioneers who had strong influence in supporting male dancing during the 1930s and 1940s. Today, an increasing number of boys and men appear to be entering dance; certainly, in colleges and community programs, more male dance teachers are being employed. There is a growing respect for the sheer physical and athletic demands of performing dance; one leading physical educator describes his experience in seeing an outstanding male dancer:

> Never before had I witnessed such a display of sheer power, quickness, and body control. . . . his . . . presence on stage captured my complete attention while raising disturbing simple questions. Who is this dancer? Why is he the only male performer in the company? And why is such a superb athletelike male pursuing a career in dance? His performance made me uneasy.[9]

More and more, educators are realizing that boys can actually *like* dancing, and take part in it enthusiastically, when it is approached seriously as a fine art and when it involves a significant creative and physical challenge. Despite the progress that is being made, however, the stereotype of dance as a feminine activity continues to be held by many, and poses a serious restriction to the full acceptance of dance education for all students.

Dance as Highbrow Activity A last negative attitude to be considered is the belief by many in community life that dance—particularly modern dance —is a "highbrow" or incomprehensible activity. In this context, ballet tends to be somewhat more acceptable to a broad audience, in part because it is known to have had a long and respected tradition. Like opera, it has established a base of support in many communities. Civic leaders serve on the boards of ballet organizations, and ballet is widely accepted as a form of training for young girls of wealthy and socially prominent families.

But perhaps more important than these factors is that audiences can watch ballet without being disturbed about understanding what they are seeing. On the other hand, modern dance (by nature more exploratory and innovative in movement and theme) often stuns and puzzles its audience. Not knowing what to look for and accustomed to seeing either frankly abstract movement or else a fairly literal approach to communication in ballet, the unsophisticated audience tends to react badly to much modern dance. Because the audience new to modern dance often feels uncomfortable for lack of a known reference point, they often are reluctant to see more of this dance form, denying it not only their physical and financial support, but also becoming skeptical of its artistic and educational merit.

All of these are reasons why dance, and particularly modern dance, has failed to gain a larger measure of support in community life. To these must

[9]Dennis Fallon, "A Man Unchained," *Journal of Physical Education and Recreation,* May 1977, p. 43.

be added the view that dance is a "frill," a decorative adjunct to education but not a matter for serious curricular concern. Recognizing the problems which stem from a lack of public understanding and whole-hearted support for dance, what can dance educators, physical educators, and school or community leaders who are interested in this art form do to promote its fuller acceptance in education?

STEPS NEEDED TO PROMOTE DANCE IN EDUCATION

Essentially, the steps needed to promote dance in education fall within two categories: (1) programs that will enrich and strengthen dance in community life at large, both as a significant cultural experience and as a form of positive recreation, and (2) actions that will expand the scope and improve the quality of instruction in dance education in schools and colleges.

How is the first task to be accomplished?

First, as earlier sections of this book have demonstrated, a great deal that is positive is already being done. On the federal level, the government is assisting touring companies, providing subsidies for performance and special workshops in schools and colleges, and supporting major conferences devoted to the promotion of the arts both in the community and in schools and colleges. Through such programs, as well as through the increased efforts of state governments, arts councils, and foundations, much help is being provided for the performing arts. If, in the continued development of arts centers around the country, greater attention is given to the need for supporting locally sponsored performing groups—rather than simply providing an audience for touring companies—dance in community life will be greatly strengthened.

Furthermore, dancers themselves can do much to promote fuller understanding of the dance, and to improve its public image as an important cultural and artistic option within the community. Certainly, it will be helpful for male dancers to assert themselves as spokesmen for their art, in an attempt to dispel the stereotype of it as a predominately feminine activity. One of America's leading male dancers, Jacques d'Amboise, has done this successfully, both on national television programs and in major publications, where the special classes he has conducted for boys (including his own son) were favorably publicized. Other dancers, including Edward Villella, have carried out similar efforts to promote the acceptance of male dancing.

Other dancers have accepted the obligation to help audiences understand and appreciate their work. Erick Hawkins, for example, has toured widely throughout the United States and Canada, often under college and university auspices. However, he has not assumed that, for this reason, his audiences were knowledgeable about modern dance. Instead, he and the members of his company have worked hard to orient their audiences. On the day of a university-sponsored dance performance, a member of the company might give a master class while Hawkins lectures on dance to students in the English or philosophy department. Sometimes his composer-accompanist, Lucia Dlugoszewski, gives a lecture-demonstration to music students. Not infrequently, the company may remain in a university community an additional day or two, without charge, in order to promote dance interest and understanding.

The most effective technique used by Hawkins to orient audiences has been to make a short talk to the audience before the performance. Typically, in such an address, Hawkins talks about the arts and American society, about the role of the male dancer, and about how to view all art, particularly dance. Giving the audience some basic principles as well as a sense of security about the works they are to see, he then goes ahead with the performance. Frequently, when performing before an audience that has seen little modern dance before, he presents a work titled *John Brown,* based on the American historical figure. His purpose in this is to illustrate the function of art as literal communication, and to give audiences a work to which they can relate somewhat more easily than more abstract or symbolic dances.

This sort of effort by dancers and choreographers is extremely helpful in creating a more favorable audience for dance. Local and regional dance organizations also are in a position to promote understanding by sponsoring festivals, workshops, film series, and seminars, directed to both educational and lay audiences. In so doing, strength can be gained by allying dance to the other performing arts. In a number of communities, a variety of concerts, performances, exhibitions, poetry readings, or film showings have combined to draw large audiences and promote total public interest in the arts. In such a setting, modern dance or ballet tends to be one of the most exciting and successful program events.

In a presentation before the Second National Conference on the Arts in Education, Gertrude Lippincott made a number of recommendations for dance educators to promote this field in both the community and in educational institutions. Dance educators in the community were urged to:

1. Establish liaison with dance groups and institutions where dance is taught, such as private studios, YMCAs, cooperatives, regional dance festivals both ballet and modern, conferences, museums, extension divisions, etc., in an effort to promote and further dance as an art form.
2. Encourage art festivals in which dance is included, dance symposiums, programs, etc. Encourage state and local art councils to include a dance performing unit among their activities, both professional and amateur. (Professional units should be sought after first.)
3. Establish a loosely organized clearing house to aid in sponsoring professional dance performances in educational institutions.

Throughout, Lippincott stressed that it is necessary for dance educators, like practitioners in all the arts, to be personally active in supporting legislation and other governmental activities that promote cultural activities in American life.[10] Her recommendations have, in fact, been widely followed throughout the 1970s. Dancers and dance educators have joined forces with each other and with representatives of the other performing arts fields in

[10]Gertrude Lippincott, *Proceedings of the Second National Conference on the Arts in Education,* National Council of the Arts in Education, 1963, pp. 12–13.

the promotion of the arts in community life, and in seeking government and business support for creative development and performance. Organizations such as the National Dance Association have been successful in gaining recognition of dance as a major art form, and have promoted numerous conferences and cooperative programs strengthening its role in community life.

But what of the other problem—the need to improve the scope and quality of dance education itself, in schools and colleges?

DANCE IN ELEMENTARY EDUCATION

As Chapter 14 has indicated, dance education in elementary schools is at best sketchy and inadequate. There is a pressing need, if this aspect of child development is to be more fully realized, for classroom teachers to become more highly skilled in dance and creative movement instruction. They must be helped to recognize the value of creative rhythmic movement and of structured dance activities, and should be given improved teaching skills in these areas. This can be accomplished both in their preservice training in undergraduate colleges, and also through in-service education and graduate study. Those in allied fields, such as music or art education, or physical education on the elementary level, must also become more knowledgeable about dance and creative movement if they are to assist classroom teachers in this field. While dance specialists have not yet been integrated into elementary education, they have demonstrated their impact in random school systems (usually when a classroom teacher or physical educator has displayed a high level of interest and competence). Administrative flexibility in teaching assignments makes possible this highly desirable arrangement.

As a rule, those who teach dance in elementary schools must be certified in another area, such as physical education. While many such teachers have a strong background and interest in dance, too often it is presented in an extremely limited way. Although efforts have been made to approve separate certification in dance so that well qualified dance specialists might obtain teaching licenses without having to meet requirements in another field, these have been approved in only a few states (see Chapter 14). In addition, in such states as New York, New Jersey, Colorado, and Hawaii, special dance instructors have been placed in schools without separate certification, on projects funded by the Elementary and Secondary Education Act (Title III/IV), by the Artists in the Schools program, or by special state or arts council funding.[11]

In terms of the participation of boys and men in dance, it is during the elementary grades that patterns are set and attitudes developed that prevail

[11]A survey to determine the status of certification in dance was carried out by Sarah Chapman, as chairperson of the Certification Committee of the Commission on Higher Education of the National Dance Association, in 1976. It found that limited progress had been made, with the exceptions cited above.

throughout upper grades and college. Therefore, every effort must be made to involve boys meaningfully in dance experience throughout the elementary school, if the harmful and unjustified stereotype of dance as a feminine activity is to be dispelled.

How can this be accomplished? First, it should be recognized that boys usually have little prejudice against the recreational forms of dance; indeed, they tend to enjoy the lively rhythm and sociability of singing games, play parties, folk dancing and square dancing when they are effectively taught. This may be a convenient starting point, but every effort should also be made to have boys participate in creative dance activity.

For this to be successful, the activity should be presented in a physically challenging way—if dance requires strength, coordination, and ability, it will tend to command respect in its own right. For creative improvisation and performance, boys should be given themes of a dramatic and exciting nature. At the outset, movement themes based on sports, primitive dancing, animals, combat, machinery, or similar ideas are likely to have great appeal. Boys should have the opportunity to develop their own accompaniment with percussion instruments or other forms of music and improvised sound. They should also be able to draw their ideas for creative movement from the subjects studied in the classroom—social studies, science, literature and poetry, music, and the graphic arts.

Efforts should be made to have dance become a recognized activity. If performance—as part of assembly programs, parents' day, arts festivals, or other special events—can be a culminating activity of a particular focus in dance instruction, it will reinforce the interest of children. Obviously, such performances should not be the sole goal of dance instruction and should not be permitted to dominate the actual process of learning to move and of creating dance for its own sake. However, they provide visible goals for classes, as well as a means of demonstrating the outcomes of dance instruction—in terms of physical skills, creative growth, and integrated learning. If they are not approached in a drill-like, boring series of rehearsals, and if they are vital and exciting, rather than stilted and mechanical, they will provide interest and enthusiasm for dance classes. Further, such experiences reinforce the concept of dance as a performing art as well as an educational medium.

In terms of the actual teaching of dance techniques in the upper elementary grades to help children acquire a vocabulary of movement, it is probable that many classroom teachers will be unable to gain the competence needed to do this effectively. Physical educators and other specialists comprehensively trained in dance techniques should be able to provide such instruction. In many school systems, it should be possible to bring in qualified teachers from the community as curriculum resources specialists, to give special instruction in dance in physical education classes—even though they may not possess regular teaching credentials.

Skilled parents may even be willing to contribute their services, in order to promote better dance education. However, this is not a desirable way of providing for such instruction on a permanent basis. Children's dance is a specialized form within the field of dance, and it is the responsibility of parents and professional educators to insist on instruction from persons adequately prepared to teach dance to young children. If dance is taught as a piecemeal activity with little or no clear direction in movement progressions and artistic components, the experience often does more to misrepresent dance than to provide an alternative learning mode or to heighten the child's cultural experience.

DANCE IN SECONDARY SCHOOLS

A number of persons who are familiar with the problems of dance instruction in secondary schools feel that dance would be best promoted by having it presented in a separate department and taught by highly skilled teachers with special certification in dance itself. They argue that historically physical educators have tended to approach it only as a minor form of physical activity and have not presented dance as an art form; indeed, given their own limited skills in the area, the size of classes and the nature of facilities, it would be almost impossible to provide high-quality dance programs in most physical education departments. However, while this would be an ideal solution to the teaching of dance as an art form in the secondary school, it offers little hope of actual implementation in more than a few educational settings. There has been only limited success in having dance specialists certified on the state level. Nor would many school administrators be willing to establish new departments of dance or to identify this as a separate curriculum field, in the light of the severe budgetary problems which exist today and which have compelled many school systems to cut back on already established arts programs.

Even from a theoretical point of view, some educators have challenged the justification for having studio instruction in the arts on the secondary level, beyond a rudimentary level, as part of general education. A leading curriculum authority, for example, in a speech before the Third National Conference on the Arts in Education, argued that it is the high school's responsibility to carry creative artistic experience to a higher level than in the elementary grades, but that this must necessarily fall short of advanced training. Instead, it is suggested that art, music, dance, and theater can be presented more fully through the co-curriculum. Realistically, many secondary school administrators today support this position. In most high schools, the advanced opportunities for participation in the fine and performing arts are found in clubs, choruses, bands, student orchestras, and dance groups—rather than in classes that are part of the actual curriculum.

This situation reflects an unfortunate paradox—that while the American public increasingly values the arts in national life, it still does not give sufficient priority to them as part of the educational experience for all children and youth. David Rockefeller, Jr., chairman of the Panel on the Arts, Education and Americans, wrote in 1977:

> Consider especially the low importance we have assigned to the arts in the education of our children. In most public schools, training in the arts is still limited to painting and music. A survey of 67 schools in major population centers shows that after kindergarten, arts instruction virtually disappears. Faced with increasing demands and tighter budgets, school administrators move almost by reflex to cut the arts curriculum. . . . And apparently this is the

way most Americans want it. . . . the Gallup organization reported that a majority of parents prefer schools that emphasize the three Rs and strict discipline.[12]

To overcome this situation, the Panel on the Arts, Education and Americans has recommended a widely ranging program to strengthen the arts in education, particularly on the secondary level. These include the following kinds of recommendations: a) integration of the arts with each other, and linkage with other academic disciplines; b) programs developed jointly with other community arts agencies and performing companies; c) innovative school structures, including "open" and "alternative" schools, and "schools without walls;" d) a heavier emphasis on studio and performing courses, and less emphasis on courses in criticism or art "appreciation;" e) increased use of professional artists within the schools, either in isolated performances or in residencies continuing over a period of time; f) special efforts to identify gifted and talented students and to encourage them to pursue advanced work, in some cases with schedules that permit them to study in outside, professional settings; and g) the establishment of more performing and fine arts schools in larger cities or on a regional basis.[13]

It has become increasingly clear to many dance educators that dance as part of general education has been inadequately supported. The fact that audiences for dance have escalated dramatically during the past decade, that commerical dance studios are thriving, and that television has heightened the awareness of new millions of dance enthusiasts vividly illustrates the growth of dance as a significant art form within the American society. What then prevents its fuller entrance into the overall educational system?

Perhaps the key factor lies within the dance community itself. While choreographers and dancers have struggled to maintain themselves financially, solve management problems, recruit audiences, and contribute to the artistic enrichment of their field, it has been difficult to provide the necessary leadership and energy to strengthen public understanding of and support for dance as an educational medium. Individual states, dance organizations, and varied arts agencies have effected some change. However, until a consolidated, organized approach is achieved, progress will remain unsteady and fragmented. The most obvious solution would be to press for the state certification of dance as a recognized academic subject and teaching specialization. This would make possible high level instruction at all educational levels, and would strengthen existing college dance major programs.

While progress is being made in a number of these directions, any realistic discussion of dance in secondary schools must assume that it will for the most part continue to be offered by departments of physical education, and that it will not constitute a separate curricular offering or academic

[12]David Rockefeller, Jr., "Wanted: A New Policy for the Arts in Education," *The New York Times,* May 22, 1977, p. D-10.

[13]Drawn from the recommendations of the Arts, Education and Americans Panel, *Coming to Our Sense: The Significance of the Arts for American Education* (New York: McGraw-Hill, 1977).

sequence in most schools in the near future. If this is so, what can be done to improve its scope and quality?

First, it is necessary to strengthen the teaching of dance. Hayes pointed out a number of years ago that many physical education teachers who are required to teach dance have had only a minimum of training in it and in addition often lack the temperament or creative interest to be successful in it. Many of them recognize their own lack of ability in dance and are therefore extremely reluctant to teach it. The danger exists in those who fail to recognize their incompetence and attempt to teach despite their lack of knowledge, skills, and understandings.

As long as physical educators continue to maintain the primary responsibility for dance, their professional preparation should be strengthened on the undergraduate and graduate levels. Not only should a stronger core of basic dance courses be provided in college physical education major departments, but there should be a wider provision of dance "concentrations," or "minors," for physical education majors with a special interest and skill in dance. Thus, such students could become identified at an early point as dance specialists, and could build their competence in a sustained way throughout their college program. A considerable number of colleges in the 1978 Dance Directory published by the National Dance Association have established educational dance majors, minors, or concentrations, which include enough physical education courses so graduates can meet state certification requirements, but also have a solid and comprehensive core of courses in dance. Such programs do much to develop skilled teachers of dance who are able to move into secondary schools. Beyond this, it would be extremely helpful if state education departments could develop a special physical education certification requirement which gives credit to a large block of courses in dance, and which keeps other skills areas to a minimum.

Though this would not be appropriate for those physical education teachers who must serve as generalists—teaching the entire range of physical activities—it should be recognized as useful for those schools which are large enough so that there are several members on the physical education staff. In such schools, it is common policy to have teachers specialize in different areas of activity—team sports, dual sports, aquatics, gymnastics, etc. The well-developed dance specialist is badly needed in such programs, and a modified certification requirement (still under the heading of physical education) would encourage more students interested specifically in dance to enter this field.

Hayes suggests also that the professional education of dance teachers should be recognized as a distinctive area of professional preparation. The title of college departments in this broad field is usually "Health, Physical Education, and Recreation." Could the word "Dance" not be added to those departments offering majors or strong minors in dance? Hayes asks whether it would not be possible to establish it as a separate administrative unit, rather than as a subject area in the women's physical education department, which makes it either awkward or impossible for men to elect it as a field of professional training. Finally, she suggests other procedures to be taken to improve dance instruction, particularly on the secondary level:

> Those individuals who lack the necessary equipment (technical skill, movement sensitivity, and creative spark) to do justice to the teaching of dance should not be expected to do so. The educational curriculum should be made flexible enough to enable majors in other subject areas such as music, speech, or art, to minor in dance; and the administrative organization in secondary schools should be sufficiently adaptable to permit these other trained educators to teach the dance if the physical educators are unwilling or unable to do so. School administrators as well as physical education administrators will need to reorient their thinking along these lines.[14]

A second important step would be to make secondary school dance activity more appropriate and attractive for boys. While it seems unlikely that such a program can be established on a mandatory basis, particularly in terms of modern dance, certainly more schools could establish coeducational recreational dance classes than are doing so at present. Such classes usually include folk, square, ballroom, and disco dance. While many boys would be unenthusiastic, in the present climate, about a *separate* course in modern dance, it might well be feasible to establish a course on an introductory level in secondary schools, titled "Introduction to Dance." Such a course might include the recreational forms of dance *and* modern dance as well, although it is possible that the latter should be described by some name that would avoid the stigma that might presently relate to it. The assumption is that once boys became interested and challenged, many of them would gain a more favorable attitude about dance as an appropriate masculine activity.

As suggested earlier, many of our narrowly stereotypical views about appropriate behavior based on one's gender have been sharply challenged in recent years. The strong drive toward equality that has been mounted by the feminist movement in the United States has resulted in a considerable increase of female participation in a wide range of sports activities from which women formerly had been excluded. The very image of sports as a male preserve has been weakened, and there has resulted a greater readiness to accept a non-sexist view of participation—in which women might choose to be assertive, forceful, daring, or highly competitive, while men might discard the traditional "macho" image, and choose to be more aesthetic or sensitive. The right to be oneself, and to choose new modes of behavior as part of individual self-actualization has been a fundamental tenet of the human potential movement of the 1970s.

Within this framework, although traditional sexist attitudes have obviously not disappeared entirely, there is a greater climate of acceptance for male dance than was true in past generations.

If it is not possible, for administrative reasons, to offer dance classes on the curricular level for boys, then every effort should be made to develop club programs which include boys on the secondary school level. Many would welcome such a program, if it were effectively presented and did not prove embarrassing to them. It might be offered as part of a music program, a conditioning program, or in connection with school dramatic presenta-

[14]Elizabeth R. Hayes, "The Dance Teacher and the Physical Education Administrator," *Journal of Health, Physical Education and Recreation,* December 1954, p. 20.

tions. If the staff itself did not have qualified teachers to guide such club or special programs on an extracurricular basis, capable instructors might be brought in from the community, on a special-teacher basis. There are a number of examples of such special programs for boys and young men today, despite the overall pattern of exclusion from dance (see Chapter 14).[15]

In terms of promoting the overall prominence of dance, many techniques can be used to arouse interest in it in secondary schools.

Recreational dance activities—square and folk dance festivals, jamborees, clubs, and clinics—can all be developed. Students may attend master classes, seminars, and concerts at nearby colleges, or regional dance events. Student choreography may be presented in assemblies and concert programs. Throughout, it is necessary to make every effort to develop the place of the arts in secondary schools. Often, unified programs of the arts, such as special week-long festivals presenting plays, poetry readings, art exhibitions, concerts, and dance events, have this effect. In a number of cases, secondary schools have developed courses in the *related arts* which are required of all students in the ninth or tenth grades. Such courses include general sections on the history of the arts and principles of aesthetic content and design in which the elements common to all the arts are explored. Sometimes they also involve students in creative experiences in the arts which are related to the more theoretical aspects of the course. It is essential that dance be part of such courses in the arts and humanities.

If all these steps are taken to promote dance in the school program, both as part of the curriculum and in co-curricular activities, it will contribute much to the total aesthetic environment of the school—as well as to interest and skills in dance itself. Particularly, teachers should make every effort to take advantage of the kinds of help which are now available from outside sources. In a number of states, arts councils and special foundation grants have made it possible to bring professional dance companies into the schools. Such opportunities for cultural enrichment as those described in Chapter 15 are likely to increase in the future, and should be encouraged by all persons interested in the growth of arts in education.

DANCE IN COLLEGES AND UNIVERSITIES

In reality, it is only on the level of higher education in the United States that dance tends to be approached with any degree of serious concern and support today. Increasingly, as Chapter 14 has shown, more and more colleges have initiated strong programs in the performing arts, with dance an integral part of these offerings.

On the college and university level, it is necessary to confront the key issue of departmental sponsorship of dance. Unlike the situation in elementary and secondary schools (where there is really little choice, and dance for

[15]See Bruce King, "Who Says Boys Don't Like Dance?" *Journal of Physical Education and Recreation,* October, 1971, pp. 36–37; and Tobi Tobias, "It's Becoming O.K. in America for Boys to Dance," *The New York Times,* January 9, 1977, p. D-6.

the foreseeable future must continue to be offered primarily by physical education departments), there *is* a choice in higher education. In a substantial number of colleges and universities, there are separate departments of dance, or sponsorship of dance majors by departments other than physical education. Therefore, it is necessary to understand the pros and cons of the relationship with physical education.

Historically, it is true that education in dance came into being under the sponsorship of physical educators, and has long been viewed as an important activity area in that field. Many physical educators have strongly supported dance as the "aesthetic side of physical education" or for its social and physical values. Without question, the fact that it has been part of the physical education *requirement* has meant that vast numbers of students have been exposed to dance through the years.

However, those who are dissatisfied with the place of dance in physical education point out accurately that in most physical education departments dance is treated primarily as a form of exercise, rather than as a creative or artistic experience. The stated goals of physical education rarely stress these latter values. When it is sponsored by physical education, dance seldom assumes a role in school or college programs comparable to that of music or fine art. Indeed, dance educators claim that the size of classes and other administrative circumstances surrounding the provision of dance in physical education make it impossible for it to function effectively as aesthetic education.

The point has already been made that dance is often taught by physical education teachers who are poorly equipped in this field (with foreseeably disappointing, and often disastrous, results), while individuals who have excellent training in dance may not be permitted to teach it—unless they have physical education credentials. It is claimed that physical educators rarely see dance as a vital concern or promote its interests as strongly as they do sports and other aspects of the physical education program. In college programs, while they support courses in basic dance skills, they rarely are competent or willing to introduce more advanced technique courses, or courses in dance composition, production, history, or notation. Teachers of dance are often compelled to teach courses in other physical education activities, in which they have been inadequately prepared, and may also be required (because of their dance background) to coach drill teams, cheerleaders, marching units, or other forms of dance entertainment for sports events of which they personally disapprove.

Finally, as was mentioned above, the argument is advanced that having dance sponsored by women's physical education departments perpetuates the rigid separation of men and women in this field, whereas having it as a separate department would mean that both sexes would be able to study it with less difficulty.

Essentially, many dance educators feel that these reasons justify taking dance—particularly dance as an art form—out of the administrative sponsorship of physical education. On the other hand, the majority of physical educators continue to affirm the relationship, seeing dance as a valid aspect of physical education and stressing that in this setting it has administrative support that it would not readily gain if independent. In a symposium by leading physical educators on this issue, the case for keeping dance within physical education was forcefully stated.[16]

Kenneth Miller stressed both the appropriateness of dance education within physical education and the problem of administrative support:

> . . .there are those who consider dance—in its broadest sense—to be the basic phase of the well-rounded program. . . . Dance is an area rich in opportunities for meeting the aims of physical education and, except for the lack of the competitive element, it might well be considered the *sine qua non* of the field. . . .
>
> In general, the educational system in the United States is committed to required physical education and to the provision of the necessary floor space, dressing rooms, and other equipment. Dance requires the same facilities, and any separation of this area from a broader unit which already has these costly necessities by fiat is inconceivable at the present time. . . .[17]

Others stress the point that dance has been increasingly accepted in schools and colleges as a part of the physical education program and therefore as a compulsory experience. If it were not sponsored in this way, many students would never experience dance in an educational setting. Some authorities describe dance as being an essential phase of the discipline of physical education, which is the "science and art of movement." The point is made that those who contemplate dance only as an art form, placing it outside the realm of physical education, have only a partial view of the field. Celeste Ulrich makes the strongest case for this argument:

> . . .movement is our unique means of education. Certainly dance has been recognized for a long time as the purest of all movement expression. It is an activity which fosters the complete utilization of the total body in order to express meaning and interpret feelings. In a sense, dance permits and encourages the sort of body expression that sports activities only allow in rigid and stratified patterns.
>
> To be sure, such expression as dance permits may be thought of as an art form and hence it may be logical that dance ally itself with certain of the expressive art fields. But the more logical attachment is with the department of physical education—a department which is committed to the education of the individual through gross muscular movement patterns. . . .[18]

Despite the fact that increased numbers of dance curricula *have* gained academic independence from physical education, either by being established as separate departments or as programs within a larger department of theater or performing arts, this battle continues to be waged. In 1977, Ulrich continued to express the views of many physical education authorities:

[16]"Dance as an Art Form in Physical Education, A Symposium by Selected Educators," *Journal of Health, Physical Education and Recreation,* January 1964, pp. 19–21, 54–55.

[17](Kenneth D. Miller) *Ibid.,* p. 19.

[18](Celeste Ulrich) *Ibid.,* p. 55.

> . . .it seems inappropriate for dance educators to seek organizational formats which cater to the fine arts and drama. The logical place to administer and organize dance is as a viable entity of . . . physical education. Both dance educators and sport educators can touch hands in the arena of human movement. To ensure that this is an honest interface, it will be necessary for departments and schools of health and physical education to add dance to their titles—a phenomenon already under way.
>
> It will also be necessary for the new band of dance educators to acknowledge the artistry and expression found in gymnastics, sports, and aquatics. The dancers' world cannot be apart from these movement forms; it must be a part of the whole world of human movement.[19]

Although these arguments are not likely to be acceptable to dance educators whose commitment is to dance as an art form, they represent the viewpoint of many influential physical educators and college administrators today. It seems unlikely that on any level of education they will consent in wholesale numbers to a severing of the relationship between dance and physical education. On the college level, where both the theoretical justification and the practical aspects of such a shift are more reasonable than in elementary or secondary schools, one may envision three kinds of administrative possibilities.

THREE MODELS OF DANCE SPONSORSHIP

1. In those colleges which have strong liberal arts traditions, placing major emphasis on the arts and humanities, there will be an increasing tendency to promote dance as a theater art, independent of physical education. In such institutions, some dance may continue to be offered on a "service" basis for all students by the physical education department, but the advanced sequences in modern dance and ballet, as well as choreography, production, and other specialized courses, will be offered by the separate dance department. Such programs tended in the past to be found only in women's colleges with a special interest in the arts and creative intellectualism, such as Bennington or Sarah Lawrence; in these schools, special provisions were made for bringing male students in as part of performing arts programs. Today, most such colleges have become legitimately coeducational, and a much wider range of institutions have established independent dance departments. Typically, those colleges with strong departments of theater arts or music—often with a conservatorylike approach to professional development—have initiated separate programs in dance. In many cases, dance has become an equal partner with theater, in a joint department of dance and drama.
2. A second type of arrangement which is likely to grow involves two dance majors: one in dance education (to prepare teachers) in de-

[19]Celeste Ulrich, "Education for a Dynamic Lifestyle," *Journal of Physical Education and Recreation,* May 1977, p. 48.

partments of physical education, and the second in dance as a performing art, either independent or in another arts-oriented department. Such patterns are usually found in large state universities which have a tradition of teacher education and physical education, but which also have developed as liberal arts institutions. In general, the dance education major stresses a broad approach to dance (including recreational dance forms and teaching methods), while the performing arts approach emphasizes modern dance and ballet. Administrative arrangements may be worked out between the two departments so that the performing arts department offers the advanced courses needed by dance education majors, thus avoiding duplication. A key problem here is whether courses in the performing arts program should be permitted to meet physical education requirements; in a number of colleges, this remains a bone of contention.

3. The third arrangement is to be found in institutions which lack a particularly strong interest in the arts—either in terms of the background of students or the capabilities of faculty. Here, dance is likely to continue to be part of the service program in physical education or, at most, a "minor" area of specialization for physical education majors. Even here, however, there should be the opportunity to experience dance as an art form in courses, and to strengthen it as part of the cultural program of the college.

When dance *is* presented primarily as a performing art, and when students major in it as a form of preprofessional activity, certain basic questions are raised.

ISSUES AFFECTING DANCE IN HIGHER EDUCATION

First, there is the fact that undergraduate liberal education has traditionally been directed to certain general goals of learning, embodying the arts, sciences, and humanities—but not including specific advanced training in any discipline. Particularly in the arts, this has meant that there has been strong resistance to "studio" work. Often, the most acceptable kind of program has stressed courses dealing with the history, aesthetics, and criticism of a given art field—rather than the development of competence as a performer.

For this reason, some educational authorities continue to be reluctant to accept dance curricula—particularly those on the graduate level which are primarily geared to performance and stage production. However, this objection is gradually weakening, and an increased number of colleges and universities have established programs which are clearly devoted to developing professional dance competence. Accompanying this development, however, dance has also emerged much more fully as an *academic* discipline. The National Dance Association and the American Dance Guild have sponsored a number of major conferences devoted to exploring historical and critical scholarship in dance. The Congress on Research in Dance has similarly explored new directions in needed dance research, and a substantial body of experimentation linked with the physical and behavioral or social sciences today involves dance. In general, there is much stronger support for research in the arts; a recent national conference in this area identified such key areas of concern as the following:

> What are the maturational, cultural, psychomotor, cognitive, and creative factors that facilitate learning in the arts?
>
> How can we identify, evaluate, and enhance effective methods of teaching in the arts?
>
> How can we best provide for the opportunity of the arts experience outside the classroom setting?
>
> How can we enhance an "arts accountability" and, in effect, direct it into becoming a more positive force in our society?
>
> Will the optimal development of one's perceptual apparatus result in an increased appetite for "quality" arts, both from the point of view of the maker as well as the perceiver?
>
> What physiological research findings have application to the arts experience? What physiological research must be undertaken in order to establish a fundamental base for understanding the arts experience?
>
> What are the educational benefits in terms of human competencies and attitudes that may be derived from comprehensive arts-in-education programs?
>
> What contributions can comparative aesthetics make to the understanding of human nature and human culture?
>
> What are the developmental stages of human growth in aesthetic sensibilities?
>
> What contributions can the arts make to increasing student motivation in schools?[20]

In summarizing the views of conference participants, Stanley Madeja points out that research in the arts may relate to such diverse areas as aesthetic theory, anthropology, psychology, philosophy, neurophysiology, biofeedback, psychocybernetics, and other emerging scientific disciplines. In addition to an expanding of research literature in the arts in general, there has been increasing interest and concern about dance criticism in particular, both in the popular press and in books. Whereas once few newspapers had special dance critics, today they are widespread. Such writers as Selma Jeanne Cohen, Walter Terry, Deborah Jowitt, Arlene Croce, Doris Hering, Marcia Siegel, Clive Barnes, Jack Anderson, Don McDonagh, Anna Kisselgoff and Alan Kriegsman are highly respected. The point to be made is that dance can and should be approached in colleges and universities not only as an appealing or provocative stage art, but as an area of personal enrichment and serious academic scholarship.

A second question which must be raised is whether preprofessional training in dance in colleges is really feasible. Can it be done? And, even if it can, is it really worthwhile?

[20]Stanley S. Majeda, ed., *Arts and Aesthetics: An Agenda for the Future* (St. Louis: CEMREL, Inc., and the Aspen Institute for Humanistic Studies, 1977), pp. 3–11.

One may ask whether it is possible to bring a dancer to a level of professional performing competence in a college program. In the past, few institutions have had programs of the required intensity and standard of instruction. Because of all the other requirements of the college curriculum, the dance major may not be able to give enough energy and time to work in dance. A physical educator, Eleanor Metheny, questions whether the "serious artist" should be in college at all:

> . . .at best, it can only lay the foundation for the later development of the student artist's talents; at worst, it may encourage him to dissipate talents in diversity and quasi-artistic performances at the dilettante level. For the dancer, whose life-span as a performer is limited by the effects of age on the body, this delay in accepting the rigorous requirements of preparation for full use of talent and creativity may well be disastrous. . . .[21]

Indeed, the majority of students who enter college performing arts dance majors today have not had the kind of intensive training that they should have had during adolescence, if they are to have a reasonable expectation of maturing as highly skilled performing artists. Thus, since only a few colleges are able to provide the kind of intensive and highly specialized training that would be found in a professional academy or conservatory of dance, the odds are doubly stacked against them. The real professional dancer—particularly in ballet—will already have had several years of intensive training and, at the age of 18 or 19, may well be serving his or her apprenticeship in a professional or semi-professional ballet company or on the musical stage. Too often, dance majors in college have little idea of the commitment required to become a professional dancer. Murray Louis has written:

> . . .the art of dance must be approached as seriously as any art or science. It would never dawn on anyone that pre-med students would study without an enormous dedication to their art. Law or science in general could not be studied without dedication. Our art is plagued with dilettantism; I don't know why. There is something very polite that has been associated with the word *dance,* and this generally turns out a very well-placed young lady who knows how to carry herself and to sit well.[22]

This leads to the second point. Is majoring in dance a worthwhile and realistic goal for the college student today? Many students, when they select a field as a college major today, expect that it will have actual vocational value for them. Within dance, such expectations are likely to be illusory—at least in the sense of finding stable, regularly paid employment in the field. Although there has been a considerable expansion of performing companies in recent years, positions in ballet and modern dance companies, and on the musical stage or in television are comparatively few in number, with sporadic employment and an intensive level of competition by highly quali-

[21]Eleanor Metheny, "Dance as an Art Form in Physical Education," *op. cit.,* p. 19.

[22]Murray Louis, in *Dance as a Discipline, Focus on Dance IV,* Nancy W. Smith, ed. (Washington, D.C.: American Association for Health, Physical Education and Recreation, 1967), p. 35.

fied would-be performers. For such positions, a college degree is not expected or really relevant.

Therefore, it is essential that colleges and universities offering major curricula in dance as a performing art give their students realistic knowledge about the role of dance in community life, and about the limited number of professional performance opportunities that are available. They should know that most performance is essentially amateur, and that modern dancers in particular usually must earn their living in some way other than by performing.

If, recognizing all this, the college still wishes to offer a major in dance as a performing art, and students still wish to take it, the justification becomes miraculously simple. It is to view dance as part of general education, without having to have a specific vocational purpose. One accepts the idea of a college student majoring in philosophy or literature without serious expectation of making a livelihood as a philosopher, novelist, or literary critic. Likewise, the student majoring in dance will regard the field primarily as a rich and rewarding form of education, within an art form related to the other arts, to history, ethnology, philosophy—and one with many avenues for personal growth. The role of the creative artist is unique within the society. Through its artistic, educational, and therapeutic values, it enhances the human potential and enrichment of all associated with it, as participant or observer. Thus, a pressing concern for direct vocational outcomes is not felt by many students engaged in the learning process. It is when the student has unrealistic career expectations or is misled by the lack of frank advisement that discouragement, disillusionment, or frustration are most likely to occur.

Finally, the dance major may wish to consider the possibility of dance education as a career. Whether this is done through teaching in secondary schools or colleges, or in community centers, private dance schools and studios, or in a host of other settings, the fact is that many thousands of dancers are able to support themselves in this way. Anne Ingram has done a comprehensive study of the role of dancer-teachers in schools and colleges, as part of a doctoral investigation at Columbia University; her analysis revealed a continuing shortage of well-trained persons in this field.[23] Surely, such a career should be of interest to many college-trained dance majors, as a means of combining a major life interest with secure employment.

Indeed, only if the quality and number of dance teachers on all levels of education throughout the United States are increased is there likely to be developed the kind of mass audience for dance that is still lacking today. This, of course, is an essential goal of dance education; the development of a literate, sensitive, and enthusiastic audience, as well as greater participation on all age levels.

When dance becomes recognized as a creative and academic discipline and is included more fully as a part of education on every level, in keeping with the overall pattern of growth in public interest and involvement that has been evidenced during the past decade, the prophecy of Isadora Duncan will at last be fulfilled: "I see America dancing."

[23]Anne G. Ingram, "The Dancer-Teacher," *Journal of Health, Physical Education and Recreation,* March 1965, pp. 29, 54–56.

Index